Gender Justice and the Law

The Fairleigh Dickinson University Press Series in Law, Culture, and the Humanities

Series Editor: Caroline Joan "Kay" S. Picart, M.Phil. (Cantab), Ph.D., J.D., Esquire Attorney at Law; Adjunct Professor, FAMU College of Law; former English & HUM professor, FSU

The Fairleigh Dickinson University Press Series in Law, Culture, and the Humanities publishes scholarly works in which the field of Law intersects with, among others, Film, Criminology, Sociology, Communication, Critical/Cultural Studies, Literature, History, Philosophy, and the Humanities.

On the Web at http://www.fdu.edu/fdupress

Recent Publications

Elaine Wood, *Gender Justice and the Law: Theoretical Practices of Intersectional Identity* (2020)
Orit Kamir, *Betraying Dignity: The Toxic Seduction of Social Media, Shaming, and Radicalization* (2019)
Marouf A. Hasian, Jr., *Lawfare and the Ovaherero and Nama Pursuit of Restorative Justice, 1918–2018* (2019)
George Pate, *Enter the Undead Author: Intellectual Property, the Ideology of Authorship, and Performance Practices since the 1960s* (2019)
Victor Li, *Nixon in New York: How Wall Street Helped Richard Nixon Win the White House* (2017)
Marouf A. Hasian, Jr., *Kafkaesque Laws, Nisour Square, and the Trials of the Former Blackwater Guards* (2017)
Michaela Stockey-Bridge, *The Lure of Hope: On the Transnational Surrogacy Trail from Australia to India* (2017)
Ted Laros, *Literature and the Law in South Africa, 1910-2010: The Long Walk to Artistic Freedom* (2017)
Peter Robson and Johnny Rodger,*The Spaces of Justice: The Architecture of the Scottish Court* (2017)
Doran Larson, *Witness in the Era of Mass Incarceration: Discovering the Ethical Prison* (2017)
Raymond J. McKoski, *Judges in Street Clothes: Acting Ethically Off-the-Bench* (2017)
H. Lowell Brown, *The American Constitutional Tradition: Colonial Charters, Covenants, and Revolutionary State Constitutions 1578–1786* (2017)
Arua Oko Omaka, *The Biafran Humanitarian Crisis, 1967-1970: International Human Rights and Joint Church Aid* (2016)
Marouf A. Hasian, Jr., *Representing Ebola: Culture, Law, and Public Discourse about the 2013–2015 West Africa Ebola Outbreak* (2016)
Jacqueline O'Connor, *Law and Sexuality in Tennessee Williams's America* (2016)
Caroline Joan "Kay" S. Picart, Michael Hviid Jacobsen, and Cecil E. Greek, *Framing Law and Crime: An Interdisciplinary Anthology* (2016)
Caroline Joan "Kay" S. Picart, *Law In and As Culture: Intellectual Property, Minority Rights, and the Rights of Indigenous Peoples* (2016)

Gender Justice and the Law

Theoretical Practices of Intersectional Identity

Edited by Elaine Wood

FAIRLEIGH DICKINSON UNIVERSITY PRESS
Vancouver • Madison • Teaneck • Wroxton

Published by Fairleigh Dickinson University Press
Copublished by The Rowman & Littlefield Publishing Group, Inc.
4501 Forbes Boulevard, Suite 200, Lanham, Maryland 20706
www.rowman.com

6 Tinworth Street, London SE11 5AL, United Kingdom

Fairleigh Dickinson University Press gratefully acknowledges the support received for scholarly publishing from the Friends of FDU Press.

British Library Cataloguing in Publication Information Available

Library of Congress Cataloging-in-Publication Data

Names: Wood, Elaine (Lecturer on women's and gender studies), editor.
Title: Gender, justice, and the law : theoretical practices of intersectional identity / [edited by] Elaine Wood.
Description: Lanham, Maryland : Fairleigh Dickinson University Press, [2018] | Series: The Fairleigh Dickinson University Press series in law, culture, and the humanities | Includes bibliographical references and index.
Identifiers: LCCN 2020035230 (print) | LCCN 2020035231 (ebook) | ISBN 9781683932390 (cloth) | ISBN 9781683932406 (epub)
Subjects: LCSH: Sex discrimination--Law and legislation. | Women--Legal status, laws, etc. | Women's rights. | Intersectionality (Sociology) | Feminist theory.
Classification: LCC K3243 .G464 2018 (print) | LCC K3243 (ebook) | DDC 342.08/78--dc23
LC record available at https://lccn.loc.gov/2020035230
LC ebook record available at https://lccn.loc.gov/2020035231

To Davood Majnoon, per aspera ad astra

Contents

Introduction

Elaine Wood

Gender Justice and the Law: Theoretical Practices of Intersectional Identity examines how gender, as a category of identity, must continually be understood in relation to how structures of inequality define and shape its meaning. It asks how notions of "justice" shape gender identity and whether the legal justice system itself privileges notions of gender or is itself gendered. By investigating how theoretical practices of intersectionality relate to structures of inequality and relations formed as a result of their interactions, this collection contributes to understanding how activism and politics resist systemic oppression.

The book's coherence centers around theoretical practices of intersectional identity at the thematic nexus of "gender and justice." Correspondingly, its subsections relate to specific issues of politics and policy shaped by sexuality, race, and class. Chapters are grouped into three parts—"Praxis and Policy," "Policing Bodies," and "Activist Politics of Resistance"—offering key insights into areas of debate related to ongoing discourses at these intersections of gender, justice, and the law.

PART I: PRAXIS AND POLICY

Close to twenty years after the significant *R. v. Gladue* (1 SCR 688) decision, carceral admissions for Indigenous women in prisons continue to rise across Canada. As the first to apply the 1996 criminal code provision, section 718.2(e), *Gladue* serves as a blueprint for the racialized and gendered structure of the Gladue process that criminalizes several Indigenous women. Arunita Das's chapter, "Constructing Criminality: *R. v. Gladue*, Intersectionality, and the Criminalization of Indigenous Women" utilizes a critical feminist/

intersectional lens of *Gladue* to explore how criminal courts operate within particular cultural and institutional contexts that perpetuate and reinforce systems of oppression. Producing broader constructions of race, crime, and female criminality, it is evident that *Gladue* missed the overarching goal to address systemic inequalities that bring Indigenous women into conflict with the law. An analysis of the critical points within case proceedings indicates how the language used by both judges and lawyers created particular images of Jamie Gladue. The androcentric language of the law serves to reify knowledge of Indigenous women while simultaneously constructing power relations, social identities, and other systems of representations. Arguably, the courtroom serves as a site for meaning making, where exclusionary definitions of female criminality are discursively constructed. These overlapping considerations underscore the racist and classist challenges that hinder the chance to seek meaningful justice.

Specifically, Das's chapter analyzes the use of 718.2(e) in *R. v. Gladue*, a reform intended to promote sentences that seek alternatives to imprisonment. Though indeed there is an abundance of literature to tackle the problem of overrepresentation among Indigenous offenders, little is written on the focus of Indigenous women specifically, and their unique experiential factors that propel them into conflict with the law. The core of the information from this chapter derives from Supreme Court–produced transcripts from the trial, Court of Appeal, and Supreme Court proceedings within *Gladue.* Significantly, narratives within the proceedings and transcripts of the trial are often not found in public records and case summaries. Thus, the chapter's major contribution is in its research that explores the more nuanced aspects of colonial history, while exploring relations among gender, culture, class, and patterns of victimization and offending. Compellingly, this chapter engages with critical feminist criminology and intersectionality as a unique and vital perspective on the limitations of the law. It is erroneous to say that all Canadian women face the same barriers; this notion is inadequate when researching the complex hindrances associated with overlapping social, racial, economic, and political factors that condition women's lives. Das illustrates, therefore, that it is important to critique the power of law, because it is a socially constructed platform that holds potential to reproduce domination and marginalization. With careful theoretical discussion, Das ultimately examines how the law has been misapplied in *Gladue* and served as a platform that reified meanings of female criminality.

Laura Lane-Steele's chapter, "Losing Custodial Mothers in Child Support Reform," employs feminist legal theory and critical race theory to address how reforms to the child support enforcement regime, derived in response to the incarceration of noncustodial fathers who are severely delinquent on their child support payments, prioritize the needs of men over women and children, and reinforce oppressive and essentialist division of labor norms. These reforms—namely, reducing the amount of support fathers owe and requiring these fathers to enter job-search programs—are designed to lessen the financial burden of child support on men and to ensure they are not jailed for contempt (for not paying court-ordered support). Lane-Steele argues that reforms ignore, or at least marginalize, custodial mothers' and children's needs. Moreover, inherent in the current child support regime, and in these reforms, is the assumption that men provide financial support to children while women provide caretaking and emotional labor. Rather than creating child support policies that allow men to provide nonfinancial assistance and redistribute the nonmonetary costs of children, such policies uphold long-standing gender norms regarding the market-home division of labor. Accordingly, Lane-Steele argues that child support law and policy can and should redistribute these costs away from low-income custodial mothers. Ultimately, Lane-Steele illustrates that the exclusion of low-income custodial mothers' interests from child support reform discourse forms part of a broader pattern of prioritizing men's interests over women's in antiracist and class-based discourse.

Drawing from theories of anti-caste thinkers, such as Sharmila Rege and Anupama Rao, and juxtaposing them with the conceptual frameworks of Michel Foucault and Gilles Deleuze, Lissa Lincoln examines the particular power of feminist Dalit testimonio to lay bare the intersecting structures of systemic oppression, violence, and exclusion that lie at the crossroads of gender and justice. Long recognized by feminist anti-caste scholars as radical counternarratives that challenge dominant voices, be they "Indian," "feminist," or even "Dalit," Lincoln argues that Dalit women's narratives are crucial to thinking and theorizing the ever-shifting and overlapping power relations that mobilize and inform these discourses.

In "Justice, Gender, and Caste: A Case for Dalit Feminist Testimonio," Lincoln illustrates how thinking caste through the lens of narrative fiction brings to the fore literature's unique capacity to interrogate and destabilize discourses of domination in general. Caste, despite its intricate and complex specificities (specificities that are critically important to identify, to recognize, and to situate and address, in order to counter and resist their subsumption under hegemonic conceptions of oppression) is ultimately a structure of exclusion and oppression—and the identification of the generalizable lines of this structure is a crucial factor in its demystification and dismantling.

Lincoln demonstrates that nowhere else do we see this function of dismantling and demystification more powerfully than in the case of Dalit feminist testimonios which, both in form and content, challenge the oppression and legitimacy of the discourses of caste, patriarchy and, indeed, literature itself. Dalit feminist testimonios expose the laws and norms that at once construct, perpetuate, and enforce them. Notably, Lincoln's chapter presents a specific focus on gender and justice issues that is not widely addressed at the crossroads of current discussions around representation, silencing, and transnational feminism. By engaging with contemporary French philosophy, intersectionality, anti-caste studies, feminism, and critical legal theory, Lincoln ultimately asserts the existence of Dalit feminism and the radicality of Dalit feminist testimonios within politics of resistance.

Shirley Lin demonstrates that as the state increasingly ceded its role in administering and defining sex, from federal and state governments to the courts, a post-2016 consensus of rights-positive decisions from federal courts returned to the statute's broader definition of sex discrimination. "Dehumanization 'Because of Sex': The Multiaxial Approach to the Title VII Rights of Sexual Minorities" reveals how such decisions reify binary sex through more granular classification methods. Most scholars propose Title VII sex-stereotyping theory as an all-encompassing tool for detecting harmful social norms tied to sex, particularly animus against LGBTQIA-identified individuals, but ignore the theoretical costs of relying on intact rigid binary sex categories as the paradigm for interpreting "because of sex." Lin's chapter is the first to provide a full account of the principles driving the doctrinal correction now undertaken by the majority of lower courts hearing cases of LGBTQIA-identified individuals.

Recontextualizing the full potential of the statute's trait-causation provision ("because of" sex), this chapter introduces multiaxial analysis. Its framework identifies the breadth of Title VII's protections along the following axes—the individual self, the harasser, society, and the state—that account for intersectional dynamics, such as race, sex, and class, salient in the discrimination. Multiaxial analysis fundamentally reconceptualizes the relationship between the self, socially constructed identity, and the state via contextual sources of subordination while respecting self-identification. Lin's chapter registers essentialist definitions of sex as immutable, biological classes reflecting entrenched norms that courts and litigators uncritically adopt in pursuing equality for LGBTQIA communities. As the Supreme Court evaluated the role of sex in sexual orientation and transgender status during the 2019–2020 term, liberals and conservative advocates deployed sex essentialism in ways that have broad implication for other socially defined traits. Foundationally, Lin proposes multiaxial analysis as a doctrinal intervention in cases brought under Title VII of the Civil Rights Act. Lin's study is the first to identify and theorize a consensus of courts since 2015 that adopted a neutral approach in which "sex," like race and religion, is a socially defined trait, ironically outpacing the ability of scholars to theorize a pluralistic view of sex.

Moreover, equality discourse has centered on constitutional models based upon broad, non-pluralistic, groups-based methods. Within equality discourse, leading experts, such as William Eskridge, have not been challenged when elevating classification-only approaches to interpreting a civil rights statute, such as Title VII. By looking at more conservative Supreme Court trends, Lin identifies that this may be true as a descriptive matter, but not as a matter of jurisprudence since 2015. Within queer theory, recent commentary regarding sexual complexity and the disestablishment of sex from state determinations have largely arisen only in constitutional or administrative-law discourse, but commentary addressing Title VII tended to treat textualism as the ascendant (and promising) means of statutory interpretation to argue LGBTQIA communities' inclusion in "because of . . . sex," notwithstanding the ideology's stark rejection of context in favor of text. Within critical race theories and intersectionality theory, scholars, such as Darren Hutchinson and Robert Chang, called for actionable and "very specific points of intervention with regard to legal doctrine," yet the scholarship has rarely gone beyond descriptive or political critique with respect to sex and race.

The diffuse sources and manifestations of power eludes easy descriptions of theory that avoid essentializing the categories that interventions wish to challenge. Critically, Lin illustrates that a transformative anti-subordination statute like Title VII can account for less familiar but equally harmful subjectivities that oppress. Multiaxial analysis can do so if the individual self, the defendant employer, society, and the state interactively generate stigma or other forms of subordination based upon differing views of the protected trait or traits. A fully contextual, contingent approach to subordination can account for intersectional dynamics that inhere in all discrimination.

PART II: POLICING BODIES

Christin M. Mulligan's chapter, "Divorce Ruling without Consent: Gender, Penal Law, and the *Faminized* Body in Nuala O'Faolain's *My Dream of You*," examines British colonial divorce and Penal Laws and how their various structures of inequality for both Anglo-Irish women and non-Anglicans of all genders are depicted through Nuala O'Faolain's historical novel *My Dream of You* (2001). It illuminates details of the infamous Talbot divorce case as well as the lack of legal protections and physical privations for tenants during the Great Famine period in Ireland. Mulligan considers the limits in addition to the ethics of the practice of supposedly intersectional historical feminist recovery work regarding writing historiographic metafiction when the legal record is largely silent for certain marginalized individuals. Further, it traces the continuing impact of bodily, socio-juridical, and ecosystemic traumas in the context of current debates concerning the rights of women and other vulnerable populations in Britain, Ireland, and beyond.

Particularly, Mulligan's chapter shows that this ostensibly intersectional feminist recovery project/novel is actually undermined by the protagonist's biases and the inherent, enduring patriarchal and racist structures of colonial laws and prejudices that are inured long after the Great Famine. Mulligan's argument presents the significance of historical, legal, archival, and contemporary theoretical materials that continue to impact cultural attitudes and the legal status of the Irish before, during, and after the Great Famine period through the use of close textual analysis that brings these discourses together. Both archival research and theories of the feminine body/psychoanalysis in terms of legal and emotional dispossession are key to understanding what happens to both the historical and the modern subjects in the novel. Convincingly, Mulligan argues that just because a project claims to be well-intentioned and feminist does not mean that it is possible to erase over two hundred years of patriarchal and racist legal precedents that silenced subjects via fiction. Notably, Mulligan identifies the continued need to understand the colonial history of Ireland and the intersection of socioeconomic, religious, and gendered representations that emerged as part of that long history between the tenancy and the Anglo-Irish Ascendancy and how that repertoire of cultural and legal signifiers continues to impact contemporary Ireland after the Great Famine.

While the concept of sexual and reproductive health and rights (SRHRs) has grown in legitimacy at the regional and international levels of the human rights system in recent decades, it continues to face significant challenges. Not least among these is that liberal, masculinist understandings of human rights continue to inform and limit the legal reasoning of the United Nations, Inter-American, and European human rights systems, often inadvertently perpetuating the very stereotypes of the female legal subject that need challenging to prevent violations of women's human rights. As a result of these problematic conceptual underpinnings, these institutions often take an inconsistent, flawed approach to cases that do not fit comfortably into androcentric understandings of rights violations. In response, Rebecca Smyth's chapter, "Gender and Justice in International Human Rights Law: The Need for an Intersectional Feminist Approach to Advance Sexual and Reproductive Health and Rights," undertakes a close reading of sample cases from the UN treaty monitoring bodies, Inter-American system, and European system to highlight these issues. It proposes an alternative, explicitly intersectional feminist approach to legal reasoning that can contribute to jurisprudence that better represents and responds to the lived experiences, needs, and realities of women and gender-diverse people.

Smyth's chapter focuses on international human rights law, particularly sexual and reproductive health and rights, as an emerging area within international human rights law. It offers an overview of the origins and evolution of SRHRs, which is timely, given the twenty-five-plus review conferences for the major UN world conferences at which the concept was first articulated (Vienna, Cairo, and Beijing). Also, Smyth engages in a critical reading of sample jurisprudence from the UN, Inter-American, and European human rights systems, informed by the growing popularity and importance of feminist judgment projects taking place around the world. Smyth's chapter provides a clear understanding of the origins and evolution of sexual and reproductive health and rights, their current scope and content in international human rights law, and the importance of continued critical engagement with international human rights law to ensure it represents and responds to the needs of marginalized and oppressed groups. Ultimately, Smyth engages with feminist legal theory and discourse analysis to articulate a critique of traditional liberal understandings of human rights and the law.

Lisa Beckmann's chapter, "'Like Cats and Dogs in the Streets': Disability and Sexuality in the Eugenic Legal Imagination" focuses on the representation of disability and sexuality in eugenic forced-sterilization laws at the beginning of the twentieth century in the United States. In eugenic ideology, disabled women were perceived as having an animalistic sex drive, which led to the "uncontrolled production of unfit offspring." As a consequence, forced sterilization laws were passed, denying these women ownership of their bodies and assigning them subordinate legal and societal status. Beckmann explores this power dynamic by analyzing selected forced-sterilization laws with a focus on their genesis in the eugenic legal system and the images of disability and sexuality that these laws conjure. Correspondingly, Beckmann argues that the gendering of disabled women through the law contributes to the notion of gender injustice in two ways. First, the construction of a sexualized and disabled identity reflects eugenic fears and punishment of non-normative bodies through intersectional identity crossing. Second, it reveals a legal system which is deeply gendered in itself, a system in which disabled women are discriminated against on multiple levels while the dominant legal actors—white male lawyers and judges—remain in a position of power.

Significantly, Beckmann contributes to discourses of disability, sexuality, gender, and the law by showing how they are historically and culturally specific as well as legally mediated. Beckmann indicates how eugenic forced-sterilization laws function to perpetuate disability-specific gender injustice as these laws construct and perpetuate derogatory images of disabled women as hypersexual animals. Therefore, the law emerges as an ideological tool of oppression and marginalization that is essential to the gender injustice that disabled women experienced at the turn of the twentieth century in the United States.

Beckmann's argument intervenes in ongoing discourses about the sexuality and agency of disabled women, particularly as it relates to intellectual and developmental disability (I/DD). It exposes the role that stereotypes serve in framing disabled women as either hypo- or hypersexual and the subsequent loss of sexual agency that disabled women experience even today, including having control over one's own body, having access to birth control as well as adequate sexual education, and possessing reproductive rights. The stereotypes discussed in Beckmann's chapter (disabled women as hypersexual "animals" and hyposexual innocent "children") resurface in contemporary discussions about disability and sexuality. Examples include the case of "Alan," the cognitively disabled man who was banned under UK law from being in a queer relationship with his male partner because of a "vigorous" sex drive, as well as "Ashley," a severely disabled woman in the United States, whose reproductive organs were removed so that her body remained childlike for life; her parents chose this treatment to prevent future sexual abuse in the institution where she was living. In both cases, the stereotypes discussed can be linked to contemporary issues regarding the sexuality, sexual agency, and reproductive rights of disabled people.

Overall, Beckmann engages with two schools of thought and adopts an approach that combines disability history with the social model of disability. In so doing, Beckmann disagrees with the medicalization and pathologization of disability. Further, Beckmann's chapter works with an approach toward law that moves beyond seeing law as legal rule alone. Instead, Beckmann perceives the law as a tool of control and punishment that reveals deep-seated ableism and sexism in the eugenic legal system. Disability—both as a category of analysis and as a state of being—moves medical diagnoses and definitions of impairment. Disability, as it is argued in Beckmann's chapter, is inherently political as it takes into account the discrimination and marginalization that disabled people perceive due to ableism and sexism. Finally, Beckmann illustrates how stereotypes and the loss of reproductive rights and sexual agency disable individuals much more than a medical diagnosis.

As a nation, Canada has long been struggling to respond to issues related to sex work and women's involvement. Since the 1970s, attempts aimed to change the law governing prostitution at the federal, provincial, and municipal levels. These legal changes, which often reflected the social fabric of the country, moved from protecting the public from the harms of prostitution to protecting the so-called vulnerable female prostitutes from patriarchal violence. Drawing on the experiences of forty racialized and Indigenous sex workers' interactions with law enforcement, Menaka Raguparan's chapter, "Victims of State Violence: Indigenous and Women-of-Color Sex Workers' Interactions with Law Enforcement in Canada," argues that police officers' discretion to determine the eligibility of sex workers' victim status heavily relies on historical/colonial presumptions of racialized and Indigenous women's sexuality and the victim rhetoric of the white slave trade panic. Specifically, policing practices often cast sex workers of color as less credible, hyper-disposable, and less deserving of police protection. Raguparan reveals how the occupational and racial bias of police officers and their failures to protect the safety and security of sex workers of color can be conceptualized through Crenshaw's (1991) structural, representational, and political intersectionality to highlight the ongoing effects of colonialism, racism, classism, sexism, and the social stratification system underpinning Canadian society.

The individual stories of sex workers of color presented in Raguparan's chapter highlight how, at the intersection of race and sex work, women are not able to subvert power relations during their encounters with police officers. Many participants in the study outlined were subjected to insults, humiliation, verbal abuse, false arrest, unlawful detention, and even physical and sexual abuse in their interactions with police officers. Raguparan's research participants' encounters with law enforcement are consistent with existing literature that focuses on police–sex worker interactions. The unique contribution of Raguparan's chapter is that it brings the experiences of indoor sex workers, which remains an understudied area, to the forefront of discussion. To this end, Raguparan clarifies the following: even with the relative privilege of working in indoor sectors, at the intersection of race and sex work, women of color are not immune to police abuses of power.

At present, public policy discourse and other reform initiatives claim that the sex industry is inherently violent and that women's participation in sex work is essentially a form of violence against women. Given such perceptions, law enforcement's response toward sex workers, especially police officers inflicting violence or not responding to sex workers' complaints of violence, contradicts public views and policy initiatives. By presenting evidence, Raguparan's arguments illuminate this paradox and provide an opportunity to understand the disconnect between law/policy in books and action. Grounded in critical race theory, Raguparan's chapter ultimately illustrates that racism is deeply ingrained in systems/structures of domination; police offices' personal biases shape/influence their discretionary power; and discretionary powers influenced by biases disproportionally affect the most marginalized members of society.

PART III: ACTIVIST POLITICS OF RESISTANCE

Catherine Cymone Fourshey and Marla L. Jaksch's chapter, "Intersections of Gender and (In)Justice: Bibi Titi Mohamed and Women's Struggles during and after Independence in Tanzania" critically examines how notions of "justice" are differently shaped by gender identity in a global context. In particular, applying a race, class, gender, and locational lens to an examination of Bibi Titi Mohamed's lived experience extends intersectional methodologies and epistemologies to transnational contexts in which pan-African socialist approaches to justice minimized gendered realities in a distinctly patriarchal construct, which reinforced women's inability to achieve being seen and treated justly, despite their desires and efforts.

Despite her importance as the president of the Women's Division of Tanganyika African National Union (TANU) as an efficacious political activist in igniting the masses to action, Bibi Titi Mohamed was in many ways dismissed during and following independence. Fourshey and Jaksch outline how issues of justice were deployed to paint Bibi Titi Mohamed as treasonous, asking whether these accusations were unjust and compounded by what Adrien Wing referred to as her multiplicative identities. Indeed, Bibi Titi Mohamed's case raises interesting issues for understanding how her identity—as a Muslim woman of limited economic means with minimal formal education living in a socialist, developing postcolony—brought her into contest with the patriarchal colonial, postcolonial, and neocolonial states she lived through. Tension arose first in her home country, not only because of her gender but also her intersectional identities as a Muslim single mother from a lower socioeconomic status with strong political and economic views, in a newly formed state headed by university-educated, well-traveled and well-resourced men.

Fourshey and Jaksch connect intersectional theoretical approaches to African feminism to the case of struggle experienced by this leader, thus revealing the limits of traditional approaches in understanding women's political activism and agency historically and contemporarily. Their argument builds upon and expands current discourses regarding intersectionality and justice. Ultimately, their chapter argues that intersectional thought, as it connects with African feminisms, allows for an intervention into conventional pan-African, masculinist narratives of the liberation struggle in Tanzania. Thereby their chapter engages with intersectional theories as they emerge from and expand Black feminist thought, as well as critically engages with African feminisms to explore the specificities of women liberation activists and their strategies for building a strong and successful movement for independence. It addresses the necessity for intersectional approaches in establishing deeper, more complex understandings of historical moments that erase, minimize, and distort the contributions of women activists, their agency, and their potential for justice.

Ava Ladner's chapter, "Policing and Place-Making: Trans* Persecution and Resilience," addresses the intersection of gender and justice in a way that is not about policing or law enforcement. When addressing justice, the systems of enforcement tend to center the discussion; however, Ladner's chapter examines how societal efforts, through religion and representation, stand in the way of trans* persons being recognized. Ladner combines historical elements with contemporary cultural aspects to present a case as to the ongoing treatment of trans* persons. Ultimately, Ladner blends a historical approach, pop culture analysis, feminist perspective, and interdisciplinary approach used in American studies to highlight problems facing the trans* community. Ladner argues that the policing of trans* bodies is at the core of American society, having been established by the Puritans and carried forward. This chapter presents the message that trans* persons have always existed and that they show amazing resilience against a culture and society that has trouble accepting them.

Theodore Davenport's chapter, "Becoming Theodore: Spatial Legal Consciousness and Transgender Name Changes," understands gender justice beyond the binary through an exploration of how trans and gender-nonconforming people experience legal violence every day. Specifically, legal name changes are a powerful way that transgender people render their gender transition visible to the state. Drawing from socio-legal studies and feminist geographies, Davenport's chapter centers around the question: How do transgender people experience legal name changes in everyday spaces?

Davenport utilizes autoethnography as a queer method to place the author's everyday experiences around a recent legal name change, signifying gender transition while living in a major city in the western United States. By relating this autoethnography to broader questions around gender and intersectional legal justice, Davenport identifies how the fragmented lived experiences of legal name changes are further complicated at the intersection of transgender identity—and the need for intersectional work around transgender legal consciousness, particularly during moments when gender transition is rendered painfully visible.

Prominent work within trans socio-legal studies exists on how legal administrations that center binary sex uniquely affect transgender people and shape legal consciousness around identity documents with gender markers. However, little work has explored how transgender people experience legal name changes, which are a more common and accessible legal signifier of gender transition than changing gender markers nearly everywhere in the United States. Davenport intervenes with discourses around transgender rights by exploring how legal systems affect trans people outside of trans-specific laws, including antidiscrimination and hate-crime legislation, typically evaluated through both popular and academic avenues. Drawing on trans geographies and trans socio-legal studies, Davenport demonstrates how the presence of gendered names on legal documentation presents unique challenges for trans and gender-nonconforming people in the United States. Further, Davenport proposes that addressing logistic and economic barriers to obtaining court-ordered name changes may ameliorate these issues.

First Amendment jurisprudence claims to focus on speech and speaker, but in areas involving erotic or potentially erotic speech, the speaker is usually ignored. The law operates under the fiction that it is the director, photographer, gallery, or store or theater proprietor who is speaking. But in doing so, as John Felipe Acevedo argues, the law silences the model—who serves as both object and subject of the artwork. Models are the object of the artwork as they, or their image, are being observed, but they are also the subject of the artwork because they are speaking through their actions. Acevedo's chapter, "The Model Speaks?: Obscenity Laws in the United States," emphasizes the disregard of models' speech at the intersection of gender, age, class, and sexual orientation in both the relationships of models to artists and to the law. Even when the models themselves are deemed First Amendment speakers, such as in erotic dancing, the court provided less protection than similarly situated performative speakers. Drawing on subaltern studies theory, Acevedo examines the reasons why courts have been unable, indeed unwilling, to hear the model speak.

Moreover, Acevedo asserts that the intersection of categories prevents the court from hearing the model as it would then have to grapple with the law's middle-class heteronormative hegemony. Acevedo's major contribution merges social science and humanities scholarship with traditional legal scholarship to intervene in the ongoing debate on speech protection. In doing so, Acevedo traces the limits of legal theory and practice. Specifically, Acevedo argues that First Amendment obscenity jurisprudence ignores the people doing the most talking—the models—in favor of distributors and sellers. Ultimately, Acevedo challenges critical legal and feminist theories that claim to speak for women by pointing out that they, too, ignore the desires and beliefs of the models.

Comprehensively, *Gender Justice and the Law: Theoretical Practices of Intersectional Identity* registers how gender, as a category of identity, must continually be understood in relation to how structures of inequality define and shape its meaning. Given its theme, the book examines theoretical practices of intersectional identity at the nexus of "gender and justice" that might also relate to issues of sexuality, race, class, age, and ability. Shaped by politics and policy, *Gender Justice and the Law* contributes to understanding how theoretical practices of intersectionality relate to structures of inequality and relations formed as a result of their interaction.

I

Praxis and Policy

Chapter One

Constructing Criminality

R. v. Gladue, *Intersectionality, and the Criminalization of Indigenous Women*

Arunita Das

In 1996, in an effort to reduce the disproportionate rate of incarceration that Indigenous Canadians are subject to, the federal government enacted Bill C-41. This bill, later becoming section 718.2(e) of the Criminal Code of Canada, contained proposals that encouraged "judges to consider historical and systemic issues when sentencing Aboriginal and Inuit offenders."[1] This reform aimed to promote alternatives to imprisonment by assessing the individual's historical and systemic factors that led to the decision to commit a crime. During sentencing, presiding judges must now "account for any relevant aggravating or mitigating circumstances relating to the offence or the offender."[2] In 1999, *R. v. Gladue* was the first to adopt the Criminal Code provision, opening discussion on the somewhat vague directive under section 718.2(e).[3] *Gladue* was praised for recognizing the need for culturally appropriate sanctions and sentences, receptive to the importance of intersectionality as a means to reduce over-incarceration rates among Indigenous offenders.

Nearly two decades after the significant *Gladue* decision, carceral admissions for Indigenous women in the prison system have risen. In the current federal prison population, Indigenous women account for 31 percent of female admissions to sentenced custody, while only comprising 4 percent of the country's female population.[4] This means that Indigenous women are not benefitting from Gladue reports and restorative justice practices the way the reform intended.[5] Such trends indicate that legal practitioners fail to provide an appropriate intersectional analysis that carefully assesses the factors propelling women to be in conflict with the law. Utilizing critical race, intersectional feminist, and sociolegal theories to examine *Gladue*, this chapter illuminates how Indigenous women are implicated in the systems through "unique history and experiences of oppression."[6] For analysis, this chapter contextualizes the Canadian justice system as an institutional apparatus of the colonial state, with entrenched biases toward Indigenous peoples, along with patriarchal biases experienced by Indigenous women. With an analysis of *Gladue* proceedings, I argue that the courtroom is a space that can define, racialize, and criminalize Indigenous women through practices of representation and contextualization. I center my analysis on the following research question(s): Considering the information presented by counsel, did the sentencing judge in *Gladue* produce an appropriate sanction that considered systemic and background factors tied to colonization? How does the courtroom then, serve as a site for meaning making, where exclusionary definitions on female criminality are constructed? Responding to these questions, this chapter works to illuminate two interrelated findings. First, the relationship between the defendant's counsel and judges becomes an important one, as their legal interpretations construct and attribute certain meanings about Indigenous women as defendants. Second, judicial interpretations of the systemic and historical pathways that bring Indigenous women in conflict with the law were obscured at every level of the court process.[7] These material and symbolic constraints make it difficult to produce appropriate, rehabilitative sentences beyond imprisonment, ultimately contributing to rates of over-incarceration.

The significant increase in over-incarceration, and the increase in the recognition of alternative dispute resolutions make it a valuable time to reflect on *Gladue.* A very limited number of research and theoretical reports critique the gendered and racial implications that *Gladue* set. The selected literature surveyed for this chapter emphasizes that, since *Gladue*, there is reason to challenge the assumption that initiatives undertaken actually have the intended remedial and positive impact on the excessive use of incarceration (for example, Lash 2000; Cameron 2008; Williams 2008; Balfour 2012; Murdocca 2013). They all concluded that not applying an intersectional lens underscores the importance of evaluating how Indigenous women are implicated in the systems and processes of oppression.[8] Thus, we must continue to examine *Gladue* and what it can tell us about the entire Gladue process, to better understand how race and gender interlock, and simultaneously structure social and legal relations. This chapter is informed by Carmela Murdocca's (2013) extensive research in this area, applying her finding that the criminal procedure in Gladue provides a "blueprint for the racialized and gendered structure of the Gladue process," setting the terrain under which Indigenous women are sentenced.[9] To conduct this study, I analyze transcripts from Supreme Court proceedings, decisions from lower courts, appeals, and judgments of *Gladue* using a feminist critical discourse analysis.[10] I focus on the role of sentencing judges because "the dominance of legal ideology is manifest not only in what judges say about their interpretive practices but also in their organization of the courtroom discourse."[11] These transcriptions provide snapshots into how and why Gladue was discursively constructed as a violent aggressor, illustrating how traditional applications of deterrence and denunciation continue to be valued more than alternatives to imprisonment. The rigidity and limiting directions provided to specialized courts serve to individualize Indigenous women's experiences while erasing the historical and systemic context of racism, sexism, and poverty. This chapter provides background and overview of *Gladue*, followed by a discussion of the theoretical framework used to examine critical points within the case proceedings, decision from lower courts, appeals, and judgments of *Gladue.* Then, I analyze *R. v. Chickekoo* as an important example of the complex difficulties that legal actors continue to have when applying an intersectional lens for female Indigenous offenders.[12] A comparative analysis between the two cases demonstrates that representations of identity serve to devalue certain Indigenous women in the sentencing process, casting them as responsible for their own criminalization.

I. BACKGROUND AND CONTEXT

In 1996, the federal government of Canada enacted Bill C-41, which contained proposals that "encourage judges to consider historical and systemic issues when sentencing Aboriginal and Inuit offenders."[13] In an effort to promote restorative justice practices, this amendment opposed the conventional practice of judicial discretion that was at the core of the sentencing process. During sentencing, judges would now have to inquire into the distinct personal background of defendants, analyzing what factors brought them before the court, when deliberating on offenses committed by the individual.

Interestingly, since its formation in 1995, several Indigenous women's groups opposed Bill C-41. Activists protested this proposal because it would generalize, individualize, and heavily discriminate against the pathways that bring Indigenous women to confront the law. The Native Women's Association of Canada (NWAC) argued that this bill would "result in less protection for Indigenous women in their communities."[14] Additionally, this controversial provision would also "transfer responsibility for incarceration rates of Aboriginal communities with the intent of having the community deal with the problem."[15] Despite this caution, the reform was passed in an action that highlights the contradictory aspirations of the Canadian government. Revealed in *Gladue*, this reductionist method of sentencing produces boundaries around cultures and identities, legitimizing the need to "police these boundaries to regulate internal membership and 'authentic' life-forms."[16] Ultimately, the government ignored the protests of the groups this bill was meant to "help." In part, moving forward with the reform can be rooted in the federal government's responsibility to "manage/control the affairs of the Aboriginal peoples, as well as its jurisdiction over the *Criminal Code*."[17] Passing the bill despite cautions illuminates "the relationships between histories of colonization, contemporary racisms, and reparative justice in liberal, multicultural states."[18] The subtext of colonialism informs what Sherene Razack (1998) understands as "white judicial cultural sensitivities," which informed the recommendations to pass Bill C-41, in a system run by an entirely male cast as spokespersons for Indigenous communities.[19]

R. v. Gladue: Case Overview

On September 1995, after her nineteenth-birthday party, Jamie Tanis Gladue stabbed and killed her common-law husband, Reuben Beaver, in Nanaimo, British Columbia. Gladue, Beaver, and other guests were drinking heavily at the time, and then Beaver left the party with Gladue's sister, Tara Chalifoux. Suspecting him of an affair, Gladue reportedly became enraged and began to search for him. After finding Beaver in her sister's apartment, having an affair with her sister, an argument ensued in Chalifoux's apartment. At this time, Beaver taunted Gladue, calling her several insults including that she was "fat, and ugly, and not as good as the rest."[20] Gladue stabbed Beaver in the arm, and when he began running, she started chasing him with a larger knife. Gladue later caught up to him and stabbed him in the chest, ultimately killing him. Confirmed by her neighbors, father, and some witnesses, Gladue felt deep remorse for her actions and did not realize what she had done at the time. She was charged with second-degree murder, but she ultimately pleaded guilty to manslaughter.

Gladue and Beaver had a strained relationship, one that would often become abusive with alcohol involved. Previously, Beaver was convicted of assaulting Gladue while she was pregnant with their first child. Gladue had no prior criminal record (apart from an impaired-driving charge), she had a supportive family, attended alcohol abuse counseling, and was attending education classes. These steps taken while awaiting trial show that Gladue would have been a strong candidate for rehabilitation.[21] Instead, however, the trial judge sentenced Gladue to three years imprisonment. During trial, counsel neither raised Gladue's Indigenous status nor applied section 718.2(e), which directs the courts to assess the history of the offender "with particular attention to the circumstances of Aboriginal offenders" during sentencing.[22] Justice Hutchinson, the trial judge, held that the section did not apply because Gladue did not live on a reserve.[23] Believing the trial judge erred in his sentence, Gladue's counsel motioned to appeal. While the Court of Appeal of British Columbia agreed that the trial judge made an error; the court upheld the sentence because the offense "was a particularly serious one."[24] Her appeal was dismissed, which was later grounds to move the case to the Supreme Court of Canada.

On December 10, 1999, *Gladue* became the first Supreme Court decision to consider section 718.2(e).[25] Given that the case garnered little public recognition and lacked universality, the case attracted three interveners: the attorneys general of Canada and Alberta and Aboriginal Legal Services of Toronto, who detailed the importance of properly applying this provision.[26] Yet all three judgments from the trial, the Court of Appeal, and the Supreme Court stated that "special consideration" did not apply to Gladue based on her Indigenous status. Gladue's indigeneity is an experiential factor which separates Jamie Gladue from most women who are criminalized. Gladue's conflict with the law stemmed from factors steeped with ongoing, colonial legacy, such as poverty, domestic violence, single parenthood, and other circumstances. A thorough intersectional assessment is difficult when courts do not consider the aforementioned factors as relevant to the decision to commit a crime. By considering her identity to be irrelevant, there was a clear mishandling of interpretation and application. The court did not connect her responsibility as a single parent to the "high rates of child apprehension in Aboriginal communities" which stem from the "legacy of residential schools in separating parents and children, and other parenting obstacles faced by Indigenous women due to poverty and racism."[27] Nonetheless, *Gladue* set an important precedent for advancing restorative justice practices. Now commonly known as the "Gladue paradigm," this case motivated the creation of Gladue Courts, a specialized court system that handles the cases of Indigenous offenders, which integrate more traditional Indigenous legal procedures.[28]

II. INTERSECTIONALITY AND *GLADUE*

In *Gladue*, Gladue's identity as female cannot be analyzed separately from her Indigenous identity and class experience. Social dislocation, colonization, and years of systemic cultural genocide produced marginalization and exclusion, contributing to the high rate of incarceration among Indigenous women. Indigenous women face additional difficulties when securing acquittals or mitigated sentences, due to overlapping social, racial, economic, and political factors that condition women's lives. It is critical to recognize the structural, socioeconomic, and historical contexts of violence that affect the treatment of all Indigenous peoples, and sexism in Indigenous women's lives.[29] The power of law is a socially constructed platform that holds potential to reproduce domination and marginalization. The key tenet of intersectional theory is that interlocking systems of "race, gender, sexuality, and class simultaneously structure social and political relations."[30] In the words of Angela Cameron (2008), it is not that regimes of "difference" operate separately and then interact during particular moments:

> Considering gender in sentencing is not about adding gender discrimination to racial discrimination to arrive at double discrimination, nor is it an exercise in bare comparison between Aboriginal men and women . . . it is an attempt to understand the ways in which systems of sexism and racism reinforce and maintain each other in the lives of Aboriginal women, with a view to how these insights can serve as a tool of anti-subordination for both Aboriginal men and women in conflict with the law.[31]

As a legal concept, intersectionality is foundational to the understanding that race intertwined with gender and class is a social phenomenon, which is interwoven into all aspects of society, including criminalization. Applying an intersectional lens to the courtroom and sentencing can be vital when considering different remedies to violence that reflect the needs and rehabilitation specific to the offender.

III. CRIMINALIZING GLADUE: JUDICIAL INTERPRETATION, POWER DYNAMICS, AND LEGAL DISCOURSE

Mohawk lawyer, activist, and educator Patricia Monture-Angus repeatedly posits that overrepresentation is merely "the first layer of discrimination."[32] It is more the fact of colonialism that correctional services in Canada have historically failed to account for the degree to which colonialism is also gendered.[33] These practices serve as a process of "legitimation of culture-controlling elites through a lack of open confrontation with their cultures inegalitarian and exclusionary practices.[34]

Had a more detailed examination of the crime in relation to intersecting markers of disadvantage been undertaken by the Supreme Court, it would have revealed that the double effects of colonialism and patriarchy have severely impacted the lives of Indigenous women. For example, within a series of encounters between the defense lawyer and the chief justice of the Supreme Court, it becomes clear that the relationship between the defendant's counsel and the judges become important, as they carry a dominant role in precedent, to create and sustain definitions of cultural difference and criminality. Since the trial began, Gladue's counsel (Mr. King) and the court relied on their own knowledge of Indigenous communities during evaluation. The following excerpt reveals the limitations that exist when a judge fails to consider intersectionality. Gladue's criminality was assessed in connection with her "ancestry, identity, and circumstances," rather than by critically assessing the historical and social contexts of criminalization.[35] The following excerpt began as a conversation regarding the background factors of the offense, including exhibits and statements of Beaver's abusive patterns toward Gladue. To validate the request for a rehabilitative sentence, Mr. King discussed Gladue's role in raising five sisters and brothers, along with caring for her two children and father. With her father always working and her mother absent, the incarceration of Gladue would render her children and her siblings without guardianship for three years, a systemic and background factor critical to her case. The conversation then switched into discussing where the Gladues resided and in which communities. This exchange raises "legal and political questions about what kinds of practices, commitments, and performances come together to constitute a legally discernable 'Aboriginal person' and/or a legally comprehensive notion of 'aboriginality.'"[36] In the following exchange, the court asks:

> The court: Where is McLennan?
>
> Mr. King: McLennan, my understanding, My Lord, is in northern Alberta.
>
> Mr. Wallensteen (prosecutor): High Prairie would be the largest community closest to it, I believe, My Lord.
>
> The court: High Prairie.
>
> Mr. Wallensteen: Would be the closest, maybe about seventy kilometres away.
>
> The court: And this is a Native community or an open community?
>
> Mr. King: I believe it's just a regular community, My Lord.
>
> The court: Yes. And are they from the Native—are they aboriginals or not?
>
> Mr. King: My client is aboriginal.
>
> The court: Is she?
>
> Mr. King: Yes.
>
> The court: Of what kind?
>
> Mr. King: My understanding, is she—she informed me that she is Cree. Both Parents are Cree[37]

How judges speak seems to have "logic and rationales of its own that are separate from and cannot be found in written law."[38] This exchange distinguishes between "Native" and "open" community. The court framed the questions to reason that such categories were separate and opposing. By creating this distinction, an "us" versus "them" narrative is produced through which a "vivid image of the drama and dilemma of cultural difference" in "foreign" spaces emerges.[39] In doing so, the court ignored how race and gender interlock with the social and historical legacies of colonization.

The language within *Gladue* can help explain how power works in the legal system, specifically when giving weight to certain "aggravating" factors, while concealing critical "mitigating" factors. As Razack notes, decision makers in North American courts "come from a cultural, social, and economic background different from that of the majority of persons in the communities where they serve."[40] Challenging cultural assumptions within the courts can offer an insightful account of discrepancies within court rulings. In doing so, one can identify additional resources that would continuously improve the criminal justice system, creating more inclusive, decolonizing approaches tailored to reflect the needs of various defendants.[41]

Judges then hold power to recontextualize this relationship by producing new meanings of the event within courtroom talk using their own knowledge on particular Indigenous communities. The courtroom used Gladue's status to create a symbolic boundary, creating a distinction between what characteristics make up a "Native" community or an "open" community—prompting the question "are they aboriginals or not?" After learning where she lived, the case deemed to identify Gladue as a criminal coming from a background with poverty, manifesting certain assumptions from those axes of identity. As a result, the words Mr. King and the court used signify negative assumptions about "aboriginal" communities and criminality. This focus on Gladue's "personal history, family, and community shifts attention away from questions about societal discrimination."[42] Her identity thereby informs the power relations between her and the judiciary, which adds to the process and power of silencing information when "rewriting" Gladue's experiences as undeserving for special consideration. Becoming an interaction between two economically unequal social groups, it is crucial to consider the ways race, ethnicity, and gender inform the interaction between the lawyers and the judges.

Furthermore, the majority of women in Indigenous communities who have histories of being abused by men and attempt to cope with abusive relationships are often criminalized. There is lack of discussion in the courts on the gendered violence that is rampant within particular Indigenous communities and the significant role that such abuse can play in a woman's decision to commit a violent offense. Of course, judges and lawyers manifest unintentional biases, which can influence them to "make decisions a certain way, based on the sum total of the individual's own cultural and social experiences," producing a "'misinterpretation' of cultural differences."[43] In regard to using the battered-women's syndrome as a defense, many Indigenous women tend to be overlooked as they continue to be stereotypically portrayed as aggressive and violent. This fact is illustrated in Gladue's appeal, which was denied on the grounds that her identity had no bearing on the sentence, as the offense was "near murder" despite the "years of documented abuse perpetrated against her."[44] Hence, courtroom "talk" serves as a function that determines worthiness by selectively inviting Indigenous women into "universal" Canadian values, as well as segregates them as the Other.

For example, in his submissions by defense, Mr. King submitted some photographs taken of Gladue shortly after her arrest. These exhibits entered as evidence show Gladue suffering detailed instances of abuse and neglect by Beaver. Photographs revealed bruises suffered on the night of the murder and included faded injuries from previous days. Gladue advised her counsel that Beaver was a "very good man . . . until he drank," and at this time, he was abusive.[45] Relevantly, Beaver was previously convicted of an assault while she was four months pregnant with her daughter Tanita. In the preliminary inquiry, Gladue's father, Lloyd Chalifoux, testified that he was suspicious of Beaver. Chalifoux stated that Beaver engaged in predatory behavior beginning when his children were younger.[46] Beaver's actions showed evidence of coercive control, and actions that would make Gladue a victim of intimate partner violence. However, her extensive counts of abuse at the hands of Beaver were never mentioned as one of the mitigating factors in the final judgment. The Crown maps a legal understanding of intent onto Gladue's actions after the murder.

> Mr. Wallensteen: I was suggesting the fact that she was washing her hands immediately after the fact, was observed by a number of people. That does reflect an individual who understands what she is doing and what has happened, as opposed to someone who is so intoxicated that the events have simply escaped her by, and is not, in other words, acting in a drunken rage. She is acting in a rage created by the infidelity of her common-law husband, and there is a difference.[47]

Intimate-partner violence, and the "battered-woman" defense was never considered because her actions and words were interpreted to be aggressive, which from the court's perspective, made it "impossible" for her to be a victim.[48] Put before the court, the Crown prosecutor (Mr. Wallensteen) suggested that Gladue was in a clear state of mind before and after the murder was committed. In terms of "suggesting a range for sentencing on a charge of manslaughter or domestic violence," Mr. Wallensteen used the fact that she washed her hands immediately after the murder to indicate that she committed the murder with intention and motive. This intriguing facet sheds light on how judges and lawyers understand Indigenous women as defendants, and the pathways that bring them in conflict with the law. Mr. Wallensteen described Gladue's actions as cold and calculated, arguing that it was impossible for her to be subject to violence. Weakened by a mentality that Gladue did not carry herself in a way that would make her seem "helpless," the court concealed the particular context of her actions. These ideals are typically constructed from stereotypical depictions of White, middle class, and heterosexual femininity, which raises concerns on the application of the testimony to women of visible minorities and classes. Women who do not fit the definition of a "helpless victim" can meet challenges in producing a successful self-defense plea. The passive and helpless portrayal to fit a battered-women syndrome defense is highly problematic in the legal sphere, as it can hinder the ability for *all* women to access meaningful justice.

Indeed, the trial judge considered mitigating factors including the accused's age, her supportive family, her attending alcohol-abuse counseling and education classes, her hyperthyroid condition, her deep remorse and emotional reaction, and Beaver's provocation in the form of insulting remarks on the night of the stabbing.[49] However, the extent to which Gladue suffered abuse by Beaver was largely overlooked in the trial verdict. It is apparent that the way the sentencing judges used Gladue factors excluded gendered conditions of endangerment in Indigenous women's communities as a systemic factor.[50] To justify this exclusion, the trial judge said:

> As she pursued the accused, she warned him to run away. She was intent on harming him seriously and in fact did so. After the event she said, "I got you you fucking bastard," which indicates that she intended to do so, although she lost her self control and I have gone over that aspect of it earlier.
>
> The accused was not afraid of the deceased that night, rather he was afraid of her.[51]

When women commit a violent crime such as manslaughter, judicial discourses suggest they not only violate the law but also "betray" preconceived notions of femininity, and must construct their story to fit the mold of helplessness.[52] For example, defendants must establish the "reasonableness" of their actions to fulfill the requirement of self-defense.[53] However, self-defense laws require that a defendant use "equal force" to an attacker's when combating an attack.[54] By stating Beaver was "afraid of her," Justice Hutchinson suggests Gladue was "an equal partner or initiator in the violence."[55] This description exemplifies how judicial narrations of Gladue "reinforces stereotypical assumptions about Aboriginal drunkenness, violence, and intraracial quarrels" to contrast the definitions of a "helpless, battered woman."[56] In *Gladue* the images produced are distorted from the reality, by representing her as equally violent and aggressive as Beaver. As well, this interpretation discounts a number of material and symbolic constraints that make it difficult to acknowledge the systemic and historical factors of violence. It reveals the "interpretive structures that limit what can be known, heard, and said in a court of law" when the subject of violence against Indigenous women arises.[57] Thus, the "histories of being abused and feelings of low self-esteem are scrutinized as risk factors and criminal justice discourse constructs these women as dangerous and 'risky' victims."[58] With the powerful positions of the recontextualizing agents (i.e., the Crown prosecution and the trial judge) in *Gladue,* her words "I got you, you fucking bastard" were used to make her appear as a callous murderer, rather than a battered woman who, arguably, killed Beaver in self-defense. Crucially, the trial judge's characterization of Gladue appeared to significantly impact the Court of Appeal and Supreme Court's sentencing. Justice Hutchinson's sentencing decision affirms the prosecution's theory that Gladue's actions were tantamount to a "very serious offence," warranting incarceration. The issue of violence against Indigenous women is obscured at every level of the court process, contributing to the discriminatory discursive practices that determine legal outcomes.

The judges discounted Gladue's unique experiences with intimate partner violence, single parenthood, substance abuse, and other factors which stemmed from legacies of colonization, historically dismissed by the legal systems and its various actors. Having isolated the offense from the context, the court reverted to traditional sentencing jurisprudence that valued deterrence and denunciation over rehabilitation.[59] An analysis of how Gladue's intergenerational history of abuse led to her decision to commit the offense illuminates the significance and prevalence of violence against women in Indigenous communities. Considering the realities that several Indigenous peoples face on and off reserves can result in confusion as to how to assess aggravating and mitigating factors, and how the assessment should be incorporated into decision making. Various actors within the criminal justice system articulate "aggravating and mitigating factors" by drawing upon underlying socioeconomic influences, myths, and stereotypes prevalent within any culture. Ehrlich, among others, explains that via the semiotic process of erasure, the facts seen as inconsistent with the official story are "filtered through cultural and institutional ideologies."[60] This practice renders the defendant's interpretations of the events as "unrecognizable," ultimately erasing her voice and story in the courtroom.[61] The court did not analyze the connection between the experience of violent victimization with the intergenerational conditions of violence, that its decision to commit a violent criminal offense. Her experience with partner violence, poverty, single parenthood, and substance abuse means that the violence Gladue was subjected to is more extensive than described in the decision to sentence her. The above proceedings excerpt serves as a great example of how lawyers can control a person's story and then construct a competing version. It is clear in this excerpt that the victim's version of her own experiences was transformed to fit the needs of the legal process. Gladue's lawyer listed these reasons to distinguish Gladue from non-Indigenous offenders, to give evidence to the judge that her case is unique. These narratives produce imagined boundaries, which "can guide human action and behaviour as well as any other cause of human action."[62] This case sheds light on how legal practitioners view Indigenous women under the court of law, by voicing representations of idealized notions of femininity. Judges interpreted Gladue to be an immoral, deviant criminal, while also defining "aboriginality" to be culturally inferior.

Gladue reveals the ways Indigenous women are "invariably portrayed as aggressors," which constitutes a practice of negation of past historical injustices, and racially codifying Indigenous women before the court.[63] The context of the judges' reasoning affirms Gayatri Chakravorty Spivak's (1987) insight that in the struggle to "decolonize women's voices, contexts . . . issues are structurally marginalized and frequently erased both by the colonial mainstream and within the indigenous collective."[64] Through interwoven processes of colonial discourse within the courts, cultural difference is reified and exaggerated, and presented in contrast to dominant society. The justice system fails to understand the lived experiences of women who cope with abuse, producing a skewed definition of "syndrome" which serves to "pathologize the woman" as opposed to perceiving their actions as "a normal response to trauma."[65] Sheehy (2013) argues that this model of understanding misses the underlying theory. It is not that battered women become helpless; rather, they "lost the ability to predict that what [they] do will make a particular outcome occur."[66] Ultimately, the justice system does not tackle structural conditions of circumstances that permit masculine aggression against females in high numbers. As a result, the law works to produce gender, "through a series of strategies that constitute both the identities of legal subjects and their social relations with each other."[67] Continuing to apply racialized ideologies contributes to the social constructions of race and crime as we know it today. Gladue was an Indigenous woman, raised outside a reserve, primarily in an impoverished neighborhood. These axes of identity became crucial to her status as a violent aggressor, embedding underlying labels to her identity, producing hidden meanings and misconstrued definitions of gendered domestic violence that informs legal practitioners. These imagined boundaries produced barriers toward a culturally appropriate sentence.

IV. *GLADUE* AS A BLUEPRINT FOR THE RACIALIZED PROCESS

Gladue should continuously be examined for its effectiveness and the ramifications it produced.[68] The incorporation of alternative dispute resolutions and penal reforms meant to "redress" systemic inequalities raise important questions about what sorts of knowledges are relied upon, and the types of subjects that are produced through such measures. For Gladue, each part of the court process is lived through her experience and perspective with intersecting identities: female, Indigenous, and criminal, which makes a dramatic difference in terms of legal outcomes. In the twenty years since *Gladue*, however, statistics show that Indigenous offenders are disproportionately excluded by specific aspects of the Gladue process. A 2017 Statistics Canada survey confirms that in the last decade, the total rate of carceral admissions for Indigenous women increased from 28 percent to 43 percent, while the number of non-Indigenous women sentenced to prison decreased from 72 percent to 57 percent of total admissions.[69]

The judicial reframing process from *Gladue* serves as the "official story," where future decisions will use it as precedent. According to Balfour, in over 70 percent of Gladue cases involving female offenders, little attention was given to the systemic and background factors and the particular features which led their way to criminality.[70] An analysis of *R. v. Chickekoo*, for example, illustrates the continued disregard for the particular circumstances of an Indigenous female offender, and the failure by the court to properly analyze the impact that colonial policies potentially had on Indigenous women in Canada. The vast prison population increase of Indigenous women indicates that criminal courts operate within particular cultural and institutional contexts that perpetuate and reinforce systems of oppression.

R. v. Chickekoo

In 2009, Ruby Chickekoo, an Indigenous woman, was charged with aggravated assault and sentenced to an eighteen-month imprisonment term. The offense took place during a social gathering and involved the consumption of an excessive amount of alcohol. During the course of the night, an argument ensued between Chickekoo and another Indigenous woman, Margaret Boyce. The argument resulted in Chickekoo smashing a beer bottle over Boyce's head, leaving her with severe permanent injuries. Chickekoo's counsel appealed the decision of the court, arguing that the sentence was excessive, and that the presentence report used during the trial did not meet Gladue standards. Defense counsel argued that an incomplete assessment of systemic and background factors affected the ability of the sentencing judge to determine an appropriate sentence. To address these issues, Aboriginal Legal Services presented a detailed Gladue report. The report prepared by Aboriginal Legal Services indicated that the original presentence report did not contain a detailed description of the sexual assault that Chickekoo experienced as a child, outlining how she was gang raped after trying to get away from her older sister, who was physically assaulting her. Additionally, the original report lacked an analysis of how the murder of her partner was linked to conditions that characterized her life on the reserve, as well as an acknowledgment of the verbal and physical abuse that Chickekoo was subjected to from other kids in the community and its generational effects. [71] Though, indeed, the Ontario Court of Appeal allowed for fresh evidence to be introduced, Justice John dePencier Wright, the sentencing judge, deemed the sentence to be "fit and appropriate." He states:

> Given the serious violence of the offense and the extreme consequences to the victim, the sentence appropriately meets the need for denunciation and deterrence. It falls at the lower end of the range appropriate in this case and reflects the full benefit of the mitigating factors, despite the fact that the sentencing judge had a less fulsome explanation of those factors than that provided to this court. [72]

Chickekoo's appeal was dismissed because the court deemed that the seriousness of the offense eliminates the consideration for the multitudes of barriers and systemic forces which led her decision to commit a criminal offense. The Supreme Court focused on the nature of the crime rather than on Chickekoo, which again went against the sentencing guideline to "proceed on an individual (or case-by-case) basis."[73] The suggestion that serious offenses do not fall under the application of Gladue principles remains antithetical to the spirit of Gladue reports. While the idea that section 718.2(e) cannot be used for "serious offences" has been rectified and clarified in subsequent cases,[74] the problem is illustrated by the lack of Gladue reports being made for Chickekoo and several other Indigenous women.

The language used by judicial actors within *Chickekoo* is similar to that of *Gladue*, serving as a reminder of how judges continue to lose sight of the impact that Canada's colonial history has had on the lives of both Indigenous men and women. The details within *Chickekoo* thus serve as an important example of the ways in which *Gladue* becomes a "blueprint for the racialized and gendered structure of the Gladue process" that criminalizes several Indigenous women. *Chickekoo*, and perhaps for many other Indigenous women, reveals that the issue is not that the legal system ignores systemic and background factors tied to criminality.[75] The dilemma lies within the mismanagement of these links when the law actively conceals the relationships among historical conditions of genocide and violence, alcohol abuse, sexual assault, intimate-partner violence, and other violence experienced by Indigenous women.[76]

A reexamination with an intersectional lens uncovers how the seriousness of the crime continues to overshadow the effects of the Gladue principle, to compel judges to consider alternative sentences, contributing to the exacerbating rates of over-incarceration. It is clear that in the judiciary's unwillingness to liberally apply Gladue factors lies a component of misunderstanding of the ways systemic and historical factors affect Indigenous women, distinctively bringing them in conflict with the law. While section 718.2(e) introduces unique case law, *Gladue* and *Chickekoo* reveal that the cases of subsequent female Indigenous defendants are handled as "contingent on how that story has been told before," where race, gender, and social position were made to disappear during the trial. Indigenous women consistently fare at least 10 percent higher rates of incarceration than Indigenous males in Canada. These rates lead most critics to believe that *Gladue* has not "sensitized the judiciary" in a way that would end over-incarceration among Indigenous offenders.[77] Rather, the principles and guidelines established in *Gladue* are manifest of colonial policies that discursively constructed Jamie Gladue as undeserving of a non-carceral sentence. *Gladue*, thereby constructed a "reparative logic . . . an ontological and temporal framework that ultimately structures discourses of human/racial difference for Indigenous people in the criminal justice system."[78] This rigid framework hindered *Gladue* and possibly limited other Indigenous women from rehabilitative sentences alternative to imprisonment.

Imprisonment continues to be used as an appropriate "solution" for the myriad factors that bring Indigenous women into conflict with the law. It is vital to "pay attention to the interpretive structures we use to reconstruct events."[79] Creating a space for Indigenous defendants to speak is a tool for social change that accounts for the voices silenced through legal discourse. Crime, like all actions, is shaped by personal and collective experiences, expressed through competing discourses of legitimacy between Indigenous communities and mainstream society. Therefore, legal participants involved with sentencing need additional information about the accused's background, as well as "available and appropriate alternatives to incarceration or to the traditional sentencing process."[80] However, to be made aware of alternative approaches to incarceration, more justice initiatives must target education about the needs of Indigenous offenders. While engaging with issues of healing, rehabilitation, and treatment, various actors in the criminal justice system structure sentencing in ways that suggest prison is an ideal place for healing traumas. In doing so, disproportionate prison rates increase, and Indigenous women are criminalized for violence committed "in situations of social and economic deprivation with a lack of opportunities and limited options for positive development."[81] With more training and recognition of viable options alternative to imprisonment, counsel and judges can thoughtfully integrate understandings of how victimization constrains Indigenous women's options, and "foments vulnerability to criminalization within the broader context of colonization."[82] That being said, additional obligations are required not just of defense counsel, but of judges, prosecutors, correctional officials, as well as community organizations.

V. STRATEGIES OF RESISTANCE

In spite of controversies during enactment, section 718.2 was significant for criminal justice reform, as it outlined the purpose of sentencing and sentencing objectives and principles. Within our criminal justice system, the provision "offers the most meaningful direct alternative to imprisonment to assist in ameliorating the overincarceration of indigenous peoples."[83] The Native Woman's Association of Canada (NWAC) released a 2015 report that addresses the "decrease in the numbers of Indigenous women and girls referred to diversion [to incarceration]."[84] The report highlights that the criminal law system is a significant institution, and there is "ongoing distrust of how laws made to benefit Aboriginal People will in practice benefit Aboriginal women and girls."[85] There needs to be more effort in producing measures to consider the varying complexities that bring Indigenous women into conflict with the law. While section 718.2(e) provides a window to examining the contextual basis of the individual and the offense, it is problematic in that the reform is introduced at the end stage of the criminal justice process. Therefore, additional resources must be required at every step of the sentencing process for *Gladue* to properly reflect all who utilize this reform. Within these reports, examining the experiences of marginalization and exclusion can vastly impact the final sentence. In doing so, while "providing a socio-legal record of such practices and processes, we might get closer to a more robust account of how dominance is produced and experienced in settler colonialism."[86] If experience particular to Indigenous women is not discussed in other parts of the process, then it does not become apparent to the judge when determining a sentence. Such measures yield inconsistent application throughout the country, as the subject experiences of Indigenous women vary depending on the individual.

Individuals tend to think comparatively when they learn about other groups and their experiences, comparing and contrasting based on their identities in relation to others. With *Gladue*, I explored the idea of how "the production of Aboriginal identity through the idea of cultural difference obscures histories of colonialism and gendered racism" which preceding cases followed, setting a terrain that contributes to contemporary incarceration rates among Indigenous women.[87] It is evident that the framework under which Gladue was sentenced was characterized by a simple narrative that failed to consider the link between colonial violence and overrepresentation of Indigenous peoples in prison. Exploring these intricacies helps to advance a framework for understanding how the legal system may socially construct racialized identities through practices of representation in projects concerned with reparative justice. The rigidity and limiting directions provided to specialized courts serve to individualize Indigenous women's experiences while erasing the historical and systemic context of racism, sexism, and poverty.

As a consequence, section 718.2(e) becomes more about addressing numbers rather than recognizing historical violence or providing reparation.

VI. CONCLUSION

Within details of *Gladue,* it is evident that the way Indigenous women are conceptualized is controlled by historical colonizers who have generally dominated the resources, markets, and institutions of the colonized territory, maintaining power to implement the sociocultural structure. *Gladue* demonstrates the apparent disregard for the unique considerations which bring Indigenous women to commit criminal acts. This determination points to a rigid interpretation of section 718.2(e), effectively missing the opportunity to fight systemic discrimination against Indigenous women in the criminal justice system.[88] Prison then continues to be promoted as a rehabilitative sanction, which indicates a rigid dichotomy between victim and offender, categories which are not necessarily mutually exclusive.

Law remains a contested terrain, analyzed to interpret social and moral regulation, ideology, and discourses surrounding trial proceedings and the problematics of criminalization. An intersectional feminist analysis of *Gladue* and the Gladue process thus provides a unique and vital perspective on the limitations of the law.[89] *Gladue* can be re-imagined, focusing the attention of judicial behaviours towards Indigenous women as defendants. The trial, appeal, and Supreme Court proceedings provide a snapshot of the ways judges and lawyers played a role in constructing the experiences and actions of Jamie Gladue. Rather than erasing the racial and gender dimensions of the crime, judges explained her identity in terms of their cultural knowledge, to reproduce and perpetuate definitions of female criminality. Legal actors conceptualized Gladue without a demonstrated and thorough understanding of Indigenous peoples, especially Indigenous women. Consequently, agents of the law produced assumptions and meanings of what "factors" matter in the legal sphere.

The Supreme Court was presented with the opportunity to take an intersectional application in *Gladue*; however, they undertook a gender-neutral analysis that failed to set the stage for future judicial decisions involving Indigenous women as defendants. In *Chickekoo*, the seriousness of the offense appears to silence any need for a deeper analysis, as a simple "recognition" of the systemic factors in the case is considered to warrant a proper application of the principles set out in *Gladue.* An analysis of *Chickekoo* provides a deeper insight into the problems that continue to arise in cases involving Indigenous women. While the courts may not have trouble imposing a lesser sentence, they do have trouble with the imposition of a conditional sentence in cases involving violent, serious offenses. These factors make

Gladue a significant medium to assess the active and creative role that law has in shaping and understanding criminality. Universalizing women's experiences is ignorance, and we must continuously challenge the inattention to how identity and gender, combined, produce discrimination under the law. If women are unable to participate and voice their concerns due to lack of representation combined with outside responsibilities, their perspective is absent, which further perpetuates the effects of racialization.

Though indeed many minorities face similar intersections of race, sex, and class, Indigenous women face a special context of difference grounded in a legacy of colonial violence and assimilationist policies. Part of the problem is that while section 718.2(e) is in the Criminal Code, there is little to no legal training designed to enforce the provision. Legal actors, including lawyers and judges, become important figures responsible to interpret this code and impose a sentence based on their construction of "Aboriginality." This practice is problematic, for it gives judges power to contextualize the actions of the defendant to be that of a violent aggressor, serving a misleading idea of what constitutes female criminality. For this reason, imprisonment continues to be identified as a place of healing and rehabilitation, when non-carceral sentences can better reflect the rehabilitative needs of Indigenous women in conflict with the law. Thus, further research must focus on the details of everyday language practice, to better understand the process of constructing discriminatory policies that target Indigenous peoples and, more specifically, Indigenous women in Canada. These investigations continue to produce deeper understandings on social orders and trends of social relationships, interaction, and culture.

NOTES

1. Canadian Criminal Code R.S.C. 1985,c.C-46,s. 718.2(e) asam.by S.C. 1995, c.22, s.6.
2. Ibid.
3. *R. v. Gladue* [1999] 1 SCR 688.
4. Statistics Canada, *Adult correctional statistics in Canada, 2015/2016* by J. Reitano. (Ottawa, ON: Juristat, 2017) https://www150.statcan.gc.ca/n1/pub/85-002-x/2017001/article/14700-eng.htm
5. Per the Constitution Act of 1982, "Aboriginal" peoples includes First Nations, Inuit, and Métis peoples of Canada. This chapter recognizes that the term "Aboriginal" has been broadly criticized as yet another "colonial construct" that does not individualize nations, diversity among them, and their autonomy in naming themselves. I use "Indigenous" throughout this chapter to align with the goals of decolonization. The only time "Indigenous" is not used is when I am quoting directly from authors or statutes. While I recognize its limitations, my intention is that it include all those individuals and community members who claim Indigenous ancestry in Canada. There is great diversity among Indigenous peoples, in language, cultures, and location across Canada. Indigenous communities in Canada include First Nations, Métis, Inuit peoples, status and non-status Indians, treaty and non-treaty Indians who reside in urban, rural, reserve, and off-reserve settings. In these communities, laws, and social norms, and the needs vary in different communities. Despite this diversity, Indigenous peoples tend to share similar worldviews, concepts of justice, mechanisms of dispute resolution, and cultural and

ethical considerations. For the discussion in this project, I generalize Indigenous perspectives to understand the differences between them. Importantly, we must acknowledge that what may be generally true for Indigenous peoples may not be true in a specific nation or community. Accordingly, no single solution to any problem is going to work for all Indigenous peoples and communities, given their great diversity. For further information see Native Women's Association of Canada [NWAC]. "Culturally Relevant Gender-Based Models of Reconcilliation" (2010). https://www.nwac.ca/wp-content/uploads/2015/05/2010-NWAC-Culturally-Relevant-Gender-Based-Models-of-Reconciliation.pdf

6. Margaret Jackson, "Canadian Aboriginal Women and Their 'Criminality': The Cycle of Violence in the Context of Difference." *Australian and New Zealand Journal of Criminology* 32, no. 2 (1999): 203.

7. With a discourse analysis, scholars gain a fresh look into the politics of language and its operations within legal interactions as a critical tool for the exercise of socio-legal power. A feminist critical discourse methodology (FCDA) permits a focus on "the complex, subtle, and sometimes not so subtle, ways in which frequently taken-for-granted gendered assumptions and hegemonic power relations are discursively produced, sustained, negotiated, and challenged in different contexts and communities." Adopting intersectionality, this method of analysis demystifies the interconnection between gender, power, and ideology, uncovering "how power and dominance are discursively produced . . . through textual representations of gendered social practices, and through interactional strategies of talk." This practice illuminates how social practices are gendered, and how hierarchies of oppression affects Indigenous women. For additional reading, see Michelle Lazar, "Feminist Critical Discourse Analysis: Articulating a Feminist Discourse Praxis." *Critical Discourse Studies* (2007): 141–64.

8. While I am mindful that these excerpts have been cited and conceptualized by many scholars (for example, Murdocca 2013; Sheehy 2013; Lash 2000) I assess these examples with context to the judicial behaviors of trial court judges and how it informs the outcomes of legal procedures.

9. Carmela Murdocca, *To Right Historical Wrongs: Race, Gender, and Sentencing in Canada* (Vancouver: UBC Press, 2013), 81.

10. My analysis of *Gladue* was based on the official court transcripts retrieved from the Supreme Court official records. While institutionally produced court transcripts may not be completely accurate or detailed, these transcripts serve as the official representation of trials, which lawyers, litigants, and court official use to cite. These reports thus have an influence on outcomes, as legal participants rely on them during trials, appeals, and preparations of Gladue reports.

11. Susan Phillips, *Ideology in the Language of Judges: How Judges Practice Law, Politics, and Courtroom Control*. (New York: Oxford University Press, 1998), 117.

12. *R. v. Chickekoo* ([2008] ONCA 488).

13. Murdocca, *To Right Historical Wrongs*, 1.

14. Ibid., 95.

15. Ibid.

16. Glen Sean Coulthard. *Red Skin, White Masks: Rejecting the Colonial Politics of Recognition* (Minneapolis: University of Minnesota Press, 2014), 82.

17. Ibid., 89.

18. Murdocca, *To Right Historical Wrongs*, ix.

19. Sherene Razack, *Looking White People In the Eye: Gender, Race, and Culture in Courtrooms and Classrooms*. (Toronto: University of Toronto Press, 1998), 77.

20. Court of Appeal of British Columbia. #26300 Application for leave to appeal, "Statement of Facts," BC, Completed on November 12, 1997.

21. Ibid., para 4.

22. Canadian Criminal Code R.S.C. 1985,c.C-46,s. 718.2(e) asam.by S.C. 1995, c.22, s.6.

23. Born one of nine children to a Cree Mother and a Métis father, Gladue had been raised in a small Albertan community before moving to Nanaimo, British Columbia; see Elizabeth Sheehy, *Defending Battered Women on Trial: Lessons from the Transcripts* (Vancouver: UBC Press, 2013).

24. Court of Appeal of British Columbia. #26300 Application for leave to appeal, "Statement of Facts," BC, Completed on November 12, 1997, para 18.

25. Sheehy, *Defending Battered Women on Trial*, 161.

26. Jonathan Rudin, "Aboriginal Over-Representation and R. v. Gladue: Where We Were, Where We Are and Where We Might Be Going." *Supreme Court Law*. (2008).

27. Angela Cameron, "R v. Gladue: Sentencing and the Gendered Impacts of Colonialism," In *Moving Toward Justice: Legal Traditions and Aboriginal Justice*, by John D. Whyte (Saskatoon, SK: Purich Pub. in association with the Saskatchewan Institute of Public Policy, 2008), 175.

28. I will refer to the Gladue court process as the "Gladue process" repeatedly throughout the chapter. This specialized court system was developed after the 1999 Supreme Court decision, and is not to be confused by the case *R. v. Gladue*, or *Gladue*. See Kelly Hannah-Moffat and Paula Maurutto, "Aboriginal Knowledges in Specialized Courts: Emerging Practices in Gladue Courts," *Canadian Journal of Law and Society* 31, no. 3 (2016): 451–71.

29. Razack, *Looking White People In the Eye*, 77.

30. Carmela Murdocca, "Racialization, Criminalization, and Representation," in *Criminalization, Representation, Regulation*, ed. Deborah Brock, Amanda Glasbeek, and Carmela Murdocca, 107–32, 128–29. (Toronto: University of Toronto Press, 2014).

31. Cameron, "R v. Gladue," 166.

32. Monture-Angus, Patricia, "The Lived Experience of Discrimination: Aboriginal Women Who Are Federally Sentenced." (Submission of the Canadian Association of Elizabeth Fry Societies to the Canadian Human Rights Commission, 2002): 1. http://www.caefs.ca/wp-content/uploads/2013/04/The-Lived-Experience-of-Discrimination-Aboriginal-Women-Who-are-Federally-Sentenced-The-Law-Duties-and-Rights.pdf.

33. Ibid.

34. Coulthard, *Red Skin, White Masks*, 82.

35. Toni Williams, "Punishing Women: The Promise and Perils of Contextualized Sentencing for Aboriginal Women in Canada." *Cleveland State Law Review* (2007): 286

36. Murdocca, *To Right Historical Wrongs*, 109.

37. *R. v. Gladue*, Proceedings at Sentence Day 1, no.34897 (February 12, 1997), Supreme Court of British Columbia, Nanaimo, BC. "Submissions by Defense," 42–43.

38. Phillips, *Ideology in the Language of Judges*, 123.

39. Leti Volpp, "Framing Cultural Difference: Immigrant Women and Discourses of Tradition." *Differences: A Journal of Feminist Cultural Studies* 22, no. 1 (2011): 93.

40. Razack, *Looking White People In the Eye*, 74.

41. Elspeth Kaiser-Derrick's research on the sentencing of Indigenous women reveals that when appropriately contextualized, Indigenous women can receive sentences that adequately reflect their needs. Within *R. v. Fineday*, *R. v. Pawis*, and *R. v. Woods*, for example, judges provide an appropriate contextualization framework using a thoughtful Gladue analysis. Rehabilitative sentences alternative to incarceration are achievable, and the judges within these cases illuminate "how community sentences serve the rehabilitation needs of the women whereas imprisonment would exacerbate their problems" (178). Nonetheless, there is inconsistency in the application of s.718.2(e), which is partly due to the lack of training and understanding legal practitioners have of the reform. For additional reading, see E. Kaiser-Derrick, "Listening to What the Criminal Justice System Hears and the Stories It Tells: Judicial Sentencing Discourses About the Victimization and Criminalization of Aboriginal Women." Thesis (LLM). Vancouver: University of British Columbia, 2012. See also *R. v. Pawis*, 2006 ONCJ 386. [Toronto], *R. v. Fineday*, 2007 SKPC 2, and *R. v. Woods* (*R. v. C.I.W.*), 2007 SKPC 54.

42. Williams, "Punishing Women," 286.

43. Razack, *Looking White People In the Eye*, 74–75.

44. Balfour, "Do Law Reforms Matter?" 90.

45. Ibid., 41.

46. Ibid., 192.

47. Ibid., 21.

48. Ibid.

49. *R. v. Gladue* [1997] 98 B.C.A.C. 120 para 20.

50. Balfour, "Do Law Reforms Matter?" 90.
51. Ibid., para 30.
52. Research confirms that defendants are judged more harshly when they deviate from the stereotypical version of a "battered woman" that is constructed via BWS. See also Sheehy, *Defending Battered Women on Trial.*
53. Sheehy, *Defending Battered Women on Trial*, 48.
54. Ibid., 23.
55. Ibid., 54.
56. Sheehy, *Defending Battered Women on Trial*, 196.
57. Razack, *Looking White People In the Eye*, 18.
58. Shoshana Pollack, "An Imprisoning Gaze: Practices of Gendered, Racialized, and Epistemic Violence." *International Review of Victimology* 19, no 1 (2013): 106.
59. Ibid., 174.
60. Susan Ehrlich, 2001, *Representing Rape: Language and Sexual Consent* (London: Routledge, 2001), 4.
61. Ibid., 1.
62. Coulthard, *Red Skin, White Masks*, 10.
63. Sheehy, *Defending Battered Women on Trial*, 16.
64. Gayatri Chakravorty Spivak. *In Other Worlds: Essays in Cultural Politics* (New York: Routledge, 1987).
65. Ibid., 53.
66. Ibid., 55.
67. Elizabeth Comack and Gillian Balfour. *The Power to Criminalize: Violence, Inequality, and the Law* (Halifax, NS: Fernwood Publishing, 2004), 34.
68. Murdocca, *To Right Historical Wrongs*, 523
69. Statistics Canada, "Adult Correctional Statistics," https://www150.statcan.gc.ca/n1/pub/85-002-x/2017001/article/14700-eng.htm. The last year this report was made available was 2017.
70. Balfour, "Do Law Reforms Matter?" 95.
71. *R. v. Chickekoo* [2008] ONCA 488.
72. Ibid., para 13.
73. Jean Lash "Case Comment: R v. Gladue." *Canadian Women Studies* 20 (2000): 88.
74. See *R. v. Ipeelee* 2012 1 S.C.R. 433.
75. Murdocca, *To Right Historical Wrongs*, 81.
76. Ellen Adelberg and Claudia Currie. *In Conflict With the Law; Women and the Canadian Criminal Justice System.* (Vancouver, BC: Press Gang Publishers, 1993), 79.
77. Stack 1999, 481.
78. Carmela Murdocca, "Ethics of Accountability: Gladue, Race, and the Limits of Reparative Justice." *Canadian Journal of Women and the Law* 30, no. 3 (2018): 526.
79. Razack, *Looking White People In the Eye*, 55.
80. "Spotlight on Gladue: Challenges, Experiences, and Possibilities in Canada's Criminal Justice System." Research and Statistics Division. Department of Justice, Canada. Ottawa, ON. https://www.justice.gc.ca/eng/rp-pr/jr/gladue/index.html
81. *R. v. Ipeelee*, para. 73.
82. Kaiser-Derrick, Listening to What the Criminal Justice Hears, 136.
83. Elspeth Kaiser-Derrick, *Implicating the System: Judicial Discourses in the Sentencing of Indigenous Women*. (Winnipeg: University of Manitoba Press, 2019), 9.
84. NWAC, 38.
85. Ibid., 39.
86. Murdocca, "Ethics of Accountability," 528.
87. Murdocca, *To Right Historical Wrongs*, 24.
88. Lash "Case Comment," 85.
89. First coined by Kimberlé Crenshaw (1991), intersectionality voices that consideration must be given to interlocking systems of oppression, including patriarchal, racial, or economic systems that converge to entrap women. Crenshaw illuminates the complex nature of our identities and the value in acknowledging the difference. She problematized the belief that

women's experiences with marginalization could be understood through gender alone, pointing to the overlapping axes of identity, including race and class, which contribute toward a marginalized individual's experience. For additional reading see Kimberle Crenshaw, "Mapping the Margins: Intersectionality, Identity Politics, and Violence against Women of Color." *Stanford Law Review* 43, no. 6 (1991): 1241–99.

BIBLIOGRAPHY

Adelberg, Ellen, and Claudia Currie. 1993. *In Conflict with the Law: Women and the Canadian Criminal Justice System*. Vancouver: Press Gang Publishers.

Angermeyer, Philipp. 2018. "Adapting Existing Data Sources: Language and the Law." In *Data Collection in Sociolinguistics: Methods and Applications*, by C. Mallinson, B. Childs and G. Van Herk, 182–85. New York: Routledge.

Balfour, Gillian. 2012. "Do Law Reforms Matter? Exploring the Victimization Criminalization Continuum in the Sentencing of Aboriginal Women in Canada." *International Review of Victimology* 19 (1): 85–102.

Cameron, Angela. 2008. "R v. Gladue: Sentencing and the Gendered Impacts of Colonialism." In *Moving Toward Justice: Legal Traditions and Aboriginal Justice*, by John D. Whyte, 160–80. Saskatoon: Purich Pub in association with the Saskatchewan Institute of Public Policy.

Comack, Elizabeth, and Gillian Balfour. 2004. *The Power to Criminalize: Violence, Inequality, and the Law*. Halifax: Fernwood Publishing.

Coulthard, Glen Sean. 2014. *Red Skin, White Masks: Rejecting the Colonial Politics of Recognition.* Minneapolis: University of Minnesota Press.

Crenshaw, Kimberle. 1991. "Mapping the Margins: Intersectionality, Identity Politics, and Violence against Women of Color." *Stanford Law Review* 43 (6): 1241–99.

Department of Justice, Canada. "Spotlight on Gladue: Challenges, Experiences, and Possibilities in Canada's Criminal Justice System." Ottawa, ON: Research and Statistics Division. 2017. Accessed July 13, 2019. https://www.justice.gc.ca/eng/rp-pr/jr/gladue/index.html.

Ehrlich, Susan. 2007. "Legal Discourse and the Cultural Intelligibility of Gendered Meanings." *Journal of Sociolinguistics* 11 (4): 452–77.

———. 2001. *Representing Rape: Language and Sexual Consent*. London: Routledge.

Jackson, Margaret. 1999. "Canadian Aboriginal Women and Their 'Criminality': The Cycle of Violence in the Context of Difference." *Australian and New Zealand Journal of Criminolo gy* 32 (2): 197–208.

Kaiser-Derrick, Elspeth. 2019. *Implicating the System: Judicial Discourses in the Sentencing of Indigenous Women.* Winnipeg: University of Manitoba Press.

———. "Listening to What the Criminal Justice System Hears and the Stories It Tells: Judicial Sentencing Discourses about the Victimization and Criminalization of Aboriginal Women." L.L.M Thesis (University of British Columbia, 2012).

Lash, Jean. 2000. "Case Comment: R v. Gladue." *Canadian Women Studies* 20: 85–91.

Manley-Casimir, Kirsten. 2012. "Creating Space for Indigenous Storytelling in Courts." *Canadian Journal of Law and Society* 27 (2): 231–47.

Maurutto, Paula, and Kelly Hannah-Moffat. 2016. "Aboriginal Knowledges in Specialized Courts: Emerging Practices in Gladue Courts." *Canadian Journal of Law and Society* 31 (3): 451–71.

Monture-Angus, Patricia. 2002. "The Lived Experience of Discrimination: Aboriginal Women Who Are Federally Sentenced." Submission of the Canadian Association of Elizabeth Fry Societies to the Canadian Human Rights Commission. Accessed July 13, 2019. http://www.caefs.ca/wp-content/uploads/2013/04/The-Lived-Experience-of-Discrimination-Aboriginal-Women-Who-are-Federally-Sentenced-The-Law-Duties-and-Rights.pdf.

Murdocca, Carmela. 2018. "Ethics of Accountability: Gladue, Race, and the Limits of Reparative Justice." *Canadian Journal of Women and the Law* 30 (3): 522–42.

———. 2014. "Racialization, Criminalization, and Representation." In *Criminalization, Representation, Regulation*, by Deborah Brock, Amanda Glasbeek, and Carmela Murdocca, 107–32. Toronto: University of Toronto Press.

———. 2013. *To Right Historical Wrongs: Race, Gender, and Sentencing in Canada*. Vancouver: UBC Press.

Native Women's Association of Canada (NWAC). 2015. "What Is Gladue?" Native Women's Association of Canada. Accessed August 10, 2019. https://www.nwac.ca/wp-content/uploads/2015/05/What-Is-Gladue.pdf.

Phillips, Susan. 1998. *Ideology in the Language of Judges: How Judges Practice Law, Politics, and Courtroom Control*. New York: Oxford University Press.

Pollack, Shoshana. 2013. "An Imprisoning Gaze: Practices of Gendered, Racialized, and Epistemic Violence." *International Review of Victimology* 19 (1): 103–14.

Razack, Sherene. 1998. *Looking White People In the Eye: Gender, Race, and Culture in Courtrooms and Classrooms*. Toronto: University of Toronto Press.

Roach, Kent, and Jonathan Rudin. 2000. "Gladue: The judicial and Political Reception of a Promising Decision." *Canadian Journal of Criminology* 6 (4): 355–88.

Rudin, Jonathan. 2008. "Aboriginal Over-Representation and R. v. Gladue: Where We Were, Where We Are and Where We Might Be Going." *Supreme Court Law*, 687–713.

R. v. Gladue, Proceedings at Sentence, no.34897 (February 12, 1997), Supreme Court of British Columbia, Nanaimo, BC.

R. v. Gladue [1997] 98 B.C.A.C. 120.

R. v. Gladue [1999] 1 S.C.R. 688.

R. v. Ipeelee, 2012 SCC 13, [2012] 1 S.C.R. 433.

R. v. Chickekoo (2008), 79 W.C.B. (2d) 66, 2008 ONCA 488 C.A.

Sheehy, Elizabeth. 2013. *Defending Battered Women on Trial: Lessons from the Transcripts*. Vancouver: UBC Press.

Spivak, Gayatri Chakravorty. 1987. *In Other Worlds: Essays in Cultural Politics*. New York: Routledge.

Stack, D. 1999. "The Impact of RCAP on the Judiciary Bringing Aboriginal Perspectives into the Courtroom." *Saskatchewan Law Review*, 472–81.

Statistics Canada. Adult Correctional Services Survey, Table 6: "Admissions to Adult Custody, by Aboriginal Identity, Sex and Jurisdiction, 2006/2007 and 2016/2017." Ottawa, ON: Canadian Centre for Justice Statistics, 2018. Accessed July 13, 2019. https://www150.statcan.gc.ca/n1/pub/85-002-x/2018001/article/54972/tbl/tbl06-eng.htm.

———. "Adult Correctional Statistics in Canada, 2015/2016," by Julie Reitano. Statistics Canada Catalogue no. 85-002-X. Ottawa, ON: Juristat, 2017. Accessed August 24, 2003. https://www150.statcan.gc.ca/n1/pub/85-002-x/2017001/article/14700-eng.htm.

Truth and Reconciliation Canada. Calls to Action (Winnipeg: Truth and Reconciliation Commission of Canada, 2015). http://nctr.ca/assets/reports/Calls_to_Action_English2.pdf.

Volpp, Leti. 2011. "Framing Cultural Difference: Immigrant Women and Discourses of Tradition." *Differences: A Journal of Feminist Cultural Studies* 22 (1): 90–110.

Williams, Toni. 2008. "Intersectionality Analysis in the Sentencing of Aboriginal Women in Canada: What Difference Does It Make?" *In Intersectionality and Beyond: Law, Power, and the Politics of Location*, edited by Emily Graham, 79–100. London: Routledge.

———. 2007. "Punishing Women: The Promise and Perils of Contextualized Sentencing for Aboriginal Women in Canada." *Cleveland State Law Review* 55 (3): 269–87.

Chapter Two

Losing Custodial Mothers in Child Support Reform

Laura Lane-Steele

Child support law and policy has undergone various stages of reform throughout its existence. Until the 1970s, child support was not heavily regulated, and noncustodial parents were typically not pursued for support. As state expenditures on welfare programs increased, Congress overhauled child support enforcement because it recognized child support as a way to reimburse the government for funds dispersed to custodial mothers. With these reforms came harsh enforcement mechanisms for noncustodial parents who were not paying child support. For middle- and high-income noncustodial parents, these reforms have been fairly effective in collecting support payments. However, for low-income noncustodial parents, the reforms have resulted in child support orders that these parents cannot afford to pay, causing the accumulation of massive arrears, and in some cases, ending with a contempt order that jails the noncustodial parent for not paying. In response, governments have recently implemented, and scholars have proposed, various reforms to child support enforcement that are aimed at right-sizing child support orders, reducing child support debt, and decriminalizing the failure to pay child support.

The intended and actual beneficiaries of these reform efforts have been primarily, and sometimes exclusively, low-income noncustodial parents. On the other hand, reform efforts aimed at improving the child support system for low-income custodial parents have been scarce. Existing child support laws and policies generally do not provide low-income custodial parents with the necessary financial and nonfinancial supports to raise their children. Yet child support reform discourse has not prioritized the system's neglect of these parents and children.

This chapter intervenes in the scholarship on child support reform to expose how the current wave of reform is disproportionately focused on fixing child support enforcement for the benefit of low-income noncustodial parents, who are overwhelmingly men, while largely ignoring low-income custodial parents, who are overwhelmingly women. Although low-income custodial mothers often bear most of the responsibility of childrearing and breadwinning, the current legal regime has posed nothing meaningful to address this form of sex inequality. This chapter posits that child support law should be expanded to include policies that provide low-income mothers with both monetary and nonmonetary forms of support.

This chapter proceeds as follows. Part I provides an overview of the current child support enforcement system and argues that it is particularly punitive for low-income noncustodial fathers and mostly indifferent to alleviating the financial and parenting burdens on low-income custodial mothers. Part II reviews the main child support enforcement reforms that have been either implemented by state and federal governments or proposed in the scholarship. It concludes that these reforms conceptualize child support's problems primarily through the perspective of low-income noncustodial fathers and thereby function to address those problems, as opposed to ones faced by low-income custodial mothers. Part III situates the prioritization of fathers over mothers in child support reform in a larger pattern of placing men's interests over women's in race and class-based discourses and movements. Part IV details why reform efforts should include the interests of these mothers, highlighting the structural sex and class inequities perpetuated by a system that requires low-income custodial mothers to assume full responsibly for raising children. Part V provides examples of how child support reform might include custodial mothers' interests.

Three introductory notes: First, this chapter's primary purpose is to identify, and critique, the male-centered focus of recent reform efforts. Some custodial mother-centered reforms are discussed at the end of the chapter, but it is beyond the scope of this project to detail exactly what a child support system that prioritizes low-income custodial mothers should look like. Second, this chapter focuses on child support law and policy as it affects low-income parents because those are the parents who are most negatively impacted by its problems. Although many of the reforms in this chapter can be applied to parents of all income levels, this chapter understands child support, its failures, and its potential through the lens of low-income parents. Third, this chapter discusses custodial parents as women and noncustodial parents as men because an overwhelming majority of custodial parents are women (80 percent) and because the use of these categories is helpful in understanding the problems of child support as problems of sex inequality. However, this choice erases non-binary parents, noncustodial mothers, and custodial fathers, and also may indirectly serve to further essentialize women as parents. This chapter should be read with those limitations in mind.

I. OVERVIEW OF CHILD SUPPORT ENFORCEMENT FOR LOW-INCOME PARENTS

The modern child support system began with the Social Security amendments of 1974. These amendments created a federal child support enforcement program under Part D of Title IV of the Social Security Act and required each state to create state-level agency counterparts.[1] The motivation behind these amendments was not primarily about supporting children or ensuring that custodial parents had adequate funds to raise their children. Rather, Congress thought that the increasing demand for government assistance was caused by absent parents and viewed child support enforcement as a way to reimburse the government for money distributed to low-income mothers.

Congress then passed two Child Support Enforcement Amendments in 1984 and 1988, and the Personal Responsibility and Work Opportunity Reconciliation Act (PRWORA), passed in 1996, included additional changes to child support policy and collection. The result of these various statutes is a child support enforcement system full of rigorous collection mechanisms. Child support agencies can order paternity testing and then locate biological fathers through various databases.[2] Courts have streamlined processes to quickly calculate how much money noncustodial parents should pay in support. If noncustodial parents fail to pay, child support agencies can automatically withhold child support payments from their paychecks and tax refunds, seize their bank accounts, and revoke their drivers, occupational, and professional licenses.[3]

For noncustodial parents who have the means to pay, these mechanisms are fairly effective in collecting support. This is evidenced by the fact that out of the billions of dollars owed in past-due child support payments, only 30 percent is owed by noncustodial parents who make more than $10,000 per year.[4] However, when it comes to low-income noncustodial parents, the child support system has proven ineffective in collecting payments primarily because these fathers are often ordered to pay more child support than they can realistically afford. This happens for a number of reasons. For one, courts frequently set child support orders based on the father's imputed income, or the amount of money he should and could make, not his actual income.[5] This typically happens when fathers fail to appear in court for the hearings, and the judge sets a default order, but this can also happen when a judge thinks a father is intentionally underemployed. When low-income fathers do attend their hearings, it is often without legal representation, which can result in child support orders that do not reflect their actual ability to pay.[6]

A second reason child support payments are too high for many low-income noncustodial parents is that many states allow noncustodial parents to request a reduction in their child support order (i.e., a downward modification) only when the change in their income is deemed "involuntary." Depending on the state, underemployment or unemployment may not qualify as involuntary. Even incarceration is not deemed involuntary in many states, causing child support arrears to accrue when noncustodial parents are in prison and incapable of making any income.[7] Moreover, to seek a modification when income changes are deemed involuntary, noncustodial fathers still need to know that they are eligible for a downward modification and either hire an attorney or navigate the legal process themselves. Thus, child support orders that are too high to begin with and difficult to modify result in low-income noncustodial parents accruing a large amount of child support debt. And unlike other forms of debt, past-due child support debt generally cannot be discharged or modified.[8]

Not only does the current system strap noncustodial fathers with massive and often nondischargeable debt, it also permits the imprisonment of these parents. Noncustodial parents who are extremely delinquent in their child support payments can be incarcerated for civil or criminal contempt of court. Low-income parents without the ability to pay are not supposed to be jailed for contempt under Supreme Court precedent. In theory, due process requirements prohibit courts from holding a noncustodial parent in civil contempt absent a finding that the parent has the ability to pay but intentionally and willfully failed to pay court-ordered child support.[9] However, low-income noncustodial fathers often do not have an attorney in civil proceedings, and the Supreme Court has not extended this same rule to criminal contempt.[10] Thus, in practice, thousands of noncustodial fathers are jailed for failure to pay child support. Indeed, one study estimates that around fifty thousand people nationwide are incarcerated for child support–related reasons.[11]

The child support system often overcharges poor noncustodial fathers and punishes their inability to pay; meanwhile, it also fails to provide low-income custodial mothers with sufficient assistance, financial or otherwise. Because custodial mothers are disproportionately low income, poverty reduction should be a primary goal of child support.[12] Yet this is not and has never been a central priority of the child support system; rather, child support has functioned as a reimbursement mechanism for the government. To receive benefits under Temporary Assistance for Needy Families (TANF), custodial mothers are required to assign their child support collection rights to the government so it can reimburse itself for TANF payments. Some states have implemented "pass through" policies, meaning that between $50 and $200 of the support payment is passed through to the custodial mother before the remaining amount is withheld by the government. However, these policies do not provide adequate financial support to custodial mothers, and often, there are no funds to "pass through" because the noncustodial parent is also low-income and making no or minimal payments. Moreover, when custodial mothers assign their child support collection rights to the government, child support court proceedings are separated from custody and visitation court proceedings—unlike other domestic relations proceedings where support and visitation/custody are adjudicated together. Thus, low-income mothers who want to share childrearing responsibilities through a custody or visitation order must navigate a second court proceeding.[13]

Additionally, over half of custodial parents with child support orders receive either no payments or incomplete payments, and the child support system has not devised any way to fill the financial gap between what noncustodial parents have provided and the amount custodial parents need to support their children.[14] Indeed, the child support system is so ineffective that more than half (60 percent) of low-income custodial mothers do not pursue child support orders.[15] Receiving adequate child support payments can be crucial for low-income custodial parents. For the limited number of custodial parents below the poverty line who do receive full payments, the average payment represents 58 percent of their average income.[16]

In sum, the "child support system" is a misnomer for low-income custodial mothers. The system does not, and was not intended to, meaningfully support low-income custodial mothers and children. Rather, it primarily operates as a revenue-generating service for the government. Meanwhile, the child support system punishes, and sometimes incarcerates, low-income noncustodial fathers for being poor. Child support enforcement is ripe for substantial reform.

II. RECENT REFORMS ARE PREDOMINANTLY FOCUSED ON LOW-INCOME NONCUSTODIAL FATHERS

In response to these problems with child support enforcement, federal and state governments have recently implemented—and scholars have proposed—a number of legal and policy changes. This section will review these reforms and explain how they are primarily designed to improve the ways in which existing child support laws and policies are detrimental to noncustodial fathers. It will also explain how these reforms leave the interests of custodial mothers largely unaddressed.

Government Reforms

In 2016, the Obama administration issued a regulation called "Flexibility, Efficiency, and Modernization in Child Support Enforcement Programs."

According to the Department of Health and Human Services (DHHS), this rule aimed to increase "timely payments to families," decrease "the nonpayment rate," and increase "the number of noncustodial parents working and supporting their children."[17] These stated goals ostensibly provide custodial mothers with more financial support and do not explicitly prioritize noncustodial fathers' interests. However, the regulation's major provisions do not directly support these goals. These provisions: (1) ensure child support orders are based on noncustodial parents' actual ability to pay; (2) require governments to abide by due process safeguards before filing civil contempt petitions for failure to pay (this includes providing the court with information regarding the parent's ability to pay and providing clear notice to the parent that his ability to pay "constitutes the critical question in the civil contempt action"); (3) require states to treat incarceration as involuntary unemployment, thereby allowing incarcerated parents to reduce their child support payments; (4) require states to provide notice to both parents of their right to request a downward modification if the parent who owes support will be incarcerated for 180 days or more; (5) give states greater flexibility to close cases when child support is extremely unlikely to be paid, as when the noncustodial parent has a serious work-limiting disability; and (6) allow a custodial parent to use the state's assistance in establishing paternity without requiring the court to impose a child support order.[18]

To be sure, many of these provisions may increase the amount of support custodial mothers receive; for example, keeping fathers out of prison allows them to work and to make support payments. But none of these major provisions places custodial mothers' interests at the fore. Rather, this regulation primary benefits low-income noncustodial fathers by ensuring that they are not paying more than they can afford, easing their ability to decrease amounts in orders, and increasing procedural safeguards so that fewer fathers who are too poor to pay are incarcerated.

States have also reformed their child support policies with similar noncustodial father-focused goals in mind. A number of states have instituted diversion programs for fathers who have been held in contempt for failure to pay child support. These programs allow participants to either avoid or reduce their period of incarceration, and some also help participants secure employment. For instance, in Georgia, participants reside in a diversion center, are permitted to travel to and from their job, and may participate in educational and counseling programs.[19] Programs also exist for noncustodial fathers who are incarcerated for reasons unrelated to child support and help these men seek downward modifications of their existing child support orders. For example, Minnesota's Child Support Liaison program connects incarcerated parents with a child support enforcement representative who helps them navigate the enforcement system and request reductions.[20] In this same vein, a number of states have recently passed legislation that either eases the modification process or suspends child support obligations for incarcerated parents.[21] Here again, these reforms are meant to ensure that noncustodial fathers who are incarcerated do not leave prison with insurmountable debt. However, they also decrease the support available to custodial mothers, without offering anything in its place.

In addition to limiting the effects of incarceration on child support debt, many states have passed laws or instituted policies that prevent child support payments from bankrupting noncustodial fathers. First, the majority of states have built in a Self-Support Reserve (SSR) into their child support statutes and regulations.[22] The SSR is the amount of money the state determines noncustodial parents need to support themselves and is typically tied to federal poverty guidelines. If the noncustodial parent's income is less than the SSR, the court can decrease the presumptive child support payment to a nominal amount, usually $25 or $50 per month. SSR amounts vary by jurisdiction but hover around $15,000 to $16,000 per year. Although the SSR may indirectly increase child support payments by ensuring that noncustodial fathers are not overcharged for child support, this policy generally results in less money reaching custodial mothers and child(ren).[23] Moreover, it shifts the financial burden of raising children further onto custodial mothers, who are on average poorer than noncustodial fathers.[24] For instance, in 2007, when Washington, DC incorporated an SSR into its child support guidelines, a noncustodial parent earning 133 percent of the poverty line paid $50 per month in support, but a custodial parent earning the same amount would not be eligible for TANF and would be responsible for the remainder of the child's financial needs.[25] In other words, she would likely be paying more than $50 per month to support her child, even though she earned the same amount of money as the noncustodial father.

Additionally, "responsible fatherhood" programs abound throughout the country and are generally focused on helping noncustodial fathers find employment, though some programs also provide additional services, including parental education, financial management assistance, and treatment for substance abuse.[26] Employment programs that target poor noncustodial fathers have the potential to benefit custodial mothers and children through increased and reliable child support payments. Some, in fact, do.[27] However, many of these programs have proved ineffective, with high dropout rates.[28] Moreover, increasing child support payment is a residual, not a primary, intended benefit of these fatherhood programs. As the names of these programs indicate, they are for the benefit of fathers. Helping men find reliable employment is prioritized over increasing custodial mothers' income or quality of life, by for instance, also helping them find reliable employment or providing free childcare.

These reforms are not problematic in their substance or intent—just in their scope. Noncustodial fathers should not be required to pay more child support than they can afford, nor should they go to jail for failing to pay unrealistically high orders. Paying child support should not force men to live below the poverty line, accrual of insurmountable debt should be avoided, and noncustodial fathers should have help securing jobs. However, with few exceptions, recent government reforms have improved child support enforcement for noncustodial fathers but have failed to broaden their reach to address the needs of custodial mothers.

Proposed Reforms from Scholarship

Many proposed reforms in the literature also disproportionately target child support enforcement's harmful effects on noncustodial fathers. This section examines three common proposals: (1) reducing the amount of support noncustodial fathers owe, (2) expanding child support to include in-kind contributions, and (3) eradicating incarceration as an enforcement mechanism.

Reducing Support Owed

Like some of the government policies discussed, proposals in the scholarship also strive to prevent the accumulation of insurmountable child support debt. For example, Cortney E. Lollar suggests that child support debt should be dischargeable through bankruptcy proceedings.[29] Similarly, Tonya Brito has criticized "states' practice of charging unjustifiable interest rates . . . particularly when child support officials are well aware that the parents who fall behind in their payments live far below the poverty line."[30] These interest rates are often appallingly high—many states charge up to 12 percent—and accumulated interest accounts for a large percentage of the total amount of outstanding arrears.[31] Additionally, many scholars have emphasized the need to change child support formulas to ensure that the amount of child support ordered matches the noncustodial father's actual ability to pay and have called for removing any imputed or potential income from the calculation.[32]

These reforms present the laudable goal of preventing poor fathers from amassing substantial debt, but by decreasing the amount noncustodial fathers owe, they shift the financial responsibility for childrearing even further onto custodial mothers, who, on average, earn less than noncustodial fathers. Thus, if these policies do not include a mechanism where the government fills the gap between what the noncustodial father can afford to pay and the amount of money it takes to raise a child, the custodial mother must fill that gap.

In-Kind Support

Some scholars have critiqued how child support is limited to cash contributions, arguing that in-kind contributions (i.e., goods and services) should be credited to noncustodial fathers' child support obligations.[33] The federal regulation of child support on Native American lands is an existing model that scholars argue states should adopt. These regulations permit noncash forms of child support, which is defined as "support provided to a family in the nature of goods and/or services, rather than in cash, but which, nonetheless has a certain and specific dollar value."[34] Noncash payments must directly contribute to the children's needs and may include tasks like helping with transportation and making repairs to the child's home.

Including goods and services in the definition of child support has numerous upsides. As scholars note, it would "allow poor fathers, who cannot fulfill the role of economic provider, to support their children in other equally important ways,"[35] "serve to reduce barriers to paternal involvement and minimize the impact on noncustodial fathers of the collateral consequences of staggering child support arrears,"[36] and rebut the restrictive "father as breadwinner" narrative. Moreover, many low-income noncustodial fathers already provide some form of in-kind support.[37] Thus, broadening the definition of child support to account for in-kind support would credit fathers for contributions they are already making. Not only would more low-income noncustodial fathers be able to contribute in this way, but they also may be more willing. According to a study on low-income noncustodial fathers and their children, these fathers "recoil at the notion that they are just a paycheck" and prefer an "'as needed' approach to financial provision, which seldom puts [the] cash in the hands of the child's mother but is directly responsive to particular needs of the child."[38]

At first glance, in-kind child support is promising because it is a form of support that fathers at any income level can provide and may be more inclined to provide. Moreover, through lowered financial payments and higher compliance, it may reduce incarceration rates for failure to pay support. Unlike many other reforms, it also directly benefits custodial mothers and children. However, counting both goods and services as child support can have negative consequences. Although the two are generally discussed together in the literature, the implications of including services as child support versus goods are meaningful.

Expanding child support to include services, from car repairs to child care, is critically important to child support reform for the reasons scholars have given. In contrast, allowing goods to count toward child support arrears may prove to be problematic. First, allowing goods to count is internally contradictory when proposed (as it usually is) in the context of critiquing child support enforcement as overly punitive for low-income fathers. If noncustodial fathers have the money to buy goods for their children, then they (probably) have the money to pay child support. Thus, including goods in the definition of child support transfers the discretion from the custodial mother to the noncustodial father to buy diapers, clothes, school supplies, and so on, for their children. Indeed, one reason noncustodial fathers prefer in-kind and informal child support to formal support is that they can bypass the custodial mother and give directly to their children.[39] Thus, because a goods-inclusive model of in-kind support both reduces (or eliminates) the amount of money custodial mothers receive in support payments and shifts decisional authority to noncustodial fathers regarding how money should be spent on children, this reform also prioritizes noncustodial fathers over custodial mothers, though perhaps less so than the others addressed in this chapter.

Moreover, this shift in power from custodial mothers to noncustodial fathers reinforces the harmful narrative that low-income mothers (and particularly Black mothers) are "bad mothers" because they misuse child support payments, spending the money on themselves rather than their children.[40] This narrative bears similarities to that of the Black "welfare queen." Just as "welfare queens" are deemed "overindulgent users of public resources," who misuse government dollars, Black mothers, according to this narrative, misuse child support dollars and should not have discretion over child support funds.[41]

The benefits of in-kind support can be achieved by broadening child support to include services, and examples of such service-only models are discussed in section V. Including goods (through its redistribution of buying power to noncustodial fathers) contributes to the harmful bad-mother rhetoric, fails to undercut the "father as provider" narrative, and is internally contradictory as a reform for low-income noncustodial fathers.

Incarceration for Failure to Pay

Another major area of reform focuses on decriminalizing the failure to pay child support and removing incarceration as a punishment for civil contempt for failure to pay.[42] Lollar argues that the extremely punitive nature of child support enforcement and the resulting criminalization of poor fathers serve as punishment for having children that fathers cannot afford to support. According to Lollar, our society seeks to deter and punish "'irresponsible sex' among heterosexuals," and "moral condemnation of and a desire to stigmatize poor, and often minority, fathers . . . is at the heart of the criminalization of a father's failure to pay child support."[43] She likens the failure to pay child support to a new debtors' prison and questions this practice's constitutionality.[44] Other scholars have also questioned the constitutionality of incarcerating noncustodial parents for failure to pay child support.[45]

The criminalization of the failure to pay child support is indeed constitutionally questionable, fueling mass incarceration and being counterproductive and morally dubious. This reform is indisputably important and necessary. Its focus remains, however, on noncustodial fathers and is another example of how reform to child support enforcement centers on noncustodial fathers.

III. PRIORITIZING MEN IN CHILD SUPPORT REFORM

This section argues that the current prioritization of low-income noncustodial fathers in child support reform is one manifestation of a larger pattern of placing men's interests before women's in race- and class-equality movements. When it comes to issues of race and class injustice that affect both low-income men and women of color, the male-centered vision of antiracism/anticlassism tends to control the majority of discourses and directs advocacy and intervention to low-income men of color.

Recent calls for reform have framed the problematic aspects of child support policy as ones of racial and class injustice, as they should. Indeed, the failures of child support enforcement have disproportionately affected both custodial and noncustodial low-income parents, and these effects are more stark for low-income parents of color. Noncustodial fathers who are also racial minorities are more likely to be arrested for nonpayment,[46] and criminalizing the failure to pay child support disproportionately affects Black noncustodial parents.[47] The incarceration of noncustodial fathers who do not pay child support has been a major contributor to the mass incarceration of people of color, and Black men in particular.

Moreover, child support's failure to alleviate the burdens of custodial parenthood have proved particularly harmful to custodial mothers of color. First, a disproportionate number of custodial unmarried mothers are Black, and almost nine of ten Black single parents are women.[48] Second, while custodial mothers of all races are more likely to live in poverty than custodial fathers or cohabiting parents, custodial mothers of color are more likely than their white counterparts to live in poverty.[49] Third, Black custodial parents are more likely than any other racial group to receive no child support payments.[50] Thus, the current child support enforcement system negatively affects both low-income custodial mothers and noncustodial fathers of color. Yet reformers view the problems of child support enforcement predominantly through the lens of low-income noncustodial fathers. Consequentially, formulated policy reforms respond to these problems.

This prioritization of men's interests over women's in child support reform is part of a broader pattern in equality discourse and movements. Critical race theorists have examined this focus on Black men and the resulting neglect of Black women in antiracist discourse and policies across different areas of law and policy. Kimberlé Crenshaw has exposed how Black women are largely marginalized in both feminist and antiracist discourses that center white women and Black men, respectively.[51] Black women are subsequently erased due to both their racial and sexed identities. Other critical race scholars, including Devon Carbado and Paul Butler, have built on Crenshaw's work. Relevant here, these scholars have critiqued the centrality of Black men's interests in antiracist discourse and policies. Carbado refers to this narrative as the "privileged victim status of black men," which instructs that "Black men are perceived to be significantly more vulnerable and significantly more endangered that Black women." Therefore, they "become the quintessential example of the effects of racial subordination."[52] Butler calls this discourse "Black male exceptionalism," whose central premise is that "by almost every index of inequality, Black males are on the bottom—exceptionally burdened and marginalized."[53]

Class-based movements have also marginalized women, and women of color in particular. The central image of the labor movement is one of a white, working-class man, and this image has subsequently shaped both the priorities of the movement and the public's understanding of the movement's substance.[54] Even though the working class is primarily made up of people of color and women, the movement has not fully incorporated these populations into its membership or its platforms. Legal scholar Marion Crain has critiqued the male-dominated nature of the movement, writing:

> Lacking an avenue in which to voice their concerns, working class women have become politically invisible: their issues are given low priority on union lobbying agendas, deemphasized in organizing campaigns, missing from collective bargaining agreements, and absent in the pressure strategies boycotts, rallies, and pickets-that labor utilizes to publicize its cause.[55]

Antiracist and labor organizations have responded to demands to develop a more intersectional understanding of the issues within their respective movements and to devise a political agenda that represents their marginalized membership. However, this is an ongoing project, and dominant antiracist and class-based discourse and movements remain primarily male centered. Moreover, while race- and class-based movements have generally ignored women's interests, feminism has traditionally not questioned how sex inequality interacts with class and race to produce forms of oppression that are different from those faced by the white middle- and upper-class leaders of the movement. Child support reform cannot be characterized as central to dominant feminist discourse, but it probably would be if the victims of the child support system's failures were middle- and upper-class white women. However, "white feminism" is not the primary culprit of current reforms' male centeredness. Thus, feminism's role in abandoning low-income custodial mothers of color is beyond the scope of this chapter and should be explored in future projects.

When seen through these theoretical lenses, the centrality of noncustodial fathers in recent child support reform efforts is revealed as another example of male centeredness in race- and class-equality discourse. Overly punitive child support enforcement punishes low-income Black men for not achieving the middle-class, white, breadwinner model of ideal fatherhood. Meanwhile, these same systems also punish low-income Black women by requiring them to provide all, or mostly all, of the financial and nonfinancial resources necessary to raise children. However, because the of the male-centric narratives embedded in antiracism and antipoverty discourses, the central problems of child support remain contextualized as harm to noncustodial fathers.

IV. LOW-INCOME CUSTODIAL MOTHERS' INTERESTS SHOULD BE INCLUDED IN REFORM EFFORTS

This section argues that child support laws and policies can and should be used to address a significant source of structural sex and class inequality: namely, that low-income custodial mothers are doing both caretaking and breadwinning for themselves and their children. These mothers are tasked with all the chores of maintaining a household, like cooking, cleaning, shopping, and doing laundry. They are also typically in charge of administrative duties like paperwork, finding medical care, paying bills, organizing child care, and managing household finances.[56] The labor associated with child care also falls primarily on women, including supervision, bathing, changing, feeding, playing, and so on. Some estimates set the total time spent on this unpaid labor at around fifty hours per week.[57]

Additionally, most custodial mothers also must provide financially for their children. Time limitations created by child care and household responsibilities combine with other structural barriers to employment these women often navigate, including racism and sexism, to significantly restrain their liberty and result in more limited employment options. Yet, despite these barriers, the majority of custodial mothers are employed: 80 percent of custodial mothers work full or part-time.[58] To be sure, women do a disproportionate amount of unpaid labor at home even when they are not custodial mothers.[59] But this "second shift" problem is exacerbated when single custodial mothers work outside of the home, run a household, and raise children without much assistance.

The burden of single parenthood cannot just be measured in unpaid hours worked. Robin West has described the physiological costs of performing menial domestic labor, particularly when one is doing "more than one's fair share" of this work. She argues that domestic labor and child care are often "repetitive, under-stimulating, [and] physically demanding . . . [and] boring"[60] and highlights the rage induced by knowing that the consequences of not performing this labor are "child neglect and an unacceptable degree of filth."[61] Middle- and upper-class custodial mothers can avoid these costs by delegating menial tasks to lower-class women of color, but low-income custodial mothers cannot; rather, they are often the ones performing menial labor for wealthier women.[62]

To be sure, raising children is not exclusively, or primarily, a burden for many custodial mothers; rather, is it often both onerous and empowering. Patricia Hill Collins comments on this duality of parenthood, explaining that some mothers view motherhood as a "truly burdensome condition that stifles their creativity, exploits their labor, and makes them partners in their own oppression." Meanwhile, other women, or even these same women, also "see motherhood as providing a base for self-actualization, status in the Black community, and a catalyst for social activism."[63]

The child support system cannot, in and of itself, remedy the deeply rooted structural inequalities exacted on low-income custodial mothers. But the current system is not even orientated around these problems, and the majority of reform discourse fails to seriously consider how child support can be reformulated to address how custodial mothers, and low-income custodial mothers in particular, "are weighed down by the incessant responsibilities of mothering."[64]

V. CUSTODIAL-MOTHER-CENTERED REFORMS

While the weight of recent child support reforms targets noncustodial parents, some scholars have argued for shifts in the law that prioritize the interests of low-income custodial mothers. This section provides examples of these arguments in order to demonstrate what including custodial mothers in child support reform efforts could look like. Due to the limited scope of this chapter, this section does not discuss all of the details of these proposals nor does it engage with all of their potential drawbacks. Many of these proposals constitute major changes in child support enforcement and raise numerous complicated issues that this chapter does not address. My goal in providing these examples is to show child support's potential to alleviate current burdens on low-income custodial mothers.

Redistribution of Custody

Custody is the precursor to child support in the sense that custodial mothers need child support in the first place because they have custody of their children. Absent the stark sex disparity in custody, the burdens of childrearing would be more equally distributed among the sexes. As such, redistributing custody more equally between mothers and fathers would reduce the demand for formal child support orders, and in turn, could benefit mothers (by sharing costs and responsibilities with fathers) and fathers (by reducing their financial child support obligations). The law cannot force parents to share custody of their children. But the law does play a large role in creating and enforcing social norms and can therefore influence societal expectations regarding child custody.[65]

Some scholars have advanced legal changes that would promote joint custody. Solangel Maldonado, for instance, argues that the law should adopt a presumption of joint legal custody in divorce proceedings.[66] Under Maldonado's proposal, any parent who does not want joint custody would attend a "Refusal of Parental Responsibilities" hearing during which the court would inform the parent that their rejection of joint custody means that he concedes unfitness or has been found unfit by the court, and that he is "legally bound to pay child support even if the other parent has sole custody."[67] He would then be required to state on the record the "reasons for rejecting the children" which would, "in effect, ask a parent to admit that he is a 'bad' parent in order to avoid receiving joint custody."[68]

Maldonado's proposal is limited in scope because it requires interaction with the court system, and many low-income, unmarried parents often do not interact with the court system because they are not required go through court proceedings to dissolve their relationship. Although these parents could, in theory, seek custody, visitation, or child support orders through the court system, legal costs and other access-to-justice barriers often make obtaining such court orders difficult. In response to these barriers for unmarried parents, Clare Huntington argues for a presumption of joint legal and physical custody that is assigned at birth and applies to both parents regardless of marital status.[69] Currently, most states do not have a default rule for custody of children born to unmarried parents, and thus, under prevailing societal pressures and scripts, women typically assume the duties of custodial parents. The fifteen states that do have such child custody laws grant sole custody to the mother automatically, and the father must petition the court for custody or visitation.[70]

Adopting a presumption of joint custody is one possible way that the law could reduce the amount of paid and unpaid labor associated with childrearing performed by the low-income mothers at issue in this chapter. This reform could potentially increase women's autonomy by giving mothers the choice to have children without also automatically signing up to be the default custodial parent if their romantic relationship ends. Some scholars, however, do not view this reform as beneficial for mothers. Specifically, they argue that a presumption of joint custody would make it more difficult for women to obtain primary custody of their children and may reduce women's bargaining power in divorce negotiations because they cannot use the sole-custody presumption as leverage.[71] Moreover, this reform presupposes that some custodial mothers want to share the costs of childrearing with their children's fathers. For mothers who do not want to share custody of their children, the labor-reducing effects of this reform might not be worth it. Increased joint custody can operate to equalize the financial and nonfinancial costs of raising children, but whether equality in this context is a good thing or not is a debate outside the scope of this chapter.

Service-Based Support

Expanding child support to include service-based child support contributions is another possible reform that foregrounds custodial mothers. Frequently, this reform is discussed in the context of in-kind support, which involves both goods- and service-based support, as explained in section II. But some scholars have discussed service-based child support models beyond the context of a goods and services in-kind model. One interesting option, introduced by Margaret Ryznar, is to have noncustodial fathers provide labor to third-party commercial actors. The custodial mothers then could "pay" the third party for goods or services using the noncustodial parent's labor as a credit. Ryznar offers examples, including the noncustodial parent donating time to a child-care organization in exchange for free or reduced child-care for the custodial mother; the noncustodial parent contributing time to a food bank where the custodial parent would receive credit; and the employer of the noncustodial parent providing free services to the custodial parent in exchange for extra services contributed by the noncustodial parent.[72]

Previously, I proposed a child support program where noncustodial fathers could perform household chores or child care for the mother of their children. If the parents' relationship was strained or abusive, the noncustodial father could provide these services for another custodial mother in the program. The program is designed to give custodial mothers optimal control and autonomy in these arrangements, allowing them to dictate what kinds of labor they need and feel comfortable with the father performing. A child support officer would work as an intermediary between the parties, helping negotiate the tasks to be performed and mediating conflicts between the parties. The time the noncustodial father worked would then be converted to a dollar amount and deducted from his current or past-due child support obligations.[73]

Government-Funded Support

Service-based support and redistribution of custody work to reduce the nonmonetary costs of raising children for custodial mothers. Reforms that increase monetary support for low-income custodial parents typically involve increased expenditures by state and federal governments. One relatively simple reform involves ending a state's practice of intercepting child support payments from noncustodial fathers in order to reimburse itself for welfare payments. Some states currently pass through child support payments directly to families, but not all states pass through the entirety of what is permitted under the law.[74]

However, pass-through policies alone are insufficient to provide adequate support to custodial mothers because often there is not much money to pass through. Scholars have proposed other policies that involve more robust government support. Under one approach, called the "assured child support benefit," the "government would act as a guarantor for child support, ensuring that custodial parents receive a minimum support payment each month."[75] In other words, if the "support collected from a noncustodial parent was less than the minimum level, the government would subsidize the payment up to the amount of the guaranteed benefit to ensure a minimal standard of living."[76] Huntington has discussed another potential reform where the government would supplement a noncustodial father's paycheck for the specific purpose of paying child support to the custodial mother.[77] Although this program would only benefit noncustodial fathers who are employed, it may be easier to achieve politically because, as Huntington notes, initiatives that provide cash payments with no work requirement are often characterized as an "unearned handout."

VI. CONCLUSION

Child support reform cannot be a panacea for ensuring that low-income mothers have sufficient financial and nonfinancial support to raise children. Large-scale structural reform outside of the child support context—such as raising the minimum wage, expanding affordable housing, providing free or sliding-scale child care, reparations, and other poverty-reduction mechanisms—is also probably necessary. However, child support law and policy does have the potential to redistribute the labor of childrearing away from women by, for example, promoting joint custody and expanding child support to include service-based support. By combining these reforms with increased government support for parents, the child support system can be reformulated for the benefit of mothers.

NOTES

1. Social Security Act, 42 U.S.C. §§ 651–69.
2. Personal Responsibility and Work Opportunity Reconciliation Act (PWORA) of 1996, Pub. L. No. 104-193, 110 Stat. 2105 (1996).
3. Tonya L. Brito, "Fathers behind Bars: Rethinking Child Support Policy Toward Low-Income Noncustodial Fathers and Their Families," *Journal of Gender, Race & Justice* 15, no. 3 (Spring 2012): 650.

4. Elaine Sorensen, Liliana Sousa, and Simone G. Schaner, *Assessing Child Support Arrears in Nine Large States and the Nation* (Washington, DC: The Urban Institute, 2007), 22, https://www.urban.org/research/publication/assessing-child-support-arrears-nine-large-states-and-nation/view/full_report.

5. See Elizabeth G. Patterson, "Civil Contempt and the Indigent Child Support Obligor: The Silent Return of Debtor's Prison," *Cornell Journal of Law and Public Policy* 18, no. 1 (2008): 108.

6. Patterson, "Civil Contempt," 108.

7. Laura W. Morgan, *Child Support Guidelines: Interpretation and Application* (New York: Wolters Kluwer Law & Business, 2010), § 5.01; Ann Cammett, "Deadbeats, Deadbrokes, and Prisoners," *Georgetown Journal on Poverty Law and Policy* 18, no. 2 (Spring 2011): 151.

8. 42 U.S.C. § 666(a)(9).

9. *Turner v. Rodgers*, 546 U.S. 431 (2011).

10. Cortney E. Lollar, "Criminalizing (Poor) Fatherhood," *Alabama Law Review* 70, no. 1 (2018): 143–44.

11. Carmen Solomon-Fears, Alison M. Smith, and Carla Berry, *Child Support Enforcement: Incarceration as the Last Resort Penalty for Nonpayment of Support*, CRS Report No. R42389 (Washington DC: Congressional Research Service, 2012), 2.

12. Timothy Grall, *Custodial Mothers and Fathers and Their Child Support: 2015*, Current Population Reports No. P60-262 (Washington, DC: U.S. Census Bureau, 2018), https://perma.cc/6DUX-E5C2.

13. See Stacy Brustin and Lisa Vollendorf Martin, "Paved with Good Intentions: Unintended Consequences of Federal Proposals to Integrate Child Support and Parenting Time," *Indiana Law Review* 48, no. 3 (2015): 805–6.

14. Grall, *Custodial Mothers*, 9.

15. Office of Child Support Enforcement, Administration for Children and Families, U.S. Department of Health and Human Services, *Why Don't More Poor Custodial Parents Have a Child Support Order?*, Child Support Fact Sheet Series No. 6, 1, https://www.acf.hhs.gov/sites/default/files/programs/css/why_dont_more_poor_cps_have_a_cs_order_sbtn_6.pdf.

16. Grall, *Custodial Mothers*, 13.

17. Office of Child Support Enforcement, Administration for Children and Families, U.S. Department for Health and Human Services, *Overview—Final Rule 2016 Flexibility, Efficiency, and Modernization in Child Support Enforcement Programs*, 1, https://www.acf.hhs.gov/sites/default/files/programs/css/overview_child_support_final_rule.pdf.

18. Office of Child Support Enforcement, *Overview*, 2–4.

19. H.R. 310, 2015-2016 Gen. Assemb., Reg. Sess. For an overview of similar programs in other states, see "Child Support and Incarceration," National Conference of State Legislatures, March 4, 2019, http://www.ncsl.org/research/human-services/child-support-and-incarceration.aspx.

20. Minnesota Department of Corrections, "Adult Offender Reentry Services and Programming," Policy 205-140, *Policies, Directives and Instructions Manual*, March 15, 2015, http://www.doc.state.mn.us/DocPolicy2/html/DPW_Display_TOC.asp?Opt=205.140.htm.

21. For example, see Utah Code Ann. § 78B-12-203 (6); see also "Child Support and Incarceration."

22. For example, see Vt. Stat. Ann. tit. 15, § 656(b).

23. Stacy Brustin, "Child Support: Shifting the Financial Burden in Low-Income Families," *Georgetown Journal on Poverty Law and Policy* 20, no. 1 (Fall 2012): 20.

24. Unmarried fathers earn around $15,800, whereas unmarried mothers earn around $10,700. See Sara S. McLanahan and Irwin Garfinkel, "Fragile Families: Debates, Facts, and Solutions," in *Marriage at the Crossroads: Law, Policy, and the Brave New World of Twenty-First-Century Families*, eds. Marsha Garrison and Elizabeth S. Scott, (Cambridge: Cambridge University Press, 2012), 141.

25. Brustin, "Child Support," 21.

26. See Jessica Pearson, *State Approaches to Including Fathers in Programs and Policies Dealing with Children and Families*, May 2018, http://centerforpolicyresearch.org/wp-content/uploads/FINAL-FRPN_StateApproaches-Brief_052918_R2-2.pdf.
27. Daniel Schroeder and Nicholas Doughty, *Texas Noncustodial Parent Choices: Program Impact Analysis (2009)* (Austin, TX: Ray Marshall Center for the Study of Human Resources, Lyndon B. Johnson School of Public Affairs, University of Texas at Austin, 2009), https://raymarshallcenter.org/files/2005/07/NCP_Choices_Final_Sep_03_2009.pdf.
28. See, for example, Karin Martinson et al., *The Implementation of the Partners for Fragile Families Demonstration Projects* (Washington, DC: The Urban Institute, 2007), http://www.urban.Org/UploadedPDF/411511_fragile_ families.pdf.
29. Lollar, "Criminalizing (Poor) Fatherhood," 180.
30. Tonya L. Brito, "The Child Support Debt Bubble," *UC Irvine Law Review* 9, no. 4 (May 2019): 982.
31. Sorensen et al., *Assessing Child Support Arrears*, 1.
32. For example, see Lollar, "Criminalizing (Poor) Fatherhood," 174.
33. See, for example, Lollar, "Criminalizing (Poor) Fatherhood," 177–78; Laurie S. Kohn, "Engaging Men as Fathers: The Courts, the Law, and Father-Absence in Low-Income Families," *Cardozo Law Review* 35, no. 2 (December 2013): 566; Maldonado, "Deadbeat or Deadbroke," 1007–8.
34. Tribal Child Support Enforcement (IV-D) Program, 45 C.F.R. § 309.05.
35. Maldonado, "Deadbeat or Deadbroke," 1017.
36. Kohn, "Engaging Men as Fathers," 541.
37. Steven Garasky et al., "Toward a Fuller Understanding of Nonresident Father Involvement: An Examination of Child Support, In-Kind Support, and Visitation," *Population Research and Policy Review* 29, no. 3 (June 2010): 364.
38. Kathryn Edin and Timothy J. Nelson, *Doing the Best I Can: Fatherhood in the Inner City* (Berkeley: University of California Press, 2013), 111.
39. See Edin and Nelson, *Doing the Best I Can*, 111.
40. For a fuller discussion, the demonization of Black mothers, see for example, Dorothy E. Roberts's work.
41. Ann Cammett, "Welfare Queens Redux: Criminalizing Black Mothers in the Age of Neoliberalism," *Southern California Interdisciplinary Law Journal* 25, no. 2 (Spring 2016): 367.
42. Lollar, "Criminalizing (Poor) Fatherhood," 125; Brito, "Fathers behind Bars," 626–30; Cammett, "Deadbeats, Deadbrokes, and Prisoners," 19.
43. Lollar, "Criminalizing (Poor) Fatherhood," 159.
44. Lollar, "Criminalizing (Poor) Fatherhood," 142–44.
45. For example, see Noah D. Zatz, "A New Peonage: Pay, Work, or Go to Jail in Contemporary Child Support Enforcement and Beyond," *Seattle University Law Review* 39, no. 3 (2016): 956.
46. Rebecca May, *The Effect of Child Support and Criminal Justice Systems on Low-Income Noncustodial Parents* (Madison, WI: Center for Family Policy and Practice, 2004), 19.
47. Solomon-Fears et al., *Child Support Enforcement*, 2.
48. Gretchen Livingston, "About One-Third of U.S. Children Are Living with an Unmarried Parent," Fact Tank: News by the Numbers, Pew Research Center, April 27, 2018, https://pewrsr.ch/2Fm1qO1; Gretchen Livingston, "The Changing Profile of Unmarried Parents," Social & Demographic Trends, Pew Research Center, April 25, 2018, https://www.pewsocialtrends.org/2018/04/25/the-changing-profile-of-unmarried-parents/.
49. Office of Child Support Enforcement, *Custodial Parents Living in Poverty*, Child Support Fact Sheet Series No. 3 (Washington, DC: U.S. Department of Health and Human Services, 2014), 2, https://www.acf.hhs.gov/sites/default/files/programs/css/sbtn_custodial_parents_living_in_poverty.pdf.
50. Grall, *Custodial Mothers*, 7.
51. See Kimberle Crenshaw, "Mapping the Margins: Intersectionality, Identity Politics, and Violence against Women of Color," *Stanford Law Review* 43, no. 6 (July 1991): 1241; Kimberle Crenshaw, "Demarginalizing the Intersection of Race and Sex: A Black Feminist Critique

of Antidiscrimination Doctrine, Feminist Theory and Antiracist Politics," *University of Chicago Legal Forum* 1989, no. 1 (1989).

52. Devon W. Carbado, "Black Male Racial Victimhood," in "Emerging Male Writers: A Special Issue, Part II," special issue, *Callaloo* 21, no. 2 (Spring, 1998): 337.

53. Paul Butler, "Black Male Exceptionalism? The Problems and Potential of Black Male-Focused Interventions," *Du Bois Review* 10, no. 2 (Fall 2013): 485. See also Luke Charles Harris, "My Two Mothers, America, and the Million Man March," in *Black Men on Race, Gender, and Sexuality: A Critical Reader*, ed. Devon W. Carbado (New York: New York University Press, 1999), 59.

54. Marion Crain and Ken Matheny, "Labor's Divided Ranks: Privilege and the United Front Ideology," *Cornell Law Review* 84, no. 6 (September 1999): 1544.

55. Marion Crain, "Between Feminism and Unionism: Working Class Women, Sex Equality, and Labor Speech," *Georgetown Law Journal* 82, no. 6 (July 1994): 1908.

56. See Elizabeth F. Emens, "Admin," *Georgetown Law Journal* 103, no. 6 (August 2015): 1409. Emens expands the definition of domestic labor to include "admin," or the "secretarial and managerial" tasks required to run a life or a household.

57. Suzanne Bianchi et al., "Housework: Who Did, Does or Will Do It, and How Much Does It Matter?" *Social Forces* 91, no. 55 (September 2012): 57–58.

58. Grall, *Custodial Mothers*, 5.

59. See Emens, "Admin," 1433–34; Bianchi et al., "Housework," 57–58.

60. Robin West, *Caring for Justice* (New York: New York University Press, 1997), 126.

61. West, *Caring for Justice*, 126.

62. Dorothy E. Roberts, "Spiritual and Menial Housework," *Yale Journal of Law and Feminism* 9, no. 1 (1997): 51.

63. Patricia Hill Collins, *Black Feminist Thought* (Boston: Unwin Hyman, 1990), 176–77.

64. Collins, *Black Feminist Thought*, 197.

65. See Solangel Maldonado, "Beyond Economic Fatherhood: Encouraging Divorced Fathers to Parent," *University of Pennsylvania Law Review* 153, no. 3 (January 2005): 921.

66. Maldonado, "Beyond Economic Fatherhood," 989.

67. Maldonado, "Beyond Economic Fatherhood," 989.

68. Maldonado, "Beyond Economic Fatherhood," 989.

69. Clare Huntington, "Postmarital Family Law: A Legal Structure for Nonmarital Families," *Stanford Law Review* 67, no. 1 (January 2015): 227.

70. See Huntington, "Postmarital Family Law," 204. See also Ark. Code Ann. § 9-10-113(a).

71. See Katharine T. Bartlett and Carol B. Stack, "Joint Custody, Feminism and the Dependency Dilemma," *Berkeley Women's Law Journal* 2, no. 1 (September 1986): 9.

72. Margaret Ryznar, "In-Kind Child Support," *Journal of the American Academy of Matrimonial Law* 29, no. 2 (2017): 378.

73. Laura Lane-Steele, "Working It Off: Introducing a Service-Based Child Support Model," *University of Pennsylvania Journal of Law and Social Change* 19, no. 2 (2016).

74. See Brustin, "Child Support," 46.

75. Andrew Burwick, *Idea Brief: Child Support Assurance* (New York: The Century Foundation, 2004), 1.

76. Burwick, *Child Support Assurance*, 1.

77. Huntington, "Postmarital Family Law," 235.

BIBLIOGRAPHY

Bartlett, Katharine T., and Carol B. Stack. "Joint Custody, Feminism and the Dependency Dilemma." *Berkeley Women's Law Journal* 2, no. 1 (September 1986): 9–41.

Bianchi, Suzanne M., Liana C. Sayer, Melissa A. Milkie, and John P. Robinson. "Housework: Who Did, Does or Will Do It, and How Much Does It Matter?" *Social Forces* 91, no. 55 (September 2012): 55–63.

Brito, Tonya L. "The Child Support Debt Bubble." *UC Irvine Law Review* 9, no. 4 (May 2019): 953–87.

———. "Fathers Behind Bars: Rethinking Child Support Policy toward Low-Income Noncustodial Fathers and Their Families." *Journal of Gender, Race & Justice* 15, no. 3 (Spring 2012): 617–74.

Brustin, Stacy. "Child Support: Shifting the Financial Burden in Low-Income Families." *Georgetown Journal on Poverty Law and Policy* 20, no. 1 (Fall 2012): 1–53.

Brustin, Stacy, and Lisa Vollendorf Martin. "Paved with Good Intentions: Unintended Consequences of Federal Proposals to Integrate Child Support and Parenting Time." *Indiana Law Review* 48, no. 3 (2015): 803–52.

Burwick, Andrew. *Idea Brief: Child Support Assurance*. New York: The Century Foundation, 2004.

Butler, Paul. "Black Male Exceptionalism? The Problems and Potential of Black Male-Focused Interventions." *Du Bois Review* 10, no. 2 (Fall 2013): 487–91.

Cammett, Ann. "Deadbeats, Deadbrokes, and Prisoners." *Georgetown Journal on Poverty Law and Policy* 18, no. 2 (Spring 2011): 127–68.

———. "Welfare Queens Redux: Criminalizing Black Mothers in the Age of Neoliberalism." *Southern California Interdisciplinary Law Journal* 25, no. 2 (Spring 2016): 363–94.

Carbado, Devon W. "Black Male Racial Victimhood." In "Emerging Male Writers: A Special Issue, Part II." Special issue, *Callaloo* 21, no. 2 (Spring, 1998): 337–61.

Collins, Patricia Hill. *Black Feminist Thought*. Boston: Unwin Hyman, 1990.

Crain, Marion. "Between Feminism and Unionism: Working Class Women, Sex Equality, and Labor Speech." *Georgetown Law Journal* 82, no. 6 (July 1994): 1903–2002.

Crain, Marion, and Ken Matheny. "Labor's Divided Ranks: Privilege and the United Front Ideology." *Cornell Law Review* 84, no. 6 (September 1999): 1542–1636.

Crenshaw, Kimberle. "Demarginalizing the Intersection of Race and Sex: A Black Feminist Critique of Antidiscrimination Doctrine, Feminist Theory and Antiracist Politics." *University of Chicago Legal Forum* 1989, no. 1 (1989): 139–67.

———. "Mapping the Margins: Intersectionality, Identity Politics, and Violence against Women of Color." *Stanford Law Review* 43, no. 6 (July 1991): 1241–99.

Edin, Kathryn, and Timothy J. Nelson. *Doing the Best I Can: Fatherhood in the Inner City*. Berkeley: University of California Press, 2013.

Emens, Elizabeth F. "Admin." *Georgetown Law Journal* 103, no. 6 (August 2015): 1409–81.

Grall, Timothy. *Custodial Mothers and Fathers and Their Child Support: 2015*. Current Population Reports No. P60-262. Washington, DC: U.S. Census Bureau, 2018. https://perma.cc/6DUX-E5C2.

Harris, Luke Charles. "My Two Mothers, America, and the Million Man March." In *Black Men on Race, Gender, and Sexuality: A Critical Reader*, edited by Devon W. Carbado, 54–67. New York: New York University Press, 1999.

Huntington, Clare. "Postmarital Family Law: A Legal Structure for Nonmarital Families." *Stanford Law Review* 67, no. 1 (January 2015): 167–240.

Kohn, Laurie S. "Engaging Men as Fathers: The Courts, the Law, and Father-Absence in Low-Income Families." *Cardozo Law Review* 35, no. 2 (December 2013): 511–65.

Lane-Steele, Laura. "Working It Off: Introducing a Service-Based Child Support Model." *University of Pennsylvania Journal of Law and Social Change* 19, no. 2 (2016): 163–83.

Livingston, Gretchen. "About One-Third of U.S. Children Are Living with an Unmarried Parent." Fact Tank: News by the Numbers. Pew Research Center. April 27, 2018. https://pewrsr.ch/2Fm1qO1.

———. "The Changing Profile of Unmarried Parents." Social & Demographic Trends. Pew Research Center. April 25, 2018. https://www.pewsocialtrends.org/2018/04/25/the-changing-profile-of-unmarried-parents/.

Lollar, Cortney E. "Criminalizing (Poor) Fatherhood." *Alabama Law Review* 70, no. 1 (2018): 125–81.

Maldonado, Solangel. "Beyond Economic Fatherhood: Encouraging Divorced Fathers to Parent." *University of Pennsylvania Law Review* 153, no. 3 (January 2005): 921–1009.

———. "Deadbeat or Deadbroke: Redefining Child Support for Poor Fathers." *UC Davis Law Review* 39, no. 3 (March 2006): 991–1022.

Martinson, Karin, John Trutko, Demetra Smith Nightingale, Pamela A. Holcomb, and Burt S. Barnow. *The Implementation of the Partners for Fragile Families Demonstration Projects.* Washington, DC: The Urban Institute, 2007. http://www.urban.Org/UploadedPDF/411511_fragile_ families.pdf.

May, Rebecca. *The Effect of Child Support and Criminal Justice Systems on Low-Income Noncustodial Parents.* Madison, WI: Center for Family Policy and Practice, 2004.

McLanahan, Sara S., and Irwin Garfinkel. "Fragile Families: Debates, Facts, and Solutions." In *Marriage at the Crossroads: Law, Policy, and the Brave New World of Twenty-First-Century Families*, edited by Marsha Garrison and Elizabeth S. Scott. Cambridge: Cambridge University Press, 2012.

Minnesota Department of Corrections. "Adult Offender Reentry Services and Programming." Policy 205-140 in *Policies, Directives and Instructions Manual.* March 15, 2015. http://www.doc.state.mn.us/DocPolicy2/html/DPW_Display_TOC.asp?Opt=205.140.htm.

Morgan, Laura W. *Child Support Guidelines: Interpretation and Application.* New York: Wolters Kluwer Law & Business, 2010.

National Conference of State Legislatures. "Child Support and Incarceration." March 4, 2019. http://www.ncsl.org/research/human-services/child-support-and-incarceration.aspx.

Office of Child Support Enforcement. Administration for Children and Families. U.S. Department of Health and Human Services. *Custodial Parents Living in Poverty.* Child Support Fact Sheet Series No. 3. January 2014. https://www.acf.hhs.gov/sites/default/files/programs/css/sbtn_custodial_parents_living_in_poverty.pdf.

———. *Overview—Final Rule 2016 Flexibility, Efficiency, and Modernization in Child Support Enforcement Programs.* January 9, 2017. https://www.acf.hhs.gov/sites/default/files/programs/css/overview_child_support_final_rule.pdf.

———. *Why Don't More Poor Custodial Parents Have a Child Support Order?* Child Support Fact Sheet Series No. 6. June 2016. https://www.acf.hhs.gov/sites/default/files/programs/css/why_dont_more_poor_cps_have_a_cs_order_sbtn_6.pdf.

Patterson, Elizabeth G. "Civil Contempt and the Indigent Child Support Obligor: The Silent Return of Debtor's Prison." *Cornell Journal of Law and Public Policy* 18, no. 1 (2008): 95–142.

Pearson, Jessica. *State Approaches to Including Fathers in Programs and Policies Dealing with Children and Families.* May 2018. http://centerforpolicyresearch.org/wp-content/uploads/FINAL-FRPN_StateApproaches-Brief_052918_R2-2.pdf.

Roberts, Dorothy E. "Racism and Patriarchy in the Meaning of Motherhood." *American University Journal of Gender, Social Policy & the Law* 1, no. 1 (1992): 1–38.

———. "Spiritual and Menial Housework." *Yale Journal of Law and Feminism* 9, no. 1 (1997): 51–80.

Ryznar, Margaret. "In-Kind Child Support." *Journal of the American Academy of Matrimonial Law* 29, no. 2 (2017): 351–76.

Schroeder, Daniel, and Nicholas Doughty. "Texas Noncustodial Parent Choices: Program Impact Analysis (2009)." Ray Marshall Center for the Study of Human Resources. University of Texas, Austin. August 31, 2009. http://www.utexas.edu/research/cshr/pubs/pdfINCPChoicesFinalSep_.03_2009.pdf.

Solomon-Fears, Carmen, Alison M. Smith, and Carla Berry. *Child Support Enforcement: Incarceration as the Last Resort Penalty for Nonpayment of Support.* CRS Report No. R42389. Washington DC: Congressional Research Service, 2012.

Sorensen, Elaine, Liliana Sousa, and Simone G. Schaner. *Assessing Child Support Arrears in Nine Large States and the Nation.* Washington, DC: The Urban Institute, 2007. https://www.urban.org/research/publication/assessing-child-support-arrears-nine-large-states-and-nation/view/full_report.

West, Robin. *Caring for Justice.* New York: New York University Press, 1997.

Zatz, Noah D. "A New Peonage: Pay, Work, or Go to Jail in Contemporary Child Support Enforcement and Beyond." *Seattle University Law Review* 39, no. 3 (2016): 927–55.

Chapter Three

Justice, Gender, and Caste

A Case for Dalit Feminist Testimonio

Lissa Lincoln

In a powerful illustration and mobilization of what Black American radical feminist bell hooks has called "marginality as a site of resistance" (hooks 1990b, 341), India's Dalit communities (peoples formerly known as "untouchables") effectively uprooted conventional discourses on democracy and modernity, defying official representations of the Indian social, cultural, and political arenas. Historically excluded and stigmatized, as evidenced by their systemic expulsion to the extreme margins of India's social, cultural, economic, and religious borderlines, it is unsurprising that Dalit communities often claim to be homeless and nationless. The untenable ambivalence of this position was perhaps made most explicit during India's independence movement, when many Dalit militants aligned themselves with the British to counter centuries of oppression that they experienced under Brahmin rule prior to colonization (Zecchini 2016, 72). In stark opposition to the trope of the voiceless, docile victim in need of rescue (reflected in the name *Harijan,* or "children of God"[1] given to them by Gandhi), and breaking with "progressive" representations of their subjugation that sidestepped or invisibilized the question of caste, whether Gandhian or Marxist, Dalit insurgency aggressively laid claim to public space and collective resistance, thus "re-constructing themselves as a dissident political and cultural minority over the course of the 20th century" (Zecchini 2016, 59).

Michel Foucault refers to the social space created by and for the perpetuation of accepted standards of behavior as the "normative space": a space that is characterized by something that traverses and exceeds the traditional concept of justice: "I do not mean to say that law fades into the background or that the institutions of justice tend to disappear, but rather that the law operates more and more as a norm, and that the judicial institution is increasingly incorporated into a continuum of apparatuses (medical, administrative, and so on) whose functions are for the most part regulatory" (Foucault 1998, 144). Law, then, cannot be reduced to the forms of its expression (constitution, codes, laws) but, rather, consists of an ensemble of procedures that prescribe behaviors through reference to norms. Dalit insurgence, then, might be seen as a calling out of these invisible laws, or norms, of exclusion, oppression, and stigmatization incorporated into the continuum of apparatuses that constitute the caste system. In this social, political, and cultural insurgence, Dalit literature plays a vital role as an instrument of collective resistance.

Traditionally, and long before the advent of feminism, intersectionality, or other discourses of social theorization, literature has been associated with the exposure and subversion of the power structures that undergird and inform all human societies and cultures and served a powerful function in the representation (and denunciation) of systemized oppression and injustice. Thinking caste through the lens of narrative fiction brings to the fore literature's unique capacity to interrogate and destabilize discourses of domination in general. Nowhere do we see this function of dismantling and destabilization more powerfully than in the case of Dalit feminist testimonios which, both in content and form, challenge the discourses of caste, gender, and indeed literature itself, exposing the laws and norms that at once construct, perpetuate, enforce, and connect them. As feminist anti-caste scholars have long pointed out, Dalit women's testimonios have always presented counter-narratives that radically challenged the "selective memory and univocal history" of the dominant voices, be they Indian, feminist, or even Dalit (Rege 2006, 99). In this way, this chapter argues that Dalit women's narratives provide a critical tool for thinking and theorizing justice, gender, and the law.

The urgency of addressing issues at the crossroads of gender, justice, and the law erupted into the public spotlight with the advent of the *#MeToo* movement, its reverberations and reiterations around the world contributing to international recognition of the impact—if not the legitimacy—of the movement. However, despite the throwback to a call for "sisterhood" solidarity implied in the movement's name, #MeToo also highlighted the problematic nature of the concept of "sisterhood" and, with it, the fact that feminist solidarity itself is constructed and fissured along lines of power and marginalization, complicating strategies of collective resistance against gender-based violence and oppression.

A striking illustration of this complication is evident in India, in the 2017 controversy incited by the circulation of a list of names of alleged sex offenders in institutions of higher education. The list, compiled by a Dalit law student (whose status as a Dalit was itself a subject of controversy), was allegedly collected from women who had been subject to the kind of sexual harassment denounced by the #MeToo movement, provoking a reprimand from thirteen high-profile progressive feminists (Banerjee and Ghosh 2018, 1). These powerful and respected figures in the feminist and intellectual community requested a withdrawal of the list, citing their collective concern that such a "manner of naming can delegitimize the long struggle against sexual harassment, and make our task as feminists more difficult" (Menon, 2017, cited in Banerjee and Ghosh 2018, 3). Such a stance was considered by some to substantiate anti-caste historian Anupama Rao's earlier critiques of Indian feminism's unilinear normative gendered approach while developing strategies for intervention which, from a Dalit perspective, rendered it politically sterile, replicating the very power relations it claimed to denounce. In the end, the critique itself of the statement contributed to a fragmentation and galvanization of the debate around the controversy into opposing factions (Banerjee and Ghosh 2018, 5). The final result, then, of this #MeToo-inspired intervention, was a blurring, if not complete neutralizing, of the original issue of accountability for sexual predators, obscuring it with questions of caste hierarchy, competing solidarities, and representation . . . *within feminism.*

We might say, then, that #MeToo brought an awareness to the public sphere of something feminist scholars have long known. Namely, that the politics of representation are fraught with issues particularly problematic for feminists. What was being attested to, again and again, in the public arena was the fact that, as one feminist commentator on the above controversy observed, "the multiple power imbalances within the feminist movement draw on not only one's gender but also sexual orientation, caste, class and other factors, and [these factors] determine whose views are taken seriously when a feminist stance is espoused" (Shreya Iliya Anasuya, 2017 cited in Banerjee and Ghosh 2018, 2).

In short, #MeToo brought to the public sphere a recognition that issues at the crossroads of gender and justice cannot be understood by a blind faith in universal sisterhood. Indeed, this "universal" was shown to be defined, not just by gender, but by a myriad of other social factors as well, and it was one's position within this social hierarchy that determined "who defined feminism and whose actions, to the contrary, would be met with censorship" (Srila Roy 2017, cited in Banerjee and Ghosh 2018).

Feminist scholars, then, are deeply implicated in the processes of speaking for, and representing, others. Thus, feminist debates around representation are steeped in the acute awareness that these practices are fundamentally of an ethical and political nature, inextricably linked, as they are, to the production of knowledge and power. What emerges is the degree to which the feminist project of addressing questions of gender and justice is complicated by the contradictory and complex problems of representing the subjectivities and identities of others. On the one hand, as Alia Loomba contends, "we are interested in recovering subaltern voices because we are invested in changing contemporary power relations" (Loomba 1998, 243), and in this respect, feminist theorists have large investments in "recovering" the voices of oppressed groups in order to challenge dominant social (and global) structures (Hinterberger 2017, 80). On the other, as Hinterberger reminds us, it is often these very investments that lead feminist theorists to the problematic endeavor of seeking "authentic voices" to represent oppressed groups, bringing to the forefront what Spivak points to as the radical untranslatability, or incommensurability, of the subaltern voice into dominant discourse. It involves the ensuing risk of thereby introducing a new absolutism via the concept of cultural relativism. Hence:

> Feminist theorists must be attentive to how, through references to "liberation/oppression," or to "western/non-western," practices of representation end up reproducing the very categories that they seek to escape. Similarly, it is crucial that theorists are self-critical of how particular arguments are implicated in legitimizing who can (and who cannot) employ representation of "others" for resistance purposes. (Hinterberger 2017, 80)

This tension is reflected in the fact that one of the most persistent critiques of Dalit studies resides increasingly in the challenging of notions of "authenticity" and "identity" that, according to some, infuse and delimit Dalit politics, preventing it from becoming "generalizable" and, ultimately, from forming alliances with other politics of resistance (Jawaare 2012). For caste, despite its intricate and complex specificities (specificities that are critically important to identify, to recognize, to situate, and address, in order to counter and resist their subsumption under hegemonic conceptions of oppression) is ultimately a structure of exclusion and oppression, and the identification of the generalizable lines of this structure is a crucial factor in its demystification and dismantling. bell hooks, albeit in a different context, troubles this critique of identity politics, writing, in *Postmodern Blackness*, "it never surprises me when black folk respond to the critique of essentialism, especially when it denies the validity of identity politics, by saying 'yeah, it's easy to give up identity, when you got one.' . . . We should indeed [be] suspicious of postmodern critiques of the subject when they surface at a historical moment when many subjugated people feel themselves coming to voice for the first time" (hooks 1990a). The debate around identity politics clearly delineates why the problem of representation is one of the most pressing questions for thinking caste in "global" contexts. How/might caste, as a generalizable structure of oppression and exclusion, be *productively* analyzed "from the outside"?

Sociologist and anti-caste feminist scholar, Sharmila Rege, elaborates on this tension in the specific framework of Dalit feminism. Rege recognizes that it is imperative for feminist politics that "difference" be historically located in the real struggles of marginalized women. Indeed, much of her work is dedicated to the identification of these historical locations and to tracing the "different voices" there within, at once exposing and challenging their exclusion from mainstream feminist discourses. She further argues that the assertion of Dalit women's voices in the 1990s brought to the fore significant issues for feminist politics' revisions. At the same time, Rege insists that the assertion of Dalit women's voices cannot be reduced to the sole issue of naming their difference and warns that this very "naming of difference" itself inevitably leads to a narrow identity politics (Rege 1998, 39). Rege's concerns thus echo some of the urgent issues informing the debate around representation. The vital question becomes, then, how to respond to the critiques and limitations of essentialist or identity-based politics, given the historically substantiated danger of subjugated voices being subsumed, consumed, or appropriated by those coming from a location of privilege?

One response to this problem, particularly in feminist approaches to questions of gender and justice, has been, of course, an engagement with the theoretical/methodological framework of intersectionality. Although it is beyond the scope of this chapter to provide an overview of the debate around intersectionality, it is nonetheless useful to remind ourselves that the concept is an increasingly polemical issue. This, despite (if not partly due to) the fact that it has become celebrated and popularized to the point of becoming somewhat of a buzzword in contemporary scholarship and, in a diluted form, popular culture. To consider a few points of the debate, intersectionality is critiqued by many for obscuring history (and in particular, the history of its own roots) and considered by some to be at risk of depoliticization, due to its appropriation, instrumentalization, and consequent promotion by international funding institutions, becoming in effect an aspect of gender mainstreaming (Menon 2015). Mary E. John summarizes: "Intersectionality is the latest example of the imperialism of categories, whereby only Western/Northern concepts have the power of being universal and even replacing non-Western/Southern understandings" (John 2015, 1). Specifically, intersectionality can be used to deflect attention from racism or caste: "When treated as a shopping list of categories, intersectionality can result in the commodification of these analytical categories, further marginalizing specific experiences of oppression" (Banerjee and Ghosh 2018, 7). It follows, then, that a central danger of intersectionality is the fact that it can be used to avert attention from the specific experiences of oppression related to racism or casteism.

However, and although recognizing the legitimacy of the critiques levied against it, for much of current feminist scholarship, intersectionality remains a conceptual framework or "organizing principle" that is considered to hold significant potential for projects of social change and resistance.

> Intersectionality [. . .] is primarily an organizing principle, a principle which asks for reflexivity in the study of social characteristics, such that one marginality is not substituted by another and lived experiences are not treated as generic and undifferentiated. The value of intersectionality does not lie only in locating hierarchies of social characteristics but also in examining ways in which they become currencies of power. (Banerjee and Ghosh 2018, 7)

Banerjee and Ghosh, for example, point to what could be a compelling conceptual framework for examining the specific currencies of power that are gender, law, and caste in their reference to what Valerie Purdie-Vaughn and Richard Eibach call "intersectional invisibility." They outline how Purdie-Vaughn and Eibach effectively identify the processes through which the intersectionality of social characteristics produces specific experiences of marginalization along three channels of invisibility: historical, cultural, and political.

> Historical invisibility through misrepresentation or de-emphasis in the mainstream historical narrative which reproduces - in this case Brahminical - patriarchy; cultural invisibility through the failure of cultural representations to capture the distinctive experiences of these subordinate groups by organizing themselves around the dominant prototypes which are then stereotyped into generalities; and finally political invisibility through the neglect by advocacy groups of the issues concerning these communities. (Purdie-Vaughn and Eibach 2008, cited in Banerjee and Ghosh 2018, 2-3)

The promise of this conceptual framework warrants an exploration beyond the purview of this chapter. For the present aim, it suffices to recognize that despite the finesse it may bring to an intersectional framework in the analysis of interlocking systems of oppression, it too is eventually confronted with the limitations of theoretical discourse.

> Researching and writing about multiple forms of differentiation without essentializing these categories or fragmenting the research subject, poses a significant methodological challenge. How does the researcher locate the relevant categories of difference in a particular context in answering a specific research question? How does one ensure that such a research does not re-essentialize fixed categories of belonging, but rather looks into their interaction and thus mutual constitution. (Carstensen-Egwuom 2014 cited in Banerjee and Ghosh 2018, 8)

In the end, our problem remains intact: How might caste, as a generalizable structure of oppression and exclusion, be productively analyzed "from the outside"? How might the invisible laws of caste and gender be made visible in such a way as to deghettoize the caste question without co-opting or essentializing the experience of the "other"?

As long as we seek to study caste primarily as an "object of analysis" (as theoretical discourses must), there will perhaps never be a satisfactory response to these questions. Given the attention that Dalit studies brought to the vital role literature serves as an instrument of collective resistance, it may provide a powerful complement to the crucial ethnographical, sociological, and historical analyses of social oppression and political violence.[2] For however critical to projects of social and political emancipation any study of caste that regards it primarily as an object of analysis will necessarily, by its very method, produce a certain "dispossession" of subjective experience. Indeed, trying to think caste from outside of its specificity brings to the fore literature's unique capacity to interrogate and destabilize all discourses of domination.

Of course, Dalit and anti-caste scholars and activists have long drawn attention to this fact. Indeed, the emergence of Dalit activism itself is inextricably linked to the activity of literature. In the early second half of the twentieth century, Dalit voices of protest against the rise of atrocities broke into the political and literary arenas simultaneously, investing and transforming them with their revolutionary presence. As is often noted, the founding of the radical resistance group the Dalit Panthers (after the Black Panthers) by three *auteurs*, testifies to the origins of a movement that is indistinguishably literary and political. As one of them (Namdeo Dhasal) famously writes, "I had found my weapons and I sharpened them" (Zecchini 2016, 63).

And yet, the question remains: to what extent can any literature truly escape the structures of power that in part produce and perpetuate it? After all, literature, too, is a currency of dominant power (as the multitude of debates and controversies surrounding the translation and publication of Dalit literature amply testify to).[3] What are the limitations of its legitimacy to represent the oppressed, given what Ajay Sekher has called "fiction's affiliations with the dominant and hegemonic ideologies and affects" (Sekher 2008)? For, literature itself is dependent on the laws, codes, and norms of language and culture (even when it sets out to expose them). And, as such, it is inherently plagued by the danger of what Gilles Deleuze calls "dogmatic thought" (via categorization, identification, definition) and, consequently, of being rendered sterile (in its project of subversion or revolt) through the blockage of real creative thought. For Deleuze, the latter implies the "encounter" of thought with something *irreducible* to itself.[4] It is precisely this problematic rapport with language that underscores literature's ambiguous relationship to power. For the *real* power of language is precisely that of forcing us to assume, despite ourselves, its normative power. The reason is simple: all discourse, whether it wants to or not, exercises a form of power, and, however strong the revolt that incites it, any discourse will invariably degenerate into terror and tyranny if it does not turn against its own power. Any creation of values, including that of literature, is a seizing of power, and any power that instates itself slides into tyranny. Deleuze reminds us of this in terms of the literary machine:

> Let no one say that this line [of escape] is present only in spirit, as though writing isn't also a machine, as though it isn't also an act, even when it is independent of publication. As though the machine of writing isn't also a machine [. . .] sometimes taken up by capitalist, fascist or bureaucratic machines, sometimes tracing a modest revolutionary line. Let us note Kafka's constant idea: even with a solitary mechanic, the literary machine of expression is capable of anticipating or precipitating contents into conditions that, for better or worse, concern an entire collectivity. (Deleuze and Guattari 1986, 59–60)

How, then, to challenge the invisible laws and norms of oppressive "apparatuses" when one's tools of resistance are themselves produced by the dominant powers of representation that traverse them? Or, to borrow Audre Lorde's vocabulary, how can the master's tools ever really dismantle the master's house? This question is in many ways a literary extension of the fundamental problem that hooks identifies in her conceptualization of marginality as a site of resistance.

Marginality is a space that nourishes one's capacity to resist. And hooks vigorously defends this position as more than a site of deprivation. It is the central location for the production of a counterhegemonic discourse. As such, hooks states, it "offers the possibility of radical perspectives from which to see and create, to imagine alternative, new worlds" (hooks 1990b, 341). Yet she warns, this site of "radical possibility" is also a space that requires a constant vigilance and struggle to maintain. For, when it is recounted, as it must be recounted to make it visible to the center, it is always in danger of being reduced, arrogated, assimilated, or subsumed by the "center." Thus it risks being transformed, in one way or another, by the discourse of the dominant via a tokenization, fetishization, in short, by an instrumentalization of difference, even if this instrumentalization comes from within. This is, of course, one of the central dangers (and critiques) of representational literature that is written from the margins. Indeed, in some ways, hooks might be said to be warning us here of the "single dream" of what Deleuze calls "major literature." "How many styles or genres or literary movements, even very small ones, have only one single dream: to assume a major function in language, to offer themselves as a sort of state language, an official language" [5] (Deleuze and Guattari 1986, 27)?

The "single dream" of major literatures, then, is to attain the authority invested in theoretical discourses, "to attain a major function in language." The aim is not necessarily to align themselves with an existing state language, but rather to "offer themselves" as an alternative, or a usurpation, of it. In other words, establishing an "apparatus" comprising discursive laws and codes, in short, norms that would prescribe a new set of values and behaviors: those of "resistance." Even in this brief description of major literature, Deleuze attends to the fact that literature cannot escape the dangers inherent to theoretical discourses. As such, literature cannot be considered a straightforward "solution" to the problems of representation—including those facing the feminist project of exposing gender-based injustice. Literature, by its very nature, always runs the danger of falling into dogmatism, establishing itself as a kind of authoritative representation (a kind of a "state language") of social injustices, prescribing, justifying, or legitimating particular codes of behavior as moral solutions. It risks, invariably, degenerating into terror and tyranny if it does not turn against its own power.

This limitation of literature as a solution to the problem of representation is evidenced in the frustration expressed by Dalit feminists regarding, for example, autobiographies of resistance. On the one hand, the vast majority of women's autobiographies, until recently almost always penned by upper-caste women, elide the issue of caste (often replacing it with "class") thus invisibilizing the social realities of Dalits, while arrogating Dalit women's struggles under the rubrics of their own upper-caste experience of subjugation. As a result, the solutions envisaged by these calls for a collective resistance to social inequality and injustice never address the structural problem of caste—a factor that fundamentally shapes, dictates, and determines Dalit women's everyday lives on all levels of experience.[6] On the other hand, the politically powerful genre of Dalit autobiography, revolutionary in its style and impact, was until recently almost entirely dominated by autobiographies of Dalit men. Caste, and in particular the systematized atrocities and dehumanizing abuse Dalits are subjected to by the upper castes in their everyday lived experiences, was at the forefront. Gender, however, was ignored, and the uniquely gender-specific subjugation and abuse inflicted on Dalit women by upper-caste *and* Dalit men as a result of competing patriarchies was invisiblized. Solutions envisaged in the collective resistance embodied in these autobiographies left gender-based violence intact and unaddressed.

How, then, to make visible that which has been erased? How to lay bare the hidden laws and norms that the apparatuses of systemic oppression, violence, and exclusion comprise? How might subaltern voices be heard without risking their instrumentalization by discourses of the dominant on one hand, or perpetuating the very strategies of power they seek to expose on the other?

French political philosopher Emmanuel Renault, in *L'Experience de l'injustice* (The Experience of Injustice) underlines the particular power with which poetry can destabilize discourses of justification/legitimation of the social order.[7] Due to poetry's capacity to observe the world through a language of description rather than judging it through a language of prescription: "The destabilization of the modes of justification of the social order is precisely what [the poet] attempts to do. Not to denounce nor to demystify but to subvert from the bottom up through a cancellation of the established logical forms"[8] (Renault 2004). What Renault suggests is that poetry (which in this sense is aligned with *minor*, not major, literature) is possibly a more effective model for social change than the more theoretical discourses typically associated with it. Rather than engaging with its "object of analysis" through a discourse of prescription as theoretical discourses do, the poet engages with their object through observation via a language of description. The poet, then, by their very relation to language, deliberately distances themselves from the ever-present danger of any theoretical approach: that of falling into dogmatic thought (definition, categorization, identification) and the consequent collaboration with and/or perpetuation of the very social orders aimed to be challenged. The poet would seem, thus, to be responding to Deleuze's call to "create the opposite dream [of major literature]: know how to create a becoming-minor" (Deleuze and Guattari 1986, 27).

It is precisely here that Dalit feminist literature finds its power and capacity to destabilize: in its refusal of prescriptive discourse, eschewing grand narratives of "definition" that would seek to prescribe a given overarching interpretation on the reader. It favors rather a method of description or, in Foucauldian terms, "an activity of diagnostics."[9] An activity Foucault describes, in the context of philosophy, as primarily interested in describing the experience of one's immediate entourage. It involves the framework of specific, individual cases that refuse and disrupt a dominant narrative that would impose grand universal theories for the interpretation of reality.

Nowhere do we see this capacity of literature to disrupt and destabilize dominant narratives more powerfully than in Dalit women's testimonios. These testimonios, in both form and content, challenge the normative discourses of caste, gender, and indeed literature itself. Exposing the invisible laws and norms that perpetuate and enforce them. Dalit women's testimonios thus provide a crucial instrument for thinking and theorizing gender and justice. Not because their epistemic privilege provides a site from which to unproblematically represent an objective truth that somehow escapes being traversed by the norm, but rather because they destabilize all dominant discourses that set themselves up as truth, and in so doing reveal the complexities, contradictions suppressions and erasures that invisibilize the normative discourses of caste and gender (Rege 2006, 99). Anti-caste feminist scholars, including Rege and Shailaja Paik, have meticulously documented the trajectory of Dalit women's testimonios that, in "agitating" their way into the public sphere in the 1980s, ripped through the multiple veils of invisibility put in place by the Dalit men and upper-caste women who claimed to represent them.

> In Dalit men's testimonios, Dalit women were only selectively remembered as sacrificing wives and mothers, or victims of caste-based violence. The repro-

> duction of hegemonic patriarchal practices within the Dalit community were only inadequately remembered, if not entirely forgotten. At best, Dalit women were written into these testimonios of Dalit struggles as supporters of a "larger cause," which men assumed to be a "male cause." Likewise, the narratives of the second wave of the women's movement, in their redefining of feminist identity through a retrieval of "forgotten" women of history, as well as women's written remembrances of the past "officially" forgot caste. Similarly, in "modern" ideologies and practices such as feminism, caste was "forgotten." Or, caste belonged only to Dalit women, (upper caste women having moved "beyond" the backward "ideology" of caste) who were then addressed only as victims to be saved, and never as active historical agents of feminism. (Rege 2006, 98)

Dalit women's testimonio, then, is not simply about resisting "colonization" from the "center" of dominant culture. As hooks reminds us, "that struggle may not even begin with the colonizer [ie., dominant culture]: it may begin within one's segregated colonized [ie. subjugated] community and family" (hooks 1990b, 242). And this resistance to the "colonizer within" must simultaneously guard against its tokenization and instrumentalization by the "colonizer without." In Dalit feminist testimonio, we remark the same preoccupations as those observed in intersectional approaches discussed earlier. Specifically, a taking into account of multiple axes of an individual's identity that cannot be reduced to one aspect of that identity without an effect of distorting, or simply eliding, others. It is this awareness in Dalit feminist testimonio of multiple and overlapping identities within interlocking systems of power, and the consequent impossibility of claiming difference in the simplistic sense of the word, that invests them with a perspective of radical resistance (hooks 1990b, 341). A perspective inextricably linked to the interrogation of its own relationship to power. This commitment to self-interrogation, this "turning against its own power" is the foundation and indeed a prerequisite for what Rege has called "a shift of focus from 'difference' and 'multiple voices' to the social relations which convert difference into oppression" (Rege 1998, 40).

This self-interrogation, to take but one emblematic example, is evident in Faustina Bama's classic work *Karukku*, which chronicles the narrator's life as an untouchable woman and her ascent to arenas of power. The narrator describes the unfathomable obstacles she overcomes, despite acute, systemic discrimination, oppression, and stigmatization, to attain the previously unimaginable social achievement, for a Dalit woman, of becoming a teacher, and then, rarer still, a nun. As the narrator's proximity to power increases with her advancement through the education system, we note her growing inner tension. A tension that reflects the narrator's awareness of her own seemingly inescapable complicity with power that expands in tandem with her proximity to it. Regardless of her fervent determination to challenge and resist those discourses of power and to implement social change as she becomes progressively more conscious that her access to arenas of power carries an inherent danger of becoming complicit with it, Bama's narrator deliberately takes actions she believes will limit or prevent that complicity.

Recognizing her limitations as a teacher (the schools were run by convent nuns and catered uniquely to the interests of upper-caste children, particularly those from wealthy families), the narrator feels forced in this role to replicate the caste system implicit in the discursive codes and laws of both the convent and the curriculum. Thereby, the narrator concludes that she will be able to more effectively address the caste injustice embedded in the school system if she infiltrates it. This involves relinquishing her teaching position and becoming a nun herself, "but to be different" (Bama 2012, 104).

Any interpretation of this passage as an uncontestably positive choice, or as an act of solidarity for Dalit resistance, is rendered problematic by the entirely negative reception of the narrator's decision by her community: "When I discussed my plan at home and with my close friends, not one of them supported me. Everyone thought I was joking [. . .] in spite of all the people who advised me against it, in spite of some of them downright forbidding me to do it, I resigned from my [teaching] job and prepared to enter a religious order" (Bama 2012, 105). Likewise, complicating any reading of the text that would find in it solutions to the problem of representation faced by Dalit women, the narrator instead underscores the fact that the Dalit community itself does not consider her choice to represent them in the arenas of power as being strategic, courageous, or even useful. Nor do they provide her with support or expressions of solidarity. To the contrary, her choice is denounced as foolhardy, irresponsible, and selfish and—particularly as it entailed forfeiting her teacher's income—detrimental to the community. Complicating matters further, the narrator herself seems to agree with these critiques, retrospectively referring to her determination to represent her community and to resist its oppression by becoming a nun, as a disastrous free fall, with only negative repercussions: "Today I realize what an extremely foolish thing I did. But at that time[,] I didn't understand in the least what I was doing. I was like one who was falling into a well, blindfolded" (Bama 2012, 103). Further, any interpretation of the narrator as a figure of solitary defiance, and as such recuperating her choice within a narrative of resistance, is likewise undercut by the latter's description of her new life. Readers observe the narrator's gradual realization that complicity with the discourses of power, and hence with the perpetuation of Dalit oppression, are as inescapable for a nun as they were for a teacher, if not more so.

> Many people in the convent did not even know what was meant by Dalit. [. . .] If ever they had to speak about something unpleasant or ugly, they tended to categorize it as *Harijan*.[10] All the time my conscience kept hurting me that

> although I heard, observed and experienced all this, I too [now] lived a privileged life like an upper-caste person. (Bama 2012, 116)

Once again, the narrator decides to eliminate this complicity in the only way that seems possible: by leaving the convent. That is, by extricating herself from the realms of power that she sacrificed so much to enter. But even this decision is difficult to align with community solidarity or resistance. Her decision to leave the convent, just like her decision to enter it, is not one that is easily interpretable as a "solution" to the problems of inequality and social injustice that she first set out to challenge. Moreover, it does not provide a solution to her own moral quest to refuse complicity with power.

Indeed, this final attempt to resolve her inner tension is impossible to set up as an example to follow. Escaping at last from the alienating prison of convent life where she observed a veritable erasure of Dalit experience and existence, Bama's narrator discovers that rather than finding relief in community and kinship, what awaits her is an even more extreme form of alienation that is compounded by material concerns. Furthermore, she is having to confront these material concerns in isolation for the first time in her life: "After I dared at last to leave the convent, it was as if I had arrived at a place where I had no connections. [. . .] I feel afraid of everyone and of everything" (Bama 2012, 118). Having for so many years struggled to represent Dalit women from within institutions of power, the narrator discovers she has been scarred by the perversity she observed in the intellectual abstraction of poverty: "It is really very hard to return to a life in this world after seven or eight years of hiding away from reality" (Bama 2014, 120). No longer "hiding from reality," she now finds herself living in the "real world" of a Dalit woman's experience. She finds herself confronted by the impossibility of finding employment as a teacher, despite her high qualifications. "Why? Because I am a Dalit" (Bama 2012, 119). Further, she is confronted with the illusory nature of "education" as the grand solution for the elimination of casteism and a dawning realization of how her gender compounds that stigmatization: "If it is so difficult even to find a means of living [as a Dalit], there is also another great difficult, the difficulty I find in moving about in the outside world, alone. [. . .] We are compelled to wander about, stricken and unprotected" (Bama 2012, 119).

Indeed, it is this awareness of her positionality as a poor, Dalit woman, having neither employment nor marriage to validate her, that prevents her from returning home after the convent in the first place. Rather than her family providing the solidarity, support, and community she longs for, she fears, rather: "My father is likely to speak impulsively and hurtfully. [. . .] If I sit at home with nothing to do now, he might even start talking to me once again about getting married. [. . .] Now they are sure to treat me as a criminal" (Bama 2012, 130). Despite having overcome overwhelming odds to access realms of power that are rarely attainable for Dalit women, Bama's narrator depicts for us the immense inner tension that results from calling into question one's relationship to that power. Recognizing, on the one hand, the urgency of infiltrating these realms in order to interrupt the discourses of oppression, marginalization, and cultural invisibility that target her community. She is forced to acknowledge, on the other, the impossibility of not becoming complicit with that power and perpetuating, however indirectly, the very laws, codes and normative behaviors sought to be challenged.

Ultimately, the narrator leaves us with no site from which to observe a possible solution to this tension. She does not present a viable road map for negotiating the multiple layers and instances of social injustice that she encounters. Having extricated herself from the realms of dominant power altogether, she discovers that she has been profoundly changed by the experience and not in a way that allows readers to construct her as a figure of feminist resistance. "I am like a bird whose wings were broken. After its wings have been broken, it is protected only if it stays within its cage. But if it comes out, it can only flap its wings uselessly, unable to fly. [. . .] With all their words and rules in the convent, they cut me down, sculpted me, damaged me. Today I blunder and stumble about in the world outside" (Bama 2012, 121). Further, her experience brought an acute awareness of another level of marginalization and stigmatization, that of "the colonizer within" her own community. In the years that follow her departure from the convent, she feels unable to return to her village and finds herself progressively rejected or abandoned by the few in her community with whom she maintained contact. Her isolation is complete.

In sum, Bama's narrator is intensely conscious of her own complicity with the structures of oppression and takes action to limit that complicity at great, and at times severe, expense to herself, and often to others. However, these actions are never unambiguously presented as effective resistance, never undertaken in a way that could be unequivocally regarded as having made the right or even ethical choice. As a result, and despite her compelling appeal to readers' sense of outrage at social injustice and the strength of her revolts, Bama's narrator never allows us to see her unproblematically as a role model or as a representative heroine of the Dalit cause. The novel's multiplicity of perspectives, its contradictions, and the final, self-inflicted alienation of its central character make it impossible to interpret the latter either as a representative case of Dalit victimhood or as a prescription for resistance. Indeed, Bama seems to eschew providing the reader with solutions for the social injustices described by her narrator. Instead, readers are left with many disturbing and unanswered questions.

Thus, Bama's narrator, both in her language—what Rege more generally describes as Dalit women's testimonio's challenge to "the hegemony of Brahminical linguistic practices" (Rege 2006, 100)[11]—and in her perpetual interrogation of her own complicity with power, provides us with an example and indeed a performance of what we've seen Renault identify as the particular power of poetry to destabilize established logical forms. In so doing, she furnishes us with a tool of radical resistance to dogmatic thought, creating a possibility for dismantling "fiction's affiliations with the dominant and hegemonic ideologies" (Sekher 2008). Not through a language conducive to prescribed interpretation (identification, recognition, categorization) that either denounces or demystifies (and thus runs the risk of degenerating into the very established logic it sets out to denounce) or that "flees the world" through abstraction, but rather by a movement of *subversion*, an act of sabotage of the very rules that bind and define it. Otherwise stated, Bama's writing creates a becoming-minor: "instead of [. . .] being related to some preexistent category or literary genre, [minor literature] will henceforth serve as a *rallying point* or *model* for certain texts and [. . .] writing practices that, until now, had to pass through a long purgatory before even being read, much less recognized."[12]

Finally, like Bama's disruption of dogmatic thought on the level of autobiographical fiction, it might be said that Dalit literature as a whole, and Dalit feminist literature in particular, disturbs and disrupts the tradition of postcolonial literature overall. Indeed, much contemporary anti-caste scholarship posits that Dalit and Dalit feminist literature, despite being particularly aligned with postcolonial concerns of thinking the margin from the center, has been largely absent from the "selective tradition" of postcolonial literature and its canon (Zecchini 2016, 60). For Dalit literature effectively disrupts some of the generalizations and abstractions (i.e., "the established logical forms") of postcolonial theory. At strict variance with some of the most common colonial/postcolonial binaries that have themselves become normative literary structures, Dalit fiction introduces the troubling question of "whose post-colonialism" is being represented in and by the discipline, and whose is being silenced, censured, or erased. As Laeticia Zecchini, leaning on Ganguly, argues (and as Bama's narrator in *Karukku* illustrates), "if Dalits have come to represent a convenient trope to address the gaps and elisions in dominant discourse," the intractable violence, inner contradictions and even, as in the case of Bama's narrator, self-destruction portrayed in Dalit texts "make their theoretical commodification difficult, and also prevent from fetishizing the figure of cultural difference or subalternity" (Zecchini 2016, 59). Dalit feminist texts compound this difficulty by disrupting Dalit (masculine voiced) texts. As a result, they remain fundamentally unassimilable, refusing to legitimize the normative discourses that would seek to represent and/or silence them. Dalit feminist testimonios, then, force an *encounter*[13] between caste and "the outside" on its own terms.

However critical to projects of social and political emancipation, the study of caste as an object of analysis necessarily produces, in its very method, a certain dispossession of subjective experience. Literature allows for a different manner of circulating subjective experience, permitting it to radically interrogate the laws and norms of oppression and exclusion without dispossessing the "other" of their specificity despite, or perhaps because of, robust internal debates about the limits of its legitimacy to represent the oppressed. Indeed, as Derrida reminds us, it is precisely literature's position of being something that at once "shares a certain power and a certain destiny [. . .] with jurisdiction and . . . the political production of institutions" *but which can also* "at a certain point . . . exceed them, interrogate them, 'fictionalize' them," that subverts attempts to subsume or assimilate it to dominant discourse. Indeed, to borrow again from Derrida, it is precisely "by producing events whose 'reality' or duration is never assured" that literature finds its political power, allowing it to both destabilize and transcend assertions of appropriation and legitimacy (Derrida 2017, 32).

Hence, for example, many of the central concerns grappled with in Dalit literature find an echo—but, precisely, *not* a reproduction or a reduction—in the questions Jacques Rancière invites us to engage with in the "lines of poetry" of the "non-representative individuals" who are the "worker-writers" in *Proletarian Nights*. Indeed, Rancière makes clear that his presentation of their writing is "explicitly intended to prompt an examination of that jealous concern for the purity of the masses, the plebeians or the proletariat" (Rancière 2012, 11). Likewise, we see in Holocaust testimonial literature a reflection of Dalit autobiography (but precisely *not* a reiteration or representation of its specificity) in its testimony of human suffering and resilience, its rendering visible that which has been erased, and its laying bare deep hidden structures of systemic oppression, violence, and exclusion, without co-opting the experience of the violated other.

In the *History of Sexuality*, Foucault addresses the urgency of "thinking otherwise": *de penser autrement*.

> There are times [. . .] when the question of knowing if one can "*penser autrement*," think otherwise than one thinks and perceive otherwise than one sees, is absolutely necessary if one is to go on looking and reflecting at all. For in what does the critical work of thought consist if not in the endeavor to know how and to what extent it might be possible to *penser autrement*, instead of legitimating what is already known? (Foucault 2012, 8–9)

In allowing readers to think caste "outside its specificity," yet without co-opting the experience of the other, Dalit women's testimonios permit us to "think otherwise" all systems of exclusion and oppression, including, but not in isolation, caste itself. Dalit women's testimonios are thus at once an illustration of and an invitation to "*penser autrement*" the relationship between justice, gender, and the invisiblized laws of normativity.

NOTES

1. This name is now generally considered to be condescending and offensive and has been replaced by the term *Dalit* (oppressed), which was given political traction when adopted by the Dalit Panthers.

2. See, for example, Joshil Abraham and Judith Misrahi-Barak's outstanding collective volume *Dalit Literatures in India.*

3. For an overview of this debate, see Joshil Abraham and Misrahi-Barak's introduction to *Dalit Literatures in India.*

4. The dogmatic image of thought is a key concept in Deleuze's work (specifically *Difference and Repetition*). In that text, it signifies a set of implicit presuppositions operative throughout the history of philosophy about what it means to think and that makes up the true exercise of thought. In short, philosophy and common sense alike (or rather, philosophy as compromised by its unexamined common sense) have assumed certain things about thought, what it is and what it does. Deleuze calls this image of thought "dogmatic," first because it has been drawn from the very realm of opinion and common sense from which philosophy has classically claimed to break and get its start, and second because it assumes that *recognition* is the vocation of thought (i.e., thought = recognition). With recognition as its aim, thought is reduced to a task of *identification,* and, as a consequence of its drive to recognize, dogmatic thought threatens to assimilate all of its potential encounters (with things, others, texts, etc.) into the very concepts and categories used to assimilate them. It is thus the suppression of encounters that makes thought dogmatic. According to Deleuze, the essence of dogmatism is the assumption, implicit or explicit, that everything encountered can be recognized . . . *an approach that seeks only to recognize is dogmatic* because it a priori assigns a *representational* form to the outside, it presumes that the encountered thing is only another identifiable instance of an existing concept.

5. Deleuze and Guattari, *Toward a Minor Literature*, 27.

6. This evokes bell hooks's observation pertaining to the ghettoization of women of color by White feminism: "white women rarely question whether or not their perspective on women's reality is true to the lived experiences of women as a collective group. Our presence in the movement's activities did not count, as white women were convinced that 'real' Blackness meant speaking the patois of poor, black people, being uneducated, streetwise, and a variety of other stereotypes. If we dared to criticize the movement, to assume responsibility for reshaping feminist ideas and introducing new ideas, our voices were tuned out, dismissed, silenced. We could be heard only if our statements echoed the sentiments of the dominant discourse. Attempts by white feminists to silence black women are rarely written about" (hooks, *From Margin to Center*).

7. Emmanuel Renault, *L'Experience de l'injustice: Reconnaissance et clinique de l'injustice*, Paris: La Decouverte, 2004.

8. Ibid.

9. Foucault, in another context, speaks of philosophy as an activity of diagnostics, contrasting the "grand epoque of philosophy, that of Sartre or Merleau-Ponty," which he sees as an enterprise of "totalization," to an activity of diagnostics: "There was the grand epoque where a philosophical text, a theoretical text, told you, finally, what life was, what death was, what sexuality was, whether God existed or not etc. . . , one now has the impression that this kind of philosophy can no longer take place. . . . I would say that if there is perhaps now an autonomous philosophical activity, it could be described as follows: an activity of diagnostics." (Foucault, Dits et ecrits, 1967, vol. 1, 66, my translation).

10. Gandhi's name for the untouchables; see note 1.

11. See Rege's chapter, "Debating the Consumption of Dalit Autobiographies," in *Writing Caste/Writing Gender* (2006) for a full discussion of this. In the passage cited above, Rege's comment is made within the context of the difficulty of translating Dalit feminist testimonio: "The testimonios produced in a consciously defined modern sense of what it means to be a dalit woman, challenging the hegemony of brahmanical linguistic practices. One has to guard therefore against stereotypical sanskritisation in 'translation' often in the name of accessibility to the 'common reader'" (Rege 2006, 100).

12. Réda Bensmaïa, forward, in Deleuze and Guattari, *Toward a Minor Literature*, xiv.

13. Again, we allude here to the Deleuzian sense of the word, whereby encounters - contrary to dogmatic thought - force themselves on thought and compel it under their pressure to think and experience something new; something that is "irreducible to itself" (see note 4).

BIBLIOGRAPHY

Abraham, Joshil K., and Judith Misrahi-Barak, eds. 2015. *Dalit Literatures in India*. Routledge.

Bama, Faustina. *Karukku*. Oxford India, 2012.

Banerjee, Supurna, and Nandini Ghosh. 2018. "Introduction. Debating Intersectionalities: Challenges for a Methodological Framework." *South Asia Multidisciplinary Academic Journal* 19.

Bilge, Sirma. 2013. "Intersectionality Undone: Saving Intersectionality from Feminist Intersectionality Studies." *Du Bois Review: Social Science Research on Race* 10, no. 2: 405–24.

Deleuze, Gilles, and Felix Guattari. 1986. *Toward a Minor Literature*. University of Minnesota Press.

Derrida, Jacques. 2017. "'This Strange Institution Called Literature': An Interview with Jacques Derrida." In *Acts of Literature*, by Jacques Derrida and Derek Attridge, 33–75. Routledge.

Foucault, Michel. 1998. *The History of Sexuality*. Vol. 1: *The Will to Knowledge*. Vintage.

Foucault, Michel. 2012. *The History of Sexuality*. Vol. 2: *The Use of Pleasure*. Vintage.

Hinterberger, Amy. 2007. "Feminism and the Politics of Representation: Towards a Critical and Ethical Encounter with 'Others.'" *Journal of International Women's Studies* 8, no. 2: 74–83.

hooks, bell. 1990a. "Postmodern Blackness." *Postmodern Culture* 1, no. 1.

hooks, bell. 1990b. "Marginality as a Site of Resistance." *Out There: Marginalization and Contemporary Cultures* 4: 341–43.

Jaaware, Aniket. 2012. "Destitute Literature." University of Mumbai.

John, Mary E. 2015. "Intersectionality." *Economic and Political Weekly* 50, no. 33: 72–76.

Loomba, Ania. 1998. *Situating Colonial and Postcolonial Studies*. Routledge.

Menon, Nivedita. 2015. "A Critical View on Intersectionality from India: Is Feminism about 'Women'"? *Economic and Political Weekly* 50, no. 17: 37–44.

Paik, Shailaja. 2014. "Building Bridges: Articulating Dalit and African American Women's Solidarity." *WSQ: Women's Studies Quarterly* 42, no. 3: 74–96.

Purdie-Vaughns, Valerie, and Richard P. Eibach. 2008. "Intersectional Invisibility: The Distinctive Advantages and Disadvantages of Multiple Subordinate-Group Identities." *Sex Roles* 59, no. 5–6: 377–91.

Rancière, Jacques. 2012. *Proletarian Nights: The Workers' Dream in Nineteenth-Century France*. Verso Trade.

Rao, Anupama. 2003. "Introduction." *Gender and Caste*. Zed Books.

Rao, Anupama. 2009. *The Caste Question: Dalits and the Politics of Modern India*. University of California Press.

Rege, Sharmila. 1998. "Dalit Women Talk Differently: A Critique of 'Difference' and Towards a Dalit Feminist Standpoint Position." *Economic and Political Weekly*, WS39–WS46.

Rege, Sharmila. 2006. *Writing Caste, Writing Gender: Reading Dalit Women's Testimonios*. Zubaan.

Renault, Emmanuel. 2004. *L'expérience de l'injustice: reconnaissance et clinique de l'injustice*. La Découverte.

Sekher, Ajay S. 2008. *Representing the Margin: Caste and Gender in Indian Fiction*. Gyan Publishing House.

Turner, Elen. 2014. "Reconciling Feminist and Anti-Caste Analyses in Studies of Indian Dalit-Bahujan Women" *Gender and Sexuality in Asia and the Pacific* 34.

Zecchini, Laetitia. 2016. "'No Name Is Yours Until You Speak It': Notes Towards a Contrapuntal Reading of Dalit Literatures and Postcolonial Theory." In *Dalit Literatures in India*, edited by Joshil K Abraham and Judith Misrahi-Barak, 74–91. Routledge India.

Chapter Four

Dehumanization "Because of Sex"

The Multiaxial Approach to the Title VII Rights of Sexual Minorities

Shirley Lin

In 1983, Judge John F. Grady presided over a trial of the sex discrimination claims of Karen F. Ulane, a commercial airline pilot and a decorated Vietnam veteran with an excellent flying record. Ms. Ulane revealed her transgender identity to her employer after undergoing sex reassignment surgery. The airline fired her, claiming that she was mentally ill and unfit to fly despite federal certification to the contrary. In a post-trial opinion weighing extensive party and expert testimony, the court concluded without hesitation that Ms. Ulane's firing was "related to" sex or "because of" her sex.[1]

Unlike many courts that applied essentialist sex classifications to such claims, the court in *Ulane v. Eastern Airlines, Inc.* advanced a socially pluralistic approach that was profound for its time, and it remains so nearly four decades later. The airline engaged in sex discrimination against Ms. Ulane, it held, when it became hostile to her "transsexual" status because a fair reading of "sex" raised "a question of one's own self-perception [and] also a social matter: How does society perceive the individual?"[2]

Analogizing to recognition of a new Hispanic "race" more than a decade after Congress passed Title VII of the Civil Rights Act of 1964, Judge Grady observed that subordination necessarily includes evidence of "stereotypes, misperceptions, and other motivations" against Hispanics even while national opinion as to their "non-White" status remained divided.[3] The court emphasized its responsibility to interpret the plain language of statute text neutrally in applying the law in spite of, and specifically because of, social recriminations against sexual minorities and extant beliefs about sex, including his own.[4]

Ulane I reflects an understanding that, no differently from race, the causes of sex discrimination must extend beyond "dominant concepts of discrimination," as Kimberlé Crenshaw argued in critiquing compartmentalized legal approaches to discrimination.[5] However, merely five months after the trial court's opinion, the Seventh Circuit reversed it. Rejecting a socially constructed view of sex, the appellate court invoked the "ordinary, common meaning" of sex—limiting Title VII to "discriminat[ion] against women because they are women and against men because they are men."[6] Thus, the employer's hostility toward Ms. Ulane's change in sex was deemed lawful.

During the 2019–2020 term, the Supreme Court decided that discrimination based upon transgender status and sexual orientation is sex discrimination.[7] Regardless of the outcome, history, precedent, and social movements continue to pose important public narratives regarding legitimacy, interpretive neutrality, and the dignitary goals of antidiscrimination law. In fact, since 2015, *Ulane I* inspired years of sustained judicial resistance to essentialist classification methods in favor of a contextual approach to discrimination where traits are socially contested, as exemplified in the cases of sexual minorities.[8] With *Ulane I* and its progeny as a point of departure, this chapter introduces multiaxial analysis as a means of establishing discrimination for socially contested identities. Multiaxial analysis is an evidentiary and narrative framework to identify the breadth of Title VII's traits under the following axes representing evidentiary viewpoints: the individual self, the defendant employer, society, and the state. These viewpoints interactively generate animus based upon any dissonant views regarding the trait or traits.

It may surprise the general public that Title VII prohibits discrimination, but it does not expressly define "discrimination" nor many of the traits to be protected, including "race," "color," "sex," and "national origin."[9] The open-ended nature of these key terms is remarkable and reflects the scale of privation and threat of violence that excluded minorities from the ballot box, public accommodations, and full economic participation.[10] Formal frameworks aimed to define the protected traits were unnecessary because lawmakers understood that eliminating prejudice required close scrutiny of how mistreatment operates.[11] Under a classic canon of statutory interpretation, courts are to interpret remedial statutes broadly to effectuate their purposes. However, difficulties in conceptualizing discrimination outside of unidimensional, majoritarian constructs allowed some courts to hamstring the reach of antidiscrimination law. Relatedly, Critical Race Theory (CRT) and intersectionality theory provided insightful yet often descriptive social and political critique, prompting calls for actionable and "very specific points of intervention with regard to legal doctrine."[12]

This chapter begins with an analysis of classification doctrine in Title VII sex cases. Some jurists continue to champion oversimplified classification rules as familiar, fair, and inevitable. As Angela Harris argued, categories may be necessary tools for advancing moral responsibility and social change, but they should be "explicitly tentative, relational, and unstable" to avoid reinscribing essentialist social beliefs.[13] As a prominent theory of discrimination, sex-stereotyping framing largely ignores the costs of limiting Title VII to a binary paradigm of sex in ways that fail to reach other manifestations of discrimination. Its ascendance in its current form is particularly troubling as local governments are increasingly willing to cede their traditional role in defining one's sex to constituents themselves.[14] This chapter proposes multiaxial analysis as a contextual approach to subordination that accounts for intersectional dynamics. It provides a theoretical model for what lower courts intuitively implemented in the post-2015 consensus.[15] A multiaxial framework is non-formulaic by design, but it is necessary to restore the full reach of our distinctly normative civil rights laws.

I. THE RISE OF TITLE VII CLASSIFICATION

The notion that "sex" is a fixed binary trait arises from the medically inaccurate view that it is strictly determined by "biological" factors, such as sexual and reproductive anatomy and chromosomes.[16] This approach has been consistent with jurists conforming their interpretation of "sex" with a state-administered sex binary.[17] Since Title VII's passage, courts unduly narrowed the law's reach under a reductive classification paradigm originating from constitutional jurisprudence. Relying on ideas about "biological" differences between men and women, the Supreme Court justified less-searching constitutional review of government policies or classifications based on sex through "intermediate scrutiny, in comparison to race, which received strict scrutiny."[18] But unlike the Equal Protection doctrine that courts developed for constitutional interpretation, Title VII's statutory language does not allocate different methodologies among the five protected traits. By the 1970s, however, the court treated Title VII as a classification statute despite the lack of any basis for doing so.[19] Binary classification neatly elided with society's open prejudices against sexual variation and in favor of an isomorphic, binary view of sex.[20] Notably, equality scholar William Eskridge adopts only a slightly broader view, arguing that Title VII is "not simply class-based legislation" but operates as "*classification*-based legislation."[21]

A class-based approach is considered the hallmark of formal equality, which does not consider material, substantive inequality occurring outside of group contexts.[22] For Title VII, a substantive approach to sex discrimination arrived via legislative rebuke in 1978. Congress passed the Pregnancy Discrimination Act (PDA), with the commentary that the court "disregarded the intent of Congress in enacting Title VII."[23] Then, in its definitions section, lawmakers included the amendment: the clause "because of sex" includes "pregnancy, childbirth, or related medical conditions,"[24] all of which are mutable sex-linked traits. Thereafter, intersectionality theorists sought to expose the analytical inadequacies of a compartmentalized approach to discrimination evidence, particularly with reference to race and sex discrimination.[25] The classification paradigm nonetheless remains the most influential basis for rejecting sexual minorities' claims today. Correspondingly, in 2018, the Second Circuit *en banc* ruled that discrimination against workers based upon their sexual orientation is sex discrimination in *Zarda v. Altitude Express, Inc.*, drawing a dissent from Judge Gerard Lynch that "actual biological and genetic differences" in sex justify treating "men and women" differently from "races" (the latter of which he conceded can be defined "socially").[26] As discussed below, stereotyping theory is considered the foremost social-construction theory for proving sex discrimination, but by anchoring itself to dimorphic "birth sex," it remains a classificationist regime.

The meaning that courts historically attribute to sex reveals the close, intentional development with constitutional jurisprudence horizontally into Title VII cases. The court sought to remediate centuries of harmful sex-based norms by declaring in 1973 that "sex, like race and national origin, is an immutable characteristic determined solely by the accident of birth."[27] This articulation of sex—from an Equal Protection case involving the male spouse of a servicewoman receiving fewer benefits than female spouses—had an immediate and lasting hold on workplace law. Although "immutability" does not appear anywhere in *United States v. Carolene Products*, which famously posited the judiciary as a counter-majoritarian institution, immutability remained a prerequisite to recognizing rights, including those under Title VII.[28] Essentialist definitions of sex as immutable, biological classes reflected entrenched norms that courts and litigators uncritically adopted in pursuing formal, group-based equality, that is, only as "between the sexes."

Early rulings that rejected status-based claims by gay, lesbian plaintiffs then relied on lines of cases that excluded transgender plaintiffs on the grounds that only mutable conduct was at issue. Although the PDA's passage the year prior disproved class-wide favoritism theory, appellate courts still held that sex was a "traditional" concept that could not be extended to include "sexual preference."[29] This approach contradicted the advice that LGBT advocates sought and received from the Equal Employment Opportunity Commission during the 1960s and 1970s. The commission was receptive to their sex discrimination claims, and at times, invited and adjudicated them.[30] Similarly, during this time, Phyllis Schlafly prominently argued that passing the Equal Rights Amendment would mean that same-sex marriage would become legal and that discrimination against homosexuals would become illegal.[31]

As U.S. history reflects, a primary tool for dehumanization practice is through sex, in tandem with race, color, religion, and national origin.[32] By the late 1990s, some justices continued to resist broad substantive definitions of harm ostensibly because they viewed Title VII as the harbinger of Equal Protection doctrine. By 1998, a unanimous Supreme Court retired a comparators-only approach in favor of relational, facts-based contextual clues regarding what may constitute sex-related causation in *Oncale v. Sundowner Offshore Oil Services*. In this case, the court finally confirmed that male-on-male sexual harassment is discrimination.[33] The import of this history is that the only doctrinally consistent approach is to treat Equal Protection as the lower boundary of rights, and not as a ceiling to contextual Title VII analysis.

Sex Stereotyping as a Species of Classification

Limiting categorical formalism to certain instances of discrimination is distinct from the question of whether sex-stereotyping theory is a panacea to restoring the law's reach. Advocates and legal scholars celebrated the adoption of sex-stereotyping theory as a basis for prohibiting gender policing in workplaces due to the important successes it occasioned. However, as a non-intersectional approach, sex stereotyping theorizes limited social roles that reflect majoritarian thinking and, through legal channels, reinforce them.

In *Price Waterhouse v. Hopkins*, the Supreme Court expressly interpreted "sex" to encompass Congress's intent to forbid employers from "tak[ing] gender into account" in its decisions.[34] Ann Hopkins, a senior accounting manager, alleged that she was denied a promotion to partner because she was considered "macho" and "overcompensated for being a woman."[35] The firm told Ms. Hopkins that she would have to "walk more femininely, talk more femininely, dress more femininely, wear make-up, have her hair styled, and wear jewelry."[36] Six justices agreed that the comments indicated discrimination based upon sex: here, her employer penalized her for conduct and appearance defying its expectations of her sex.[37] Justice Kennedy, a seventh, agreed that sex-stereotyping evidence is "quite relevant to the question of discriminatory intent" in his dissent.[38] In other words, proscribing sex as a factor in harmful employment decisions meant that "gender must be irrelevant to employment decisions."[39]

By excavating Title VII from the hold of group-based essentialism, *Price Waterhouse*'s analysis made it possible to argue that antidiscrimination laws' traits may be socially constructed. In 1991, Congress passed the Civil Rights Act to clarify Title VII's causation standard as broad. Nevertheless, it left the substantive sex-stereotyping holding of *Price Waterhouse* intact.[40] Moreover, sex stereotyping provided the theoretical foundation for a supermajority of appellate courts to recognize that animus against those identified as lesbian, gay, or transgender can constitute sex discrimination based upon sex stereotypes.[41] For instance, a person fails to conform to gender stereotype by being attracted to the "wrong gender."[42] Current sex-stereotyping theory also reflects incipient multiaxial analysis by requiring courts to skeptically interrogate the perpetrator's conceptions of "sex" as invidious stereotypes, without upholding the perpetrator's categorization as valid, as "classification" theory does. Also, it recognizes that the policing of those individuals, whose gender departs from sex roles, is unlawful discrimination. Examples include pregnancy and employee-benefits stereotyping cases.[43]

The theory, however, is persuasive only to the extent that binary "birth sex" remains the core metaphor in the mind of the harasser. Current stereotyping theory tends to constrain readings of sex that acknowledge actual sexual variation. Courts deemed Title VII to encompass "sex" as physical differences between only men and women and "gender" as cultural attributes self-determined and ascribed by others.[44] Tensions surface between sex-stereotyping theory and a fully theorized causation framework. *Price Waterhouse* did not interrupt the cascading syllogism of body-equals-sex-equals-gender-equals-sex/gender identity.[45] Instead, this case reinforced it. Hopkins was a woman and therefore punished by supervisors at work for not expressing her gender "like a woman" through her behavior or appearance.

Because our own "sex" could be our harasser's solipsism, courts and advocates must clarify that stereotyping theory is not limited to a binary framework. Indeed, it is necessary to account for sexual diversity.[46] Without further doctrinal reform, binary-presenting transgender plaintiffs would be expected to easily prevail under sex-stereotyping theory. In its most basic articulation, the theory detects symmetrical crossing between two limited categories. It is a rare court that tries to go further. In the 2018 decision *Harris Funeral Homes v. Equal Employment Opportunity Commission*, the Sixth Circuit recognized that transgender plaintiff Aimee Stephens, who transitioned during her employment, proved that she faced sex discrimination, both "because of sex" and through sex stereotyping. Aware of *Price Waterhouse*'s potential to be misread, the Sixth Circuit observed that a trait such as transgender status "need not be exclusive to one sex to nevertheless be a function of sex."[47] The court rejected the categorical symmetry of male-versus-female group harm, observing that discrimination exists "even if [an employer] expects both biologically male and female employees to conform to certain notions of how each should behave."[48]

To insist that sex stereotyping must be theorized beyond majoritarian viewpoints is to require more of advocacy than stratagem. Legal theories that fail to reflect lived experience reinstate and legitimize dominant views of sex and gender.[49] Notably, all parties arguing the *Zarda-Bostock-Harris Funeral Homes* trio of LGBT cases during the Supreme Court's 2019–2020 term—

employees' counsel, defendant employers' counsel, and the U.S. Solicitor General—narrowly focused on binary, male-or-female "biological sex," constricting the harms that Title VII can remediate.[50] Indeed, the theory's origin story of a sex-gender *mismatch* further allowed courts to misgender transgender and intersex plaintiffs before them and to reify "birth sex" as biological sex. This result left intact normative barriers for individuals who identify with communities that include intersex, non-binary, and gender-fluid.

While sex stereotyping supported rights-positive outcomes for some individuals, a narrow starting point for sex-based stereotypes conflicts with dignitary interests in self-determination. As third, or non-binary, sex increasingly gains formal recognition among states, the question becomes: What is the stereotype associated with non-binary sex or intersex individuals who identify as non-binary?[51] Increasing use of the qualifier "birth sex" in recent litigation alleviates only one problem with sex stereotyping for transgender litigants, absent a broader doctrinal correction that acknowledges sexual variation.[52]

Also, current sex-stereotyping arguments universalize limited gender norms to the exclusion of race, class, geography, and other determinants of social interaction before a case may be presented to a jury. Psychologists recognize that sex has always been inherently racialized, then and now.[53] Questions remain: Can sex stereotyping expressly account for the confluence of sexual identity with race and class cues? Can the unsolicited advice Hopkins received to wear jewelry and talk femininely at her accounting firm apply regardless of the occupational culture that once caused the Utah Transit Authority to openly worry about the "image" that a transgender female bus driver, Krystal Etsitty, created for the public after her transition?[54] If not, then courts inherently, but not transparently, make judgments about which kinds of harm are socially verifiable.

II. FROM INTERSECTIONALITY TO MULTIAXIAL ANALYSIS

As introduced here, multiaxial analysis is a contextual approach to defining the role of a protected trait under Title VII. Because formalistic evidentiary rules hide the fact that the Supreme Court has an exceptionally limited substantive theory of discrimination, multiaxial analysis reconceptualizes animosity as traceable to fact-specific social dynamics. Multiaxial analysis normatively expands analysis in these cases beyond trait essentialism and the most common patterns of discrimination. In this way, the harms of stereotyping and misrecognition are not "legally enshrin[ed]" by attempts to define discrimination.[55]

The Axes

Under a multiaxial approach, each axis represents a distinct viewpoint regarding the protected trait, generating both evidentiary and narrative frameworks for any disagreement regarding a plaintiff's sex. This approach is akin to the familiar investigation and presentation of evidence to a fact finder in a civil case by the parties.[56] The distinct axes that could be triggered during adjudication with respect to the sex trait are as follows: (1) the plaintiff's conception of their own sex; (2) the defendant employer's conception of the plaintiff's sex; and to the extent relevant to the defendant's conceptions, (3) broader society's and (4) the state's conception of the plaintiff's sex.[57] (See figure 4.1.) Stigma or animus resulting from conflicting views of the plaintiff's sex or other statutory traits is *prima facie* evidence of trait-based discrimination. If established, the court must adjudicate the case as to the trait and proceed to questions of fact as to causation. As a situational model, the axes may shift relative to each other depending on the workplace or point in time because discrimination based on social traits, such as identity-related status, arise relationally.

The latter three axes represent potential sources of subordination and evidence of the subordination to the extent that it substantially differ from the Plaintiff axis. This conceptualization realizes the "fair reading" of sex and its

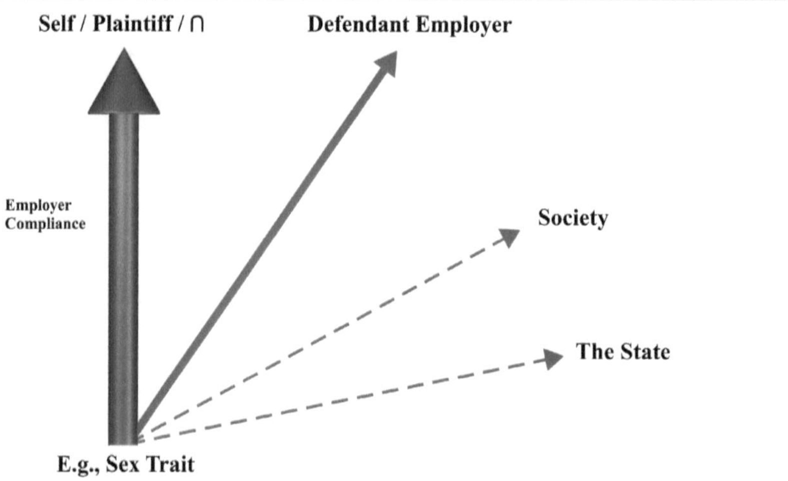

∩ refers to plaintiffs' self-realized conception of all dimensions of their identities that became salient because of the discrimination, e.g., accounting for influences of race, geography, class, and other important concepts in the construction of one's sex or other protected traits.

Figure 4.1. Multiaxial analysis reflecting situational separability of viewpoint axes. ***Source:*** **Ken Lee**

"denotations" originally raised in *Ulane I* as "a question of one's own self-perception [and] also a social matter."[58] Interactively, the axes may generate evidence sufficient to answer whether the protected trait was tied to the characteristic, as reflected in figure 4.1.

The chief axis is the plaintiffs' self-determination as to their own trait or, in the intersectional context, multiple traits. Self-identification is a dignitary interest respected throughout adjudication of the civil rights. It is the starting point of the inquiry. Relatedly, D. Wendy Greene cogently theorized that "perceptions or misperceptions that are observable or ascertainable characteristics signify an individual's physical and mental capability, morality, and self-worth, among other individual characteristics," making the harm of discrimination ascriptive or descriptive.[59] Accordingly, where more than one trait is also prominent in the discriminatory harm, each of the axes is intersectional as to dynamics toward the (non-compartmentalized) plaintiff. The plaintiff's self-identification is separable from the discrimination itself because the courts within the post-2015 consensus expressly or implicitly understand dignity as despite, and not because of, discrimination.[60]

Further, the minimum additional axis necessary for a claim is a Defendant Employer axis. It is significantly misaligned with the Plaintiff axis. Separation of the axes evinces a dissonant view of the plaintiff's trait, for instance, as a basis for actionably subordinating treatment. The subordination may manifest as a gravitational "pull" from the Defendant axis to shift the plaintiff's self-attestation of their trait. Or, dissonance between the axes may represent stigma that was a factor in the employer's adverse decision, even absent a prescriptive stereotype. A defendant's animosity toward actual or perceived "biological sex" attributes, sexual orientation, gender presentation, gender identity, or other sex-linked traits can be evidence that it impermissibly relied on the plaintiff's sex. As Zachary Kramer previously argued, these traits encompass both status and conduct, aligning with sex discrimination doctrine.[61]

Two final potential axes are Society and the State (government). Their relevance to each case depends on particular circumstances. The Society axis may reflect occupational culture, geographically specific practices, or political and historical context, with experts or *amici* as possible aids.[62] The axis would often encompass traditionally relevant witness viewpoints, such as non-defendant coworkers, customers, or those whose involvement in the matter as members of society may provide evidence of the defendant's state of mind.

The state's position may be relevant with respect to defining and administrating sex and regulating the sex-linked trait at issue. As an institution of the state, jurists must focus on its task of determining the scope of the forbidden criterion and to avoid prior courts' errors in adopting its own conception of the plaintiff's sex. Title VII's other statutory traits—race,[63] color, religion,[64] and national origin[65] —are socially and often privately defined. The court's conflation of Equal Protection with workplace antidiscrimination law raises the public/private division that Mary Dunlap and Dean Spade prominently advanced. Fundamental to their critiques is that the state directly purveyed harm to sexual minorities and is inherently suspect in administering matters arising from sex with life-and-death consequences through binary sex designation, heteronormative regimes, and failing to recognize gender identity.[66] Indeed, the state's political branches engage in variable and oppositional politics regarding sex, as currently illustrated by the Trump administration's policies rescinding gender identity and sexual orientation from federal nondiscrimination protections. Meanwhile, states and localities expand their laws and policies expressly memorializing such protections, defining sex and gender broadly, offering non-binary or third-sex markers, and other policies. As to sexual orientation, laws that excluded homosexuality "put the imprimatur of the State itself on an exclusion that soon demeans or stigmatizes those whose own liberty is then denied."[67] Like the Defendant Employer axis, Society and State axes are conceptually separable from the plaintiff's self-definition as to their sex trait.

A fairly common state intervention arises in employees' disclosures of government documents to their employers in order to verify identity or work authorization. Sex markers on governmental identification is a structural form of notice and commonly triggers intolerance against sexual minorities. Those who identify as non-binary or as a different sex from that assigned at birth often face challenges when attempting to amend the identity documents necessary to navigate sex-segregated spaces. Examples include schools, workplaces, and government-sanctioned modes of transportation.[68] Transitioning sexes and other sex-linked conduct motivated employers to deny designating new, accurate names, requested pronouns, and other public markers of sex, which may precipitate workplace harassment or assault,[69] and create barriers in accessing health insurance for gender minorities.[70]

The multiaxial approach recognizes the force between the axes that function dynamically like ascriptive and prescriptive forms of discrimination. Unlike sex stereotyping, however, this approach clarifies from a compliance perspective that the employees' self-identification of sex is to be respected. Sex is not limited to a finite set of categories such that, for example, intersex, non-binary, gender-fluid, or agender plaintiffs may accurately self-identify with respect to their sex. A plaintiff may provide evidence of the defendant's disagreement with their sex trait, irrespective of whether the state recognizes it. Conversely, the policies of government agencies that do recognize, for example, a third, non-binary sex, could be evidence supportive of plaintiffs' identification of their sex.

When an employee is known or perceived to defy heterosexual norms, this model demonstrates that Title VII already has the ability to account for increasingly visible sexual variation with society beyond classes or "statuses."[71] An intellectually honest approach to Title VII's reach does not define the *malum* of discrimination through the categorizing gaze or the identity politics of the harasser.

Multiaxial Analysis in Application

It is important to note the components of a discrimination claim that multiaxial analysis does not replace. At all times, plaintiffs must marshal a preponderance of evidence that the trait motivated the mistreatment. Also, plaintiffs must show that they were qualified for the position (except in harassment cases). Further, plaintiffs must show that the employer's conduct was sufficiently serious to alter the terms and conditions of their employment. For the defendant's part, the defenses of business necessity or other valid, otherwise nondiscriminatory reasons remain unchanged.

Courts have yet to adopt aspects of this approach to trait-causation beyond iterations of formalistic categorical approaches, such as sex stereotyping, comparator, and associational discrimination theories that "isolate the significance of sex to the employer's decision."[72] Employers will find that the multiaxial model reflects best practices for training and prevention. Centering employee dignity and self-identification simplifies compliance over discrimination remediation. Employers that are multijurisdictional or based in states or localities with laws that extend beyond the fixed-sex binary or recognize "perceived-as" status-based discrimination will find that they implicitly comply with multiaxial analysis.[73] Dissonance among the axes (viewpoints) can be supported by circumstantial or direct evidence of discriminatory motive, after which the court must proceed to questions of fact regarding whether the employee can prove factual causation and the requisite severity of harm.

This case reporting workplace claims also addresses intersexuality: *Wood v. C.G. Studios*. Here, multiaxial analysis conceptually recognizes the sex-based harms that an employee experiences upon revealing an identity outside of fixed binary sex.[74] C.G. Studios denied Wilma Wood a promotion and terminated her employment after discovering that she underwent gender-corrective surgery for a so-called hermaphroditic condition.[75] The contextual nature of the multiaxial approach has the capacity to account for an externally ascribed identity, as Wood now self-identifies as a binary female, prevailing against mere labels to detect socially contested sex characteristics.

The court rejected Wood's claims by relying on *Ulane II*, limiting the "plain meaning" of sex to encompass only discrimination against women *qua* women and men *qua* men.[76] Nor would she be recognized under the classification approach, as the court identified her group animus as "individuals [who] have undergone gender-corrective surgery" and related "transsexual" status.[77] The comparative binary approach recently advanced in *Zarda* and *Hively v. Ivy Tech Community College* is also inapt, as in its unique context it detects the role of sex in animosity against same-sex sexual orientation.[78] Here, Wood fares no differently from an individual whose later-affirmed sex and gender is female, given that the harm arises from the stigma of having changed sexes. The critical clarification to be made is that unlawfulness is not dependent on the dimorphic classes being relatively favored or disfavored, but that the significance of someone's sex, here a change in sex, need not be exclusive to one sex to nevertheless be a function of sex."[79]

Thereby Wood's dignitary interest remained in being recognized as a woman, having obtained surgery to affirm her sex and gender identity as female (the Plaintiff axis). The employer was hostile toward Wood because of her former intersex status and subsequent change in sex, rather than her current binary-presenting identity (the Defendant Employer axis), generating dissonance between the two axes in the form of stigma that harmed Wood's livelihood. Her change in sex from intersex to female (literally, trans-sexualism) should have been treated under extant doctrine as direct evidence that Wood's sex (both former and current) were decisive. Summary judgment should have been granted to Wood. Further, the court, as the state, joined the defendant employer in viewing her as having a "hermaphroditic condition" and being "transsexual," rather than dignifying Wood's self-identification. The relative positions of the axes in Wood's case are illustrated in figure 4.2.

Under this approach, animosity with the inverse chronology of events would also be cognizable. If C.G. Studios thought its employee was a binary female with respect to sex and gender identity but fired the employee for planning to adopt an original intersex sex and non-binary gender identity, it too would be sex-based discrimination.

Intersectionality

By focusing on the context of the particular parties and evidence in each case, the multiaxial framework fundamentally expands our evidentiary and narrative abilities to articulate how intersectional discrimination operates. The *sui generis* approach of multiaxial analysis avoids what CRT theorists Devon Carbado and Cheryl Harris identified as intersectionality and sex dominance-theory critiques simply generating new forms of essentialism.[80] Employees discriminated against (based upon a confluence of traits, for example, racialized sexual hostility) have an exceedingly low chance of success in courts due to the compartmentalized evidentiary rules that drive substantive fact finding.[81] Some judges spurn overlapping or mutually defined theories of harm "governed only by the mathematical principles of permutation and commutation, clearly rais[ing] the prospect of opening the hackneyed Pandora's box"[82] or creating a "many-headed Hydra . . . splinter[ing] Title

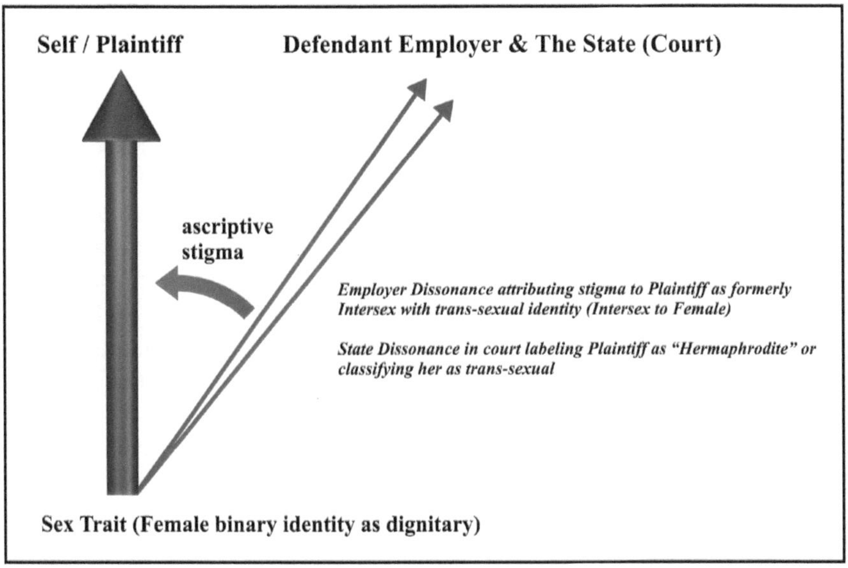

Figure 4.2. Multiaxial analysis, trans-sexual dissonance in *Wood v. C.G. Studios*. *Source:* Ken Lee

VII beyond use and recognition."[83] Rather than statutory overreach, these courts are beholden to an imagined duty to apply formulaic and unenlightening rules to all forms of discrimination, particularly those less familiar to them.[84]

Current trends shift to theorize plaintiffs who include a sex claim under sex alone or a sex-plus analysis.[85] However, those doctrines fail to capture the full competence of the statute or courts. Moreover, they presuppose too much about the facts of every Title VII case. Indeed, the judiciary's application of intersectionality theory reached a high-water mark in the 1980s, after the Tenth Circuit held in *Hicks v. Gates Rubber Co.* that a plaintiff who experienced hostility as a Black woman could aggregate general evidence of anti-Black racial animus *with* evidence of sexual hostility in support of her sex-based hostile work environment claim.[86] A situationally variable approach understands that one's identity as a Black woman does not delimit the forms of discrimination she may face.[87] The multi-perspective approach embodied in multiaxial analysis addresses the important critique of intersectionality theory that, for example, there is no singular Black women's experience within a static hierarchy, and that subordination and privilege can be concurrent and contextually defined.[88]

Unfortunately, few opinions recognize the simultaneous dimensions of identity. This leads litigants and counsel to theorize Title VII cases in compartments and to limit characterization of the evidence at the pleading stage. Consider the following atomized approach at summary judgment in the following case alleging only color-based discrimination, although it could have alleged sex. In *Brack v. Shoney's, Inc.*, a Tennessee district court concluded that Jerry Brack, a gay African American employee who is dark skinned, would be unable to prove discrimination based upon color with respect to his demotion and termination.[89] The court believed that he could, however, prove such discrimination only with respect to hostile work environment and retaliation. Brack was a restaurant supervisor whose boss, Victoria Chevalier, referred to him as "the little black sheep" or "the black sheep" on several occasions. The boss stated that a promotion to a store with a higher sales volume required someone "fair-skinned." She made these remarks around the time that she denied Brack the position and instead demoted him to a lower-volume store. Chevalier, who is also black, referred to Mr. Brack as "unusual." A witness interpreted this statement to refer to his sexual orientation. "Princess Diana" was a phrase that Brack (or his counsel) interpreted to refer only to sexual orientation.

Although Brack was also reprimanded for cash shortages at closing on three occasions, the court considered the "fair-skinned" comment as direct evidence of colorism only as to one act. Specifically, it referred to the defendant's failure to assign Brack to the higher-volume store. It did not consider whether a jury could interpret Chevalier's view of Brack as compromised with regard to all employment decisions. Nor did it determine whether the "Princess Diana" comment intended to mock his skin tone along with his sexual orientation. Significantly, multiaxial analysis would have obligated the court to consider whether Chevalier pejoratively viewed Brack as "unusual" for a Black man because he is gay, even though she demoted a lighter skinned peer for the same cash handling violations and replaced him with a darker-skinned employee.

The Supreme Court has been willing to discipline lower courts to meaningfully evaluate the influence of other dimensions of social identity in trait-based bias, even those that are not based on statutory grounds.[90] In 2003, the court considered a case in which a Tyson poultry plant failed to promote two Black petitioners, Anthony Ash and John Hithon, to shift manager positions by promoting two White males instead.[91] After Mr. Ash and Mr. Hithon prevailed at trial, the district and appellate courts believed that a new trial was warranted, disregarding evidence that the plant manager referred to each of the petitioners as "boy" multiple times. A unanimous Supreme Court disagreed with the panel's holding that the "boy" comments required "modifi[cation] by a racial classification like 'black' or 'white'" before they could evidence a connection to race (and rather than require a supplemental age-discrimination claim). Rather, the "speaker's meaning may depend on various factors including context, inflection, tone of voice, local custom, and historical usage."[92] Certainly, socio-historical usage of the word "boy" to humiliate and subordinate adult Black male peers illustrates how the Eighth Circuit went awry with evidentiary rules and ignored the normative requirements of antidiscrimination law.

Interpreting Title VII to broadly detect and reach socially contested traits is a task delegable to trial courts. The multiaxial approach is critical to institutional legitimacy, given that lower courts recently cast doubt on the validity of the old rules. Moreover, decades of cases effectuated Title VII's unique role as a normative statute. Judicial responses hostile to contextual, non-formulaic inquiry in civil rights cases reflect the fact that some courts fundamentally disagree with the obligations that Congress delegated to them.

Also, multiaxial analysis may encounter resistance from conservatives and civil rights advocates. One reason is that it does not provide a one-size-fits-all rule. Rather, it requires fact-sensitive analysis to operate. As one court opined, courts should not be tasked with "grading competing doctoral theses in anthropology or sociology."[93] Setting aside the divide-and-conquer approach of the old rules, however, is necessary to achieve the socially informed, circumstantial approach in *Ash*. In part, it was developed by a few circuits as a totality-of-the-circumstances or "mosaic" approach to the trait underlying discriminatory intent or motive in Title VII cases.[94]

Indeed, practicability has not prevented the post-2015 groundswell of federal trial and appellate courts from finding unlawful discrimination because of sex-based traits. Moreover, in the 1991 CRA, Congress stated its preference that juries, not courts, resolve factual questions regarding the cause of discrimination in Title VII cases.[95] This approach empowers a diachronic, local assembly of peers capable of being close to social facts. As Deborah Malamud noted, psychological studies revealed that juries make sense of complex facts better than complex law.[96] Ultimately, the problem is not a lack of broad legal authority, duly entrusted to the courts, but the courts' neutrality.

III. CONCLUSION

Title VII causation doctrine remains fraught with conceptual error and is statutorily inadequate. Treating "sex" as a binary, fixed, and homogenous classification misapprehends actual sex and what an aggrieved worker may articulate and ultimately prove under Title VII. Such approaches exhausted theoretical legitimacy and utility under the current statute. Title VII is "capable of contextually variable answers" [97] and may navigate the socially contested nature of traits, as *Ulane I* did for sex. Stakeholders including counsel, parties, and jurists must resist totalizing approaches that undermine the law's normative core and undercut equality for all individuals, without disfavor.

NOTES

This chapter is adapted from an article first published in *Lewis & Clark Law Review* 24, no. 3 (2020), which provides a more detailed discussion of these issues and is available at https://law.lclark.edu/law_reviews/lewis_and_clark_law_review.

1. The above facts are drawn from the trial court opinion, *Ulane v. E. Airlines, Inc.*, 581 F. Supp. 821, 822-23, 827 (N.D. Ill. 1983) (hereinafter "*Ulane I*"); and the appellate opinion, *Ulane v. E. Airlines, Inc.*, 742 F.2d 1081, 1082-83 (7th Cir. 1984) (hereinafter "*Ulane II*").

2. *Ulane I*, 581 F. Supp. at 823 (referring to sexual identity, today commonly referred to as gender identity, as a component of sex).

3. Ibid., 823–24. See also Gloria Sandrino-Glasser, "Los Confundidos: De-Conflating Latinos/as' Race and Ethnicity," *Chicano-Latino Law Review* 19 (1998): 69, 128–29.

4. *Ulane I*, 581 F. Supp. at 823. For the purposes of this chapter, "sexual minorities" refers to the broad array of self-identified sexes, genders, and sexual orientations, including but not limited to lesbian, gay, bisexual, transgender, queer, intersex, non-binary, gender-fluid, and agender individuals. The term's meaning here is distinct from its alternative usage referring to marginalized sexualities and does not imply homogeneity among all communities or permanent minority status. Sex-linked traits are not mutually exclusive and overlap.

5. Crenshaw pioneered intersectionality theory in her article "Demarginalizing the Intersection of Race and Sex: A Black Feminist Critique of Antidiscriminatory Doctrine, Feminist Theory and Antiracist Politics," *University of Chicago Legal Forum* 1989 (1989): 139, 140, 139–49.

6. *Ulane II*, 742 F.2d at 1085. Ms. Ulane petitioned for Supreme Court review and—perhaps concerned the justices would side with Judge Grady's broader recognition of traits as socially contested—the employer successfully settled the case for more than what the trial court calculated in actual damages.

7. The trio of cases comprises *Bostock v. Clayton Cty. Bd. of Comm'ners*, 723 Fed. App'x 964 (11th Cir. 2018), cert. granted, 139 S. Ct. 1599 (2019); *Equal Employment Opportunity Comm'n v. R.G. &. G.R. Harris Funeral Homes, Inc.*, 884 F.3d 560 (6th Cir. 2018), cert. granted, 139 S. Ct. 1599 (2019) (hereinafter "*Harris Funeral Homes*"); *Zarda v. Altitude Express, Inc.*, 883 F.3d 100 (2d Cir. 2018) (en banc), cert. granted, 139 S. Ct. 1599 (2019).

8. The post-2015 trend is tidal, encompassing four circuit courts reading Title VII sex discrimination to encompass hostility toward transgender status, *EEOC v. R.G. & G.R. Harris Funeral Homes*, 884 F.3d 560 (6th Cir. 2018); *Chavez v. Credit Nation Auto Sales , LLC*, 641 Fed. App'x 883, 884 (11th Cir. 2016) (per curiam), and hostility toward sexual orientation, *Zarda v. Altitude Express, Inc.*, 883 F.3d 100, 121 (2d Cir. 2018) (en banc); *Hively v. Ivy Tech Comm. Coll. of Ind.*, 853 F.3d 339, 346-47 (7th Cir. 2017) (en banc) (same). Three appellate courts further opined that transgender students are covered under Title IX's analogous provisions, *Whitaker v. Kenosha Unified Sch. Dist. No. 1*, 858 F.3d 1034 (7th Cir. 2017); *Dodds v. U.S. Dep't of Educ.*, 845 F.3d 217 (6th Cir. 2016); cf. *Doe ex rel. Doe v. Boyertown Area Sch. Dist.*, 897 F.3d 518 (3d Cir. 2018) (rejecting claims based upon Title IX and constitutional privacy brought by cisgender plaintiffs challenging policy allowing transgender students to use bathrooms and locker rooms aligned with their gender identity and sex, and noting a ruling for plaintiffs would violate transgender students' Title IX rights), pet. for cert. denied (U.S. May 28, 2019), as did a majority of district courts nationwide during this period.

9. 42 U.S.C. § 2000e-2(a). "Religion" is defined in Title VII's definitions section. 42 U.S.C. § 2000e(j).

10. See Maria L. Ontiveros, "The Fundamental Nature of Title VII," *Ohio State Law Review* 75 (2014): 1165, 1166–67, 1173–74.

11. Congress's bipartisan Interpretative Memorandum of Title VII from the 1964 deliberations declined to define any of the five protected "traits," and omits any reference to "classes" or "categories" in using the term "trait." See also *Webster's Third New International Dictionary of the English Language, Unabridged*, 3rd ed. (1961), s.v. "trait" (defining "trait" to include "a characteristic of behavior or a typical artifact that distinguishes a human culture—called also *culture trait*") (emphasis original).

12. Darren Lenard Hutchinson, "New Complexity Theories: From Theoretical Innovation to Doctrinal Reform," *University of Missouri-Kansas City Law Review* 71 (2002): 431, 439–40 (quoting Robert S. Chang and Jerrome McCristal Culp Jr., "After Intersectionality," *University of Missouri-Kansas City Law Review* 71 (2002): 485, 490).

13. Angela P. Harris, "Race and Essentialism in Feminist Legal Theory," *Stanford Law Review* 42 (1990): 581, 586.

14. Jessica A. Clarke, "They, Them, and Theirs," *Harvard Law Review* 132 (2019): 894, 905–33 (discussing the diversity of non-binary gender identities and overlaps and divergences with other civil rights struggles); www.lgbtmap.org/img/maps/citations-id-drivers-license.pdf (reflecting that 36 states permit residents to update the sex marker on a driver's license without requiring proof of surgery, and 11 states permit an update to the sex marker upon proof of surgery).

15. See cases cited at note 9

16. Julie A. Greenberg, "The Roads Less Traveled: The Problem with Binary Sex Categories," in *Transgender Rights*, ed. Paisley Currah et al. (Minneapolis: University of Minnesota Press, 2006), 51, 52.

17. Mary C. Dunlap, "The Constitutional Rights of Sexual Minorities: A Crisis of the Male/Female Dichotomy," *Hastings Law Journal* 30 (1979): 1131, 1147–48.

18. Erwin Chemerinsky, *Constitutional Law*, 3rd. ed. (New York: Aspen Publishers, 2006), 764, 766 (discussing tension between discredited opinions such as *Geduldig v. Aiello*, *Michael M. v. Superior Court*, *Rotsker v. Goldberg* and issues "whenever the Court purports to rely on biological differences as a justification for differences in treatment, are whether these differences are real or social constructs and whether they should matter").

19. Compare 42 U.S.C. § 2000e-2(a)(1) (excluding reference to classification as a prohibited practice) with 42 U.S.C. § 2000e-2(a)(2) (referring to "classify[ing]" individuals adversely as only one of several prohibited practices).

20. Cf. Charles R. Lawrence, "The Id, the Ego, and Equal Protection: Reckoning with Unconscious Racism," *Stanford Law Review* 39 (1987): 317, 336–37 ("Cognitivists see the process of 'categorization' as one common source of racial and other stereotypes. All humans tend to categorize in order to make sense of experience. . . . When [] the category of black person or white person—correlates with [beliefs regarding] the range of human intelligence or the propensity to violence—there is a tendency to exaggerate the differences between categories on that dimension and to minimize the differences within each category" [citing studies from 1952 to 1977]).

21. William N. Eskridge Jr., "Title VII's Statutory History and the Sex Discrimination Argument for LGBT Workplace Protections," *Yale Law Journal* 127 (2017): 322, 343.

22. See Serena Mayeri, *Reasoning from Race* (Cambridge, MA: Harvard University Press 2011), 107, 106–43 (discussing initial feminist legal strategies in the 1970s that pursued formal equality and, later, more expansive contextual and structural discrimination theories of sex discrimination).

23. *Pregnancy Discrimination Act of 1978: Hearing on S. 995 Before the Subcomm. on Labor of the S. Comm. on Labor & Human Res.*, 95th Cong. 1 (1977) (statement of Senator Harrison Williams).

24. 42 U.S.C. § 2000e(k). Although the statutory definitions section does not refer to any other recognized forms of discrimination as "because of sex"—e.g., sex stereotyping, hostile work environment, sexual assault, or sexual harassment—the foregone viability of these forms of sex discrimination did not raise congressional intent questions that appellate courts have similarly resolved as to sexual minorities facing discrimination based upon sex traits.

25. See Crenshaw, "Demarginalizing the Intersection of Race and Sex," 144 (illustrating how "dominant conceptions of discrimination condition us to think about subordination as

disadvantage occurring along a single categorical axis" and the norming of white women's experiences in the doctrine).

26. 883 F.3d 100, 149 (2d Cir. 2018) (en banc) (Lynch, J., dissenting).

27. *Frontiero v. Richardson*, 411 U.S. 677, 688 (1973). As the scholarship acknowledges, race is considered a social, rather than biological or genetic, construct. Alice Littlefield et al., "Redefining Race: The Potential Demise of a Concept in Physical Anthropology," *Current Anthropology* 23, no. 641 (1982) (noting complete shift in anthropological textbooks by the 1970s); D. Wendy Greene, "Categorically Black, White, or Wrong: 'Misperception Discrimination' and the State of Title VII Protection," 47 (2013): 87, 133; Ian Haney Lopez, "The Social Construction of Race," *Harvard Civil Rights-Civil Liberties Law Review* 29 (1997): 1.

28. Janet Halley has argued that the text of footnote 4 of *Carolene Products* does not use the word "immutable" anywhere, and argues that at best it should be treated as a nonessential factor. "Sexual Orientation and the Politics of Biology: A Critique of the Argument from Immutability," *Stanford Law Review* 46 (1994): 503, 509–11. On the evolving conceptions of legal immutability, see Leora F. Eisenstadt, "Fluid Identity Discrimination," *American Business Law Journal* 52 (2015): 789, 803 nn.65–66. However, in an early interpretation imagining immutability to be an element of Title VII, an appellate court held: "Equal employment opportunity may be secured only when employers are barred from discriminating against employees on the basis of immutable characteristics, such as race and national origin." *Willingham v. Macon Telegraph Pub. Co.*, 507 F.2d 1084 (5th Cir. 1971).

29. E.g., *Desantis v. Pacific Tel. & Tel. Co.*, 608 F.2d 327, 329-30 (9th Cir. 1979).

30. Brief of Historians as *Amici Curiae* in Support of the Employees, *Bostock, Zarda, R.G. & G.R. Harris Funeral Homes,* 22–28, Nos. 17-1618, 17-1623, 18-107, at 23-29 (U.S. July 3, 2019).

31. See Cary Franklin, "The Anti-Stereotyping Principle in Constitutional Sex Discrimination Law," *New York University Law Review* 85 (2010): 83, 17–18, 163–72 (historicizing links between sex-role stereotyping arguments during the 1970s in connection with lesbian and gay activism and constitutional litigation strategies) (citing Phyllis Schlafly, *The Power of the Positive Woman* [1977], 90).

32. See, e.g., *City of Belleville v. Doe*, 119 F.3d 563, 588 (7th Cir. 1997), *vacated and remanded for reconsideration in light of Oncale v. Sundowner Offshore Services, Inc.*, 523 U.S. 1001 (1998) (sex-based harassment "is often motivated by issues of power and control on the part of the harasser, issues not necessarily related to sexual preference.").

33. 523 U.S. 75 (1998).

34. 490 U.S. 228, 239 (1989) (plurality opinion).

35. 490 U.S. at 235 (plurality opinion).

36. Ibid.

37. Ibid.; ibid., 258–61 (White, J., concurring); ibid., 272–73 (O'Connor, J., concurring). See also *University of Texas Southwestern Medical Center v. Nassar*, 570 U.S. 348, 348 (2013) (noting same).

38. *Price Waterhouse*, 490 U.S. at 294–95 (Kennedy, J., dissenting).

39. Ibid., 240 (citing 42 U.S.C. § 2000e-2(a)(1)(2)).

40. The bill's sponsors stated in committee reports that the bill only "overrules one aspect of the [*Price Waterhouse*] decision." H.R. Rep. No. 102-40, pt. 1, at 48 (1991); H.R. Rep. No. 101-644, pt. 1, at 29, n.17 (1990).

41. *Zarda*, 883 F.3d 100, 120-23 (2d Cir. 2018) (en banc); *Hively*, 853 F.3d 339, 346-47 (7th Cir. 2017) (en banc); *E.E.O.C. v. Boh Bros. Constr. Co.*, 731 F.3d 444, 457-60 (5th Cir. 2013) (en banc); *Glenn v. Brumby*, 663 F.3d 1312, 1316 (11th Cir. 2011); *Prowel v. Wise Bus. Forms, Inc.*, 579 F.3d 285, 287–88 (3d Cir. 2009); *Smith v. City of Salem*, 378 F.3d 566, 574 (6th Cir. 2004); *Nichols v. Azteca Res. Enters.*, Inc., 256 F.3d 864, 870, 874-75 (9th Cir. 2001); *Schmedding v. Tnemec Co.*, 187 F.3d 862, 865 (8th Cir. 1999).

42. *Zarda*, 883 F.3d at 112; *Hively*, 853 F.3d at 346, 350; see also *Bostock v. Clayton Cty. Bd. of Comm'rs*, 894 F.3d 1335, 1339 (11th Cir. 2018) (Rosenbaum, J., dissenting) (noting the "considerable calisthenics" to explain why gender nonconformity claims are cognizable except for when a person fails to conform to the "ultimate" gender stereotype by being attracted to the "wrong" gender [quoting *Hively*, 853 F.3d at 346, 350]).

43. See, e.g., *L.A. Dep't of Water & Power v. Manhart*, 435 U.S. 702, 707 n.13 (1978).

44. See, e.g., *Schwenk v. Hartford*, 204 F.3d 1187, 1201 (9th Cir. 2000); see also *J.E.B. v. Alabama ex rel. T.B.*, 511 U.S. 127, 157 n.1 (1994) (Scalia, J., dissenting) ("The word 'gender' has acquired the new and useful connotation of cultural or attitudinal characteristics (as opposed to physical characteristics) distinctive to the sexes").

45. Jason Cromwell originated the metaphor in a different context. "Queering the Binaries: Transsituated Identities, Bodies, and Sexualities," in *The Transgender Studies Reader*, ed. Susan Stryker and Stephen Whittle (New York: Routledge, 2006), 509.

46. Only a few commentators have been willing to critique *Price Waterhouse*'s incomplete theorizing of sex stereotyping as discrimination. See, e.g., Zachary A. Kramer, "The New Sex Discrimination," *Duke Law Journal* 63 (2014) 891, 925–27; Sharon M. McGowan, "Working with Clients to Develop Compatible Visions of What It Means to "Win" a Case: Reflections on *Schroer v. Billington*," *Harvard Civil Rights-Civil Liberties Law Review* (2010): 205, 218 (describing client Diane Schroer's reaction to her counsel's potential sex stereotyping argument as: "I haven't gone through all this only to have a court vindicate my rights as a gender non-conforming man.")

47. Ibid., 578.

48. 884 F.3d 560, 574 (6th Cir. 2018).

49. See Paisley Currah, "Defending Genders: Sex and Gender-Nonconformity in the Civil Rights Strategies of Sexual Minorities," *Hastings Law Journal* 48 (1997): 1363, 1364.

50. Transcript of Oral Argument, Oct. 8, 2019, *Bostock v. Clayton Cty. Bd. of Comm'ners*, No. 17-1618 (U.S.) and *Zarda v. Altitude Express, Inc.*, No. 17-1623 (U.S.), 7:18-24 (employees' counsel), 44:10-23 (employers' counsel); 60:21-61:9 (U.S. Solicitor General); Transcript of Oral Argument, Oct. 8, 2019, *Equal Employment Opportunity Comm'n v. R.G. &. G.R. Harris Funeral Homes, Inc.*, No. 18-107 (U.S.), 4:3-5:1, 24:16-22 (employee's counsel), 28:10-30:22 (defendant's counsel); 46:4-13 (U.S. Solicitor General).

51. Non-binary gender markers are now available by law on some form of identification, or have been granted to at least one person under court order, in the following seventeen jurisdictions: Arkansas, California, Colorado, Connecticut, Indiana, Maine, Maryland, Minnesota, Nevada, New Jersey, New Mexico, Ohio, Oregon, Utah, Washington, New York City, and Washington, DC. "Resources," Intersex and Genderqueer Recognition Project, accessed October 13, 2019, https://www.intersexrecognition.org/resources (noting initiatives underway in Arizona, Hawaii, Massachusetts, New Hampshire, New York, Rhode Island, and Vermont).

52. E.g., *Harris Funeral Homes*, 884 F.3d at 36 (referring to transgender plaintiff-intervenor's "birth-assigned sex"); *M.A.B. v. Bd. of Educ.*, 286 F. Supp. 3d 704, 708 n.3 (D. Md. 2018) (in Title IX case, with respect to transgender boy, "[t]he Court uses terms such as "birth sex" to refer to gender designations made at birth").

53. Darren Lenard Hutchinson, "Ignoring the Sexualization of Race: Heteronormativity, Critical Race Theory, and Anti-Racist Politics," *Buffalo Law Review* 47 (1999): 1 (reviewing published accounts and statistical data regarding the use of sexualized violence against LGBT individuals of color to further racial oppression); Cecilia L. Ridgeway and Tamar Kricheli-Katz, "Intersecting Cultural Beliefs in Social Relations: Gender, Race, and Class Binds and Freedoms," *Gender and Society* 27, no. 294 (2013) (surveying social cognition research into comparisons' powerful role in organizing social relations and "evidence that people in the United States automatically and nearly instantly categories others on sex and race on the basis of quite minimal cues," with sex, race, and age as primary categories, and institutional/occupation roles or contextual identities as additional categories).

54. See *Etsitty v. Utah Transit Auth.*, 502 F.3d 1215, 1221-22 (10th Cir. 2007).

55. Richard T. Ford, "Race as Culture? Why Not?" *UCLA Law Review* 47 (2000): 1803, 1805; Mary Anne C. Case, "Disaggregating Gender from Sex and Sexual Orientation: The Effeminate Man in the Law and Feminist Jurisprudence," *Yale Law Journal* 105 (1995): 1, 76.

56. The conceptual model is that of a three-dimensional ball-and-socket joint with axes that can pivot, rather than traditional x- and y- axes along each ray, or projected identification of the plaintiff.

57. Singular usage of the word "their" is intentional.

58. *Ulane I*, 581 F. Supp. at 823.

59. See Greene, "Categorically Black, White, or Wrong," *University of Michigan Journal of Law Reform* 47 (2013): 87, 115; see also Paulette M. Caldwell, "Intersectional Bias and the Courts: The Story of *Rogers v. American Airlines*" in *Race Law Stories*, ed. R. Moran and D. W. Carbado (New York: Foundation Press, 2008), 571, 572 – 73 (discussing requirement of immutability under Title VII as blind to the "dignitary and psychological interests in racial and ethnic identity," and the "message of hostility, intimidation, and inferiority communicated by workplace rules that target . . . culturally specific behaviors").

60. See e. christi cunningham, "The 'Racing' Cause of Action and the Identity Formerly Known as Race: The Road to Tamazunchale," *Rutgers Law Journal* 30 (1999): 707, 712 ("I wish to distinguish who we are and might be from what is and has been be done to us").

61. Kramer, "The New Sex Discrimination," *Duke Law Journal* 63 (2014): 891, 940–41.

62. *Price Waterhouse v. Hopkins*, 490 U.S. at 255–56 (relying upon use of social psychology expert's testimony regarding sex stereotyping in defendant's promotion process); *Ulane I*, 581 F. Supp. at 823–25 (relying upon competing medical expert testimony regarding how sex is determined); *Schroer v. Billington*, 577 F. Supp. 2d 293 at 306–7 (D.D.C. 2008) (same). *See also* Ann C. McGinley, "Masculinities at Work," *Oregon Law Review* 8 (2004): 359 (addressing occupational culture).

63. Indeed, this societal realization came decades sooner for race than for sex as a social construct. See Greene, "Categorically Black, White, or Wrong," *University of Michigan Journal of Law Reform* 47 (2013): 145–77,146 n.284 (describing the ignominious race determination trials of the nineteenth century grounded "physical features" and "racial reputation" to grant or withhold political, social, legal, and economic rights); *Shaare Tefila Congregation v. Cobb*, 481 U.S. 615, 618–19 (1987) (in § 1982 action for right to hold property, holding that congregation of Jews were not foreclosed from claim of racial discrimination because they were distinct people that Congress intended to protect, regardless of fact society today considers them "part of the Caucasian race"); see also *St. Francis College v. Al-Khazraraji*, 481 U.S. 604, 613 (1983).

64. See Sue Landsittel, "Strange Bedfellows? Sex, Religion, and Transgender Identity Under Title VII," *Northwestern University Law Review* 104 (2010): 1147, 1172.

65. 29 C.F.R. § 1606.1 (defining national origin discrimination "broadly as including, but not limited to, the denial of equal employment opportunity because of an individual's, or his or her ancestor's, place of origin; or because an individual has the physical, cultural or linguistic characteristics of a national origin group").

66. See Mary C. Dunlap, "The Constitutional Rights of Sexual Minorities: A Crisis of the Male/Female Dichotomy," *Hastings Law Journal* 30 (1979): 1131–39 (discussing implications of the "two-sex presumption" in the law and among courts and civil rights advocates); Dean Spade, "Documenting Gender," *Hastings Law Journal* 59 (2008): 731, 738 (discussing the assumption of gender cohesiveness and stability as mythical based upon inconsistent criteria). This separability of the State axis for the purposes of Title VII adjudication is distinct from the debate over whether the state should ever track natal sex or sex, as those who rely upon updated identification of their sex to navigate institutions daily would seek an incremental approach. See A. J. (Anna James) Neuman Wipfler, "Identity Crisis: The Limitations of Expanding Government Recognition of Gender Identity and the Possibility of Genderless Identity Documents," *Harvard Journal of Law and Gender* 39 (2016): 491, 496–97, 534–38.

67. *Obergefell v. Hodges*, 135 S. Ct. 2584, 2602 (2015).

68. See, e.g., *The Report of the 2015 U.S. Transgender Survey* , National Center for Transgender Equality (Washington, DC: National Center for Transgender Equality, 2017), 85 (reporting only 11 percent of trans respondents reported that all of their identification cards and records listed both the name and gender they preferred,); *Zzyym v. Pompeo*, No. 15-CV-02362-RBJ, 2019 WL 764577, at **3–4 (D. Colo. Feb. 21, 2019) (denying motion to stay order enjoining U.S. State Department from relying upon binary-only gender marker policy to deny non-binary intersex plaintiff Dana Zzymm a passport with a sex marker of "X").

69. In the largest survey examining the experiences of transgender people in the United States, 77 percent of respondents who had a job in the past year hid their gender identity at work, quit their job, or took other actions to avoid discrimination. In only the prior year alone, as many as 14 percent of respondents reported that they were verbally harassed, physically

attacked, and/or sexually assaulted at work because of their gender identity or expression; and nearly one-quarter (23 percent) reported other forms of mistreatment based on the same during the past year, including (1) being forced to use a restroom that did not match their gender identity, (2) being told to present in the wrong gender in order to keep their job, or (3) having a supervisor or coworker share private information about their transgender status without their permission. *The Report of the 2015 U.S. Transgender Survey*, 44.

70. See, e.g., Third Amended Complaint, *Doe v. Fedcap Rehab. Servs., Inc.*, No. 1:17-cv-08220-JPO-OTW (Dkt. 58) at ¶¶ 9, 58–62 (S.D.N.Y. May 11, 2018) (alleging conduct as grounds for Title VII sex discrimination against plaintiff who identifies as trans-masculine genderqueer); Complaint in Intervention of Plaintiff-Intervenor Dr. Rachel Tudor, No. 5:15-cv-00324-C, Dkt. 24 at ¶¶ 67–69 (W.D. Okla. May 5, 2015) (describing employer's health insurance for professors explicitly excluded including medically necessary treatments health care benefits for transgender individuals connected with transition).

71. Americans are two to three times more likely to say that they are attracted to individuals of the same sex or have had same-sex sexual experiences than they are to self-identify as lesbian, gay, or bisexual. Gary J. Gates et al., *How Many People Are Lesbian, Gay, Bisexual, and Transgender?* (Los Angeles: The Williams Institute, 2011), 1, https://williamsinstitute.law.ucla.edu/wp-content/uploads/Gates-How-Many-People-LGBT-Apr-2011.pdf. Furthermore, more than 35 percent of Americans between ages 13 and 21 know someone who prefers to use gender-neutral pronouns. Kim Parker et al., *Generation Z Looks a Lot Like Millennials on Key Social and Political Issues*, (Washington, DC: Pew Research Center, 2019), https://www.pewsocialtrends.org/wp-content/uploads/sites/3/2019/01/Generations-full-report_FINAL_1.18.pdf.

72. *Hively*, 853 F.3d at 345.

73. According to one study, 55 percent of the adult "LGBT" population resides in states that prohibit workplace discrimination based on sexual orientation and gender identity through both descriptive group coverage and interpreting existing sex-discrimination laws to include sexual orientation and gender identity. "Non-Discrimination Laws," *Movement Advancement Project*, accessed July 3, 2019, http://www.lgbtmap.org/equality-maps/non_discrimination_laws.

74. *Wood v. C.G. Studios*, 660 F. Supp. 176, 177, 177–78 (E.D. Pa. 1987).

75. Ibid., 176–78. Employment claims by intersex plaintiffs are less common in that they may be less visible: members may publicly express their gender aligned with a sex binary and thereby avoid gender policing or other harassment based on their sex characteristics. See Janet Dolgin, "Discriminating Gender: Legal, Medical, and Social Presumptions about Transgender and Intersex People," *Southwestern Law Review* 47 (2017): 61, 96, 97.

76. 660 F. Supp. at 177–78.

77. Ibid.

78. Nor would the substantive-equality method of associational discrimination, akin to the Supreme Court invalidation of anti-miscegenation laws in *Loving v. Virginia*, 388 U.S. 1 (1967), apply to here as intimate associations are not an issue.

79. *Harris Funeral Homes*, 884 F.3d at 575, 578 (quoting *Hively*, 853 F.3d at 345) (holding discrimination based upon transgender status and a change in sex both constitute sex discrimination).

80. Devon W. Carbado and Cheryl I. Harris, "Intersectionality at 30: Mapping the Margins of Anti-Essentialism, Intersectionality, and Dominance Theory," *Harvard Law Review* 132 (2019): 2193, 2200.

81. Empirical research in intersectionality scholarship further substantiates the problems with anti-discrimination doctrine. See, e.g., Rachel Kahn Best et al., "Multiple Disadvantages: An Empirical Test of Intersectionality Theory in EEO Litigation," *Law and Society Review* 45 (2011): 991, 999 (reporting sampling in which plaintiffs with multiple claims were only half as likely to win their cases as other plaintiffs); Minna J. Kotkin, "Diversity and Discrimination: A Look at Complex Bias," *William & Mary Law Review* 50 (2009): 1439, 1440 (reporting sampling in which employers prevailed at summary judgment in multiple-claims cases at a rate of 96 percent, as compared to 73 percent in employment discrimination claims in general).

82. *Degraffenfried v. Gen. Motors Assemb. Div., St. Louis*, 413 F. Supp. 142, 145 (E.D. Mo. 1976).

83. *Judge v. Marsh*, 649 F. Supp. 770, 780 (1986). Rarely, if at all, do opinions in criminal opinions applying general- or specific-intent statutes bemoan the potential kaleidoscopic variation inhering in human thought.

84. This chapter acknowledges that intersectionality inheres in everyone across contexts, and that sexual minorities include racial minorities, and vice versa. Where necessary, this chapter denotes distinct groups but recognizes they comprise some of the same individuals.

85. E.g., Kate Sablonsky Elengold, "Clustered Bias," *The North Carolina Law Review* 96 (2018): 457.

86. *Hicks v. Gates Rubber Co.*, 833 F.2d 1406, 1416–17 (10th Cir. 1987) (citing *Jefferies v. Harris Co. Community Action Ass'n*, 615 F.2d 1025, 1032 [5th Cir.1980]).

87. Crenshaw called this critique the "single categorical axis."Crenshaw, "Demarginalizing the Intersection of Race and Sex," 140.

88. Hutchinson, "Identity Crisis," 312–13; *see also* Deborah King, "Multiple Jeopardy, Multiple Consciousness: The Context of a Black Feminist Ideology," *Signs* 14 (1988): 42, 51–52.

89. The facts and holdings of this case are drawn from *Brack v. Shoney's, Inc.*, 249 F. Supp. 2d 938 (W.D. Tenn. 2003).

90. e. christi cunningham, "The Rise of Identity Politics I: The Myth of the Protected Class in Title VII Disparate Treatment Cases," *Connecticut Law Review* 30 (1998): 441, 499 n. 281. ("Few courts have been willing to do the calculus for the intersection of more than two forms of oppression.") The intersectional capacity of multiaxial analysis in the areas of race, disability, and religion is beyond the scope of this chapter, and will be addressed in future work revisiting precedent and illustrating possible approaches.

91. All facts are derived from *Ash v. Tyson Foods, Inc.*, 546 U.S. 454 (2006) (per curiam).

92. *Ash*, 546 U.S. at 456.

93. *EEOC v. Catastrophe Management Solutions*, 852 F.3d 1018, 1034 (11th Cir. 2016).

94. E.g., *Paz v. Wauconda Health Care*, 464 F.3d 659, 665–66 (7th Cir. 2006) (reversing summary judgment for defendant where supervisor had made repeated disparaging remarks about Mexicans and Hispanics, courts must look at entire "mosaic of discrimination" even without any being dispositive); *Vega v. Hempstead Union Free Sch. Dist.*, 801 F.3d 72, 87 (2d Cir. 2015) (holding plaintiff's alternative to *McDonnell Douglas* is to create a "mosaic" of intentional discrimination identifying bits and pieces of evidence that together give rise to an inference of discrimination").

95. 42 U.S.C. § 1981A(c), as amended by the Civil Rights Act of 1991.

96. Deborah C. Malamud, "The Last Minuet: Disparate Treatment after Hicks," *Michigan Law Review* 93 (1995): 2229, 2323, and 2323 n. 293.

97. Kathryn Abrams, "Title VII and The Complex Female Subject," *Michigan Law Review* 92 (1994): 2479, 2533.

BIBLIOGRAPHY

Cases

Ash v. Tyson Foods, Inc., 546 U.S. 454 (per curiam 2006).

Bostock v. Clayton City Board of Commissioners, 723 Fed. App'x 964 (11th Cir. 2018), *cert. granted*, 139 S. Ct. 1599 (2019).

Bostock v. Clayton City Board of Commissioners, 894 F.3d 1335, 1339 (11th Cir. 2018).

Brack v. Shoney's, Inc., 249 F. Supp. 2d 938 (W.D. Tenn. 2003).

Chavez v. Credit Nation Auto Sales, LLC, 641 Fed. App'x 883, 884 (11th Cir. 2016).

City of Belleville v. Doe, 119 F.3d 563, 588 (7th Cir. 1997).

Degraffenfried v. General Motors Assembly Division, St. Louis, 413 F. Supp. 142 (E.D. Mo. 1976).

Desantis v. Pacific Telephone & Telegraph Co., 608 F.2d 327 (9th Cir. 1979).

Dodds v. U.S. Department of Education, 845 F.3d 217 (6th Cir. 2016).

Doe ex rel. Doe v. Boyertown Area School District, 897 F.3d 518 (3d Cir. 2018).

Equal Employment Opportunity Commission v. R.G. &. G.R. Harris Funeral Homes, Inc., 884 F.3d 560 (6th Cir. 2018), *cert. granted*, 139 S. Ct. 1599 (2019).
Equal Employment Opportunity Commission v. Boh Brothers Construction Co., 731 F.3d 444 (en banc 5th Cir. 2013).
Equal Employment Opportunity Commission v. Catastrophe Management Solutions, 852 F.3d 1018 (11th Cir. 2016).
Etsitty v. Utah Transit Authority, 502 F.3d 1215 (10th Cir. 2007).
Frontiero v. Richardson, 411 U.S. 677 (1973).
Glenn v. Brumby, 663 F.3d 1312 (11th Cir. 2011).
Hicks v. Gates Rubber Co., 833 F.2d 1406 (10th Cir. 1987)
Hively v. Ivy Tech Community College of Indiana, 853 F.3d 339 (en banc 7th Cir. 2017).
J.E.B. v. Alabama ex rel. T.B., 511 U.S. 127 (1994).
Jefferies v. Harris Co. Community Action Association, 615 F.2d 1025 (5th Cir.1980).
Judge v. Marsh, 649 F. Supp. 770 (1986).
Loving v. Virginia, 388 U.S. 1 (1967).
M.A.B. v. Board of Education, 286 F. Supp. 3d 704 (D. Md. 2018).
Nichols v. Azteca Restaurant Enterprises, Inc., 256 F.3d 864 (9th Cir. 2001).
Obergefell v. Hodges, 135 S. Ct. 2584 (2015).
Oncale v. Sundowner Offshore Services, Inc., 523 U.S. 75 (1998).
Paz v. Wauconda Health Care, 464 F.3d 659 (7th Cir. 2006).
Price Waterhouse v. Hopkins, 490 U.S. 228 (1989).
Prowel v. Wise Business Forms, Inc., 579 F.3d 285 (3d Cir. 2009).
Schmedding v. Tnemec Co., 187 F.3d 862 (8th Cir. 1999).
Schroer v. Billington, 577 F. Supp. 2d 293 (D.D.C. 2008).
Schwenk v. Hartford, 204 F.3d 1187 (9th Cir. 2000).
Smith v. City of Salem, 378 F.3d 566 (6th Cir. 2004).
St. Francis College v. Al-Khazraraji, 481 U.S. 604 (1983).
Ulane v. Eastern Airlines, Inc., 581 F. Supp. 821 (N.D. Ill. 1983).
Ulane v. Eastern Airlines, Inc., 742 F.2d 1081 (7th Cir. 1984).
University of Texas Southwestern Medical Center v. Nassar, 570 U.S. 348 (2013).
Vega v. Hempstead Union Free School District, 801 F.3d 72 (2d Cir. 2015).
Whitaker v. Kenosha Unified School District No. 1, 858 F.3d 1034 (7th Cir. 2017).
Willingham v. Macon Telegraph Publishing Co., 507 F.2d 1084 (5th Cir. 1971).
Wood v. C.G. Studios, 660 F. Supp. 176 (E.D. Pa. 1987).
Zarda v. Altitude Express, Inc., 883 F.3d 100 (en banc 2d Cir. 2018), *cert. granted*, 139 S. Ct. 1599 (2019).
Zzyym v. Pompeo, No. 15-CV-02362-RBJ, 2019 WL 764577 (D. Colo. Feb. 21, 2019).

Books, Articles, and Other Sources

Abrams, Kathryn. "Title VII and the Complex Female Subject." *Michigan Law Review* 92 (1994): 2479–2540.
Best, Rachel Kahn, et al. "Multiple Disadvantages: An Empirical Test of Intersectionality Theory in EEO Litigation." *Law and Society Review* 45 (2011): 991–1026.
Caldwell, Paulette M. "Intersectional Bias and the Courts: The Story of *Rogers v. American Airlines*." In *Race Law Stories*, edited by R. Moran and D. W. Carbado. New York: Foundation Press, 2008.
Carbado, Devon W, and Cheryl I. Harris. "Intersectionality at 30: Mapping the Margins of Anti-Essentialism, Intersectionality, and Dominance Theory." *Harvard Law Review* 132 (2019): 2193–2239.
Case, Mary Anne C. "Disaggregating Gender from Sex and Sexual Orientation: The Effeminate Man in the Law and Feminist Jurisprudence." *Yale Law Journal* 105 (1995): 1–106.
Chang, Robert S., and Jerrome McCristal Culp, Jr. "After Intersectionality." *University of Missouri-Kansas City Law Review* 71 (2002): 485–92.
Chemerinsky, Erwin. *Constitutional Law*, 3rd ed. New York: Aspen Publishers, 2006.
Clarke, Jessica A. "They, Them, and Theirs." *Harvard Law Review* 132 (2019): 894–991.

Crenshaw, Kimberlé. "Demarginalizing the Intersection of Race and Sex: A Black Feminist Critique of Antidiscriminatory Doctrine, Feminist Theory and Antiracist Politics." *University of Chicago Legal Forum* 1989 (1989): 139–68.
Cromwell, Jason. "Queering the Binaries: Transsituated Identities, Bodies, and Sexualities." In *The Transgender Studies Reader*, edited by Susan Stryker and Stephen Whittle. New York: Routledge, 2006.
cunningham, e. christi. "The 'Racing' Cause of Action and the Identity Formerly Known as Race: The Road to Tamazunchale." *Rutgers Law Journal* 30 (1999): 707–30.
———. "The Rise of Identity Politics I: The Myth of the Protected Class in Title VII Disparate Treatment Cases." *Connecticut Law Review* 30 (1998): 441–502.
Currah, Paisley. "Defending Genders: Sex and Gender-Nonconformity in the Civil Rights Strategies of Sexual Minorities." *Hastings Law Journal* 48 (1997): 1363–86.
Dolgin, Janet. "Discriminating Gender: Legal, Medical, and Social Presumptions about Transgender and Intersex People." *Southwestern Law Review* 47 (2017): 61–114.
Dunlap, Mary C. "The Constitutional Rights of Sexual Minorities: A Crisis of the Male/Female Dichotomy." *Hastings Law Journal* 30 (1979): 1131–50.
Eisenstadt, Leora F. "Fluid Identity Discrimination." *American Business Law Journal* 52 (2015), 789–857.
Elengold, Kate Sablonsky. "Clustered Bias." *North Carolina Law Review* 96 (2018): 457–511.
Eskridge, William N. Jr. "Title VII's Statutory History and the Sex Discrimination Argument for LGBT Workplace Protections." *Yale Law Journal* 127 (2017): 322–405.
Ford, Richard T. "Race as Culture? Why Not?" *UCLA Law Review* 47 (2000): 1803–14.
Franklin, Cary. "The Anti-Stereotyping Principle in Constitutional Sex Discrimination Law." *New York University Law Review* 85 (2010): 83–173.
Gates, Gary J., et al. *How Many People Are Lesbian, Gay, Bisexual, and Transgender?* The Williams Institute (2011), available at https://williamsinstitute.law.ucla.edu/wpcontent/uploads/Gates-How-Many-PeopleLGBT-Apr-2011.pdf.
Greenberg, Julie A. "The Roads Less Traveled: The Problem with Binary Sex Categories." in *Transgender Rights*, edited by Paisley Currah et al. Minneapolis: University of Minnesota Press, 2006.
Greene, D. Wendy. "Categorically Black, White, or Wrong: 'Misperception Discrimination' and the State of Title VII Protection." *University of Michigan Journal of Law Reform* 47 (2013): 87–166.
Halley, Janet. "Sexual Orientation and the Politics of Biology: A Critique of the Argument from Immutability." *Stanford Law Review* 46 (1994): 503–68.
Harris, Angela P. "Race and Essentialism in Feminist Legal Theory." *Stanford Law Review* 42 (1990): 581–616.
Hutchinson, Darren Lenard. "Identity Crisis: 'Intersectionality,' 'Multidimensionality,' and the Development of an Adequate Theory of Subordination." *Michigan Journal of Race and Law* 6 (2001): 285–318.
———. "Ignoring the Sexualization of Race: Heteronormativity, Critical Race Theory, and Anti Racist Politics." *Buffalo Law Review* 47 (1999): 1–116.
———. "New Complexity Theories: From Theoretical Innovation to Doctrinal Reform." *University of Missouri-Kansas City Law Review* 71 (2002): 431–45.
King, Deborah. "Multiple Jeopardy, Multiple Consciousness: The Context of a Black Feminist Ideology." *Signs* 14 (1988): 42–72.
Kotkin, Minna J. "Diversity and Discrimination: A Look at Complex Bias." *William & Mary Law Review* 50 (2009): 1439–1500.
Kramer, Zachary A. "The New Sex Discrimination." *Duke Law Journal* 63 (2014): 891–954.
Landsittel, Sue. "Strange Bedfellows? Sex, Religion, and Transgender Identity under Title VII." *Northwestern University Law Review* 104 (2010): 1147–78.
Lawrence, Charles R. "The Id, the Ego, and Equal Protection: Reckoning with Unconscious Racism." *Stanford Law Review* 39 (1987): 317–88.
Littlefield, Alice, et al. "Redefining Race: The Potential Demise of a Concept in Physical Anthropology." *Current Anthropology* 23 (1982): 641–55.

Lopez, Ian Haney. "The Social Construction of Race." *Harvard Civil Rights-Civil Liberties Law Review* 29 (1997): 1–62.

Malamud, Deborah C. "The Last Minuet: Disparate Treatment after Hicks." *Michigan Law Review* 93 (1995): 2229–2324.

Mayeri, Serena. *Reasoning from Race.* Cambridge: Harvard University Press, 2011.

McGinley, Ann C. "Masculinities at Work." *Oregon Law Review* 8 (2004): 359–434.

McGowan, Sharon M. "Working with Clients to Develop Compatible Visions of What It Means to 'Win' A Case: Reflections on *Schroer v. Billington.*" *Harvard Civil Rights-Civil Liberties Law Review* (2010): 205–46.

Movement Advancement Project. *Identity Document Laws and Policies: Driver's License* (2019), available at www.lgbtmap.org/img/maps/citations-id-drivers-license.pdf.

National Center for Transgender Equality. *The Report of the 2015 U.S. Transgender Survey* (2017), 44.

"Non-Discrimination Laws." Movement Advancement Project (2019), available at http://www.lgbtmap.org/equality-maps/non_discrimination_laws.

Ontiveros, Maria L. "The Fundamental Nature of Title VII." *Ohio State Law Review* 75 (2014): 1165–1206.

Parker, Kim, et al. *Generation Z Looks a Lot Like Millennials on Key Social and Political Issues.* Pew Research Center (2019), available at https://www.pewsocialtrends.org/wp-content/uploads/sites/3/2019/01/Generations-full-report_FINAL_1.18.pdf.

"Resources." Intersex and Genderqueer Recognition Project (2019), available at https://www.intersexrecognition.org/resources.

Ridgeway, Cecilia L., and Tamar Kricheli-Katz. "Intersecting Cultural Beliefs in Social Relations: Gender, Race, and Class Binds and Freedoms." *Gender and Society* 27 (2013): 294–318.

Sandrino-Glasser, Gloria. "Los Confundidos: De-Conflating Latinos/as 'Race and Ethnicity.'" *Chicano-Latino Law Review* 19 (1998): 69–162.

Schlafly, Phyllis. *The Power of the Positive Woman.* New Rochelle, NY: Arlington House Publishers, 1977.

Spade, Dean. "Documenting Gender." *Hastings Law Journal* 59 (2008): 731–842.

Webster's Third New International Dictionary of the English Language, Unabridged, 3rd ed. Springfield: Merriam-Webster, 1961.

Wipfler, A. J. (Anna James) Neuman. "Identity Crisis: The Limitations of Expanding Government Recognition of Gender Identity and the Possibility of Genderless Identity Documents." *Harvard Journal of Law and Gender* 39 (2016): 491–554.

II

Policing Bodies

Chapter Five

Divorce Ruling without Consent

Gender, Penal Law, and the Faminized *Body in Nuala O'Faolain's* My Dream of You

Christin M. Mulligan

Nuala O'Faolain's historical novel, *My Dream of You* (2001), demonstrates how the deliberately paternalistic, patriarchal, and prejudicial structures of inequality established by both nineteenth-century British colonial divorce and Penal laws for both Anglo-Irish women and non-Anglican Irish subjects of any gender, deny them what we would now consider basic rights preceding, in the midst, and following the Great Famine period. Such laws in fact silenced their voices from the record, denying them the right to advocate for themselves and actively participate in litigation. In response, O'Faolain's modern narrator, Kathleen de Burca/Burke, tries to create a possibly intersectional identity for her historical female subject, Marianne McCausland Talbot, and redress this through the practice of writing that ironically endeavors to transcend as it claims to consider class, religion, and ethnopolitical identity as well as notions of "sanity" in an effort to push back against the historical discriminations of these laws, only to indicate how such prejudices linger into the twentieth century in Kathleen's own experience.

Using the novel as a paradigm for twentieth-century cultural accounts of the (post-)Famine era, I will further examine the relations between personal accountability and historical accuracy, invoking Judith Butler and Athena Athanasiou's theorization of "aporetic dispossession" to explore the disturbed and disturbing formation of one's subject-position in the face of legal and bodily subjection and the dynamics of constructing an audience in a decidedly self-conscious story and how that impacts the possibilities for imagining gender and justice that must be impossibly delayed. Kathleen de

Burca's efforts are earnest, but she also repeatedly protests or "poor mouths" (perhaps too much) her own lack of agency as she endeavors to "perform the political" while addressing this fraught moment in Irish history through her subject Marianne Talbot's notorious divorce case.

Athanasiou insists that we must also foreground dispossession in alliance with Derridean "ontopology" or located- or situated-ness (or the lack thereof) as "practices that produce and constrain human intelligibility" (Butler and Athanasiou 2013, 18), particularly relevant as I relate them to a (neo- or post-)colonial context in Ireland and how that context contributes to the "precarity" of "those whose proper place is non-being" (ibid., 19). Their de-subjectivization occurs as a result of the Famine or its lingering effects, such as the lack of a socio-juridical context for one's language or desire—what she and Butler follow Achille Mbembe in terming the "necropolitics" of human value versus human disposability. Such accounts of precarity are often the result of long-term political and socioeconomic dispossession, such as the sixteenth- and seventeenth-century Penal Laws that denied non-Anglicans the rights to "lease land with more than one cabin or own more than two acres. They could not purchase land, and if they did own land, when they died it had to be inherited either by a Protestant heir or divided equally amongst all their sons, so as to render a large estate smaller and smaller through the generations" (Stoddard 2012, 35). These colonial prohibitions continued until the Catholic Emancipation of the 1820s were effectively reinforced by Famine-era evictions, which implicitly impact Marianne Talbot's employee, tenant, and alleged lover, William Mullan, and were not officially, fully, and completely repealed until the Government of Ireland Act of 1920.

Representing the dispossessed traumatic body in the text is an essential gesture of memorialization in the same way that many public Famine memorials and later representations of the period in contemporary art mark the disfigurement of malnourishment that not only occurs to victims' physiognomies but also represent the breakdown of codified social structures, the lack of legal protections, and the starvation of forms of community.[1] Such collapses are figured textually as the absence of adequate language to express or contain these losses for William, in order to negotiate through elision the violence, poverty, privation, fear, and ultimately, imprisonment or death that occur in his and/or Marianne's experiences, particularly because he does not speak more than a few words of English and she does not speak any Irish. This is also especially relevant because both of their direct testimonies are absent from the record.

It is my contention that the act of writing an explicitly historicized work—whether fiction, memoir, or fiction as memoir of recovery—alters the narrative and narrators and orients their narratives toward site specificity. Kathleen de Burca's and thus O'Faolain's account of Marianne Talbot's status as wifely chattel links her body to the rest Richard Talbot's property, including his estate, Mount Talbot, the eventual *faminization* of the tenancy, her expulsion and institutionalization during their divorce, and Marianne and Mount Talbot's mutual collapse, as she had no legal standing for a prior claim. Such a distinction also insists that through O'Faolain's deliberate grounding in the potato fields and cottages surrounding the "big house" endeavors to localize as well as engage with both intimate and communal sites of suffering writ large in the landscape itself. For the Great Famine period, undeniably, is also about a kind of linguistic "death" or marginalization that requires bereaved memorialization of the passing away and exodus of so many millions of Irish speakers, including William Mullan.

Whatever vocabulary one uses and whether written in Irish or English, this novel explores a constellation of experiences around *An Gorta Mór*, as well as what novelist Sean Kenny reflects on as its larger sociocultural and psycho-spiritual relevance, "a Famine repressed breeds an incipient hunger of its own, a hunger to know, to grieve, to hold accountable, to resolve, and to honour" (qtd. Kinealy and Valone 2002, 17). In that regard, I will also incorporate the Famine orature of the Folklore and School Surveys of the 1940s, both presenting the visions and recollections of those, in many cases, merely a generation removed from *An Drochshaol,* another standard term for the Famine period that literally translates as "the Bad Life." As a result, the novel offers an occasion for self-transformation and transformation of the reader's perspective on *An Gorta Mór* as one endeavors to unearth the past from the chthonic depths of the land and the language as well as the reverberations of the Famine into Kathleen's future. O'Faolain questions whether language in the face of mass death is a necessary, integumentary form that endeavors to preserve the malnourished or debilitated body and successfully commemorate individual and collective losses, whether it can offer a means of protection when all biological and legal systems fail. Can fictional language speak when the legal record of Marianne's voice is unfortunately mute, except secondhand? Can it remain to memorialize and effectively cope with cultural and corporeal remains?

I. THE LEGAL, HISTORICAL, AND PSYCHOLOGICAL SIGNIFICANCE OF THE GREAT HUNGER/FAMINE

The feminization and fetishization of place and space as well as the historically discriminatory classist and gendered laws pivot again to still impact the realm of desire and longing, but in a way that derives from hungers: material, physical, and spiritual, that rage unabated by the lapse of over 160 years. For instance, through the infamous clause that bears his name in Irish Poor Law legislation (1847), Sir William Gregory denied relief measures to tenants who owned more than a quarter of an acre, unless the family relinquished its land. In Colm Tóibín and Diarmaid Ferriter's "documentary" book *The Great Famine* (2002), Tóibín speculates that the Gregory's famous home Coole House and its park must have been haunted by the specters of the Famine and subtly implies that Lady Augusta Gregory and W. B. Yeats's desire to collect Irish legends, orature, and folklore that, as Yeats says, arise "from contact with the soil" (qtd., 3) was in fact facilitated by Sir Gregory's own prior obsession with soil, or more rightly, increasing his and other landlords' holdings, prior to his death in 1892. Coole House itself was demolished in 1941; only its plinth remains, but the initials of Lady Gregory, W. B. and Jack Yeats, George Bernard Shaw, J. M. Synge, Sean O'Casey, and several other members of their circle can still be found carved into a copper beech that is not far from where the domicile once stood.

The tree marks the impact of the Yeatses, the Gregorys, and the others not only on the scene of literary and artistic culture but on the scenery of Ireland itself, as the legacy of both the Famine and the big houses that would in turn engender the Celtic Revival, sings through its boughs and remains rooted in the earth even to the present day, representative of an *echonomical* and revenant phenomenon that is replicated in O'Faolain's novel, despite the fact that the Mount Talbot estate no longer stands other than as ruins. The shape and landscape of Ireland is still marked by memory, from woods of copper beech and birch to untilled fields nevermore to be planted and crumbling edifices of what was once meticulously laid stone. What Garret O'Connor and Deborah Peck refer to as the "malignant shame" and the "transgenerational trauma" of the Famine is a lingering psychological consequence of the experience of occupation for both the (ex-)colonizer and the (de-)colonized (Kinealy and Valone 2002, 14). Historian Joseph Lee has described "the instinct of inferiority . . . feelings of self-deception, begrudgery, contempt for authority, lack of self-confidence and poor leadership" that have arguably been exacerbated by the Famine ruins that mark the landscape as well as, I would add, by the post–Celtic Tiger "ghost estates" that similarly mark sites of socioeconomic and personal collapse in Ireland today (ibid., 15).

David Valone and Christine Kinealy point out the reticence of government officials and lawmakers in the nineteenth century to use the word "famine," or a translation of the Irish "hunger" designated, especially, "great" to distinguish it from other crop failures that had occurred at intervals since 900 AD, preferring instead more exculpatory terms like "*distress, destitution, extreme destitution, calamity, or suffering*" (ibid., 17). Although at various points in my discussion, I will use all of those as well as other terms, such diction is not meant to minimize or misrepresent the events portrayed in the text of *My Dream of You* but, rather, to give them more depth, shade, and nuance: "While [Hunger] captures more of the human dimension of the tragedy, the use of the word *famine* more fully conveys the political dimension of food shortages—especially in regard to food distribution and entitlements.

Famine is never just about food shortages but is ultimately about political choices and decisions, and what happened in Ireland in the 1840s is a clear case of this" (ibid.).

II. *FAMINIZATION*, FEMININIZATION, AND COLONIZATION

O'Faolain's own psycho-political gendering of famine is inherently feminine, which in the Lacanian or Freudian sense of the feminine is defined by lack—whether that be of a penis or in this instance, sociopolitical autonomy. "To be colonized is to be feminized, is to be a body acted upon, a category always already dependent on the inferior status of women. To be feminized is to be passive, relieved of agency, of political leadership, and voice" (Stoddard 2012, 13). Such fundamental absence is not purely figured in psychoanalytical terms by Kathleen's imagining and thus reenacting Marianne Talbot's victimhood, but it also occurs because of Ireland's colonial status during and long after the Famine period, in addition to the cultural prohibitions of de Valera's Ireland concerning democracy and the rights regarding one's own body for author/protagonist, Kathleen. Indeed, "de Valera's Ireland" operates as a "necessary condition for the . . . self-constitution of 'contemporary Ireland'" and its emergence as the antithesis and rebuke of the former (Cleary 2006, 6). Kathleen, even more indiscriminately and reductively, employs "Ireland" as a signifier of generalized conditions of socioeconomic and psycho-cultural depression and oppression, generally with little regard to temporal or other relevant historicizing nuances, as if there have been almost no such epochs or minimal shifts since the watershed of the (post-)Famine period, generally considered the tipping point of modern Irish history.[2]

O'Faolain's "Famine memoir" blended with contemporary fiction represent a postcolonial perspective. At turn of the twenty-first century, she employs a mindset that questions the notion of just how far "post," if at all, the colonial Ireland is and joins it with concerns about gender and sexual liberation, in particular by co-opting an outmoded early second-wave feminist rhetoric of women's victimization for both its would-be-novelist protagonist and her subject/heroine, with the former's account of the latter interpolated with italicized "facts" from testimony and other records of the infamous Talbot divorce case. Accused of adultery with her groom, Marianne Talbot is removed from her life at Mount Talbot to endure a future in which she was not only an impoverished pariah but also, for all intents and purposes, the real-life Anglo-Irish equivalent of the Sandra Gilbert and Susan Gubar figure of "The Madwoman in the Attic." The (de- and re-)formation of place and space in the context of the trauma of Famine gestures toward the discourse of the gendered body, as suggested by Margaret Kelleher's excellent study, *The Feminization of Famine* (1997). This text addresses depictions of women in literature from the Famine period itself in the 1840s through the sesquicentennial as well as the literature surrounding the Bengali Famine of the 1940s.

Kelleher follows feminist critics like Alice Jardine and Jacqueline Rose as acknowledging the frequent representation of the feminine body as the vehicle of the inexpressible or unfathomable, "the Lacanian *'pas tout'* or 'point of impossibility' in any system" (1997, 6). Kelleher also ascribes to a Kristevan position on the sheltering body of the mother (and implicitly Mother Nature) as an ostensible source of protection and succor that instead becomes tied to the abject or "'the unthinkable,' extending from the mother's inability to feed her child, to cases of abandonment, desertion, even infanticide" (ibid., 7). What's more, the political and cultural *mythoi* thus relate the suffering of women to the feminine State and a horrifying vision of both the figures of the *cailleach* or hag as well as the *spéirbhean* or sky-queen iterations of the Irish mother-goddess, evoked by writers from the early Irish period to Yeats himself throughout his verse and in dramas like *Kathleen Ní Houlihan* and *The Countess Cathleen.*

Woman as a signifier of Ireland in the context of *An Gorta Mór* is at once foundational and forsaken, productive and destructive, conquerable and permeable yet nonetheless incomprehensible and untouchable (in the sense of bodying forth and manifesting a landscape that is the site of otherwise inexpressible taboos). Kelleher further notes the presence of "'walking dead' . . . children prematurely aged" and emaciated by starvation or with their mouths contorted in a rictus and "stained green from eating grass" (1997, 8). This is a motif evident throughout historical Famine lore, as in the account of Ned Buckley (i.e., Ua Buachalla) from Cork: "She was found dead . . . on the roadside with a miserable child trying to suck at the dead breasts of the mother and the mouth of the poor corpse was smeared with green slime to show that the poor woman was existing on grass and weeds" (qtd. Póirtéir 2007, 95). As Athena Athanasiou claims, "dispossession as a way of separating people from means of survival, is not only a problem of land deprivation but also a problem of subjective and epistemic violence; or put another way, a problem of discursive and affective appropriation, with crucially gendered and sexualized implications" (Butler and Athanasiou 2013, 26), most especially as they relate to the historical, textual, oral, and iconographic repertoires of femininity and Irishness that I address throughout this chapter.

As a result, Kathleen perpetually finds herself wanting in all aspects of her life and invests or projects that same *ennui* and longing, which is ultimately a failure of belonging, in/on-to her portrayal of Marianne. As Marina Warner asserts, "On to the female body have been projected the fantasies and longings and terrors of generations of men and through them of women, in order to conjure them into reality or exorcise them into oblivion" (qtd. Kelleher 1997, 8). In spite of the fact that Kathleen has long been physically absent from Ireland through her work as a travel writer for the British-based TravelWrite service, she remains psychologically grounded—as in *buried* or *mired*—in the predominant and restrictive mindset regarding the role of women (or lack thereof) in the public discourse and milieu of the Ireland of her youth. She continues to be confounded in her efforts to write a full novelization of Marianne Talbot's presumed life as a desperate and lonely erotic being during the Famine because she herself cannot overcome the oppressive class and sexual dictates of the mid-twentieth century during which she came of age, even as the new millennium beckons. Thus, she reflexively figures both Marianne and herself as neurotic casualties of patriarchal culture, never to feel pleasure free of guilt, condemned to adulterous and thus unsatisfying liaisons, forbidden from experiencing sincere contentment for more than a moment.

Kathleen inadvertently but repeatedly recreates the lack of agency and the effective abhumanity of Marianne Talbot's body that occurs by conflating it with those of the *faminized.* Mrs. Talbot was legally dispossessed, but contested in the records is whether she ever endured the privations of starvation (*Talbot v. Talbot* 1854a, 1854b). The processes of Famine break down the corpus to its raw elemental parts and the mind to its pure as well as base survival instincts. Kelly Hurley's definition of "abhumanity" suits my usage best because she clarifies that the "abhuman subject is a not-quite-human subject, characterized by its morphic variability, continually in danger of becoming not-itself, becoming other" (1996, 3), which Marianne Talbot does, if not through hunger, at least socially through her ostracization, expulsion from Mount Talbot, and institutionalization.

Additionally, the theories of criminal anthropology, social medicine, and biologically based and anthropomorphically influenced racialized discourses that Hurley traces throughout numerous British *fin-de-siècle* texts in the nineteenth century in fact relate to or evolve from many prevailing prior cultural attitudes, language, and imagery surrounding the pre-Famine, what I refer to throughout as the *faminized*, and post-Famine Irish as subjects and objects of scrutiny and (post)colonial hegemony, specifically the racially feminized and supposedly dissipated body of William Mullan. Such tropes obscure and interrogate the humanity of the body in systemic peril and social as well as legal turmoil that continue to inflect the self-perceptions and depictions of the Irish in art, literature, and law.[3] At the same time, countervailing discourses, such as historical accounts of recovery, regeneration as opposed to degeneration, compassion, self-sacrifice, commemoration, and endurance could strive to palimpsestically rewrite these bodies as human once more.

III. DISPOSSESSED SUBJECT OR SEXUAL POVERTY TOURIST?

However, Kathleen often reinforces her own abhuman status in the eyes of others and fails to extend any genuine empathy to them. For example, during her travels, sex work in Manila appalls de Burca, but other than the exploitation of children, in this instance, and the exchange of cash, couldn't it not be a way of describing her own albeit consensual anonymous encounters, typically in hotel rooms in foreign places rather than her dingy basement flat in London? Rather than freeing her and providing the thrill and escape she seeks, Kathleen, avowed believer in passion, actually undergoes a kind of biblical Passion when experiencing rejection by these men, and she pities herself all the more for it, as the novel catalogues in detail the slights of racism and misogyny she endures on a daily basis. Furthermore, her revulsion at being offered sex by a young girl and the fact that "there are children living in the middle of the road" result in being scolded by her Filipino taxi driver and told, "We don't need no fuckin' grief from some old bitch" (O'Faolain 2001, 11). Kathleen is acting out her own neocolonial fantasy in these remembrances in which she, Othered by her gender and her ethnicity as an Irish expat in London, subconsciously adopts the quasi-anthropological diction in her accounts of travel. While Kathleen vociferously and rightfully resents being treated like a foreigner in Britain, when she has lived there for over twenty years, referring to it as "my own personal Anglo-Irish war," from being mistaken for a tourist when approached for a television fashion interview on the street to discovering her session with a psychiatrist is being monitored without her permission by a trainee—to which her the doctor replies, "They do it in your country, too!" The police also search Kathleen and her luggage for fear that she is a member of the IRA when in the Peak District (ibid., 264, 16, 20, 265).

In spite, or perhaps as a result, of this, Kathleen's narratives from Asia and Africa to continental Europe involve what we would now describe as a "first world problem" of making a show of supposedly sympathizing with underprivileged locals or, at their worst, what I would consider sexualized poverty tourism. Her evening in Harare, for example, revolves around pleasing men, during which she and an unnamed woman perform "a parody of excitement, and wiggled our bosoms" while serving stew (ibid., 12). This parody lacks both humor and sensitivity, only demonstrating Kathleen's desperation for connection, even as she expounds at her companion's expense. Despite her insistence that she and this woman shared "our life stories" (ibid.), de Burca exoticizes her Zimbabwean acquaintance even further beyond the pale of failing to provide her with the dignity of a name: "She took down a plastic carrier bag from a nail on the wall and showed me her treasures. Her radio that got two stations. Her conical pink bra, for best occasions" (ibid.). Kathleen is in essence inverting her own experience of emotional colonialism and then reproducing it inadvertently under the guise of charming local color in her travel recollections and articles. It begs the question of whether there is any fundamental difference between the alienization enacted in these remembrances and the disturbing accounts of many British and American visitors to Ireland, not to mention the Anglo-Irish landed gentry themselves about their Catholic tenancy, as well as racist responses to Irish émigrés prior to and even during the early twentieth century or direct provision and other responses to the so-called "new Irish" in Ireland today.

Desirability to men is always already the coin of Kathleen's realm, and with it, the attendant anxiety that she will come up wanting, instead of wanted, as she wishes to be "on any terms, by anybody" (ibid.). Then, the neocolonial double bind ostensibly shifts again when her elderly married English landlord, Mr. Vestey, offers to trade the cost of her deposit for a sexual favor, to which she submits. "I didn't have to do anything except lie down" (ibid., 37), and during the act, she reflects, "You couldn't call him English, at that moment, or me Irish. This person and I were just slabs of flesh held in by skin, one sandwiched on top of the other" (ibid., 38). The unsettling metaphor of a fleshy-sandwich to represent the experience and the troubling nature of her detachment from her being as a person as opposed to an object is only underscored by the parting well-wishes exchanged between the former tenant and landlord as seemingly as perfunctory for Kathleen as the previous exchange of fluids. Her services are rendered in lieu of payment as she must manually assist her partner in achieving his satisfaction. The bald facts are, despite the fact that she never speaks, Kathleen does not just get to lie down, and her claim that "lying down for him in silence was the only way to tell him absolutely nothing about myself" only further effaces her individuality and her autonomy, emphasizing her complicity in her own oppression (ibid., 40).

Kathleen demurs; she opts to metaphorically lie down rather than stand up, no matter how she wishes to present herself upon exiting the flat as "Orpheus ascending" (ibid., 41). More Eurydice than Orpheus, de Burca remains trapped in a psycho-cultural Underworld created by her alterity as an Irishwoman because the situation in the basement merely reverses the gender paradigm of the Talbot scandal of an English lady of the manor being serviced sexually and otherwise by her male Irish tenant and the more archetypal version of (semi-)colonial sexual abuse. Regardless of protestations to the contrary, her body and Mr. Vestey's—not only in her own mind but evident from the racialized language surrounding letting the apartment that leads to his indecent proposition—is still thoroughly imbricated within this (neo)colonial and patriarchal system. In Britain, she is never not marked as Irish in her mind, permanently an outsider, a tourist, a subjugated woman who actively participates in or at least refuses to directly contradict the processes of her own Othering beyond the occasional cutting reply. This is further underscored by the sexual manipulation Kathleen experiences with Sir David, the father of her English best friend, Caro(line), as well as with Ian, Caro's repeatedly unfaithful lover and the father of her child.

IV. MARIANNE'S HISTORY VERSUS KATHLEEN'S FICTIONS: THE LEGAL RECORDS OR "THE TALBOT BOOK"

O'Faolain tries to cast her historical protagonist as a subaltern when Marianne Talbot, despite her hardships, is actually a privileged, if possibly disturbed, member of the Ascendancy. O'Faolain uses the real historical evidence of Mrs. Marianne Talbot's so-called madness to portray her as a rejected, misunderstood, and thus wretched figure in her narrative of feminine dispossession, comparable to another colonial Other, Bertha Antoinette Mason-Rochester in Charlotte Brontë's *Jane Eyre* (originally subtitled *An Autobiography* upon publication in 1847), or even more accurately as she is presented in the reimagining of the character in Anglo-Dominican author Jean Rhys's *Wide Sargasso Sea* (1966 [1999]). However, Kathleen de Burca, thinking of herself as "like Grace Poole" (O'Faolain 2001, 66), becomes self-appointed guardian of Marianne Talbot's cathected interiority and eternal flame. De Burca selectively narrates and consciously re-imagines the life of an actual personage through a fictional viewpoint that is deliberately set at odds with Marianne's depiction in historical documents and trial transcripts in an effort to rectify what Kathleen views as an untenable and gross miscarriage of justice in how Marianne and William Mullan are depicted without their direct testimony:

> The witnesses both say they saw Mullan and Mrs. Talbot lying down together in the straw in one of one of the stalls. You have it that he was in his stable clothes, and a witness calls him a dirty, filthy-looking person; and that—that does not alarm her. Now, when you talk about the impossibility of a lady allowing an act of sexual intercourse in a stable, where, as it is said, the beasts copulate, that may sound very well, but you are to recollect that if a groveling passion of this kind engrosses a woman towards a menial servant, how is it to be gratified? Opportunities will not always occur; they must be sought. (*Talbot v. Talbot* [1854a], qtd. ibid., 4)

As a self-professed "believe[r] in passion the way other people believed in God" (ibid., 5), Kathleen's early interest and eventual determination to writing about the Talbot scandal arise not merely from her righteous indignation about the racialized and socially stratified portrayals of the lovers, particularly the opprobrium heaped on Marianne, but because she views their alleged affair as a kind of powerless submission to chaotic forces of desire beyond their control. Her views develop as a result of the shocking, almost modern brazenness of the earthy details of their acts in the testimony itself and from the paradoxical contrast of the richness within Mount Talbot and the barrenness of the landscape outside the demesne when the affair began in 1848 after the height of the Famine and continued for three years afterward.[4] Of course, Marianne will eventually lose her status when she is accused of adultery, separated permanently from her daughter, exiled from her home, institutionalized, and divorced by her husband, and the property will likewise decline.

Further, Kathleen's social interactions in Britain and especially in Ireland are frequently the result of narcissistic responses couched in the language of sympathy or pity that nonetheless remains fundamentally about *her* reactions as a means of gaining validation. Eve Walsh Stoddard claims that "Kathleen's reading [of Marianne Talbot] bears no resemblance to her own subject position as exiled Catholic Irish woman" but does also note how she conflates herself with Marianne (2012, 180). However, Stoddard neglects to address Kathleen's simultaneous and inconsistent vision of Marianne as liberated or revolutionary in terms of sexuality and as a helpless, naïve victim of patriarchal culture, which are also roles in which Kathleen alternately presents herself. While Stoddard deflects by describing de Burca as initially "Anglo-centric" but eventually developing more sympathetic responses to other Irish people, she fails to observe the ways Kathleen generally adopts the neocolonial viewpoint I described above in anecdotes from her travels. Despite Stoddard's claims that Kathleen succeeds in what I would consider reactionary efforts to be a cosmopolite "citizen of nowhere," Kathleen nevertheless experiences what Stoddard identifies through Oliver's work in *The Colonization of Psychic of Space* (2004) as "social melancholy" or "the inability to mourn the loss of a loved and lovable self" (ibid., qtd., 185). However, Stoddard pivotally neglects the ways in which de Burca's melancholia pathologizes her perspective concerning not only herself but others. Instead of considering the needs or experiences of others on their own terms, de Burca regularly externalizes her own sorrows, longings, and grievances through them or what is commonly now known in feminist internet circles as "concern-trolling." Moreover, "The Talbot Book" is just such a large-scale exercise, offering equally one-dimensional or conflicting portraits and interpretations of the motivations of Marianne and Richard Talbot, William Mullan, and the surrounding community that begins as a historical recovery project, which, as the local librarian Nan Leech rightly points out, is at first largely devoid of facts, specifically those that would dispute Kathleen's own romanticized viewpoint.

For instance, even Marianne's uncle, John Paget's, account of the Talbot case (1854b) also categorically refutes Kathleen's imaginings by presenting Marianne as neglected by Richard, frail, delicate, and infantilized—instead of hale, hardy, and lusty—starved and kept in penury at gloomy Mount Talbot, then shut away to be divorced. In these testimonies, Marianne is not "*a strong-minded woman; she was generally in low spirits*" and is the object of "*A FOUL CONSPIRACY*" by a husband in want of a male heir, a condition to fully inherit the estate (ibid. qtd. O'Faolain 2001, 339, 334). Paget charges that Richard is evidently willing to go to any lengths to break his wife's spirit and compel her to falsely admit unfaithfulness.

Paget's defense relies on equally racist assumptions like those concerning Mullan in the Talbot *Judgment* about many of the Irish servants lacking veracity, including witnesses whose very countenances betray "*habitual cunning*," alleged thievery, and dissolution (ibid.). Kathleen notes that Paget strongly implies (possible gang) rape when Halloran and other manservants, including Mullan, are "seen by a maid beside [Marianne's] bed, holding her feet" (ibid., 350). Marianne's allegedly transgressive behavior and supposed, though disputed, contravention of class- and religious-based values transport her from a position of respectability, dignity, sanity, and incredible socioeconomic privilege as a lady to that of a degraded, nearly incoherent outcast. Paget insists that she could not even understand her confession because "*no trace of levity or impurity has been discovered among the ruins of her intellect, where all is pure, simple and childish*," and she is also physically transported by the Rev. McClelland across the border of the sea from her home in Ireland to an asylum in England (*Talbot v. Talbot* 1854b). Thus, "both spatiality and location have to be reconceived once we consider the departure from within, the dispossession that demands immobility. . . . [specifically] for one who is newly, and at once, contained and dispossessed in the very territory from which one both departs and arrives" (Butler and Spivak 2007, 18), which Marianne experiences both in Ireland and England on juridical, affective, bodily, and spatial levels. The very possibility of rape and violation are both elaborated within and effaced from Paget's text.

Nevertheless, de Burca opts to largely jettison both legal records and eagerly transform the work into fiction, retelling a variation on D. H. Lawrence's *Lady Chatterley's Lover* (1929 [2011]) in an Irish setting that still remains in many respects ignorant, insensitive, or paradoxical with regard to its haphazard approach to the myriad of differing cultural nuances and historical particularities created by that specifically Irish setting and the context of the Famine period, such as language, religion, socioeconomic status, and gender norms. All of which, as I will show, make its narrative deeply problematic. Kathleen's invention of the subjectivities of these real personages out of whole cloth ultimately necessitates leaving the novel incomplete as a result of the inherent internal contradictions of its shifting fantasies as well their repeated refutation in the admittedly aporetic records. De Burca sees the couple ahistorically, like a more gratifying mirror of her own experiences, such as their supposed assignations in the Mount Talbot orchard:

> They must have seemed like luscious fruit to each other. Their bodies must have ripened on each other.
>
> I'd half an hour on the juicy grass at the edge of a sweet-smelling orchard once myself, at someone's wedding, on a hot autumn evening, somewhere in Kent. I remembered the orange moon through the branches with black apple shapes on them, and I remember the man putting a gold sandal back on my foot—I even remember the tickle of the blades of grass on my sole and then the firmness of his fingers. That wasn't making real love, of course, it was just a party thing. His wife watched us coming back up the lawn to the lights of the terrace.

The memory made me stand up, uncomfortable. (O'Faolain 2001, 101)

What Kathleen cannot fully acknowledge to herself is that Marianne Talbot's life offers the alluring possibility of intense, authentic passion that she believes has thus far eluded her and also made her urgently seek it out as often as possible.

Kathleen seeks to stage the dream of love beyond borders of class, ethnicity, and religion, even superseding boundaries of monogamous or marital fidelity:

> William Mullan and Mrs. Talbot had been builders—they had made love in the literal sense of "made"—had manufactured love. Their passion led to love. The *Judgment* was full of her acts of care for him. And he—the three years he was with her were the years in which his own world convulsed and expelled its people, but he had stayed with her when there could be nothing in it for him but punishment. All the more because it was a journey I had failed to make, I believed that the body was the way to the heart, and the heart was the way to the soul. (ibid., 67)

De Burca takes it upon herself to write and "preac[h]" her gospel from the Book of Talbot—moderation in nothing—which she ironically develops, despite all her complaints about unjust, inaccurate suppositions and hostilities based on her ethnicity and her gender—through reliance on the same feminine (and in William's case as an Irishman, feminized by his Anglo-Irish "superiors") servility and taboo sexuality inherent in earlier deeply reductive historical paradigms like Matthew Arnold's (over)emotional Celt, who lacks a measured temperament (1867); (pre-)Freudian hysteria throughout the nineteenth and early twentieth centuries, and Betty Friedan's "problem that has no name" from *The Feminine Mystique* (1963), reductive stereotypes against which she would presumably argue. In O'Faolain's novel, sensitive, lonely women, those poor creatures, that is, both Marianne and—one-hundred-fifty years later—Kathleen, who lest we forget, is doubly pitiable as a fervent native Celt, are subjected to and abjected by ruling, uncontrollable strange fits of passion that whether fulfilled or repressed, breed bedlam in their lives, particularly in Marianne's case as she is (most likely) unjustly institutionalized.

Kathleen also implicates her nationality in being "expelled from that Eden" of her London apartment for her repeated infidelities to her first beloved, a wealthy Englishman, Hugo, and she employs rendering his posh accent to transform her ethnicity and homeland into a kind of sexualized plaguing of the body as well as a location dense—even unweeded—with displaced desire but also woe: "Ahrash, he made it sound like Ahland" (O'Faolain 2001, 3). *Ah-"rash"* especially prefigures the novel's preoccupation with haptics, or modes of communication through the skin. *Ah-land* functions as both the locus of the sigh of despair and the expression of Kathleen's discontent: "Ah, land." From Hugo's introduction, Kathleen uses perceived differences in language in a way that shows her own self-consciousness regarding, and alienation from, her Irishness—for instance his use of "supper" for "when [she]'d only just got used to the meal in the evening being called dinner" instead of "tea" (ibid., 2). What she emphasizes as "*embarrassment*" at his diction and accent emphasize her own insecurities: "In the Ireland I grew up in . . . [t]he only time we ever used 'supper' was The Last Supper" (ibid.). Marianne Talbot is also claimed to have used Lapsarian language about a Catholic seducer in the transcripts in describing her affair to a nurse while confined in Dublin:

> Mrs. Talbot told me how it commenced and the way it commenced was this. She went into his room, and a part of his body [implicitly, his penis] came into contact with hers, which caused a thrill to run through whole frame, and that was the commencement of her fall.
>
> . . .
>
> Did she say, "commencement of my fall?"—Yes. (*Talbot v. Talbot* 1854a, qtd. ibid., 108)

Similarly, Tóibín describes firsthand historical accounts of the Famine period as having a tone comparable to the great Victorian poets: Tennyson, Arnold, Hardy, Hopkins, and Emily Brontë; one "of pure, flat statement which is lifted, surrounded with a shot of awed, hidden, raw cadence so that you're never quite sure where the emotion is coming from" (Tóibín and Ferriter 2001, 40). Although this may at first appear to be a rather desultory sampling of "relevant" source material, *My Dream of You* exhibits a precarious balance between deliberately elliptical reportage and deliberately chthonic, cathartic revelation alongside folk memory and historiographic revisionism. In O'Faolain's case, the circumstances of the Talbot scandal in the historical record are considered inadequate in and of themselves by Kathleen to necessarily require invention on her part. All of these instances attest to what Tóibín rightly characterizes as the use of an unexpected "shot" of pathos and offer a profound grasp of Marianne's disappointing life.

V. CONCLUSION: HISTORICAL REVISIONISM, HISTORIOGRAPHIC METAFICTION, AND VIRTUAL SPACE

At this point, it is relevant to qualify that my use of the term "revisionism" or variations thereof within this chapter do not refer to the historical revisionism practiced by some British and Irish scholars—most notably Theodore William Moody, Robert Dudley Edwards, and Roy Foster—with regard to exculpating or minimizing the role of British imperial infrastructure or the lack thereof during the Famine period, but rather that this novel stands in sharp contradistinction to this school of thought because it refuses to discount or discredit the fundamental significance that the Famine times hold in the collective *innenwelt* of both the Irish and the Irish diaspora and therefore, the enduring role it continues to play in their cultural imaginaries as a form of Foucauldian "counter-memory," a moment of historical resistance or debate (1977).[5] This is particularly so for O'Faolain, as she writes about its recurrent effects at the beginning of the twenty-first century, doubting the truth of both fiction and history through an unreliable or at least ethically questionable narrator.

Instead, it becomes vital to acknowledge that these are works of what Linda Hutcheon describes in *A Poetics of Postmodernism* (1988) as "historiographic metafiction" that deploy actual past events as the means to reconsider or reconfigure the nature of reality and the limits of supposedly factual truths (e.g., the use of excerpts from the Talbot case and other period sources in *My Dream of You*). As Kathleen observes, "I used to wonder whether something that had happened more than a hundred years ago, something that was almost forgotten, could have been so terrible that it knocked all the happiness out of people" (O'Faolain 2001, 6). Historiographic metafiction serves as an ideological challenge to what were, at prior points in history, the received notions of the Famine for many in academe as a Malthusian corrective that resulted as a natural consequence of overpopulation, notions promulgated by historians primarily trained in Britain, who claimed objectivity even as they embraced the rhetoric of dismissing their critics out of hand and disparaging their work with the charge of republicanism in the face of escalating violence in Northern Ireland post-1969 (cf. Moody et al.). Many scholars later qualified such dismissals and their views on the role of imperial Britain in the epistemic crisis of the Famine after the Good Friday Agreement.

For Kathleen de Burca, her own personal, juridical, and "received" national history[6] offer perspectival turning points that enable reconsideration and reinvention as the metaphorical children of individual necessity. *My Dream of You* employs the historical past in a way that is not far removed from the Yeats circle's use of the mythical Otherworld for catharsis and affective discharge. In actuality, the historiographic metafiction of O'Faolain (who published the novel in 2001 in the midst of the paramilitary decommissioning of the IRA under Strand 3 of the Multi-Party/Good Friday Agreement of 1998, the year in which the present sections of the novel are set) strives to further complicate "nationalist" conceptions of the Famine as a strictly Catholic travail largely orchestrated by the machinations of a Protestant government by consciously blurring or undermining the religious and class distinctions that served as the backbone of plantation or tenant farming and ultimately led to Partition. After visiting Somalia in 1998, Irish president Mary Robinson claimed that the best mode of honoring the Famine period was to "tak[e] the folk memory of this catastrophe into our present world with us and allo[w] it to strengthen and deepen our identity with those who are still suffering" (qtd. Kinealy and Valone 2002, 13), and I would insist that O'Faolain's novel does just that. Her narrative shifts offer occasion to dispel, negotiate, or perhaps even reaffirm Kathleen's and Marianne's status as victims of gendered trauma.

In turn, the territory surrounding Mount Talbot itself becomes minimal and unfamiliar, neither national nor local as it is depopulated, but also all encompassing as an abscess, a fallow and carceral void. Marianne's self is realized or fails to be realized in geography that is at once named and also falls away as amorphous, unmappable and uncontained, like her possibly *faminized* body itself, somewhere in particular but also relegated to a deliberately ambiguous nowhere as a result of various blights: agricultural, legal, political, linguistic, and physical. For O'Faolain, it is the undeniable power of such forces, whether sociocultural or what Elizabeth Grosz calls "imperceptible" and physical (i.e., time and space), that drives Kathleen's impulse to create the narrative but also ultimately leads to the incompleteness of "The Talbot Book" (2015). De Burca cannot undo the lapse of time within Marianne's life, much less her own, nor ever satisfactorily remedy or mobilize the gaps that remain in the historical record. Kathleen and Marianne's subjectivities, one largely fictionalized and the other purportedly "real," exist in a Nietzschean world of

> competing forces, wills to power, everything organic and material, all the ingredients that make up each thing are nothing but relations of forces or wills to power, whose provisional alignments make all things, including living beings, possible. The universe is a sea of wills, wills to command and obey, wills that are active or reactive. (Grosz 2015, 7)

Therefore, try as she may, Kathleen cannot reset or undo the "provisional alignments" of heteropatriarchal forces that resulted in Marianne's fall from grace, exile, and institutionalization. Therefore, she will not to strive to realign those that also exist in own life. Kathleen functions as a strictly "reactive will" that is eventually outmatched in her effort to create an alternative narrative by the preexisting "facts," and since she believes that Marianne is victimized by these facts and mores, she over-identifies with her subject and believes herself to be persecuted by similar forces.

The organic failure of over one million bodies and the systemic failure of the potato crops around Mount Talbot and across Ireland during the Famine are metonymized in Kathleen's inability to craft a satisfying ending and in the dilapidation of the big house and its outbuildings. It is also reinforced by the economic collapse of the Talbot holdings post-Famine, since as Cathal Póirtéir notes:

> A disproportionate amount of taxation to pay for the cost of relief schemes fell on the landlords and large farmers, especially those with greatly sub-divided estates, The charging of the cost of relief schemes to local taxes, and the steadily growing arrears among badly hit small farmers and middlemen, gave landlords a double burden to carry. For many landlords, the loss of rents during the Famine and the burden of taxation imposed on them by central government was their final ruin and saw many of them lose their traditional wealth, power and lands. (2007, 197)

As David Lloyd observes, "The ruin is that part of the past that lives on to find its place and meaning in a relation with the present" (qtd. Stoddard 2012, 27). Because "matter has a kind of life, a kind of will—or many of them—that makes it an agent, or many" (Grosz 2015, 7), The imaginative sensorium of Kathleen's textual world is hampered and forced to reduplicate or anticipate the conditions of material deterioration:

> Already, this early in the year, ramparts of nettles guarded the breach in the wall, and twisted saplings bent from where the earth had lodged between loosened stones. There was fallen masonry everywhere under the drenched grass. [. . .]
> Bertie stopped.
> Here you are, he said.
> Where?
> The house.
> Where's the house, I said, looking around.
> Here.
> All there was ahead of us was a wide platform, stretching away. A broad, level, stone platform covered in black moss and twigs and bird droppings. (O'Faolain 2001, 105)

Kathleen discovers that much like the aporia within the record of the Talbot scandal, the estate itself (or rather, the little of it that remains) exemplifies absence, loss, the lack of fulfillment naturalized in images that reinscribe Mount Talbot's inevitable decay: funereal black moss, dead tree detritus, bird feces.

While she had hoped to chart what she refers to as "the seven stations" of Marianne's encounters with William Talbot, like praying the Stations of the Cross, other than the long-dormant and weathered stable yard, there is no house or orchard remaining, excepting one stray arbutus, in order to undertake this cartography (ibid., 107). She is sorely disappointed and laments that no map can be made. Furthermore, Kathleen recognizes the space of the property becomes for all intents and purposes a Famine graveyard beyond the demesne, as when she has the Rev. McClelland tell Marianne, "'In the end, at the worst,' he said, 'they used to knock a few stones out of the bank at the side of the road, and push the corpse into that declivity, and then they replaced the stones'" (ibid., 304). This anecdote is also reflected in the copious amount of historical lore concerning the absence of proper and individual burials without funeral rites across all of Ireland, including this example, also from County Roscommon, where Mount Talbot once stood:

> My father was only a little fellow during the Famine but I often heard him tell that he saw a whole cart of corpses and the bodies all swollen, and they brought the cart of corpses to the graveyard and made a big hole and put the corpses in the hole as they were. They put a big mat over the corpses and then filled in clay over the mat, and that's how they were buried. (Mrs. Peter Reynolds, qtd. Póirtéir 2007, 184)

Kathleen herself reflects on the "pauper" Irish who lived and died around the exterior beyond the walls, whose turf dwellings "had melted back into the fabric of landscapes like the one before me":

> I tried to remember the worst attacks of dysentery I'd had—the shiver of cold flesh and bone, the whole of me so sick and so feverish that my head lolled on its stem and my knees buckled. But it would have been more awful than that. To lie on wet earth, under rain-sodden straw, your face greasy and gray with sweat, while hot, yellow, poisoned stuff trickles out from between your dirt-encrusted buttocks and streams down your legs. . . . Did the dying people writhe and call on God? *A Dhia! A Dhia!* Or were they dumb? . . . the ones who caught the cholera swelled up and turned black—their faces turned black—and they died lying on the roads heading into town, because they came out of places like the valley before me and tried to crawl to the workhouse. But they all knew that the death rate in the workhouse was terribly high, too. They must not have wanted to die alone. Or wanted to die fed. (O'Faolain 2001, 74)

The arrestingly primal mortification of Famine deaths, the victims' loss of dignity and control of even the most basic bodily functions, create and sustain what Kathleen considers the "genetic material of trauma" (ibid., 76). When she recalls her father's boiling rage at England and his choice to legally re-Hibernicize their surname from "Burke" to "de Burca," Kathleen presumes to speak for him in the same way she speaks for Marianne: "There was no pity in him. [My father] didn't imagine to himself the people who stumbled out of this watery, secretive landscape, squelching along the edge of the marsh, mud bubbling up between their thin toes. Old men's feet with blackened nails. Soft children's feet. Brown feet, white, purple and misshapen," contrasting this graphic image with the clean and pristine faces of keening girls in red flannel in her convent school pageant for the centennial of Black '47 (ibid.).

As a consequence of her parents' dysfunctional and abusive relationship, nearly every relationship in the novel is painted uncritically with the same sweeping brush and thus object of an overtly indistinct, morose perspective that Kathleen's expands and expounds upon, pertaining to her various relationships over the years: including her and Hugo, whom she cheats on simultaneously with both their French neighbor and a Black janitor at her cleaning job; her best friend Caro(line) and boyfriend Ian, whom Kathleen sleeps with once; her and her boss, Alex, who, after a pathetic one-night stand eventually reveals he's a Protestant lay brother; her and Shay, who like many of her other lovers is married; her colleague and best friend Jimmy's anonymous series of male lovers; her alcoholic brother and her careworn sister-in-law; Marianne Talbot and Richard Talbot; Marianne Talbot and William Mullan; and last, Marianne Talbot and her unknown, hypothetically Anglo-Irish second lover, who, of course, completely disputes the entire premise of "The Talbot Book." As Foucault explains, "We want historians [or in this case, writers of historical fiction] to confirm our belief that the present rests upon profound intentions and immutable necessities. But the true historical sense confirms our existence among countless lost events without landmark or point of reference" (1977, 155), like the single unattributed tabloid page Kathleen receives from Nan Leech. De Burca wants Famine history, specifically the aporetic Talbot divorce case, to explain her own personal history as well as all of the Irish national history that followed it, and the quest for grand passion to explain Marianne's life, just as she believes it explains her own. The knowledge of lost or profoundly unclarifiable or inexplicable events and the unbearable lacunae of the legal records without Marianne and/or William Mullan's direct testimony are what cause her to forsake "The Talbot Book."

Moreover, Kathleen frequently and paradoxically intertwines her own romantic entanglements with Marianne's, for instance when she claims, "Maybe she did indeed have a passionate affair with Mullan, and—like me when I was with Hugo—her sense of her own sexual power made her reckless, and the [unidentified] man kneeling between her legs [according to the tabloid], was the equivalent of my [French neighbor] Sasha" (O'Faolain 2001, 469). Furthermore, Kathleen insists that her friend, Jimmy; her parents, and the forbidden lovers themselves are all "tragic ghosts listening to me and waiting for me to free them" (ibid., 22). Although they do not appear visibly, it is their voices which compel her to research the Talbot case and return to Ireland after the sudden death of Jimmy. To put a fine point on it, De Burca willfully elides the cultural, historical, or social complexities and idiosyncrasies of these individual relationships under the common banner of her own frustrated and devastating passion, which she problematically ascribes to almost everyone else she encounters. For Kathleen, and implicitly O'Faolain, there is little possibility of transcendence in *My Dream of You*, which can only occur when one is able "to wrench something from the teeming chaos of the world . . . [by] creat[ing] a space for ourselves, a virtual space, in which to enable forces, chaos, to be temporarily contained, that is, framed and made to have an effect in a given way" (Grosz 2015, 8). Bound by the limits and destructions of history in her efforts to create deconstructive historiographic metafiction, Kathleen cannot fashion a pleasing frame that can contain her dreams of Marianne's life in relation to generations of innuendo beyond the extant record and her dreams for her own beyond the canvas of the sky while in flight.

Indeed, there is no "virtual space" on the page for an alternative passionate narrative to successfully exist in relation to the historical legal record, except perhaps when Kathleen imagines the death of Marianne's lover, William Mullan, whose whereabouts are unknown after he seeks Marianne in vain at Coffey's Hotel in Dublin to supposedly persuade her to flee to America with him. So, de Burca has him forced to emigrate to live in a cabin in the birch wood and work at Saratoga Racetrack:

> And the deer turned their flanks to him as they rolled and jumped away—white flanks, dun flanks. When they did, he saw in his mind's eye [Marianne's] naked side, as she turned languidly beneath him, on a bed of her dress and petticoats. . . .
>
> William Mullan was not alone when he died. . . . When the men from the stable found his body, it did look lonely. But he had seen her dolphin body above him—the white torso twisting and turning in a most beautiful way—at the very end. And the deer did not move away until he was dead. (O'Faolain 2001, 527–28)

How can love without constraints and freedom not limited by social hierarchies exist and be sustained in the reality when O'Faolain suggests they can only be attained in death? Perhaps this is based on as an intrinsically Irish understanding of the realities of one's mortality because in the Irish language, the idiom is *ag fail báis* or literally, "to obtain death," as if the act of dying is a form of accomplishment or achievement, related no doubt to lore surrounding *an fód bháis*, or "the sod of death," the specific spot where an individual will meet his or her fate. What we witness here "at the very end" of both William Mullan's imagined life and *My Dream of You* is the demise of earthly passion, its consignment to the fading memories of the newly departed, which also describes Kathleen herself, who is now en route to England, leaving Ireland, the Talbot case, and ultimately, all notions of restoration of dignity or a sense of authentic justice for Marianne—beyond anything more than a final masculinized, objectifying ephemeral erotic fantasy—far removed, trailing behind Kathleen in the clouds, an ethereal vision of what remains of a profoundly abhumanized body and dehumanized subject, whose consent was projected rather than conscientiously obtained nearly as much in fiction as it was in reality.[7]

NOTES

1. I am deeply indebted to Elizabeth Grosz for the generous use of her unpublished keynote address from the UNC Boundaries of Literature Symposium. I am thinking specifically of the gaunt and decapitated bodies exposed to the elements in Edward Delaney's Famine Memorial statues at St. Stephen's Green in Dublin, obviously informed by the deformed, distorted, and transfigured figures throughout the *oeuvre* of mid-century Irish-born painter Francis Bacon, the subject of Grosz's insightful address. The oxidization or verdigris of the "lost-wax" bronzes not only shows the decay and mutation of the body when suffering the *extremis* of starvation but also causes the more disturbing abstract figures with distended limbs to appear to be deteriorating and regressing into the landscape itself, as if they are moldering like the potatoes during the Hunger, as opposed to Delaney's nearby cast of Anglo-Irish leader of the 1798 Rebellion, Wolfe Tone, who still possesses a noble bearing, a discernible countenance, and all of his appendages, seemingly in working order.

2. In this spirit, I will also strive to unsettle the pervasive and over-determinative autobiographical tendency throughout criticism on O'Faolain's novels as variations on or extensions of her two memoirs (Stoddard, inter alia). While there are certainly overlaps between O'Faolain's life and de Burca's, this seems to me an all-too-simplistic paradigm of protagonist of metanarrative as automatically equivalent to and inherently inseparable from the author, which is as reductive and problematic a conception as single or monolithic Truth, especially in the context of the events of *My Dream of You* itself with regard not only to Kathleen, but her approach to the personage and figure of Marianne Talbot.

3. For a compelling study of linguistic justice and the death penalty, see Margaret Kelleher's superior *The Maamtrasna Murders: Language, Life and Death in Nineteenth-Century Ireland* (2018).

4. *My Dream of You* is primarily set in 1998, which is the 150th anniversary of the Great Hunger's "last" year, although, of course, its repercussions obviously continued far beyond 1848 and, as will be suggested by the novel itself and the historical material in this chapter, it was not as if there was a clear understanding or delineation of a definitive endpoint for its victims and survivors (indeed most historians would consider the final year of the Great Famine period to be 1852), particularly in light of the pervasive threat of recurrence and the later *An Gorta Beag* or mini-famine of 1879, which was significantly less severe.

5. See Kevin Whelan's "The Revisionist Debate in Ireland" *boundary 2* 31.1 (Spring 2004): 179-205 and Joe Cleary's *Outrageous Fortune*.

6. Whether fairly or not, Kathleen compares the Famine to the Holocaust (O'Faolain 2001, 86–87).

7. I am deliberately using the phrase "obtain consent" regarding de Burca's view of Marianne to contrast the fact that, meanwhile, as I have just observed, William Mullan, in the Irish sense, has just "obtained [his] death."

BIBLIOGRAPHY

Arnold, Matthew. 1867. *On the Study of Celtic Literature*. London: Smith, Elder.

Butler, Judith, and Athena Athanasiou. 2013. *Dispossession the Performative in the Political : Conversations with Athena Athanasiou*. Cambridge: Polity.

Butler, Judith, and Gayatri Chakravorty Spivak. 2007. *Who Sings the Nation-State?: Language, Politics, Belonging*. London: Seagull.

Cleary, Joe (Joseph N.). 2006. *Outrageous Fortune: Capital and Culture in Modern Ireland.* Field Day Dublin: Published by Field Day Publications in association with the Keough-Naughton Institute for Irish Studies at the University of Notre Dame.

Foster, R. F. [Robert Fitzroy "Roy"]. 1989 [1990]. "The Famine: Before and After." *Modern Ireland 1600-1972*. London: Penguin Books. 318-344.

Foucault, Michel. 1977. *Language, Counter-Memory, Practice: Selected Essays and Interviews*, edited by Donald F. Bouchard; translated by Sherry Simon. Ithaca, NY: Cornell University Press.

Grosz, Elizabeth A. 2015. "Francis Bacon, Gilles Deleuze, and Imperceptible Forces: Keynote Address at The University of North Carolina Boundaries of Literature Symposium." Chapel Hill, NC, 1–20.

Hurley, Kelly. 1996. *The Gothic Body: Sexuality, Materialism, and Degeneration at the Fin de Siècle*. Vol. 8. Cambridge Studies in Nineteenth-Century Literature and Culture, Cambridge; New York: Cambridge University Press.

Hutcheon, Linda. 1988 [2010]. *A Poetics of Postmodernism: History, Theory, Fiction*. New York; London: Routledge.

Kelleher, Margaret. 1997. *The Feminization of Famine: Expressions of the Inexpressible?* Durham, NC: Duke University Press.

———. 2018. *The Maamtrasna Murders: Language, Life and Death in Nineteenth-Century Ireland.* Dublin: University College Dublin Press.

Kinealy, Christine, and David A. Valone, eds. 2002. *Ireland's Great Hunger: Silence, Memory, and Commemoration*. Quinnipiac University Studies in the Great Hunger, Lanham, MD: University Press of America.

Lawrence, D. H. 1929 [2011]. *Lady Chatterley's Lover*, edited by John Worthen. New York: Signet Classics.

Moody, T. W. [Theodore William]. "Irish History and Irish Mythology." *Hermathena*, no. 124 (1978): 6-24. Accessed September 4, 2020. http://www.jstor.org/stable/23040380.

O'Faolain, Nuala. 2001. *My Dream of You*. New York: Riverhead Books.

Oliver, Kelly. 2004. *The Colonization of Psychic Space: A Psychoanalytic Social Theory of Oppression*. Minneapolis: University of Minnesota Press.

Póirtéir, Cathal. 2007. *Famine Echoes*. Dublin: Gill & MacMillan.

Rhys, Jean. 1966. [1999]. *Wide Sargasso Sea: Backgrounds, Criticism*. New York: W.W. Norton.

Stoddard, Eve Walsh. 2012. *Positioning Gender and Race in (Post)Colonial Plantation Space: Connecting Ireland and the Caribbean*, 1st ed. Palgrave Macmillan's Critical Studies in Gender, Sexuality, and Culture, New York: Palgrave Macmillan.

Talbot v. Talbot. 1854a. Talbot, John, and Mary Anne McCausland Talbot.

Talbot v. Talbot. 1854b. Paget, John, Thomas Tertius, Mary Anne McCausland Talbot, and John Talbot.

Tóibín, Colm, and Diarmaid Ferriter. 2002. *The Irish Famine: A Documentary*. New York: Thomas Dunne Books/St. Martin's Press.

Chapter Six

Gender and Justice in International Human Rights Law

The Need for an Intersectional Feminist Approach to Advance Sexual and Reproductive Health and Rights

Rebecca Smyth

Sexual and reproductive health and rights (SRHRs) are a prime site in which to observe the dynamics of emerging and contested rights discourses. SRHRs concern sensitive subjects related to reproduction and sexuality, including access to contraception, abortion, and assisted reproductive technology. They also pose a challenge to the current gendered political and social order by advocating an approach to human rights that requires women's and gender-diverse people's full personhood to be recognized. It is unsurprising, then, that they are often controversial and subject to resistance and opposition. These obstacles are compounded by the theoretical foundations upon which human rights and the law rest and from which they derive legitimacy. Therefore, feminist theorists and activists must make use of the language and mechanisms of human rights as they currently exist to advance their agenda while also redefining the meanings of these systems.

This chapter will first provide an overview of the origins, evolution, and scope of SRHRs, emphasizing the role of feminists—particularly those from the Global South—in developing and legitimizing the concept within international human rights law (IHRL). It will then consider the ways in which the UN, the inter-American, and the European human rights systems applied the concept in their jurisprudence. Focusing on one of the most contested aspect of SRHRs, the need for safe, straightforward and legal access to abortion, this chapter will highlight the limits and contradictions that arose in the interpretation of SRHRs at the regional and international levels. I argue that these limits and contradictions are due to the persistence of understandings of the law and legal subjects that do not fully represent or respond to women's and gender-diverse people's lived realities. To deliver its critique of this jurisprudence, this chapter will suggest ways forward for a reconceptualization of IHRL and its theoretical foundations that can better serve the human rights of marginalized and oppressed groups. Before doing so, an articulation of the theoretical approach taken in this chapter is required.

Adopting a discursive approach, the law and human rights—and the liberal concepts that inform them—are understood to be sites of struggle. Although they have been a source of and justification for oppression and exclusion, they are also potential sources of protection, advancement, and liberation. In all likelihood, they will never fully be one or the other, but attempting to reconcile these two contradictory aspects can lead to more nuanced understandings of concepts such as rights, subjectivity, and autonomy, and so can bring about positive social change.

As noted by Flax, "The liberal political theories we have inherited and depend upon in the contemporary west have produced impoverished and unsatisfactory concepts of reason, subjectivity and justice" (1992, 189). These concepts, along with Aristotelian dichotomies such as public/private and reason/emotion, are fundamental to traditional interpretations of law, which have resulted in a reductive and ideological legal construction of life, the body and society. Informed by these concepts, the understanding of human rights that has developed since the Enlightenment has taken a "white, Anglo-Western/European, Judeo-Christian, educated, propertied, heterosexual, able-bodied male" to be the normative standard (Hernández-Truyol 1999, 31). As a result, those who do not conform to this idea of a legitimate subject are unable to have their experiences properly recognized before the law, and are considered other and in need of surveillance and control (Hernández-Truyol 1999, 31). Since the 1970s, feminist and queer legal theory, and other critical approaches to legal studies, attended to the ways that the law is a discourse that upholds and perpetuates sexist, racist, class-based, ableist, heteronormative, and cis-normative assumptions about society and legal subjects (Fineman 2005b, 19). A key development in feminist legal theory is the work of Crenshaw and other Black feminist scholars in articulating the concept of intersectionality: "a method and a disposition, a heuristic and analytic tool" which names and makes visible the ways in which personal identities and power structures such as gender, race, and class overlap and interact to create differing forms of privilege and disadvantage (Carbado et al. 2013, 303).

In recent decades, feminist legal scholars analyzed these dynamics in IHRL (Bunch 1990; Charlesworth, Chinkin, and Wright 1991; Otto 2009). For example, Charlesworth and Chinkin argue that "feminists should tackle international law on a number of levels at the same time" by using existing laws where possible, reforming them where necessary, and harnessing the "symbolic force" of IHRL "to reshape the way women's lives are understood in an international context" (Charlesworth and Chinkin 2000).

To summarize, an intersectional feminist approach to IHRL is required to understand the power dynamics that inform it, and to approach it as a site of contestation where alternative, emancipatory understandings of rights and legal subjects can emerge. SRHRs are a significant and worthwhile area of IHRL where this process can be observed, as will be discussed in the next section.

I. SRHRs—THEIR CONTENT, ORIGINS, AND EVOLUTION

For over fifty years, the concept of SRHRs evolved and expanded in legitimacy in IHRL on account of efforts of feminist and LGBT+ activists. This section will first discuss the current scope of SRHRs in the international and regional human rights systems. The second part will provide a chronological overview of the origins and evolution of SRHRs. In doing so, this section will emphasize the integral role of transnational feminist activism, led by Global South feminists, in articulating this holistic and intersectional interpretation of IHRL.

SRHRs Today

SRHRs combine four distinct but interrelated fields: sexual health, sexual rights, reproductive health, and reproductive rights. They affirm the rights and freedoms of people of all sexual orientations and gender identities to enjoy safe, satisfying sexual relations free of coercion, discrimination and violence. They also emphasize the importance of having the freedom to make informed decisions about sexual and reproductive health, including if or when to have children (IPPF 2008; WAS 2014; Yogyakarta Principles 2017; UNGA 1994, para 7.3). The following human rights are necessary to realize these aims:

1. the principle of nondiscrimination and equality
2. the right to life
3. the right to be free from torture and other forms of cruel, inhuman, or degrading treatment or punishment (CIDT)
4. the right to marry and found a family
5. the right to seek, receive, and impart information
6. the right to a fair trial
7. the right to privacy
8. the right to freedom of thought, conscience, and religion
9. the right to health

10. the right to enjoy the benefits of scientific progress (WHO 2012, 19; UNFPA et al. 2014, 89–115).

In relation to abortion, the UN human rights system's position is that it should be permitted at a minimum in the case of a risk to the pregnant person's life or health, in the case of rape or incest, and in the case of lethal or fatal fetal abnormalities; otherwise some or all of these rights could be violated (Méndez 2016, paras 5–11, 43–4, 72; UN Committee against Torture 2009; CESCR 2016; CEDAW 2011; HRC 2005, 2011, 2016, 2017). This position has been more consistently asserted in recent years. For example, the UN Committee on Economic, Social and Cultural Rights (CESCR)—the treaty monitoring body which oversees the implementation of the International Covenant on Economic, Social and Cultural Rights (ICESCR)—released General Comment No. 22 in 2016, which states that "the right to sexual and reproductive health is an integral part of the right to health enshrined in article 12" of the ICESCR (CESCR 2016, para 1).

The situation varies at the regional level. The African human rights system's Maputo Protocol contains an article dedicated to reproductive rights, including the need to authorize abortion "in cases of sexual assault, rape, incest, and where the continued pregnancy endangers the mental and physical health of the mother or the life of the mother or the fetus" (African Union 2005, article 14). It is the first international human rights treaty to recognize abortion as a human right under certain circumstances (Ngwena 2014, 190; African Commission on Human and Peoples' Rights 2014). However, the Maputo Protocol has yet to be signed and ratified by many African Union member states, and it is subject to numerous reservations. Moreover, abortion remains widely restricted across the continent (Ngwena 2010, 2014, 2016). Further, the African Commission and Court on Human and Peoples' Rights have yet to engage with specific cases to the extent that the inter-American and European systems have, and for this reason will not be discussed further in this chapter. Future cases from this regional human rights system should be considered with interest, however.

The two main components of the inter-American human rights system are the Organization of American States' Inter-American Commission on Human Rights (IACHR) and Inter-American Court of Human Rights (IACtHR). The IACHR conducts country visits and work on thematic areas such as women's rights, and hears individual petitions concerning alleged violations of the American Declaration of the Rights and Duties of Man and the American Convention on Human Rights (ACHR) (OAS 1978; OAS 1979, articles 34–51; OAS 1993). The IACtHR is responsible for the application and interpretation of the ACHR, and it has jurisdiction over the twenty-five Organization of American States (OAS) member states which have acceded to the convention. It hears cases referred to it from the IACHR's individual petitions system. Also, it issues advisory opinions on the interpretation inter-American human rights treaties, and on whether domestic legislation is compatible with the Convention (OAS 1978; OAS 1979). As will be discussed in greater detail in another part of this chapter, the inter-American human rights system—particularly the IACHR—has often taken an intersectional approach to women's and LGBT+ people's rights, and it has also demonstrated a commitment to SRHRs since the early 2000s. At present, based on a survey of the IACHR's individual petitions system, thematic reports, and country reports, the IACHR's stance on abortion is that it should be decriminalized at a minimum in the case of risk to the pregnant person's life or health, in the case of rape or incest, and in the case of fatal fetal abnormality (IACHR 2010, 2011, 2015, 2017, 2018). The court has yet to hear a case on abortion access.

In contrast to the inter-American and African systems, the European human rights system has been more conservative in advocating for SRHRs. The central component of the European human rights system is the Council of Europe's European Court of Human Rights (ECtHR). The court's current stance on abortion is that states have a wide margin of appreciation to determine under which circumstances it should be legal. If states decriminalized abortion in certain circumstances, people should be able to access it under those conditions. If they are refused an abortion, they should have access to a procedure to challenge the decision (*A, B and C v. Ireland* 2010; *P and S v. Poland* 2012; *RR v. Poland* 2011; *Tysiąc v. Poland* 2007). Other bodies within the Council of Europe (CoE)—the European Committee of Social Rights (ECSR), the Parliamentary Assembly of the Council of Europe (PACE), and the Council of Europe's Commissioner for Human Rights—also engage on occasion with SRHRs, but a coherent stance on the issue, and the extent to which these bodies influence the court's jurisprudence, is difficult to discern (Parliamentary Assembly of the Council of Europe 2008; Commissioner for Human Rights 2019; *IPPF-EN v. Italy* 2013). Four potential reasons for the Council of Europe's cautious approach to SRHRs are the European Convention of Human Rights focus on civil and political rights, the centrality of the doctrine of the margin of appreciation to the court's interpretation of the convention when engaging with controversial issues, the less extensive engagement of the court (compared to the UN and inter-American human rights systems) with civil society activism, and the lack of a specialized body dedicated to women's human rights.

In summary, SRHRs have been formally recognized as an emerging "family" of rights within IHRL at the international and regional levels of the human rights system, but significant interpretative obstacles hinder their full realization. The next section will consider the root causes of these challenges by providing an overview of the origins and evolution of SRHRs.

SRHRs—Origins and Evolution

An awareness of human rights issues relating to reproduction and sexuality first emerged in IHRL at the UN in the 1960s. This section will discuss the development of the concept within the UN to the present day, before summarizing its incorporation and interpretation in the inter-American and European human rights systems.

The first reference to reproductive rights occurs in the 1968 Proclamation of Tehran, formulated at the UN's International Conference on Human Rights. The proclamation states that "couples have a basic human right to decide freely and responsibly on the number and spacing of their children and a right to adequate education and information in this respect" (UN General Assembly [UNGA] May 12, 1968, sec XVIII, para 5). During this period, feminist thinking and activism influenced both domestic and international politics: in 1972, following considerable efforts by feminists within and outside the UN, the UNGA approved a world women's conference to be held in 1975, designated as International Women's Year. The 1975 Declaration of Mexico, which was adopted at this conference, expanded upon the Proclamation of Tehran's definition of a right to family planning, referring to the right of individuals and not just couples to decide "whether or not to have children as well as to determine their number and spacing" (UNGA 1975, para 12). This evolution in language and expansion in scope would continue in the following decades.

With the growing focus on human rights work across all aspects of the UN's work, feminists more consistently and vocally articulated critiques of the population control approach to development (Corrêa and Petchesky 1994, 107, 108). According to this approach, women were "targets" and "users" of coercive family planning programs which were characterized by the use of forced sterilization and unsafe contraceptive devices, and which focused on lowering birth rates to ensure continued provision of foreign aid and development loans (Hartman 1995; Jaquette and Staudt 1998). In response to these issues, the growth of conservatism and neoliberalism in the 1980s, and increased attention to the AIDS pandemic, the concept of reproductive rights was developed. Situating issues such as contraceptive access in the context of systemic inequalities, feminists advocated for a holistic approach to dismantling the structural barriers limiting women's human rights (Antrobus 2004, 31, 67; Corrêa and Petchesky 1994, 108). Feminist activists from the Global South, such as the DAWN coalition, played a vital role in drawing attention to these issues and in advancing this approach (Petchesky 2000, 4–5; DAWN n.d.).

The work of these transnational feminist coalitions before and during the UN conferences of the 1980s and 1990s was instrumental to ensuring that women's rights, including SRHRs, were given particular attention at the

1993 Vienna World Conference on Human Rights, the 1994 International Conference on Population and Development (ICPD), and the 1995 Fourth World Conference on Women in Beijing (Petchesky 2003, 35).

As regards reproductive rights, the Vienna Declaration and Programme of Action expanded on the 1968 Proclamation of Tehran and the 1975 Declaration of Mexico further. It framed access to "the widest range of family planning services" as a woman's human rights issue in of itself, rather than in terms of population control (UNGA 1993, sec IIB, para 41). The ability of feminist transnational activists to place women's issues on the human rights agenda, and to reshape human rights to respond to these issues, would also inform the ICPD held in Cairo the following year. It was at this Conference that the contemporary definition of reproductive rights was first articulated.

The ICPD's final document, the Programme of Action, represents "years of concerted effort by women's health movements around the world to gain recognition of women's reproductive and sexual self-determination as a basic health need and human right" (Petchesky 1995, 152). In many respects it also adopted an intersectional understanding of structural inequality, and the ways in which only transformative approaches to law, politics, and economics could address it (UNGA 1994, paras 1.5, 1.6; Principles 4, 8, 10, 14, paras 4.1, 4.12, 4.24, 4.25, chapter VI, paras 7.7, 7.8, 7.9, 7.12, 7.13, chapters XIII, XIC, XV, paras 15.1–15.4). The ICPD PFA defines the concepts of reproductive health, reproductive healthcare, and reproductive rights (ibid. paras 1.8, 7.2, 7.3). These were significant advances, as was the inclusion of references to the negative health and human rights impact of unsafe abortion, albeit in heavily qualified terms due to pressures from the conservative coalition led by the Vatican (UNGA 1994, paras 7.23, 8.25; Buss 1998, 343). The cautious language of the ICPD PFA concerning abortion, as well as the absence of any discussion of LGBT+ rights, would be critiqued and developed in subsequent years, including the 1995 Fourth World Conference on Women held in Beijing.

Due to the conservative and religious right's efforts to "stem the tide of what they termed "'gender' feminism" (Buss 1998, 340), the terms "sexuality," "sexual orientation," and "sexual health" were excluded from the final Beijing Declaration and Programme of Action. However, the debates surrounding sexuality represented the first time that non-heterosexual sexualities were widely discussed at an international human rights forum. This marked the beginning of the inclusion of the "sexual" in "sexual and reproductive health and rights" (Girard 2014). In regard to reproductive rights, the definitions of reproductive rights, reproductive health, and reproductive healthcare presented in the ICPD Declaration and PFA were restated. Concerning abortion specifically, paragraph 8.25 of the ICPD PFA was restated, but it was slightly expanded in that states agreed to "consider reviewing laws containing punitive measures against women who have undergone illegal abortions" (ibid., paras 94, 95, 106[k]). The subtle but significant developments achieved by feminist human rights activists at the Vienna, Cairo, and Beijing Conferences would serve as an important starting point for further evolution in the concept and legitimacy of SRHRs from the late 1990s to the present. However, they would also face concerted resistance and opposition during this period, especially in the 2000s or "decade of stagnation" (Garita 2015, 272).

At the "plus five" review sessions of these three conferences, feminists secured commitments to ending gender-based violence, and to realizing women's and adolescents' reproductive health and rights within the UN's human rights and development work. However, "the gains of the 1990s were being significantly eroded" due to a less active transnational feminist SRHR movement, sustained fundamentalist religious opposition, and the impact of the U.S. administration's neoconservative stance (ibid. 273–77). This erosion had been predicted by feminist activists and scholars, who emphasized the need for meaningful reform of economic, political, and legal structures to ensure SRHRs' full realization. They argued that without such structural changes, SRHRs would simply be incorporated in a reductive form across disparate issue areas, and they would also be actively undermined by their opponents (Corrêa 2005; Sen 2005).

Nevertheless, feminist and LGBT+ activists, as well as responsive state governments, continue using the language and mechanisms of human rights to advance their transformative agenda. Since the 2000s, there has been growing attention to LGBT+ rights as human rights within the UN. In 2011, a UN Human Rights Council (UNHRC) resolution affirmed the rights of LGBT people and requested that the OHCHR draft a report on discriminatory laws, practices, and violence against them (UN Human Rights Council 2011). In 2014, the UNHRC adopted a second resolution on sexual orientation and gender identity which called for a report from the OHCHR on best practices for combating discrimination on these grounds (UN Human Rights Council 2014). An independent expert on sexual orientation and gender identity was mandated through UNHRC Council resolution 32/2, and it began work at the 35th session of the UNHRC in June 2017 (UN Human Rights Council 2016). SRHRs have thus been recognized by the UN system as integral to IHRL.

In regard to abortion access, since 2005 the UN human rights treaty monitoring bodies issued Views, Concluding Observations, General Recommendations, and General Comments. They represent an increased confidence in challenging states' restrictive abortion legislation that builds on and asserts the understanding of women's human rights developed at the Vienna, Cairo and Beijing Conferences. For example, the UN Human Rights Committee—responsible for overseeing states' compliance with and implementation of the International Covenant on Civil and Political Rights (ICCPR)—found states to be responsible for violations of the right to be free from torture and CIDT, the right to equality and nondiscrimination, and the right to privacy for failing to provide women and girls with access to abortion services (*KL v. Peru* 2005, *LMR v. Argentina* 2011, *Amanda Mellet v. Ireland* 2016, *Siobhán Whelan v. Ireland* 2017). The CEDAW Committee, which is responsible for overseeing states' compliance with and implementation of the Convention on the Elimination of All Forms of Discrimination against Women (CEDAW), issued Views emphasizing the importance of quality obstetric care, including access to abortion, in ensuring that women's human rights are fully respected, protected, and fulfilled (*Alyne da Silva v. Brazil* 2011; *LC v. Peru* 2011). These Views represent an assertion of the UN's stance that abortion must be decriminalized in the case of a risk to the life or health of a pregnant person, in the case of rape or incest, and in the case of fatal fetal abnormalities. They also offer some indication of an awareness of the need for intersectional approaches to challenging structural inequalities that inform and exacerbate restrictive abortion legislation. However, the inconsistencies and limitations that persist as a result of the liberal legal framework in which they are situated must be acknowledged. These will be discussed in greater detail in relation to the *Mellet* and *Whelan* Views.

While the structural transformation that SRHRs require has yet to be fully realized, the growing coherence and legitimacy of SRHRs at the UN is testament to the effectiveness of persistent transnational feminist activism. It also illustrates the importance and utility of intersectional approaches to the law. Activists and legal practitioners will not be able to properly address and eradicate one expression of discrimination (for example restrictions to abortion access) without also addressing other expressions of discrimination (for example the criminalization of homosexuality). They need to recognize that these expressions of discrimination have common origins in narrow, ideological ideas about sexuality and reproduction which serve to justify and perpetuate an unequal social order. Activists and legal practitioners will similarly be unable to address and eradicate such inequalities unless they recognize and actively challenge the ways in which such discrimination can manifest and differentially impact people because of race, ethnicity, geographical location, age, dis/ability and/or socioeconomic background. Such approaches to IHRL are becoming more apparent within the inter-American system, as will be demonstrated in the next section.

SRHRs in the Inter-American System

The IACHR and IACtHR consistently demonstrated a commitment to SRHRs in recent years. This commitment is evident in the IACHR's work since the 1990s, and in that of the IACtHR since 2012. This would appear to be for four main reasons: the IACHR's dynamic approach to the interpretation of human rights provisions in the American Declaration and Convention; the existence of a specialized body dedicated to women's human rights; their engagement with regional feminist civil society activists; and their openness to citing UN interpretations of human rights.

A survey of the origins and evolution of the inter-American human rights system (IAHRS) reveals that issues relating to what are now known as SRHRs are largely absent until the 1990s. However, women's human rights issues have often been given attention since its inception. This has been in large part through the work of the Inter-American Commission of Women, also known as the Comisión interamericana de las mujeres (CIM). CIM predates the OAS by twenty years, having been founded in 1928; now a specialized organization of the OAS, it has its origins in transnational feminist activism of the early twentieth century.

Partly because of the increased attention to women's human rights issues at the UN conferences and partly as the culmination of decades of work by regional feminist activists and CIM, from 1993 onward, there is a more pronounced focus on women's human rights issues in the work of the IACHR (CIM n.d.; IACHR 1993; IACHR 1994). In 1994, the Special Rapporteur on the Rights of Women was established within the Commission, and the Inter-American Convention on the Prevention, Punishment, and Eradication of Violence against Women (the Belém do Pará Convention) was also adopted. In 1998, the Report of the Inter-American Commission on Human Rights on the Status of Women in the Americas was published (IACHR 1998). This report included a section on the right to health and reproductive health, which it interpreted as being enshrined in the American Declaration, the ACHR, and the Belém do Pará Convention (ibid.). Country reports also increasingly drew attention to SRHR-related issues. For example, the 1999 report on the human rights situation in Colombia framed the criminalization of abortion as "a very serious problem for Colombian women, not only from a health perspective, but also considering their rights as women, which include the rights to personal integrity and to privacy" (IACHR 1999).

During the 2000s, the IACHR's annual and country reports included increasing concrete references to sexual and reproductive rights and to LGBTI rights (e.g., IACHR 2001; IACHR 2008). Moreover, two friendly settlements contributed to jurisprudence on the negative human rights impact of forced sterilization and restricted access to abortion, respectively (*María Mamérita Mestanza Chavez (Peru)* 2000; *Paulina Del Carmen Ramirez Jacinto (Mexico)* 2007).

From 2010 to the present, both the IACHR and the IACtHR increasingly focused on SRHRs, making explicit reference to them in reports, individual petitions, and cases. They emphasized the negative human rights impact of the criminalization of abortion, forced sterilization, and limiting access to

IVF. Also, they increasingly urged states to respect diverse sexual orientations and gender identities.

In the IACHR's thematic reports during this period, there is a growing focus on the rights of LGBTI people, human rights defenders (HRDs), indigenous peoples—particularly indigenous women—and women's human rights as standalone topics and in relation to SRHRs (e.g., IACHR 2014; IACHR 2015; IACHR 2017). Of particular relevance here are the 2010 and 2011 thematic reports on access to maternal health services and access to information on reproductive health from a human rights' perspective (IACHR 2010; IACHR 2011). In 2013, the IACHR mentioned the negative impact of the criminalization of abortion on women's human rights in its annual report for the first time. Also, it issued precautionary measures concerning the complete criminalization of abortion in El Salvador (IACHR 2015, chapter II, paras 42–43). The IACHR's annual reports from 2010 to the present demonstrate a growing awareness of and commitment to an intersectional approach to human rights in general, and in relation to SRHRs in particular (e.g., IACHR 2011, IACHR 2013, IACHR 2018).

In its country reports during this period, the IACHR continued to dedicate specific sections to women's human rights. It also began to focus more on LGBTI rights, and made use of the concept "intersectional" to describe forms of discrimination experienced by women and the ways in which states should address it (e.g., IACHR 2013, chapter 6; IACHR 2015, para 395; IACHR 2012, chapters V, VII). Its 2015 reports on Guatemala and Honduras and 2017 report on Venezuela make explicit references to sexual and reproductive rights and the measures states should take to ensure their full realization (IACHR 2015; IACHR 2015, paras 398–401; IACHR 2017, para 436). Following country visits in 2018 to El Salvador and Honduras, both reports specifically mention the negative human rights impact of the complete criminalization of abortion. These reports stated that abortion should be legal, at a minimum, where there is a risk to the pregnant person's life or health, in the case of rape, and in the case of fatal fetal abnormality (IACHR 2018; IACHR 2018). It can therefore be asserted that this is the IACHR's current position on access to abortion.

Numerous scholars highlighted the increased attention to women's human rights in the IACtHR's jurisprudence since the 2000s and the limits and potential of their current approach (Acosta López 2012; Celorio 2011). In relation to SRHRs, the court has yet to hear a case on the criminalization of abortion, although it did issue provisional measures in relation to the 2013 abortion controversy in El Salvador (IACtHR 2013). The 2012 *Artavia Murillo v. Costa Rica* case has significant implications for any future cases on SRHRs. In this case, the IACtHR found that the state's complete prohibition on IVF violated the applicants' right to personal integrity, personal freedom, privacy, and family life in relation to the equality and nondiscrimination provision of the ACHR. *(Artavia Murillo et al. ['In Vitro Fertilization' v. Costa Rica* 2012). Subsequent cases on the rights of people living with HIV and on forced sterilization also contributed to the court's jurisprudence on SRHRs. These cases relied on UN jurisprudence on SRHRs and employed a relatively intersectional approach in considering the interaction among factors such as HIV status, age, socioeconomic status, and gender *(Gonzalez Lluy et al. v. Ecuador* 2015; *IV v. Bolivia* 2016). In 2017, the court issued an advisory opinion on state obligations in relation to gender identity, equality and nondiscrimination of same-sex couples. In this opinion, the court declared that the right to have one's name, public records, and identity records changed to conform to a person's gender identity is protected under the ACHR, and that states must extend all existing legal mechanisms, including marriage, to same-sex couples (IACtHR 2017). It is in marked contrast to the ECtHR's jurisprudence on marriage equality, which holds that it is within states' margin of appreciation as to whether or not to allow LGBT+ couples to marry and that article 12 of the European Convention should not be interpreted to extend the right to marriage to non-heterosexual couples (e.g., *Schalk and Kopf v. Austria* 2010). In relation SRHRs in general—from access to abortion to marriage equality—the European system has been considerably more conservative than its largely progressive, intersectional inter-American counterpart.

SRHRs in the European System

The Council of Europe's Parliamentary Assembly, Commissioner for Human Rights, Committee of Social Rights (ECSR), and Court of Human Rights (ECtHR) affirmed the importance of SRHRs, albeit in a less coherent and more cautious manner than the IAHRS or UN. A survey of the ECtHR's history suggests less openness to feminist civil society activism and the UN system's interpretation of human rights. The absence of a body such as the UN's CSW or the OAS's CIM may be one contributing factor to this.

Until system reforms in 1998, the court was complemented in its functions by the European Commission of Human Rights. Now defunct, some of its rulings still exert influence on the court's jurisprudence, such as the 1978 commission decision in *Bruggeman and Scheuten v. Germany*, to the detriment of SRHRs. The applicants argued that German abortion legislation of the time—which criminalized abortion except for "in specific situations of distress"—interfered with their article 8 right to privacy (*Brüggemann and Scheuten v. Federal Republic of Germany* 1977, paras 4–5). The commission found that "pregnancy cannot be said to pertain uniquely to the sphere of private life" and that "not every regulation of abortion amounts to interference with the right to respect for private life" (ibid., para 61). This finding is indicative of the problematic nature of traditional understandings of the right to privacy that fail to capture the complexity of non-masculine embodied experiences. These issues were highlighted in one dissenting and one separate opinion, both of which argued that restrictive abortion legislation should be considered a violation of article 8(2) (Dissenting Opinion, para 7). The separate opinion asserted that "the self-determination of women" is the issue on which cases concerning restrictive abortion legislation need to focus, arguing that "the laws regulating abortion ought to leave the decision to have it performed in the early stage of pregnancy to the woman concerned" (Separate Opinion, paras 1–2). The separate opinion also highlighted that traditional understandings of the right to privacy "depended on the outlook which has been formed mainly by men" (ibid., para 3). The ideas expressed in these two opinions have yet to find full articulation in contemporary ECtHR jurisprudence.

During the 1980s and 1990s, the court heard a number of cases concerning women's rights and LGBT+ rights, in many instances finding the applicants' article 8 rights to have been violated due to the disproportionate or unjustified nature of the interference that legislation imposed (*Dudgeon v. The United Kingdom* 1981; *B v. France* 1992; *Open Door and Dublin Well Woman v. Ireland* 1992; *Burghartz v. Switzerland* 1994). Perhaps because of the court's cautious, deferential approach, there is little discussion of systemic discrimination or of how discriminatory legislation has its origins in and serves to perpetuate an unequal social order. This failure to address such concerns is in contrast to the approach of the IACHR and IACtHR.

In the 2000s and 2010s, the court heard more cases concerning SRHR-related issues such as forced sterilization and gender identity, but it did not use the term "SRHR" to describe them (*KH and Others v. Slovakia* 2009; *Christine Goodwin v. The United Kingdom* 2002). In contrast to the IAHRS and UN stance that abortion should be decriminalized at least in some circumstances to prevent violations of women's human rights, the ECtHR still maintains that states have a margin of appreciation in determining legislation on abortion. It is only where abortion is legal and not accessible that violations of the convention may arise (*A, B and C v. Ireland* 2010; *P and S v. Poland* 2012; *RR v. Poland* 2011; *Tysiąc v. Poland* 2007). This position fails to acknowledge the origins and consequences of restrictive abortion legislation vis-à-vis the status of women—an issue that the dissenting and separate opinions in *Bruggeman and Scheuten* recognized over forty years ago. The case pending before the court concerning access to abortion in Northern Ireland might finally redress this oversight and align the European system with its UN and inter-American counterparts (*A and B v. the United Kingdom* [pending] 2019).

The work of the Commissioner for Human Rights, established in 1999, might also contribute to an evolution in the Council of Europe's approach to SRHRs. Since 2007, the commissioners used the term "sexual and reproductive rights" in their reports and issue papers (Commissioner for Human Rights 2008, paras 78–80; Commissioner for Human Rights 2011, section I.7; Commissioner for Human Rights 2011, 4–5). Most notably, the 2017 report on women's sexual and reproductive rights in Europe makes use of an explicitly intersectional framework to conceptualize both SRHRs and the steps states must take to implement them fully (Commissioner for Human Rights 2017). The commissioners also issued statements on the need to decriminalize access to abortion (Commissioner for Human Rights 2019; Commissioner for Human Rights 2018).

Along with the Commissioner for Human Rights, the ECSR, which is responsible for overseeing the implementation of the European Social Charter, took a more assertive stance than the court regarding abortion rights. Two ECSR decisions concerning conscientious objection to abortion in Italy found there to be a violation of article 11(1) on the right to health, and in conjunction with it, a violation of article E on nondiscrimination (*IPPF-EN v. Italy* 2013; *CGIL v. Italy* 2015). In its survey of relevant law, the committee referred to UN human rights treaties and treaty-monitoring bodies' interpretative standards, as well as WHO guidelines on abortion and conscientious objection (ibid.).

Finally, in recent years, the court employed concepts of "vulnerability" and "vulnerable groups" in ways that partially parallel intersectional approaches to inequality. This approach potentially frames and addresses multiple forms of inequality experienced by marginalized groups and is a development worth monitoring in the coming years (Timmer 2013; Peroni and Timmer 2013).

In light of these developments, there is some hope that the European human rights system may yet adopt a more reflexive, progressive approach to SRHRs. The next section considers these issues and ways that all three human rights systems could bring approaches to SRHRs more in line with the intersectional feminist core of this family of rights.

II. CURRENT JURISPRUDENCE AND PROPOSALS FOR AN ALTERNATIVE APPROACH

SRHRs continue to face challenges in the form of concerted opposition from conservative forces. Also, full realization is hampered by the need for a more intersectional feminist approach to legal reasoning. The first cases considered will be the UNHRC *Amanda Mellet v. Ireland* and *Siobhán Whelan v. Ireland,* followed by the IACtHR *Artavia Murillo et al. v. Costa.* The final section will consider the ECtHR's *A, B and C v. Ireland.*

Key ideas underpinning this intersectional feminist approach to IHRL need to be briefly set out. It turns upon reconceptualizing the liberal legal subject so that the rights that flow from having the status of a legitimate legal subject take on new meanings. This requires disrupting the rigid dichotomy between "a liberal quasi-disembodied subject" and "a human, embodied, vulnerable subject" that the development of the law and human rights has created (Timmer 2013, 152). In doing so, the law's historical "others"—such as women, LGBT+ people, and people of color—can have their agency and concerns recognized as legitimate, and so can reshape the law and human rights to represent and respond to their experiences. In the context of advancing SRHRs, particularly access to abortion, this has implications for the ways in which the right to equality, the right to privacy, and the right to be free from torture and CIDT should be interpreted.

Formal equality, in which the same law is applied equally to everyone, has been criticized by feminists as doing little to address power imbalances and as perpetuating the imposition of a male norm against which others must be measured (Fineman 2005a; Hunter 2008). Substantive equality is proposed as a more promising alternative, given that it focuses on the outcomes of the law's application and seeks to address discrimination and oppression (Fineman 2005a, 4). Substantive equality offers a potential starting point for acknowledging the ways in which the law has historically conceptualized women's embodiment as problematic, in need of regulation, and grounds for their exclusion from full legal subjecthood. As the close reading of cases in this section will illustrate, there are some indications that the UN human rights system is moving toward a more substantive approach to equality. At the regional level, the inter-American system regularly invokes the nondiscrimination principle in conjunction with rights violations, and it has interpreted protected statuses in a dynamic and evolving way. In contrast, the ECtHR inconsistently invokes the principle of nondiscrimination, and it remains under-theorized.

In challenging the public-private dichotomy and offering a more nuanced understanding of autonomy by emphasizing its relational nature, this theoretical framework offers a more comprehensive understanding of the right to privacy than it being simply "a right to be left alone" (Neff 1991, 329). It also recognizes that the state often applies the public-private divide in a selective fashion that enables it "to interfere with" pregnancy-related decisions "in furtherance of its own policies" (ibid.). Applying this framework requires a shift from a competing-rights model to a relationship-based approach, in which the relationship between the person and their pregnancy, between them and the other people in their life, and between them and wider power structures are all taken into account. Ideally, this right to privacy would be one that simultaneously respects the deeply personal nature of deciding whether or not to continue with a pregnancy, while also ensuring that necessary state supports are provided to allow for the person's decision to be respected and realized. The extent to which the UN, IACtHR, and ECtHR aligned with such an interpretation will be discussed below.

In regard to freedom from torture, reconciling the quasi-disembodied, invulnerable subject and the human, embodied vulnerable subject leads to an understanding of vulnerability as both universal and particular. It also recognizes that it is a condition which can be exacerbated by existing power structures such as patriarchy (Turner 2008, 13–14, 259; Fineman 2008). The right to be free from torture can then be reinterpreted to better recognize the particular ways in which women's embodiment—especially in relation to reproduction and sexuality—can be a site of abuse, mistreatment, and violence. The UN and inter-American human rights systems have demonstrated some willingness to do so. Under the American Convention on Human Rights, freedom from torture falls under a broader category of the right to humane treatment, which includes not just the standard IHRL prohibition on torture and CIDT in article 5(2) but also articulates a right to physical, mental, and moral integrity in article 5(1). In contrast, article 3 of the European Convention on Human Rights only refers to "torture or to inhuman or degrading treatment or punishment" and has been narrowly interpreted by the ECtHR because of the subjectivity of the *de minimis* rule and its roots in an androcentric understanding of torture. These advances and limitations will now be explored in relation to the UN Human Rights Committee, the IACtHR, and the ECtHR.

The UN

The UN Human Rights Committee (HRC) issued two views that reveal some of the key theoretical issues concerning the interpretation of human rights in relation to abortion. In both *Amanda Mellet v. Ireland* and *Siobhán Whelan v. Ireland*, the HRC found Ireland to be responsible for violations of the right to be free from torture and CIDT, the right to privacy, and the right to equality before the law. Both Views concerned women who had to travel to the UK to obtain an abortion following the diagnosis of fatal fetal abnormalities.

In recognizing these women's experiences as traumatic and violations of the right to be free from torture, the HRC effectively reconceptualized this right to include and respond to women's lived experiences. Both women were subjected to conditions of intense physical and mental suffering amounting to cruel, inhuman, or degrading treatment due to the lack of continuity in care; the distress of having to choose between continuing their nonviable pregnancies to term or traveling abroad at personal expense to receive medical treatment; the shame and stigma arising from the criminalization of abortion; and the suffering caused by having to leave their children's remains in the UK (*Amanda Mellet v. Ireland* 2016, para 7.4; *Siobhán Whelan v. Ireland* 2017, paras 2.5, 7.5). This is an empathic and nuanced understanding of ill treatment as personal, cumulative, and both physical and psychological. The emphasis on the economic, social, and cultural aspects of a civil and political right—the cost of travel and health care, the lack of emotional support, the delays to and disruptions of the grieving process—demonstrates commitment to the indivisibility, interdependence, and interrelatedness of human rights. The acknowledgment of shame and stigma's profound effect in this context is also an important development. It seems to have been informed by the work of CAT Special Rapporteur Juan Méndez, among others (Méndez 2013, 2016; Cook 2014). Also, the HRC effectively articulated connections between the right to be free from torture and the right to privacy. In finding the state's interference in their private lives to be unreasonable and arbitrary, the committee made reference to the "intense suffering" and "mental anguish" that Ireland's restrictive abortion legislation had inflicted on the applicants (*Mellet v. Ireland*, para 7.8; *Whelan v. Ireland*, para 7.9).

However, the committee's Views, concurring opinions, and dissenting opinions also epitomized some of the continued conceptual uncertainty surrounding SRHRs. For example, the committee did not consider the applicants' allegations pertaining to the principle of nondiscrimination. While it did find that the right to equality before the law had been violated, it did so by using both a formal and a substantive understanding of equality without linking the two. First, the committee found this right to have been violated because similarly situated women (i.e., those pregnant with a nonviable fetus) who continued their pregnancy to term were given support by the state, while those who decided to terminate the pregnancy were not (*Mellet v. Ireland*, para 7.10; *Whelan v. Ireland*, para 7.12). It then acknowledged that Ireland's criminalization of abortion was informed by gender-based stereotypes of women's reproductive role, and cited the applicant's medical needs and socioeconomic circumstances as further reasons for a violation of article 26 (*Mellet v. Ireland*, para 7.11).

This muddle of promising elements reflects dissent within the committee. Two concurring opinions stated that the HRC should have considered the claims relating to the ICCPR's nondiscrimination provisions, and it should have taken the opportunity to articulate the ways in which denying women "the right to choose" is a form of gender-based discrimination (*Mellet v. Ireland*, Appendix I, paras 3, 4; Appendix II, paras 3–16). Another committee member issued a partly dissenting opinion stating the opposite: that the HRC should exercise caution and not overextend the concept of discrimination (*Mellet v. Ireland*, Appendix V). Such disagreement reflects the tension between formal and substantive understandings of equality. For Seibert-Fohr, formal equality should inform the committee's reasoning, asserting that "[d]ifference in treatment requires comparable situations in order to give rise to discrimination" (*Mellet v. Ireland*, Appendix V, para 4). In contrast, Ben

Achour and Cleveland favor a substantive approach, whereby any "distinction, exclusion, restriction or preference" that "has the purpose or effect" of inhibiting the full enjoyment of human rights constitutes discrimination (ibid., Appendix II, para 8). This more expansive and reflexive understanding of discrimination is better adapted to recognizing and challenging legislation that is informed by and perpetuates gendered stereotypes of women's social and biological role.

To summarize, the HRC's approach to interpreting the right to be free from torture marks a welcome evolution, and its recognition of its connection with the right to privacy is also commendable. This reasoning is broadly in keeping with a feminist approach to legal reasoning. The ongoing debate about how best to interpret equality suggests a need for a more coherent theoretical approach. Adopting a substantive approach to equality, one which explicitly recognizes the intersection of unequal power relations such as gender, race, and class in the violation of human rights, would be a positive development from an intersectional feminist perspective. There are some indications that the IACtHR is beginning to take such an approach, as the next section will illustrate.

IACtHR

In *Artavia Murillo v. Costa Rica*, the IACtHR found that the state's complete prohibition on IVF violated the eighteen complainants' rights to personal integrity, personal freedom, privacy, and rights of the family in relation to the equality and nondiscrimination provision of the ACHR (*Artavia Murillo et al. ['In Vitro Fertilization'] v. Costa Rica 2012*). This judgment is significant for several reasons: it articulated the inter-American human rights system's commitment to SRHRs as defined and developed by the UN system; it undertook a dynamic approach to treaty interpretation to clarify the meaning of "from the moment of conception" in relation to the right to life; and it made some attempt at an intersectional approach to recognizing human rights violations. The limits of its intersectional approach, and the persistence of ideas about the integrity of motherhood to women's identity require critique, however.

In articulating its understanding of the right to privacy as it pertained to the case, the court emphasized its interrelationship with the right to life, the right to family, the right to physical and mental integrity, the right to health, and the right to enjoy the benefits of scientific progress. The court emphasized the centrality of "the reproductive rights of the individual," as well as of "reproductive autonomy," "access to reproductive health services," and "reproductive freedom" (ibid., paras 144, 146, 147). It also directly quoted the definitions of SRHRs articulated by the 1994 ICPD Programme of Action, 1995 Beijing Declaration and Platform for Action, and the Committee on Economic, Social and Cultural Rights. This holistic approach to the interrelated nature of human rights of relevance to SRHRs, and reliance on the ICPD and Beijing PFAs indicates the IACtHR's commitment to feminist understandings of IHRL. The use of the terms "reproductive autonomy" and "reproductive freedom," which are often used by feminist activists and scholars to indicate that human rights, are a useful discursive framework to realize structural change and social justice (Hernández-Truyol 1999; Sifris 2014; Corrêa, Petchesky, and Parker 2008).

The court's dynamic interpretation of the convention, specifically the right to life as enshrined in article 4(1) ACHR, is one of the major developments this case made to its jurisprudence. Its analysis of this article was in response to the fact that the de facto ban on IVF in Costa Rica arose from the 2000 ruling by the Costa Rican Supreme Court's Constitutional Chamber that article 4(1) ACHR accorded "full recognition of the legal and real personality of the unborn child and its rights" and that the voluntary or involuntary "elimination or destruction of embryos" during IVF treatment violated this (*Artavia Murillo v. Costa Rica*, paras 73–77). To counter this assertion, the IACtHR interpreted "conception" as occurring at the moment of implantation, and any right to life of embryos as "gradual and incremental according to its development" (para 264). Moreover, since the Costa Rican court claimed that the UDHR, ICCPR, Convention on the Rights of the Child, and 1959 Declaration on the Rights of the Child also guaranteed an absolute right to life from the moment of conception, the Inter-American Court analyzed these conventions and declarations to demonstrate that such a conclusion was mistaken and would jeopardize the human rights of pregnant people (paras 191–244). In doing so, it drew attention to General Comments, Concluding Observations and Views issued by the UN Human Rights Committee and the CEDAW committee that a "total ban on abortion, as well as its criminalization under certain circumstances" violates CEDAW and could also violate women's right to life as enshrined in the ICCPR (paras 226–28). It also referred to regional human rights standards, specifically the "non-absolute scope of the protection of prenatal life in the context of cases of abortion and medical treatments related to in vitro fertilization" in the European system, and the provisions on sexual and reproductive rights in the African system's Maputo Protocol (paras 243, 235). It is surprising that the court did not allude to the work of the IACHR on SRHRs in its discussion of the inter-American system, however (paras 220–23).

This oversight, along with an assertion that "motherhood is an essential part of the free development of a woman's personality" (para 143) were nuanced by an attempted intersectional approach to the ways in which the ban on IVF differentially impacted the complainants according to disability, gender, and socioeconomic situation (para 276, 284). It emphasized the importance of the principle of nondiscrimination, and it drew attention to the importance of challenging both direct and indirect discrimination (para 286). How it approached disability, gender, and class was not entirely in keeping with intersectional feminist understandings. First, its presentation of its analysis—discussing each of the three categories under separate subheadings—makes it seem as though these categories are separate and additive, rather than interrelated and interacting in complex ways (paras 288–93, 294–302, 303–4). Second, although its attention to the social model of disability and its understanding of involuntary fertility as a disability are progressive and reasonably nuanced, it failed to reflect on the fact that one of the petitioners was paraplegic and so might have experienced additional particular barriers and prejudices in accessing IVF (paras 85, 288–93). Its discussion of gender featured some promising points. For instance, it recognized the "differentiated disproportionate impacts owing to the existence of stereotypes and prejudices in society" (paras 294, 302). It also asserted that because of the existence of these stereotypes and the resulting internalized, highly gendered expectations and pressures of becoming a parent, the complete ban on IVF had the effect of indirectly discriminating against those who wished to become parents and could not because of involuntary infertility (paras 294, 296, 299, 301).

In sum, *Artavia Murillo* sets an important precedent for SRHR cases in relation to the right to life, and it also suggests that the court is slowly adapting a more intersectional approach to judicial reasoning. Further engagement with the IACHR's work on SRHRs and a more comprehensive understanding of intersectionality will improve further on these promising beginnings. This is in marked contrast to the ECtHR, which has taken a deferential and conservative approach to SRHRs.

ECtHR: A, B, C v. Ireland

The ECtHR adopted a markedly different approach to abortion compared to the UN and the IAHRS. Rather than acknowledge the negative human rights impact of restrictive abortion legislation, it employed the following line of reasoning. First, it ruled that it is neither "desirable or possible" to decide whether the right to life (article 2 ECHR) applies to the fetus, given the absence of European and scientific consensus on when life begins (*Vo v. France* 2004). Second, it acknowledged that any potential right to life of the unborn is "implicitly limited by the mother's rights and interests" (ibid., para 80). In light of these considerations, and the fact that there is a broad European consensus to permit abortion in at least some circumstances, the court has generally found that where abortion is legal, it should be accessible (*Tysiąc v. Poland* 2007, paras 121–30; *A, B and C v. Ireland* 2010, para 235). This means that states are under a positive obligation to implement a clear legal and procedural framework under which women can establish whether they are legally entitled to an abortion and have access to an appeals mechanism should they be refused access to this procedure (*A, B and C v. Ireland*, para 154; *RR v. Poland*, para 200; *Tysiąc v. Poland*, paras 121–30). The lack of gender sensitivity or engagement with SRHRs that this approach represents resulted in a body of jurisprudence that does little to advance women's human rights.

A, B and C v. Ireland concerned three applicants who had to travel to the UK for abortions. All three experienced complications following the procedure once back in Ireland, with A having to be taken to the hospital by ambulance for emergency care and C experiencing "prolonged bleeding and infection" (para 16, 21, 26). A and B alleged that the prohibition of abortion in Ireland violated their right to be free from torture and CIDT (article 3), their right to privacy (article 8), and the right to an effective remedy (article 13) in conjunction with the prohibition of discrimination (article 14) (ibid. para 113). C alleged that her inability to establish her right to a lawful abortion in Ireland on the grounds of a risk to her life violated these rights as well as her right to life (article 2) (ibid.).

Despite considering the ICPD and Beijing PFAs (paras 104–5), and acknowledging concerns about Ireland's restrictive abortion legislation raised by the CoE's Commissioner for Human Rights, the CEDAW Committee and the UN Human Rights Committee (paras 109–11), the court found that there had been no violation of the applicants' rights, with the exception of C's right to privacy. In contrast to the UN HRC, the ECtHR ruled that the psychological, physical and financial burden of having to travel abroad for an abortion "did not disclose a level of severity falling within the scope of Article 3" (para 164). It did not engage with the applicants' allegations that "the criminalization of abortion was discriminatory" and that "the stigma and taboo effect of the criminalization of abortion" amounted to degrading treatment (para 162). This too is in marked contrast to the approach taken by the UN HRC in *Mellet* and *Whelan*.

The court also dismissed A and B's allegations that their right to privacy was violated. This was because Ireland had not exceeded the margin of appreciation afforded to it in enacting restrictive abortion legislation supposedly based on the "profound moral views of the Irish people as to the nature of life" (paras 241–42). Since the applicants had access to information and medical care in Ireland, and were legally permitted to travel abroad for an abortion, the court ruled that the Stated had struck the appropriate balance between their right to privacy and the "legitimate" aim of protecting these profound moral views (ibid.). The court was extensively criticized for this reasoning in both case commentaries and the Joint Partly Dissenting Opinion (Ronchi 2011; Ryan 2014; Westeson 2013). The latter questioned the court's finding that "these profound moral views are still well embedded in the conscience of the majority of Irish people" and stated that considering "profound moral views" as capable of overriding the European consensus marked "a real and dangerous new departure in the Court's case-law" (Joint Partly Dissenting Opinion, para 9). In contrast to the UN HRC Views and the applicants' own allegations, the Court failed to recognize that the criminalization of abortion in Ireland prevented women from making free and informed decisions about their reproductive health, thus violating their rights to privacy and to nondiscrimination.

In relation to C, the court decided that her allegation of a violation of article 2, that is, "her complaint that she was required to travel abroad for an abortion given her fear for her life." was within the scope of Article 8 (para 158). In this respect, at least, the court found that her right to privacy was violated. The reason was because the state failed to implement a legislative or regulatory regime providing an accessible and effective procedure by which she could have established whether she qualified for a lawful abortion in Ireland (paras 267–68). As for violations of the prohibition on discrimination and the right to an effective remedy, the court decided that there was no need to examine complaints separately under article 14, and that no separate issues arose under article 13 (paras 270, 274). The lack of gender-sensitive reasoning, aside from intersectional feminist reasoning, in this case is in contrast to the approach advocated for by feminist activists and that is increasingly adopted by the UN and IAHRS. It is hoped that future cases before the ECtHR will align with the growing IHRL consensus that SRHRs, including straightforward access to safe and legal abortion, are vital to ensure the respect, protection, and fulfillment of women's human rights.

III. CONCLUSION

There is a contested, difficult process underway at the regional and international levels of the human rights system to ensure that women's rights are recognized as human rights. This is especially apparent in relation to SRHRs and access to abortion specifically, as claims for reproductive agency and autonomy threaten the patriarchal social order that requires the subordination of women's reproductive function integral to its continuation. At the international and regional levels of the human rights systems, there is evidence of varying degrees of responsiveness to this approach, as well as the tensions inherent in such structures attempting to adopt a more intersectional feminist approach. The UN remains a prime site for the articulation and advancement of SRHRs, as evidenced by the origins and evolution of the concept, and the jurisprudence and policy of special procedures and treaty monitoring bodies. The IAHRS contributes to the promotion and protection of SRHRs through regional transnational feminist activists' influence on the OAS and the UN, and through the work of the IACHR, CIM, and the IACtHR. There are indications of SRHRs gaining in visibility and legitimacy at the CoE, largely through the work of the ECSR and the Commissioner for Human Rights. However, the ECtHR—arguably the cornerstone of the CoE's human rights system—needs to move away from its deferential approach to human rights protection, and instead embrace the doctrine of the convention as a living instrument. A revised understanding of article 14, and the relationship between the ECtHR and the ESR, would also be beneficial. Across all three systems, more representation of women, more dialogue with civil society and across the systems, and a clearer understanding of the ways in which violations of women's human rights are a symptom of wider structural inequalities, is required to advance SRHRs and achieve gender justice.

BIBLIOGRAPHY

A and B v. the United Kingdom (pending). 2019. Application No. 80046/17 (European Court of Human Rights, February).

A, B and C v. Ireland. 2010. Application No. 25579/05 (European Court of Human Rights, December 16).

Acosta López, Juana I. 2012. "The Cotton Field Case: Gender Perspective and Feminist Theories in the Inter-American Court of Human Rights Jurisprudence." *Revista Colombiana de Derecho Internacional* 10 (21): 17–54.

African Commission on Human and Peoples' Rights. 2014. "General Comment No. 2 on Article 14.1 (a), (b), (c) and (f) and Article 14. 2 (a) and (c)of the Protocol to the African Charter on Human and Peoples' Rights on the Rights of Women in Africa."

African Union. 2005. "Protocol to the African Charter on Human and Peoples' Rights on the Rights of Women in Africa (Maputo Protocol)."

Alyne da Silva Pimentel Teixeira v. Brazil. 2011. CEDAW/C/49/D/17/2008 (UN CEDAW Committee, September 27).

Amanda Mellet v. Ireland. 2016. CCPR/C/116/D/2324/2013 (UN Human Rights Committee, June 9).

Antrobus, Peggy. 2004. *The Global Women's Movement: Origins, Issues and Strategies.* London: Zed Books.

Artavia Murillo et al. ('In Vitro Fertilization') v. Costa Rica. 2012. Series C-257 (Inter-American Court of Human Rights, November 28).

Brüggemann and Scheuten v. Federal Republic of Germany. 1977. Application No. 6959/75 (European Commission of Human Rights, July 12).

Bunch, Charlotte. 1990. "Women's Rights as Human Rights: Toward a Re-Vision of Human Rights." *Human Rights Quarterly* 12 (4): 486–98.

Burghartz v. Switzerland. 1994. Application No. 16213/90 (European Court of Human Rights, February 22).

Buss, Doris. 1998. "Robes, Relics and Rights: The Vatican and the Beijing Conference on Women." *Social and Legal Studies* 7 (3): 340–63.

Butler, Judith. 1990. *Gender Trouble: Feminism and the Subversion of Identity.* London: Routledge.

B v. France. 1992. Application No. 13343/87 (European Court of Human Rights, March 25).

Carbado, Devon W., Kimberlé Williams Crenshaw, Vicki M. Mays, and Barbara Tomlinson. 2013. "Intersectionality: Mapping the Movements of a Theory." *Du Bois Review* 10 (2): 303–12.

Celorio, Rosa M. 2011. "The Rights of Women in the Inter-American System of Human Rights: Current Opportunities and Challenges in Standard-Setting." *University of Miami Law Review* 65 (3): 819–66.

CGIL v. Italy. 2015. Complaint No. 91/2013 (European Committee of Social Rights, October 12).

Charlesworth, Hilary, and Christine Chinkin. 2000. *The Boundaries of International Law: A Feminist Analysis.* Manchester: Manchester University Press.

Charlesworth, Hilary, Christine Chinkin, and Shelley Wright. 1991. "Feminist Approaches to International Law." *American Journal of International Law* 85 (4): 613–45.

Christine Goodwin v. The United Kingdom. 2002. Application No. 28957/95 (European Court of Human Rights, July 11).

CIM. n.d. *A Brief History of the Inter-American Commission of Women.* Accessed May 31, 2019. http://www.oas.org/en/cim/docs/BriefHistory[EN].pdf.

Commissioner for Human Rights. 2011. *Commissioner for Human Rights Positions on Women's Rights.* CommDH/PositionPaper(2011)1, Strasbourg: Council of Europe.

———. 2018. *Malta Urged to Eradicate Violence against Women and Ensure Access to Abortion Care.* January 16. Accessed May 31, 2019. https://www.coe.int/en/web/commissioner/-/malta-urged-to-eradicate-violence-against-women-and-ensure-access-to-abortion-care.

———. 2008. *Report by the Commissioner for Human Rights on His Visit to Ireland, 26–30 November 2007.* CommDH(2008)9, Strasbourg: Council of Europe.

———. 2011. *Report of the Commissioner following his visit to Slovakia, 26–27 November 2011.* CommDH(2011)42, Strasbourg: Council of Europe.

———. 2019. *We Need to Stand Up for Women's Sexual and Reproductive Health and Rights.* March 7. Accessed May 31, 2019. https://www.coe.int/en/web/commissioner/-/we-need-to-stand-up-for-women-s-sexual-and-reproductive-health-and-rights.

———. 2017. *Women's Sexual and Reproductive Health and Rights in Europe.* Issue Paper, Strasbourg: Council of Europe.

Cook, Rebecca J. 2014. "Stigmatized Meanings of Criminal Abortion Law." In *Abortion Law in Transnational Perspective: Cases and Controversies*, by Rebecca J. Cook, Joanna N. Erdman, and Bernard M. Dickens, 347-69. Philadelphia: University of Pennsylvania Press.

Cook, Rebecca J., Bernard M. Dickens, and Mahmoud M. Fathalla. 2011. *Reproductive Health and Human Rights: Integrating Medicine, Ethics and Law.* Oxford: Oxford University Press.

Corrêa, Sonia. 2005. "Holding Ground: The Challenges for Sexual and Reproductive Rights and Health: In Dialogue with Sonia Corrêa." *Development* 48 (4): 11–15.

Corrêa, Sonia, and Rosalind Petchesky. 1994. "Reproductive and Sexual Rights: A Feminist Perspective." In *Population Policies Reconsidered: Health, Empowerment, and Rights*, by Gita Sen, Adrienne Germain, and Lincoln C. Chen. Boston: Harvard University Press.

Corrêa, Sonia, Rosalind Petchesky, and Richard Parker. 2008. *Sexuality, Health and Human Rights.* London: Routledge.

DAWN. n.d. *History.* Accessed May 21, 2019. http://dawnnet.org/about/history/.

———. n.d. *Vision.* Accessed May 21, 2019. http://dawnnet.org/about/vision/.

Dudgeon v. The United Kingdom. 1981. Application No. 7525/76 (European Court of Human Rights, October 22).

Fineman, Martha A. 2005a. "Equality across Legal Cultures: The Role for International Human Rights." *Thomas Jefferson Law Review* 27 (1): 1–13.

———. 2005b. "Feminist Legal Theory." *Journal of Gender, Social Policy and the Law* 13 (1): 13–23.

———. 2008. "The Vulnerable Subject: Anchoring Equality in the Human Condition." *Yale Journal of Law and Feminism* 20 (1): 1–23.

———. 2009. "Introduction: Feminist and Queer Legal Theory." In *Feminist and Queer Legal Theory: Intimate Encounters, Uncomfortable Conversations*, by Martha A Fineman, Jack E. Jackson and Adam P. Romero, 1–8. Farnham, UK: Ashgate.

Flax, Jane. 1992. "Beyond Equality: Gender, Justice and Difference." In *Beyond Equality and Difference: Citizenship, Feminist Politics and Female Subjectivity*, by Gisela Bock and Susan James, 182–99. London: Routledge.

Fraser, Arvonne S. 1999. "Becoming Human: The Origins and Development of Women's Human Rights." *Human Rights Quarterly* 21 (4): 853–906.

Garita, Alexandra. 2015. "Moving toward Sexual and Reproductive Justice: a Transnational and Multigenerational Feminist Remix." In *The Oxford Handbook of Transnational Feminist Movements*, by Rawwida Baksh and Wendy Harcourt, 271–94. Oxford: Oxford Unviersity Press.

Gender Identity, and Equality and Non-Discrimination of Same-Sex Couples. 2017. OC-24/17 (Inter-American Court of Human Rights, November 24).

Girard, Françoise. 2014. "Negotiating Sexual Rights and Sexual Orientation at the UN." In *Sex Politics: Reports from the Front Lines*, by Richard Parker, Rosalind Petchesky and Robert Sember. Sexuality Policy Watch.

Gonzalez Lluy et al. v. Ecuador. 2015. Series C No. 102/13 (Inter-American Court of Human Rights, September 1).

Hartman, Betsy. 1995. *Reproductive Rights and Wrongs: The Global Politics of Population Control* (revised edition). Boston: South End Press.

Hernández-Truyol, Berta Esperanza. 1999. "Human Rights through A Gendered Lens Emergence, Evolution, Revolution." In *Women and International Human Rights Law Volume 1*, by Kelly D. Askin and Dorean M. Koenig, 3–39. New York: Transnational Publishers.

Hunter, Rosemary. 2008. *Rethinking Equality Projects in Law.* Oxford: Hart.

IACHR. 1993. "1992–1993 Annual Report OEA/Ser./L/V/II.83 doc. 14 corr. 1." March 12.

———. 1994. "1993 Annual Report OEA/Ser.L/V.85 Doc. 9 rev. 11." February.

———. 2009. "2008 Annual Report OEA/Ser.L/V/II.134 Doc. 5, rev. 1." February 25.

———. 2011. *2010 Annual Report.* OEA/Ser.L/V/II. Doc. 5, rev. 1 , Washington, DC: OAS.

———. 2013. *2013 Annual Report.* OEA/Ser.L/V/II. Doc. 50 Corr.1 , Washington, DC: OAS.

———. 2018. "2018 Annual Report." Accessed May 31, 2019. http://www.oas.org/en/iachr/docs/annual/2018/TOC.asp.

———. 2011. *Access to Information on Reproductive Health from a Human Rights Perspective.* Washington, DC: IACHR.

———. 2011. *Access to Information on Reproductive Health from a Human Rights Perspective.* OEA/Ser.L/V/II. Doc. 61, Washington, DC: OAS.

———. 2010. *Access to Maternal Health Services from a Human Rights Perspective.* Washington, DC: IACHR.

———. 2010. *Access to Maternal Health Services from a Human Rights Perspective.* OEA/Ser.L/V/II. Doc. 69, Washington, DC: OAS.

———. 2018. *Conclusions and Observations on the IACHR's Working Visit to El Salvador—Voluntary Interruption of Pregnancy under Certain Circumstances.* No. 011A/18, Washington, DC: IACHR.

———. 2015. *Legal Standards Related to Gender Equality and Women's Rights in the Inter-American Human Rights System: Development and Application Updates from 2011 to 2014.* Washington, DC: IACHR.

———. 2015. *Legal Standards related to Gender Equality and Women's Rights in the Inter-American Human Rights System: Development and Application Updates from 2011 to 2014.* OEA/Ser.L/V/II.143 Doc.60, Washington, DC: OAS.

———. 2014. *Missing and Murdered Indigenous Women in British Columbia, Canada.* OEA/Ser.L/V/II. Doc. 30/14, Washington, DC: OAS.

———. 2018. *Preliminary Observations on the Visit of the IACHR to Honduras.* No. 171A/18, Washington, DC: OAS.

———. 1998. "Report of the Inter-American Commission on Human Rights on the Status of Women in the Americas, OEA/Ser.L/V/II.100, Doc. 17." October 13.

———. 1999. "Report on the Human Rights Situation in Colombia. OEA/Ser.L/V/II.102 Doc. 9 rev. 1." February 26.

———. 2001. "Report on the Situation of Human Rights in Guatemala. OEA/Ser.L/V/II.111 doc. 21 rev." April 6.

———. 2012. *Report on the Situation of Human Rights in Jamaica.* OEA/Ser.L/V/II.144 Doc. 12, Washington, DC: OAS.

———. 2015. *Report on the Situation of Human Rights in the Dominican Republic.* OEA/Ser.L/V/II. Doc. 45/15, Washington, DC: OAS.

———. 2015. *Situation of Human Rights in Guatemala: Diversity, Inequality and Exclusion.* OEA/Ser.L/V/II. Doc. 43/15, Washington, DC: OAS.
———. 2015. *Situation of Human Rights in Honduras.* OEA/Ser.L/V/II. Doc. 42/15, Washington, DC: OAS.
———. December 31, 2015. "Situation of Human Rights in Honduras. OEA/Ser.L/V/II. Doc. 42/15." Washington, DC: IACHR.
———. 2017. *Situation of Human Rights in Venezuela.* OEA/Ser.L/V/II. Doc. 209, Washington, DC: OAS.
———. December 31, 2017. "Situation of Human Rights in Venezuela OEA/Ser.L/V/II. Doc. 209." Washington, DC: IACHR.
———. 2017. *Towards Effective Integral Protection Policies for Human Rights Defenders.* OEA/Ser.L/V/II. Doc. 207, Washington, DC: OAS.
———. 2013. *Truth, Justice and Reparation: Fourth Report on Human Rights Situation in Colombia.* OEA/Ser.L/V/II. Doc. 49/13, Washington, DC: OAS.
———. 2015. *Violence against Lesbian, Gay, Bisexual, Trans and Intersex Persons in the Americas.* OAS/Ser.L/V/II.rev.1 Doc. 36, Washington, DC: OAS.
IACtHR. 2013. "Provisional Measures with Regard to El Salvador, Matter of B." May 29.
Inter-American Court of Human Rights. 2015. *2015 Annual Report.* San José: IACtHR.
International Commission of Jurists. 2006. "The Yogyakarta Principles: Principles on the Application of International Human Rights Law in relation to Sexual Orientation and Gender Identity."
IPPF. 2008. "Sexual Rights: An IPPF Declaration." *Sexual Rights: An IPPF Declaration.* London: IPPF.
IPPF-EN v. Italy. 2013. Complaint No. 87/2012 (European Committee of Social Rights, September 10).
IV v. Bolivia. 2016. (Inter-American Court of Human Rights, November 30).
Jaquette, Jane, and Kathleen A. Staudt. 1998. "Politics, Population, and Gender: A Feminist Analysis of US Population Policy in the Third World." In *The Political Interests of Gender: Developing Theory and Research with a Feminist Face*, by Kathleen B. Jones and Anna G. Jónasdóttir, 214–33. London: Sage.
KH and Others v. Slovakia. 2009. Application No. 32881/04 (European Court of Human RIghts, April 28).
KL v. Peru. 2005. CCPR/C/85/D/1153/2003 (UN Human Rights Committee, November 22).
LC v. Peru. 2011. CEDAW/C/50/D/22/2009 (UN CEDAW Committee, November 4).
LMR v. Argentina. 2011. CCPR/C/101/D/1608/2007 (UN Human Rights Committee, April 28).
María Mamérita Mestanza Chavez v. Peru. 2000. Case 12.191, Report No. 66/00, OEA/Ser.L/V/II.111 Doc. 20 rev. at 350 (2000) (IACHR, October 3).
Méndez, Juan E. 2013. "Report of the Special Rapporteur on Torture and other Cruel, Inhuman or Degrading Treatment or Punishment." A/HRC/22/53.
———. January 5, 2016. "Report of the Special Rapporteur on Torture and Other Cruel, Inhuman or Degrading Treatment or Punishment."
———. 2016. "Report of the Special Rapporteur on Torture and Other Cruel, Inhuman or Degrading Treatment or Punishment." A/HRC/31/57.
Neff, Christyne L. 1991. "Woman, Womb, and Bodily Integrity." *Yale Journal of Law and Feminism* 3 (2): 327–53.
Ngwena, Charles G. 2014. "Conscientious Objection to Abortion and Accommodating Women's Reproductive Health Rights: Reflections on a Decision of the Constitutional Court of Colombia from an African Regional Human Rights Perspective." *Journal of African Law* 58 (2): 183–209.
———. 2010. "Inscribing Abortion as a Human Right: Significance of the Protocol on the Rights ofWomen in Africa." *Human Rights Quarterly* 32 (4): 783–864.
———. 2016. "Taking Women's Rights Seriously: Using Human Rights to Require State Implementation of Domestic Abortion Laws in African Countries with Reference to Uganda." *Journal of African Law* 60 (1): 110–40.
Open Door and Dublin Well Woman v. Ireland. 1992. Application Nos. 14234/88, 14235/88 (European Court of Human Rights, October 29).

Organization of American States. 1978. "American Convention on Human Rights 'Pact of San José, Costa Rica' (adopted November 22, 1969, entered into force July 18, 1978) OAS Treaty Series No. 36."

———. 1993. "Charter of the Organization of American States (signed in Bogotá in 1948 and amended by the Protocol of Buenos Aires in 1967, by the Protocol of Cartagena de Indias in 1985, by the Protocol of Washington in 1992, and by the Prot OAS Treaty Series Nos. 1-C."

———. 1979. "Statute of the Inter-American Commission on Human Rights (approved by OAS General Assembly Resolution No. 447, October 1979)."

———. 1979. "Statute of the Inter-American Court of Human Rights (Resolution No. 448 adopted by the OAS General Assembly, October 1979."

Otto, Dianne. 2009. "The Exile of Inclusion: Reflections on Gender Issues in International Law over the Last Decade." *Melbourne Journal of International Law* 10 (1): 11–26.

P and S v. Poland. 2012. Application No. 57375/08 (European Court of Human Rights, October 20).

Parliamentary Assembly of the Council of Europe. 2008. "Resolution 1607: Access to safe and legal abortion in Europe." April 16.

Paulina del Carmen Ramírez Jacinto v. Mexico. 2007. Report No. 21/07. Petition 161–02 (IACHR, March 9).

Peroni, Lourdes, and Alexandra Timmer. 2013. "Vulnerable Groups: The Promise of an Emerging Concept in European Human Rights Convention Law." *International Journal of Constitutional Law* 11 (4): 1056–85.

Petchesky, Rosalind Pollack. 1995. "From Population Control to Reproductive Rights: Feminist Fault Lines." *Reproductive Health Matters* (6): 152–61.

———. 2003. *Global Prescriptions: Gendering Health and Human Rights.* London: Zed Books.

———. 2000. *Reproductive and Sexual Rights: Charting the Course of Transnational Women's NGOs.* Occasional Paper No. 8, Geneva: UNRISD.

Ronchi, Paolo. 2011. "A, B and C v. Ireland: Europe's Roe v. Wade Still Has to Wait." *Law Quarterly Review* 127: 365–69.

RR v. Poland. 2011. Application No. 27617/04 (European Court of Human Rights, November 28).

Ryan, Christine. 2014. "A, B and C v. Ireland: A Disproportionate Response to the Violation of Women's Reproductive Freedom." *UCL Journal of Law and Jurisprudence* 3 (1): 237–61.

Schalk and Kopf v. Austria. 2010. Application No. 30141/04 (European Court of Human Rights, June 24).

Second International Panel of Experts in International Human Rights Law, Sexual Orientation, Gender Identity, Gender Expression and Sex Characteristcs. 2017. "The Yogyakarta Principles plus 10: Additional Principles and State Obligations on the Application of International Human Rights Law to Sexual Orientation, Gender Identity, Gender Expression and Sex Characteristics to Complement the Yogyakarta Principles." Geneva.

Sen, Gita. 2005. *Neolibs, Neocons and Gender Justice: Lessons from Global Negotiations.* Occasional Paper No. 9, Geneva: UNRISD.

Sifris, Ronli. 2014. *Reproductive Freedom, Torture and International Human Rights: Challenging the Masculinisation of Torture.* Abingdon, UK: Routledge.

Siobhán Whelan v. Ireland. 2017. CCPR/C/119/D/2425/2014 (UN Human Rights Committee, June 12).

Smart, Carol. 1992. "Disruptive Bodies and Unruly Sex: The Regulation of Reproduction and Sexuality in the Nineteenth Century." In *Regulating Womanhood: Historical Essays on Marriage, Motherhood and Sexuality*, by Carol Smart, 7–32. London: Routledge.

Timmer, Alexandra. 2013. "A Quiet Revolution: Vulnerability in the European Court of Human Rights." In *Vulnerability: Reflections on a New Ethical Foundation for Law and Politics*, by Martha A. Fineman and Anna Grear, 147–70. Farnham, UK: Ashgate.

Turner, Bryan S. 2008. *The Body and Society: Explorations in Social Theory* (3rd edition). London: Sage.

Tysiąc v. Poland. 2007. Application No. 5410/03 (European Court of Human Rights, March 20).

UN Committee against Torture. June 17, 2011. "Concluding Observations on the initial report of Ireland. CAT/C/IRL/CO/1."
———. December 9, 2009. "Concluding Observations on the Second Periodic Report of El Salvador. CAT/C/SLV/2."
UN Committee on Economic, Social and Cultural Rights. March 4, 2016. "General Comment No. 22 (2016) on the Right to Sexual and Reproductive Health (article 12 of the International Covenant on Economic, Social and Cultural Rights), E/C.12/GC/22."
UN Committee on the Elimination of Discrimination against Women. November 4, 2011. "*LC v. Peru.* CEDAW/C/50/D/22/2009."
UN General Assembly (UNGA). May 12, 1968. "Final Act of the International Conference on Human Rights, Tehran, April 22–May 13, 1968. A/CONF.32/41.UNGA Res 2442 (XXIII)."
UN General Assembly. September 13, 1994. "Programme of Action Adopted at the International Conference on Population and Development, A/CONF.171/13." Cairo.
UN Human Rights Committee. June 9, 2016. "*Amanda Mellet v. Ireland.* CCPR/C/116/D/2324/2013."
———. November 22, 2005. "KL v. Peru. CCPR/C/85/D/1153/2003."
———. April 28, 2011. "LMR v. Argentina. CCPR/C/101/D/1608/2007."
———. June 12, 2017. "Siobhán Whelan v. Ireland. CCPR/C/119/D/2425/2014."
UN Human Rights Council. 2011. "Resolution 17/19 Human Rights, Sexual Orientation and Gender Identity. A/HRC/RES/17/19." July 14.
———. 2014. "Resolution 27/32 Human Rights, Sexual Orientation and Gender Identity. A/HRC/RES/27/32." September 26.
———. 2016. "Resolution 32/2 Protection against violence and discrimination based on sexual orientation and gender identity. A/HRC/RES/32/2." July 12.
UNFPA. The Danish Institute for Human Rights, United Nations Office of the High Commissioner for Human Rights. 2014. *Reproductive Rights are Human Rights: A Handbook for National Human Rights Institutions.* New York: United Nations.
UNGA. 1995. "Fourth World Conference on Women: Beijing Declaration and Platform for Action. A/CONF.177/20." September 15.
———. 1994. "Programme of Action Adopted at the International Conference on Population and Development, Cairo, September 5–13, 1994. A/CONF.171/13."
———. 1975. "The Declaration of Mexico on the Equality of Women and Their Contribution to Development and Peace E/CONF.66/34."
———. July 12, 1993. "Vienna Declaration and Programme of Action. A/CONF.157/23."
Vo v. France. 2004. Application No. 53924/00 (European Court of Human Rights, July 8).
WAS (World Assocation for Sexual Health). 2014. "Declaration of Sexual Rights." *Declaration of Sexual Rights.*
Westeson, Joana. 2013. "Reproductive Health Information and Abortion Services: Standards Developed by the European Court of Human Rights." *I nternational Journal of Gynecology and Obstetrics* 122 (2): 173–76.
WHO. 2012. *Safe Abortion: Technical and Policy Guidance for Health Systems, Second Edition.* Geneva: WHO.

Chapter Seven

"Like Cats and Dogs in the Streets"

Disability and Sexuality in the Eugenic Legal Imagination

Lisa Beckmann

If God had intended them to have sex, he wouldn't make them disabled.

1. WHY DO DISABILITY, SEXUALITY, AND GENDER INJUSTICE MATTER?

For disabled women, societal, cultural, and legal responses to disability and sexuality are inextricably linked to gendered stereotypes regarding impairment, femininity, and gender. In contemporary, online disability-rights advocacy, activists emphasize the need for disability to be understood in conjunction with sexuality and gender to facilitate the empowerment that results by having ownership over your own body (Wineland 2018, n.p.; Webster 2017, n.p.). At the same time, gender-sensitive scholarship in disability studies questions medicalized definitions of impairment and pushes for disability to be regarded as a category of difference at the intersection with issues, such as sexual rights and health, feminism, and gender studies (see, for instance, Addlakha, Price, and Heidari 2017; Ahlvik-Harju 2017; Garland-Thomson 2002; Shakespeare, Gillespie-Sells and Davies 1996). Despite these developments, the history of gender injustice and disability reveals the key role sexuality serves in the systematic oppression of disabled individuals, particularly women. Across time, disabled individuals have been confronted with various forms of gender injustice—that is, the rejection, ridicule, pathologization, and othering of a disabled person's sexuality, reproductive rights, and sexual agency. Often, such forms are based on the prejudiced misconception that they are "unfit" to be sexually active and in control of their own bodies (Wilkerson 2011, 193–217). In this discourse, disability and sexuality embody what Western society stigmatizes as socially "inappropriate" and non-normative. Disability is understood as an inherent physical and mental defect. Sexuality is perceived as something so inherently shameful and unnatural to the extent that it exacerbates the perceived otherness of disability. Or, as a stereotypical response posits: "I think that's *disgusting* [. . .] if God had intended them to have sex, he wouldn't make them disabled" (Perlin and Lynch 2016, 1, emphasis original).

Techniques of othering are central to the image of disability and sexuality as that which is foreign to society. This image, in turn, plays a key role in the gender injustice experienced by disabled individuals, and it also reinforces the function of law as a tool of oppression. In this context, the pervasive animalization, criminalization, and fetishization of disability and sexuality as "dangerous" is particularly important as it perpetuates the prejudice that by being sexually active, disabled people are a danger to society (and to themselves). For example, in 2011, Alan,[1] a forty-one-year old cognitively disabled man from the UK, was taken to court because he was detected by staff, who supported him at the local housing council where he lived, as participating in a same-sex relationship. Subsequently, the judge ruled that the relationship ought to be restricted because having sexual relations with persons of both genders, which the judge took as evidence for Alan's "vigorous sex drive," is "inappropriate" for someone who is disabled, particularly if the disability in question is of cognitive or developmental nature (Gill 2015, 1). What is striking in this verdict is that Alan's disability is used as justification for his sexual relations to be labeled as seemingly "unnatural." In other words, the fact that he is in a queer relationship transgresses heteronormative gender expectations as a matter of sexuality and sexual activity. The verdict painfully exposes the private details of Alan's sex life (Gill 2015, 1). The legal rhetoric portrays queer, sexually active disabled individuals as the fundamental other. Thus, Alan is stigmatized twice—once for being disabled and second for being queer.

Further, I hypothesize that if Alan was sexually inactive and single, he would not have been taken to court. Instead, he would have been perceived as a man whose disability is normalized through the infantilized image of disability-asexuality as "innocence," as the late disability activist Claire Wineland remarks. "It's much easier to believe that sick people are cherubs—held in perpetual youth and innocence—who simply don't understand their condition because they are living up in the clouds" (2018, n.p.). By sending disabled people to court for being in a relationship, by attaching sandpaper to their thighs to prevent masturbation (Wilkerson 2011, 93–94), or by removing sexual organs to prevent abuse and rape in institutions (Waldtschmidt 2010, 38–40), disabled bodies are violated based on the image of "inappropriate sexuality," an image that is fundamentally dehumanizing. Gender injustice does more than differentiate between normative and non-normative bodies based on whether or not their sexuality is deemed "appropriate." It does more than strip disabled people of their legal rights to control over their own bodies. Under the disguise of "protection" from "inappropriate behavior," disabled people are stripped of their humanity, and their bodies are silenced into shame.

Yet, what remains absent from this discussion is the historical dimension of gender injustice, particularly the injustice and violence suffered by disabled women whose sexuality is othered as animalistic and abnormal. Of course, pathologizing and gendering disability and sexuality has a history: it is connected to historically and culturally specific, legal, institutional, and societal attitudes toward disabled people. An example is the eugenics movement in the United States. At the turn of the twentieth century in the United States, as eugenic ideology increased in power, societal attitudes toward disabled women became increasingly punitive. Such individuals were regarded as a "burden" to the state, "dependent" with no hope of living a self-sufficient life. These fears of economic dependency quickly merged into societal fears of the "immoral nature" of disabled women, whose "vigorous" sexuality would lead to uncontrolled reproduction of "defective offspring." In response, this chapter traces this development by analyzing selected forced sterilization laws with a focus on their genesis in the eugenic legal system and the images of disability and sexuality that these laws conjure. I argue that the gendering of disabled women through the law contributes to the notion of gender injustice in two ways. First, the construction of a sexualized and disabled identity reflects eugenic fears and the punishment of non-normative bodies through intersectional identity crossing. Second, it reveals a legal system that is deeply gendered itself. It reflects a system whereby disabled women are discriminated against on multiple levels while the dominant legal actors—primarily White male lawyers and judges—remain in a position of power. This chapter first discusses the development of the eugenics movement in the United States. This discussion is followed by a consideration of disability and sexuality in the U.S. eugenic cultural imagination to unpack sexist and ableist stereotypes. Finally, I explore selected laws in the section on disability in the U.S. eugenic legal imagination as a system that is deeply gendered (dominant legal actors are White and male). This chapter concludes with an overview of "the" cognitively disabled woman as a sexualized identity in the eugenic legal system.

II: THE EUGENICS MOVEMENT IN THE UNITED STATES

Following Lennard J. Davis, disability "is not a minor issue that relates to a relatively small number of people; it is part of a historically constructed discourse, an ideology of thinking about the body under certain circumstances" (1995, 2). In other words, disability is neither a "minor issue" nor a medical problem that only affects an individual. It relates to how society constructs and views impairment. Disability is "everywhere in history" (Baynton 2013, 30): it is an interpretation, a reading, and a renarrating of impairment that is historically, culturally, and legally specific.

A time in U.S. history when the historical specificity of disability became jarringly evident was during the eugenics movement in the United States. Between circa 1880 and 1940, a set of medical, legal, societal, and cultural responses to impairment occurred. These occurrences deeply influenced the ways that the disabled body was thought of, imagined, and represented as the pathologized, sexualized, and animalized other. At this time, mass industrialization and urbanization brought recurring periods of economic instability and depression. Physical disabilities were on the rise due to work-related accidents. The image of the disabled body, and the "overwhelming influx of disabled people in public," became associated with societal fears, such as chronic dependency, poverty, and homelessness (Lindstrom 2004, 406; Schweik 2009, 59–60).

On the other hand, medicine became increasingly professionalized and economized in an attempt to classify and segregate these individuals. Such persons found themselves in institutions housed with criminals, "delinquents," and "paupers," chronically poor, and "dependent" individuals. This connection aligned disability, criminality, and poverty (Lombardo 1996, 5). Consequently, eugenicists sought to calculate perceptions of social and financial "costs" that disabled individuals placed on U.S. society and the state. In the polemic and cruel words of William Lennox, a leading U.S. neurologist at that time: "Most of these patients [. . .] are physically and mentally incapable of self-support and will be a burden as long as they live," and "the bill for mental and physical disability is huge" (1927, 458, 463). Thus, as the influence of the eugenics movement unfolded, the social stigma attached to disability morphed into medical pathology, which eventually became the image of disabled people as dehumanized other.

A figure central to this development was Francis Galton (cousin of Charles Darwin), the British "father of eugenics," a "pioneer and a progenitor" of the eugenics movement as he was popularized in contemporary discourse at the end of the nineteenth century (Brauer 2009, 124-25). Galton coined the term "eugenics" in *Inquiries into Human Faculty and Its Development* (1951 [1883]) as follows:

> The brief word to express the science of improving the stock, which is by no means confined to questions of judicious mating, but which, especially in the case of man [*sic*], takes cognizance of all the influences that tend in however remote a degree to give the more suitable races or strains of blood a better chance of prevailing speedily over the less suitable than they otherwise would have had. (17)

Galton's selected quotation intends to show that the growing influence of the eugenics movement on public images of disability is connected to a specific, ableist, nationalist, and racist rhetoric. The intrinsic hubris—the smug self-assurance with which eugenicists, such as Charles Davenport, called themselves "normal member[s] of a society" (1912, 280)—reveals that eugenic ideology was formed through the use and systematic abuse of ideas and theories about the human body, impairment, reproduction, and modes of belonging and exclusion in U.S. society. Galton's rhetoric and imagery reveal this pattern of thinking. On a rhetorical level, phrases such as "the science of improving the stock," "the questions of judicious mating," and "the more suitable races or strains of blood" are inherently suggestive. Instead of dehumanizing those who are regarded as "less suitable" from the start, Galton begins with a dichotomy. He constructs an image of those he considers "more suitable or strains of blood" to create a stark contrast distinguishing those he perceives as "normal" and belonging. Thus, he fosters the notion that the function of society was to improve itself constantly (Baynton 2013, 19), a mechanism known as "positive eugenics" (Rembis 2002, 88). The image of those considered to be "more suitable" was not only deeply ableist, but also racist and classist. The eugenic idea of "fitness of the race" became virtually synonymous with being White, able-bodied, and college educated. A high fertility rate for those deemed "fit" was perceived as desirable for the entire nation (ibid.; Smith 1999, 45). Yet beneath this normative image was the unspoken assumption that if the constant strive for "improvement" was to stop, society would inevitably retreat to its "animal origins" (Baynton 2013, 19). For this assumption, Saul Dubow coins the eugenicist phrase "air of catastrophism" about progress and degeneration of U.S. society (1995, 121).

Galton's rhetoric reinforced this "air of catastrophism." The visceral terminology *race*, *blood*, *stock*, and *mating* is reminiscent of animal breeding. Therefore, it suggests a sense of objectivity through its presumable "scientific" register. Galton's eugenic view on reproduction constructs those perceived as "less suitable" as a problem to which eugenics needs to respond: a technique that whitewashes, quite literally, the movement's pervasive nationalism and racism. Here, it is important to note that Galton's language mirrors the rhetoric of other published eugenicists at that time. Publications, such as Harry Laughlin's "Report of the Committee to Study and to Report on the

Best Practical Means of Cutting Off the Defective Germ-Plasm in the American Population" (1914), suggest that there is something inherently pathological about specific parts of the U.S. population, precisely those considered "the less suitable races" (in Galton's words). By anthropomorphizing U.S. society and turning it into an organism from which the "defective Germ plasm" needs to be cut to keep the nation "healthy," disability becomes a metaphor for national sickness. As a rhetorical means of othering, this metaphor further ostracizes and pathologizes disabled individuals by suggesting that there is something inherently and physically defective about them and their bodies. It presents people as formally defective and with potential to become societally dangerous if uncontrolled (O'Brien 2013, 29).

However, there is more to the organism metaphor as it reveals an intersection of two theories that are key to the evolution of eugenic thinking: the link between Social Darwinism and hereditarianism. Based on the rediscovery of Mendel's laws and belief in the inheritance of acquired characteristics (Adams 1990, 120), both Social Darwinism and hereditarianism entered eugenic ideology. It is most prominently argued by the aforementioned eugenicists Davenport, Laughlin, and Galton.[2] In general, eugenicists supported the idea that "heredity determined everyone's potential and that science could identify those persons whose hereditary endowment made them likely to be diseased or unsuccessful in life" (McCann 2004, 299). With the publication of Charles Darwin's *On the Origin of Species* in 1860, another train of thought enters the eugenic argument as to why disabled individuals are inherently "defective." Darwin posits that in the ongoing competition between different species to succeed in different environments, naturally, the "fittest" species will thrive and spread their genotypes across different generations. Later, eugenicists used Darwinist thought to, again, create an argument as to why certain (non-disabled) human "species" are superior and "fitter" in society. By comparison, others, the "unfit," ought to die to make the success of the "fittest" species possible (Braddock and Parish 2001, 38). Akin to the distinction that Galton creates for the more "suitable" races, disabled people, as well as non-White races, were seen as atavistic "evolutionary laggards" (Baynton 2013, 19): an animal-like "throwback to a more primitive evolutionary stage" (Rafter 1994, 101). This image will become important when this chapter discusses the presumed animal-like hypersexuality of disabled women. As a consequence, the ableist and racist perspective on disability as defective is justified through the image of disability as a "species" unable to evolve. As a consequence, Social Darwinism situates the "defectiveness of disability" within disabled people themselves as individuals perceived to be biologically predetermined "defective" and thus "unfixable."

To reinforce the association between disability and "unfitness," eugenicists employed hereditarian ideology. In eugenic ideology, a "germ plasm" is understood as a "determiner" that shaped ("determined") physical characteristics, such as the shape of one's nose. From this perspective, these characteristics are passed genetically "through determiners in the germ cells" (Davenport 1912, 269). Significantly, it was not physical characteristics alone that were believed to be passed on. According to eugenicists such as Davenport, "immoral tendencies" including "socially deviant behavior," poverty, alcoholism, and criminality are inherited across generations (Davenport 1912, 269, 277–86). As a consequence, disability was understood as an incurable defect and metaphor for disease in U.S. society. Central to eugenic ideology is the assumption that disability is the root cause of social problems and that once disabled individuals are controlled through segregation and forced sterilization, social problems would be alleviated (O'Brien 2013, 8). Thus, the hereditarian response to disability is framed by a specific fear of the "degeneration" of society, which disabled individuals were thought to embody. This response reveals the fundamental tendency to pathologize and ostracize disabled individuals in U.S. society at the turn of the twentieth century.

While eugenicists supported medicalized and dehumanized views of disability, a significant portion of physical and mental impairments were caused by the environment. Lack of medical care, poor hygiene, heavy workloads in factories, and high incidence of working conditions made it more likely to become disabled (Davis 1995, 87). Further, poor medical treatment with no possibility of rehabilitation in society (as with refractory epilepsy, for instance) exacerbated suffering and social isolation (Dwyer 1997, 249–51). Thus, pathologizing and segregating disabled individuals was what the eugenic movement aimed for. Dehumanization through specific, persistent stereotypes, such as epileptic individuals as "objects of dread," remains central to supporting and popularizing eugenic ideas of disability as foreign to society. The next section explores how these stereotypes function in the move from the dehumanization to the animalization and sexualization of disabled women.

III: DISABILITY AND SEXUALITY IN THE EUGENIC CULTURAL IMAGINATION

At this moment, pathologizing disability and sexuality occurs. The connection between disability and "hereditary defect" was constructed through eugenic medical discourse. Yet images of disabled women as imminent, hypersexual threats to U.S. society shaped how disability and sexuality were perceived at the beginning of the twentieth century. To unpack this image, this section focuses on a shift of stereotypes central to the eugenic cultural imagination: the disabled woman as a perpetual "child" that is biologically predisposed to become a hypersexual animal. Here, I focus on the cultural means via narratives and stereotypes that construct this image. Moreover, I consider the identity of disabled women as child-like and hyposexual, on the one hand, and animal-like and hypersexual, on the other.

First, it is important to note that whereas hereditarian, atavistic, and Social Darwinist attitudes toward disabled individuals were applied to a broad range of disabilities (Baynton 2016, 46), the image of a disabled person as hypersexual was specific to cognitive disability. This type of impairment became synonymous with societal fears about "sex crimes," female immoral behavior, and indecency (Jarman 2012, 98–99). This perspective leads to the superstition that cognitively impaired individuals are hypersexual. Moreover, it presents criminals as cognitively disabled. In other words, the eugenic conflation of disability with defect, delinquency, and degeneration surfaces.

However, similarly to Galton's and Laughlin's rhetoric, medical professionals in the eugenics movement worked with a specific, paternalistic and dehumanizing rhetoric to construct cognitive disability as a stereotype. For Walter Fernald, cognitively disabled people are particularly dangerous because they have "the mind of a child and the body and passion of an adult [. . .] a foreign body in any community" (1907, 486). In Fernald's view, cognitively disabled individuals are dangerous in two ways. According to Fernald, similar to a child, they have no control over their actions and cannot be held accountable while also bearing intrinsic, fully developed sex drives. Returning to eugenic fears about the hereditary nature of disability as defect, the notion is that such individuals will spread their defective "germ plasms" uncontrollably. In this context, reports written by superintendents of institutions for individuals with cognitive impairments constitute a cultural narrative key to this part of eugenic ideology. Such narratives document the infantilization and sexualization of disability. In these reports, several rhetoric means are combined to create a multimodal narrative of eugenic ideology. First, the frequent use of photographs and drawings document and pathologize certain "cases" with "evidence." Second, hand-drawn tree diagrams indicate family history and intend to prove "hereditary defects." Third, the written narrative exists. To reinforce the connection between cognitive disability and hypo/hypersexuality, these reports frequently use the Binet-Simon scale, a test developed by psychologists Binet and Simon to rank children according to IQ test results.

Based on the "performance of about 300 normal children" (Domino and Domino 2002, 101), psychologists Alfred Binet and Theodore Simon developed a test to measure intelligence through thirty tasks ("items"). These include "following simple commands, telling how two objects are alike, defining common words, drawing designs from memory, and repeating spoken digits" (Wolf qtd. in ibid., 100). Three aspects remain central to the visual rhetoric of this illustration. The Binet-Simon test was based on how well "normal" children, (i.e., children whose IQ was assumed to be in the "normal" range of 90 to 110 points) performed. In the medical discourse on cognitive disability at that time, any number below 90 meant cognitive impairment: a score of 70 to 89 meant a "high-grade moron," a score of 50 to 69 an "idiot," and anything below 50 revealed the tested child to be an "imbecile" (Allen 2006, 173). The overall intention of this test was to standardize the norm and to pathologize "abnormal" results. The test sought to establish IQ levels, leading to the dichotomy of "the normal person" as having an average IQ and "the defective" as below average (Baynton 2013, 19). Consequently, intelligence emerges as a narrative of able-bodied normativity compared to disabled non-normativity. This measure links disability to being below average, non-normative, and defective.

Significantly and harmfully, this illustration depicts adults pejoratively with an emphasis on disability as incapacity. In the words of eugenicists, these adults present as future "economic burdens." Thus, "morons" were regarded as incapable of performing work that requires reason and judgment; "high-grade imbeciles" were perceived as incapable of performing complex manual work; "medium- and low-grade imbeciles" were able to do little more than simple manual work, simple menial work, and self-preservation, and below the level of self-preservation was "the idiot" as the lowest category. Step by step, category by category, test result by test result, people were stripped of their humanity. As "average" turns into "below average," the normalized able-bodied person turns into a moron, an imbecile, or an idiot who sits slumped at the bottom. What was considered "normal" range becomes a matter of what was considered "human": "Lumps of matter in human form but without human mind" (Lennox 1927, 457).

Further, accessibility issues, such as language and education barriers, made it impossible for some people to complete the tasks. IQ tests resulted in false positive results, leading psychologists and educators to believe that some were cognitively impaired when, in fact, they did not understand the language of the test (Hubbard 2013, 77). Test results remain only a single component of the image formed by the cultural narrative of cognitively disabled adults as profoundly impaired. Although the Simon-Binet test assigns a specific IQ score to each different group, aiming to develop a typology of cognitive impairment, the category of cognitive disability is pre-constructed. It is founded on the belief that cognitively disabled adults are biologically predisposed to being defective due to what was believed to be the hereditary nature of their impairment. By using the Binet-Simon test as evidence, eugenicists aimed to prove what they already assumed: that cognitively disabled adults are less than human beings.

The image's visual rhetoric is key to this mechanism of othering. The fact that adults are separated from each other through different stages of development, with each next step out of reach for the person below, leads to a pervasive form of ableism propelled by eugenic ideology. Akin to the Darwinist image of an evolutionary "ladder," this illustration employs a similar image of a ladder with different "stages of mental development." These stages correspond to an individual's place in society. The "moron," ranked highest in the group, is unable to climb the last step and reach the stage of "work requiring reason and judgement." As for "idiots" on the lowest step, climbing the ladder is virtually impossible. The illustration is subtitled "where they stumble" (*Mental Defectives in Virginia* 1915, 9), thus narrowing the focus on the limitations imposed upon each individual.

Disabled people were confronted with the prejudice of being seen as economic "burdens" to society. Relatedly, it is significant that none of the individuals in the illustration are depicted as being productive. Instead, they are shown being idle as if waiting for something that never arrives, with blank, empty expressions. They personify the eugenic conviction that disabled individuals are "burdens" to society. Another report, this time by Henry Goddard (1926), illustrates this aspect by framing cognitively disabled adults as children predisposed to become criminals. Their value to the community and to society remains unclear. In a set of images of three individuals deemed cognitively disabled, labels such as "moron" and "imbecile" refer to a disjunction between mental age and biological age. Ages vary between 10 (mental) and 16 (biological) ("Isaac Q."); 3 and 17, ("Prudence Q."); and 8 and 21 ("Wil T."). While differences vary by example (with the lowest difference being 6 years, "Isaac Q.," and the highest difference being 14 years, "Prudence Q."), this image suggests that these individuals are cognitively disabled because of their mental ages, and the image is regarded as evidentiary proof. Because cognitive disability is largely invisible, this image constructs cognitive impairment as an "infantile" condition. Bearing in mind that these images were taken by an institution, a "training school at Vineland [. . .] [for] those whose minds have not developed normally" (Goddard 1926, n.p.), the visual rhetoric of these images reinforces the notion that for these individuals, disability, pathology, and having a child-like mental age correspond. All three individuals are depicted in a set of two shots, a medium close-up of faces and another medium close-up of facial profiles. Moreover, in the case of Wil T. and Isaac Q., no medical devices, doctors, nurses, or institution are depicted. Instead, the image shows the surroundings of the institution as trees and sky. Therefore, this image evokes the sense that these are "natural" images of disabled individuals that could have been found in a family photo album. Although these images were taken for Goddard's study, they naturalize and normalize how these individuals are depicted.

This notion is reinforced by other visual narratives in the report, such as personal letters and drawings. See, for instance, a drawing by Isaac Q. This drawing suggests that, indeed, Isaac is a child. The technical simplicity and the fact that the figure on the left is Santa Claus, to whom Isaac has also written a letter (Goddard 1926, 83), serve to reinforce the sense that Isaac's mental age is that of a child. Rather than refer to Isaac by his full name, Isaac is referred to as "child" or "boy." Thus, Isaac is treated as someone much younger. Goddard writes:

> Isaac, on the other hand, is a high-grade moron, a fine-looking boy; has made great improvement since coming here. On admission at the age of nine he is reported to have had a large head, open mouth, unsteady gaze; was heedless, active, obstinate; memory and attention poor. He had been in kindergarten a year and had learned to count and tell color. In the seven years he has learned to do about what the high-grade defectives usually do. (1926, 82)

According to Goddard's rhetoric, infantilizing and pathologizing attitudes toward Isaac as a "child" clash. Phrases like "high-grade moron" and the detailed description of Isaac's appearance and body ("a large head, open mouth, unsteady gaze") and his behavior ("heedless, active, obstinate; memory and attention poor") convey the notion that Goddard bases his observations on a medical report. Yet this is not an individual medical report or a study. Instead, it is a tool to reinforce eugenic ideology. Isaac is described as a "high-grade moron," and this diagnosis is formed on the assumption that Isaac's ability to learn will not exceed "what the high-grade defectives usually do." Again, the image of cognitive disability emerges as inherently ableist. Isaac, in the illustration of the Binet-Simon test, can be imagined resting on the step of his development. Thus, he is presented as being of no real "use" to U.S. society.

There remains a political layer to this image, recalling hereditarianism and the eugenic idea that disabled people should be held accountable for social problems through their defective "germ plasms." Consequently, although the rhetoric in Goddard's study is paternalistic and infantilizing, implicit criminalization forms the narrative, despite the existence of criminal records. Instead, the image becomes the criminal record itself. This label is further supported by Goddard's narrative, marking Isaac as inherently criminalistic:

> A glance at the family chart is enough to account for the condition of these children. [. . .] Isaac, however, is extremely dangerous. He is a potential criminal or bad man, or under the best conditions would at least marry and probably become the father of defectives like himself. (1926, 85)

Creating a stark contrast to Isaac's drawings, this rhetoric deconstructs the image of Isaac as an "innocent" and, by implication, "asexual child." It favors Isaac's depiction as a "criminal in the making." In his family chart, Isaac (marked by an "F") is identified as the son of a cognitively disabled mother (equally marked by an "F") (1926, 82). Here, "F" stands for "feebleminded," an umbrella category for cognitive impairment that marks Isaac and his mother as individual carriers of "defective germ plasm." Returning to hereditarianism, this image evokes the notion that defectives genes are passed through generations. These genes, as Goddard interprets them, will lead to criminal behavior. Regardless of whether Isaac will become a criminal, he will become a father—which, in eugenic ideology, constitutes a crime because Isaac would spread his "defective germ plasm." The plasm is responsible for his disability and risks spreading pauperism, alcoholism, and criminality.

Notably, Goddard's observation attributes Isaac's predisposition to become a criminal to a matter of parentage. He is the offspring of "a feeble-minded woman with a husband who is alcoholic" (1926, 82). Thus, two conclusions follow from Isaac's family chart. First, there is a hereditary element to cognitive disability, with Isaac and his mother affected. Second, what was perceived as immoral behavior contributed to Isaac's becoming disabled. The term "feeble-mindedness" is strongly gendered in eugenic discourse as associated with women who "ostensibly threatened the social order with their irresponsible sexual proclivities and bad moral judgment" (Stern 2010, 177). A connection is drawn between criminality, gender, and disability, with the focus on female hypersexuality and the genesis of disability. This connection becomes important in the next section.

Another aspect connecting sexuality, gender, and disability complicates the stereotype of the cognitively disabled adult "child." In stark contrast to Isaac, Prudence is described as "not dangerous. She is so low grade that there is hardly any likelihood of her ever marrying, although she might be victimized by some evilly [*sic*] disposed man" (Goddard 1926, 85). In this quotation, the implicit connection between disability and lack of sexuality forms the basis for a gendered, sexualized disability narrative. The cognitively disabled woman registers as a victim of sexual abuse. It is striking that Goddard mentions the possibility of sexual abuse without offering a solution to protect Prudence. Instead, unlike Wil and Isaac, Prudence and her disability are implicitly gendered as unattractive because she is low functioning and "too disabled" to ever be considered a, normatively speaking, sexually attractive woman. Thus, although Goddard does not mention Prudence's sexuality explicitly, the fact that he considers her to be a victim of future sexual abuse reinforces a sense of gender injustice. Like "Alan," the queer disabled man in the UK, Prudence is marginalized twice: for being disabled and for being a woman, with both aspects factoring into her identity as a low-functioning, helpless victim. As a consequence, cognitive disability emerges as a concept that is medicalized and pathologized in the eugenic cultural discourse, and also it is gendered. While Wil, Prudence, and Isaac are all depicted as eternal "children," disabled women like Prudence remain victimized due to the supposed severity of their condition. In the next section, this assumption is reconsidered by a shift in stereotype: the cognitively disabled woman as hypersexual.

IV: DISABILITY AND SEXUALITY IN THE EUGENIC FORCED STERILIZATION LAWS

Similar to the infantilization of cognitively disabled adults, a counter-image suggests criminality and animality. This counter-image relies on another combination of rhetoric and imagery that aims at the systematic degradation and dehumanization of cognitively disabled individuals. Central to this section is the notion that a nexus of different laws is central to the way eugenicists understood, imagined, and gendered disability in the legal system. Apart from forced sterilization laws, so-called ugly laws (state-specific anti-mendicancy ordinances), anti-immigration laws targeted disabled people by associating disability with "deviant social behavior." Further associations included "unsightliness," homelessness, and poverty ("ugly laws," see Schweik 2009, 9) as well as uncontrolled immigration and criminality (anti-immigration laws, see Baynton 2016, 22). These laws support the overall cultural narrative of disability as a form of hereditary defect, deviancy, and delinquency, requiring legal intervention and control. In this context, legal rule becomes an ideological tool of oppression, marking bodies as able and disabled. Thus, in the eugenic legal imagination, disability becomes an embodiment of difference. Sharon Snyder and David Mitchell posit the phrase "embodiment gone awry" (2006, 39). As regards the connection between disability and (hyper)sexuality, forced-sterilization laws warrant discussion. Its legal rhetoric and imagery are key components to the concept of disabled women as hypersexual beings. The reason is that the sexualization of disability and the associated notion of gender injustice rest on the construction of a particular identity. This identity is rendered as a dangerous, hypersexual, "feeble-minded" woman.

> These feeble-minded women are notoriously immoral. One writer reported having found 15 in one almshouse in a neighboring State, who had given birth to six illegitimate children in six weeks of each other. In speaking of them, he says that they are no more able to live according to the rules of society than the cats and dogs in the streets; they come to the almshouse to be delivered, and just as soon as they are on their feet, leave, only to return at the earliest possible moment for the same purpose, and this continues to the end of their child-bearing lives. (Dew 1913, 5)

Further, Mary Storer Kostir states in her family study *The Family of Sam Sixty*:

> Inasmuch [*sic*] as our incomplete study of this group has placed on record forty-seven illicit sexual relationships, and forty-one children known to be illegitimate, the folly of framing restrictive marriage laws to remedy conditions here presented, is at once apparent. Many of these people are as irrespon-

> sible sexually as are rabbits or guinea pigs. To pass laws to prevent the marriage of such individuals, would serve only to increase illegitimacy. It would not lessen the number of offspring from the least desirable parents. (1916, 29)

Consider the following aspects of these quotations together. First, on the level of representation, the image of the disabled woman as an animal is similar to the images of disabled individuals in the illustration of the Binet-Simon test. Like the "idiot," who remains slumped and animal-like on the lowest step of human development, a disabled woman is depicted as beyond "reason and judgement." The idea is that it is in her nature to reproduce uncontrollably. The "logical" (read: eugenic) response is segregation and forced sterilization. Thus, by gendering disabled women as hypersexual, Kostir already makes an implicit argument for forced sterilization by evoking deep-seated eugenic fears of disabled women as a threat to U.S. society. Moreover, the identity constructed in these passages naturalizes the notion of "immoral" female sexuality by connecting the disabled female body to biologically determined, inherent defects. This presentation issues a sense of gender injustice as these women remain pathologized, providing no agency over their own bodies.

Notably, in eugenic discourse on sexuality, female, non-disabled bodies remained normalized through another image. Embodied through the image of the eugenic "mother of tomorrow" (Kline 2001, 16), she participates in family contests and focuses on "domestic duties" (ibid.). Female sexuality and able-bodiedness are closely linked through the normalized and gendered image of the "angel in the house." In contrast, the disabled woman has fallen, both ideologically and literally. On the streets, "like cats and dogs," she is made to represent and embody what eugenicists perceived as non-normative sexuality and femininity. Hence, the gendering of disability as hypersexual moves beyond the pathologizing of cognitive impairment. In the case of the hypersexual "fallen" woman, the eugenic narrative of disability as an inherited, biologically determined defect becomes a means to pathologize women whose sexuality was linked to "disease" and disability (for instance, prostitutes; see Kline 2001, 46). The gender injustice inherent in the sexualization of disabled women as hypersexual intersects with the moralization and normalization of feminine sexuality. The created identity is intersectional, remaining oppressed on multiple levels. Beyond society's femininity norms, a woman in an almshouse is impoverished, marginalized, and stigmatized by the assumption that her hypersexual, immoral behavior led her there. She is perceived as the carrier of a defective "germ plasm." She becomes a determiner responsible for her deviant sexuality and multiple children, who are carriers of the defective germ plasm, according to eugenic ideology.

Significantly, Kostir adopts the image of a disabled woman as hypersexual to argue *against* another law. Miscegenation laws banned "interracial" marriages between White and African American individuals as well as marriages between disabled people (Daar 2017, 38). In Kostir's view, these laws are not sufficiently effective to keep the "rabbits and guinea pigs" from procreating. Instead, her rhetoric implies that unmarried, disabled individuals produce "offspring," rendering them "immoral" and more in opposition to the eugenic "mother of tomorrow" than the hypersexual, "fallen" woman. Kostir advocates sterilization laws that respond forcibly to the "growing problem" of disabled, hypersexual individuals.

Forced-sterilization laws developed at the beginning of the twentieth century. Harry Laughlin drafted a "model law," aiming at the forced sterilization of disabled individuals who were institutionalized (Lombardo 2008, 51). From these laws, the Virginia Sterilization Act of 1924 developed:

> Be it enacted that by the general assembly of Virginia [t]hat whenever the superintendent of the Western State Hospital [. . .] or of the State Colony for Epileptics and Feebleminded shall be of opinion that it is for the best interest of the patients and of society that any inmate of the institution under his care should be sexually sterilized, such superintendent is hereby authorized to perform, or cause to be performed by some capable physician or surgeon, the operation of sterilization on any such patient confined in such institution afflicted with hereditary forms of insanity that are recurrent, idiocy, imbecility, feeble mindedness, or epilepsy. (*Acts and Joint Resolutions* 1924, 569)

In this example, the association of disability with hypersexuality and the resulting sense of gender injustice resurface as part of a specific legal rhetoric. Similar to Galton, who constructed human reproduction as a problem for eugenics to respond, terms such as "the patient" and "state colony" reinforce the sense that in the context of disability, sexuality is pathology. Consequently, cognitively disabled, "feeble-minded" people are, first and foremost, patients: they are segregated from society by the institutions that confine them. Although the tone of this law is reminiscent of a medical report, there is a political dimension to it. Institutionalized disabled people are virtually invisible to the general public. Reasons include their marginal status (as infantilized, gendered, and pathologized) and the institution. Exposure to forced sterilization renders the target group vulnerable.

The explicit terminology used in this law is "sexually sterilized." In contrast to its first draft in 1907, wherein the term "to prevent procreation" is used (Laughlin 1922, 15), the focus shifts to the sexuality of the target group, rather than reproduction. Arguably, in the 1924 Virginia act, sexuality is regarded as the core problem for the legal rule to control.[3] Within the context of this specific rhetoric, the image of disability as hypersexuality appears to be resolved. "Sexually sterilized" suggests asexuality. It presents as the "solution" to address a population believed to have an animalistic sex drive. Also, it returns to the image of cognitively disabled individuals as children.

Having an "animalistic" sex drive is framed thus as dangerous and unnatural. Being "asexualized," in contrast, is the norm reinforced by this law.

A final aspect central to this discussion is the Supreme Court case *Buck v. Bell* (1927). It connects the sexualization of disabled women and gender injustice to dominant legal actors in the eugenic law and speaks to the gendering of the eugenic legal system generally. *Buck v. Bell* is instrumental to the institutionalization of the 1924 Virginia act because it was used as a "test case of the Constitutionality of the sterilization law" (Lombardo 2008, 101). Again, eugenicists aimed to prove what they already assumed: that sterilizing disabled individuals was well within the means of the law and Constitutional limits. In the same year that the Virginia act was passed, Carrie Buck, a seventeen year-old girl who lived in the foster care system in Charlottesville, Virginia, was raped by a member of her foster family. She became pregnant and, after giving birth to a daughter, Vivian, Carrie was sent to the Virginia State Colony for the Feeble-Minded and Epileptic. There, her biological mother, Emma Buck, was already institutionalized. Scoring below average in the Binet-Simon test, Carrie was labeled a "moron" (ibid., 106). As noted in her file, she gave birth to additional, unidentified illegitimate children. And she was arrested for prostitution (ibid.). From the perspective of eugenic law and ideology, she is doubly suspect as a cognitively disabled and "fallen," immoral woman.

In 1927, Buck was delivered to the Supreme Court as her family—her mother, her daughter, and Carrie herself—were perceived to embody what eugenic ideology wanted to control and segregate, the "manifestly unfit" (Lombardo 2008, x). As a consequence, in the verdict of Justice Oliver Wendell Holmes, two contrasting images of cognitively disabled women emerge. While Carrie Buck is hypersexualized, the contrast to Prudence, the "child" too disabled to ever be considered an "attractive" woman, could not be stronger. First, by recalling the 1924 Virginia act, Holmes situates the trial in an overall legal narrative that frames disabled women as hypersexual. "An Act of Virginia, approved March 20, 1924, recites that the health of the patient and the welfare of society may be promoted in certain cases by the sterilization of mental defectives [. . .]" (*Buck v. Bell* 1927, 205). Here, Buck as "the patient" is objectified; meanwhile, forced sterilization is portrayed as the necessary means by which the "welfare" of society will be "improved." Again, Galton's rhetoric of U.S. society as a living organism resurfaces as Holmes compares forced sterilization to compulsory vaccine statues (1927, 203). The impetus for both is for the sake of U.S. social "health" and "fitness." Consequently, Holmes's verdict becomes another tool of oppressive eugenic ideology.

Notably, Holmes distinguishes able-bodied and cognitively disabled individuals:

> No legal reason appears why a person of full age and sound mind, and even though free from any disease making such operation advisable or necessary, may not by consent have the performed [. . .] Who then is to consent or decide for this appellant whether it be best for her to have this operation? She cannot determine the matter for herself both because being not of full age her judgement it not to be accepted nor would it acquit the surgeon, and because she is further incapacitated by congenital mental defect. (1927, 204)

In this quotation, ableism blends with paternalism. The rhetoric of Justice Holmes, the dominant legal actor, is reminiscent of the words of a "father knows best figure." In contrast, Carrie remains infantilized and powerless. This power relation is reinforced by the fact that the legal actors involved in the preparation of the case were all White, male individuals in equal positions of power. Figures included Harry Laughlin, the director of the Eugenics Records Office (ERO), Aubrey Strode, a lawyer who presented the Buck case before the Supreme Court, and Albert Priddy, the superintendent of the colony where Carrie was institutionalized. Remarkably, Carrie's lawyer, Irving Whitehead, "had no intention of defending her" (Lombardo 2008, xi). Consequently, the sense of gender injustice the Buck case evokes—the pathologizing of a woman's sexuality and the subsequent sterilization against her will and without her knowledge—reveals the eugenic legal system to be a gendered system. In this system, White, male eugenicists successfully argued for the validity of a legal case that was, in fact, a sham. At its core, *Buck v. Bell* was an "an elaborate campaign to win judicial approval for eugenic sterilization laws" (ibid.).

Accordingly, Justice Holmes proceeded. The rhetoric in his verdict shifts with the trial:

> Carrie Buck is a feeble-minded white woman who was committed to the State Colony above mentioned in due form. She is also the daughter of a feeble minded mother in the same institution, and the mother of an illegitimate feeble minded child [. . .] many defective persons who if now discharged would become a menace but if incapable of procreating might be discharged and become self-supporting with benefit to themselves and to society [. . .] [i]t is better for all the world, if instead of waiting to execute degenerate offspring for crime, or to let them starve for their imbecility, society can prevent those who are manifestly unfit from continuing their kind. [. . .] Three generations of imbeciles are enough. (205–6, 209)

In this quotation, the image of Buck as an "innocent" child or a "patient" requiring care and support is disrupted. Buck is represented as a "feeble-minded woman" who reproduces offspring like a "guinea pig" or a "rabbit," for which her "illegitimate" child is proof. Thus, Buck is made to embody two key narratives in eugenic ideology. On the one hand, she is regarded as a cognitively disabled woman with "defective germ plasm," for which her daughter and her mother, both diagnosed as cognitively disabled, provide evidence. Legal rhetoric substitutes for a family chart, such as in Goddard's study. On the other hand, she is "immoral" *per se* because she gave birth to a child out of wedlock, "degenerate offspring for crime." Again, Buck is gendered as hypersexual, with the implication that if she were to allowed to "produce" more "offspring," her defectiveness, both her disability and her "immoral sexual behavior," would be passed on.

In Holmes's verdict, neither Buck's financial background nor socioeconomic status are mentioned. This implies a default for cognitively disabled women. Paul Lombardo characterizes Buck as "a poor girl [who] was separated from her family at an early age and [who] was living quite literally on the wrong side of the railroad tracks" (2008, x). Further, disability theorists like Anna Stubblefield argue that in the eugenic discourse on disability, cognitive impairment is intersectional in its marginal status. Race, socioeconomic status, and gender factor in whether or not someone was diagnosed in the eugenic medical system. Such diagnosis affected poor, White women from the countryside disproportionally (2007, 162). Also, it links to Kostir's family study *Sam Sixty*. In this study, she links her image of disabled women of the Sixty family "procreating like guinea pigs and rabbits" to living conditions, "filth and desperate poverty" (1916, 12). Buck ultimately suffers as a result. Not only is she is sterilized against her will, but the surgery, disguised as an appendectomy, is performed without her knowledge (Lombardo 2008, 251). This gender injustice illustrates the pervasiveness of ableist, sexist discrimination against disabled women in the eugenic legal system. Buck was someone who was vulnerable in the eugenic legal system, which perceived her as someone who needed to be sterilized. The medical system rendered her as a "defective" and "delinquent." Socially, she remained segregated. Her financial situation and economic status were precarious. She was raped, placed in an institution, and then sterilized against her will. All of this illustrates that in the legal imagination of the eugenics movement, law is more than a set of legal rules that constituted forced sterilization and the segregation of disabled people. It is a narrative whereby disabled women are rendered outlaws in every sense of the word—they are outside of legal protection and societal participation.

V. CONCLUSION

This chapter illustrated that when we think about disability and gender injustice in the U.S. eugenics movement, neither historical context nor the impact of forced-sterilization laws as an ideological tool of oppression can be ignored. Main stereotypes include the cognitively disabled woman as a hyposexual "child" and women hypersexualized as feral "animals." Both show the different ways in which sexuality is normalized (asexuality) and pathologized (hypersexuality). In either case, cognitively disabled women are denied agency over their own bodies and positions in U.S. society and the U.S. eugenic legal system. Instead, they become embodiments of gender injustice as they remain powerless and marginalized. Forced-sterilization laws perpetuate this power dynamic. In *Buck v. Bell*, Carrie Buck is made to represent this power dynamic. The dominant legal actors in her case frame her as a stereotype for the poor, disabled, "sexually immoral" woman. This registers that in discussions about sexuality and gender injustice, disability remains intersectional in its marginality. Social class, race, gender, and disability all factor into the contested status of a disabled woman's hypo- or hypersexualized body in society. Thus, disability is more than medical impairment. Indeed, it remains deeply political in its function to embody non-normative reproduction and sexuality.

NOTES

I wish to thank Osnat Katz for her diligent proofreading.

1. The name Alan is a pseudonym; it was chosen to protect the man's anonymity.
2. See, for instance, Charles Davenport, "The Geography of Man in Relation to Eugenics" (1911) and "Influence on Heredity on Human Society" (1909); Francis Galton, *Hereditary Genius: An Inquiry into Its Laws and Consequences* (1869) and "Typical Laws of Heredity" (1877); and Harry Laughlin, *Eugenical Sterilization in the United States* (1922).
3. This is mirrored by the rhetoric of other laws that were drafted and passed in other states, such as the 1909 bill in California, which uses the phrase "to permit asexualization" to reinforce the notion that disabled people should be asexual under the rule of law (Laughlin 1922, 17).

BIBLIOGRAPHY

Acts and Joint Resolutions (Amending the Constitution) of the General Assembly of the State of Virginia (1924). Richmond: Davis Bottom.

Adams, Mark B. (1990). *The Wellborn Science: Eugenics in Germany, France, Brazil, and Russia.* New York and Oxford: OUP.

Addlakha, Renu, Janet Price, and Shirin Heidari (2017). "Disability Rights and Sexuality: Claiming Sexual and Reproductive Rights." *Reproductive Health Matters* 25, no. 50: 4–9.

Ahlvik-Harju, Carolin (2016). "Disturbing Bodies—Reimagining Comforting Narratives of Embodiment through Feminist Disability Studies." *Scandinavian Journal of Disability Research* 18, no. 3: 222–33.

Allen, Garland E. (2006). "Biological Determinism." *Encyclopedia of Disability: Volume 1.* Ed. Jerome Bickenbach et al. Thousand Oaks, London, New Delhi: Sage. 172–74.

Baynton, Douglas C. (2016). *Defectives in the Land: Disability and Immigration in the Land of Eugenics.* Chicago and London: University of Chicago Press.

——— (2013). "Disability and the Justification of Inequality in American History." In *The Disability Studies Reader.* 4th ed. Ed. Lennard J. Davis. New York and Abingdon: Routledge.17–33.

Braddock, David L., and Susan Parish. (2001). "An Institutional History of Disability." In *The Handbook of Disability Studies.* Ed. Gary L. Albrecht, Katherine D. Seelman, and Michael Bury. London et al.: Sage. 11–68.

Brauer, Fae (2009). "Framing Darwin: A Portrait of Eugenics." In *The Art of Evolution: Darwin, Darwinisms, and Visual Culture*. Ed. Barbara Larson and Fae Brauer. Hanover and London: University of New England, 124–55.

Buck v. Bell, 274 U.S. 200 (1927).

Daar, Judith (2017). *The New Eugenics: Selective Breeding in an Era of Reproductive Technologies*. New Haven and London: Yale University Press.

Davenport, Charles (1912). "Eugenics and Charity." *Proceedings of the National Conference of Charities and Corrections.* Press of Geo. H. Ellis. 280–82.

Davis, Lennard J. (1995). *Enforcing Normalcy: Disability, Deafness, and the Body.* London and New York: Verso.

Dew, H. W. (1913). "Sterilization of the Feeble-Minded, Insane and Habitual Criminals." *Virginia Medical Semi-Monthly* (April 1): 4–8.

Domino, George, and Marla Domino (2002). *Psychological Testing: An Introduction.* 2nd ed. Cambridge: Cambridge University Press.

Dubow, Saul (1995). *Scientific Racism in Modern South Africa.* Cambridge: Cambridge University Press.

Fernald, Walter (1907). "Discussions of Defectives and the Public Schools." *Proceedings of the National Conference on Charities and Corrections.* Ed. Alexander Johnson. Indianapolis: Press of Wm. E. Murford. 486.

Galton, Francis (1951). *Inquiries into Human Faculty and Its Development* [1883]. London: Eugenics Society.

Garland-Thomson, Rosemarie (2002). "Integrating Disability, Transforming Feminist Theory." *NWSA Journal* 14 no. 3: 1–32.

Gill, Michael (2015). "Sexual Ableism Exposed." *Already Doing It: Intellectual Disability and Sexual Agency.* Minneapolis: University of Minnesota, 1–22.

Goddard, Henry Herbert (1926). *Feeble-Mindedness: Its Causes and Consequences.* New York: Macmillan.

Hubbard, Ruth (2013). "Abortion and Disability: Who Should and Should Not Inhabit the World?" In *The Disability Studies Reader.* Ed. Lennard J. Davis. Abingdon and New York: Routledge, 74–99.

Jarman, Michelle (2012). "Dismembering the Lynch Mob: Intersecting Narratives of Disability, Race, and Sexual Menace." In *Sex and Disability*. Ed. Robert McRuer and Anna Mollow. Durham, NC, and London: Duke University Press, 89–109.

Kline, Wendy (2001). *Building a Better Race: Gender, Sexuality, and Eugenics from the Turn of the Century to the Baby Boom.* Berkeley: University of California Press.

Kostir, Mary Storer (1916). *The Family of Sam Sixty.* Columbus: Press of Ohio State Reformatory.

Laughlin, Harry (1922). *Eugenic Sterilization in the United States.* Chicago: Municipal Court.

Lennox, William G. (1927). "Should They Live? Certain Economic Aspects of Medicine." *The American Scholar* 7 no. 4: 454–66.

Lindstrom, Diane (2004). "Industrialization." In *Poverty in the United States: An Encyclopedia of History, Politics, and Policy: Volume I, A–K.* Ed. Gwendolyn Mink and Alice O'Connor. Santa Barbara, Denver, Oxford: ABC Clio, 405–9.

Lombardo, Paul (2008). *Three Generations, No Imbeciles: Eugenics, the Supreme Court, and Buck v. Bell.* Baltimore: Johns Hopkins University Press.

——— (1996). "Medicine, Eugenics, and the Supreme Court: From Coercive Sterilization to Reproductive Freedom." *Journal of Contemporary Health Law and Policy* 13 no. 1: 1–25.

Maxwell, Anne (2010). *Picture Imperfect: Photography and Eugenics 1870–1940.* Brighton and Portland: Sussex Academy Press.

Mental Defectives in Virginia: A Special Report of the State Board of Charities and Corrections to the General Assembly on Weak-Mindedness in the State of Virginia (1915). Richmond: Davis Bottom.

O'Brien, Gerald V. (2013). *Framing the Moron: The Social Construction of Feeble-Mindedness in the American Eugenic Era.* Manchester: Manchester University Press.

Perlin, Michael L., and Alison Lynch. *Sexuality, Disability, and the Law: Beyond the Last Frontier?* Basingstoke: Palgrave Macmillan, 2016.

Rembis, Michael (2002). "Disability and the History of Eugenics." In *The Oxford Handbook of Disability History.* Ed. Michael Rembis, Catherine Kudlick, and Kim E. Nielsen. Oxford: Oxford niversity Press, 85–105.

Schweik, Susan M. (2009). *The Ugly Laws: Disability in Public.* New York and London: New York University Press.

Shakespeare, Tom, Kath Gillespie-Sells, and Dominic Davies (1996). *The Sexual Politics of Disability: Untold Desires.* London and New York: Continuum.

Snyder, Sharon L., and David T. Mitchell (2006). *Cultural Locations of Disability.* Chicago: University of Chicago Press.

Stern, Alexandra Minna (2010). "Gender and Sexuality: A Global Tour and Compass." *The Oxford Handbook of the History of Eugenics.* Ed. Alison Bashford and Philippa Levine. Oxford: Oxford University Press, 173–91.

Stubblefield, Anna (2007). "Beyond the Pale: Tainted Whiteness, Cognitive Disability, and Eugenic Sterilization." *Hypatia* 22 no. 2: 162–81.

Waldtschmidt, Anne (2010). "Das Mädchen Ashley oder: Intersektion von Behinderung, Normalität und Geschlecht." *Gendering Disability: Intersektionale Aspekte von Behinderung und Geschlecht.* Ed. Jutta Jacob, Swantje Köbsell, and Eske Wollrad. Bielefeld: transcript, 35–60.

Webster, Lucie (2017, August 3). Retrieved September 19, 2019 fromhttps://www.buzzfeed.com/lucywebster/how-feminism-informed-my-identity-as-a-disabled-woman.

Wilkerson, Abby (2011). "Disability, Sex Radicalism, and Political Agency." *Feminist Disability Studies*. Ed. Kim Q. Hall. Bloomington: Indiana University Press 193–217.

Wineland, Claire (2018, March 19). Retrieved November18, 2018 fromhttps://www.instagram.com/p/Bgg9SgChrV4/>.

Chapter Eight

Victims of State Violence

Indigenous and Women-of-Color Sex Workers' Interactions with Law Enforcement in Canada

Menaka Raguparan

Law enforcement practices and protocols to govern sex work and sex workers vary considerably by region, in time, by the types of sites in which they occur, and by the influence of cultural and socio-structural forces. As a result, police–sex worker interactions have been described as inseparable and engendered (Dewey and Kelly 2011) and as arbitrary and abusive (Almodovar 2010; Saunders and Kirby 2010–2011; Bruckert and Chabot 2010). Policing protocols and practices are also well known for tolerating indoor sex work, which operates discreetly out of public view (Sanders and Soothill 2011; Scambler 2007), and as expressions of public patriarchy, whereby the state legitimizes interfering in the personal lives of individuals (Sanders 2009). The relationship between street-based sex workers' increased visibility in public and the associated intensive forms of policing practices has also been well documented around the world (Dewey and St. Germain 2014; Rhodes et al. 2008).

This chapter adds to critical sex work scholarship's growing realization that the relationship between law enforcement and sex workers is complex and dynamic. Drawing upon forty women-of-color sex workers' encounters with police officers, the chapter identifies how the occupational and racial biases of police officers influence their actions and behaviors toward sex workers. Analysis of research participants' lived experiences advances the literature on the forms of state violence inflicted upon marginalized and minoritized populations in Canada and other nation-states. Subjecting sex workers to differential policing practices that are discriminatory not only contradicts police mandates to serve and protect the public, but it also violates the constitutional rights of sex workers by excluding them from state protections.

Many participants in this study have been subjected to insults, humiliation, verbal abuse, unlawful detention, unwarranted arrest, and even physical and sexual abuse in their interactions with police officers. My research participants' encounters with law enforcement are consistent with existing literature that focuses on police–sex worker interactions (Stinson et al. 2014; Saunders and Kirby 2010–2011; Sherman et al. 2015; Krusi et al. 2016). The unique contribution of this chapter is that it brings the experiences of indoor sex workers, which remains an understudied area (see Benoit et al. 2016), and women of color. To this end, this chapter clarifies the following: even with the relative privilege of working in the indoor sectors, at the intersection of race and sex work, women of color are not immune to police abuses of power.

I. THEORETICAL FRAMEWORK AND LITERATURE REVIEW

It is well documented that the increased risk of violence in sex workers' lives is the result of increased isolation, social marginalization, racism, sexism, and other systemic factors that are prevalent in the Canadian Criminal Justice System (Shannon et al. 2008; O'Doherty 2011; Socias et al. 2015). Critical sex-work scholars also argue that the way Indigenous people and people of color as a whole are over-policed and under-protected contributes to the violence some sex workers experience in the sex industry (Lam 2016; Anderson et al. 2015; Amnesty 2016; Goldenberg et al. 2015). Women in the current study assert that their visible markers of skin color and body features at the intersection of race, indigeneity, and occupation often result in under-protection, over-policing, and abuse of authority. At the backdrop of widespread public and policy rhetoric, which claims that the sex industry is inherently violent and that women's participation in sex work is essentially a form of violence against women, the question becomes: How do we make sense of law enforcements' response to research participants' experiences of violence when police officers are themselves perpetrators of certain forms of violence inflicted upon sex workers?

State Violence

Yasmin Jiwani (2006) argues that everyday definitions of violence should not be limited to the "physical, psychological, and discursive dimensions" (7). According to Jiwani (2006), a comprehensive explanation of violence should include the inherent elements of use of force and abuse of power. A complete definition of violence will allow us to contextualize state-imposed violence such as "slavery, indentured labor, the internment of particular groups of people during specific historical periods," and colonization as examples of uses and abuses of power (Jiwani 2006, 7). A comprehensive definition will also allow us to understand how "the violence of colonialism" is normalized in the name of nation building and rendered invisible (Jiwani 2006, 9). Furthermore, Jiwani (2006) points out that the contextualization of violence that encompasses the use of force and abuse of power as a form of violence will allow us to comprehend how structures of discrimination are themselves deeply rooted in the violent exercise of power. That is, in hierarchical system/society, social institutions exercise power through concepts of racism, sexism, ableism, ageism, classism, and homophobia. This exertion leads to ranking identity categories and individuals "in terms of their access to varying degrees of power and privilege" (Jiwani 2006, 9). Also, it legitimizes the process of social inclusion and exclusion. In this regard, Jiwani (2006) claims that dominant structures maintain and legitimize the power and privileges of elites, as they not only "define the social order [by] producing and reproducing social inequalities" but also use violence as an instrument for describing and maintaining the differential values to different social categories (9). Extending this thinking to the legal context, David Goldberg (2002) argues that "modern law has been invoked as a technology of racial rule, promoting racial categorization and racial identification, thereby exacerbating law's abstraction" (142). In this sense, "law becomes the primary means of racial order, (the threat of) violence now the means to ensure law enforcement" (Goldberg 2002, 142).

The framework of "state violence," therefore, is a way of exploring and mapping the complex range of direct and indirect harms resulting from state policies, actions, and inactions that severely affect the everyday lived realities of minoritized and marginalized populations. As Maynard (2015) points out, given that "the state possesses an enormous, unparalleled level of power and authority over the lives of its subjects[,] [s]tate agencies are endowed with the power to privilege, punish, confine or expel at will" (3). In this regard, race remains a crucial factor in the state's use and abuse of power, such that there is extensive scholarship that documents the historical and contemporary tensions between people of color and police officers. Examples involve forms of police misconduct influenced by police racial bias (Johnson 2004; Weitzer and Tuch 2004; Wortley and Owusu-Bempah 2009; Macdonald et al. 2007; Oliveira and Murphy 2014; Buffam 2017). Furthermore, focusing on the intersections of race and gender, Black feminist scholars and activist such as Joy James (1996); Angela Davis (1998); Andrea Ritchie (2006, 2017); Robyn Maynard (2017); and others have documented state violence experienced by women of color in the United States and Canada. Ritchie (2017) argues that examining women of color's interactions with law enforcement highlights yet another manifestation of structural racism.

Following these scholars and activists, this chapter advances the conversation of state violence by including Indigenous and women-of-color sex workers' experiences interacting with law enforcement in the cities they live and work in. It aims to identify archetypes of state violence against these women.

Using the framework of state violence, the intersectional analysis (Crenshaw 1991) presented in this chapter brings to the forefront of discussion the gender- and sexuality-based violence experienced by racially marginalized and socially stigmatized groups of women. Here I demonstrate that the use and abuse of power that law enforcement personnel inflict upon sex workers of color is a severe form of violence that is often normalized and rendered invisible. Police officers, operating as moral guardians of civil society and as agents responsible for public order and public protection, continue to justify their abuse of power and use of force with impunity (Sanders and Soothill 2011). Saunders and Kirby (2010–2011) argue that such power and privilege bestowed upon police officers to govern sex workers' actions and behaviors is directly related to societal perceptions that stigmatize and dehumanize sex workers.

Police–Sex Worker Interactions

The prevalence of police officers' use of force and abuse of power through unusually harsh and punitive behaviors toward sex workers is well documented worldwide (Williamson et al. 2007; Almodovar 2010; Saunders and Kirby 2010–2011; Rhodes et al. 2008; Hubbard and Sanders 2003; Dewey and St. Germain 2014). Studies also show that sex workers in public spaces, due to their increased visibility and the criminalization of sex-work-related activities, are at increased risk of confrontation with law enforcement officers (Socias et al. 2015, Dewey and St. Germain 2014). Under such circumstances, street-based sex workers have limited choices. They either have to "cooperate with the cops, give cops sex for protection, become an informant, or go to jail" (Almodovar 2010, 251–52). More recent studies indicate that indoor sex workers are not immune to police misconduct (Goldenberg et al. 2015; Lam 2016). Studies reveal that serial killers and police perpetrators find sex workers as natural subjects for their victimization, and sex workers being raped or extorted for sexual favors by police officers happens far too often (Almodovar 2010; Rhodes et al. 2008; also see Stinson et al. 2014; Kraska and Kappeler 1995). Studies also show that police officers often threaten female sex workers, stating that because of their poor reputation in society, following an arrest no one will believe them if they dispute an officer's claims (Dewey and St. Germain 2014, Williamson and Folaron 2003).

Moreover, studies illustrate that police officers often blame sex workers for any violence they experience. Police response to complaints of violence by sex workers is normalized by claiming that violence is an inherent part of their occupation (Krusi et al. 2016). Krusi et al. (2016) acknowledge that "in a context where sex work is conceptualized as inherently dangerous, and sex workers are increasingly understood as victims in need for saving, blame for sex work related violence continues to be shifted to sex workers themselves for continuing to engage in this dangerous practice" (1142–43). Additionally, because they are perceived to be socially "disreputable" and "disposable," Indigenous sex workers are often denied police protection (Hunt 2013; Pratt 2005). Denying sex workers the status of victimhood when warranted becomes a coercive form of state violence that infringes upon the human rights and socioeconomic mobility of sex workers (Kempadoo et al. 2017; Hunt 2015/2016; Krusi et al. 2016). Such denial of rights and protection, scholars have argued, not only forces sex workers to operate in the social periphery, but also exposes them to increased structural violence (Kempadoo et al. 2017; Hunt 2015/2016; Krusi et al. 2016). In fact, participants in the Krusi et al. (2016) study said that police officers' continued "denial of their citizenship rights for police protection and legal recourse by virtue of their 'risky' occupation" (original emphasis) not only leads to normalizing "their experiences of violence as an inherent part of selling sex," but also seeking police protection felt like experiencing a form of every day/symbolic violence (1142).

Sex workers' experience of state-inflicted violence is not a unique phenomenon of contemporary society; instead, such practices are rooted in history. For instance, Carter (2000) and Moss and Gardner-O'Toole (1991), focusing on the historical legal representation of women who were perceived to be engaging in immoral sexual conduct, point out the extent to which these women were subjected to unusually harsh and often repressive policing policies. According to Carter (2000), the policing practices during that time were conditioned by the intersection of race, class, and gender underpinning Canadian societies, such that the segregationist policies adopted by the state relied on the images that Indigenous women were inherently "dissolute, dangerous and sinister" (61). Such policing practices and protocols not only make life difficult for sex workers irrespective of their guilt but also lead to sex workers' lack of trust and confidence in police officers that they will receive fair treatment (Benoit et al. 2016, Bruckert and Hannem 2013b, Sherman et al. 2015, Dewey and St. Germain 2014).

Existing literature on police–sex worker interactions can be mapped onto at least two interrelated terrains. First, police officers' decisions to enact their authority or abuse their power when interacting with sex workers are, to a greater extent, dependent entirely on the police officer, and it is a matter of their personality (Dewey and St. Germain 2014). It is in this sense that there is a disconnect between law in books and law in action (see Pound 1910) because police officers' views and perspectives of sex workers differ from law and policy definitions of sex workers and sex workers' lived realities. With the designation of police officers as benevolent protectors of social order, Sanders (2009) argues that police officers' urges to regulate women's sexual behaviors and actions can be understood through the term *public patriarchy*, "whereby the state becomes directly involved in personal life-style behaviour" (510). Sanders (2009) argues that "specifically [for] women involved in the sex industry, women become oppressed by the public patriarchy of the state as clear benchmarks regarding what behaviour is acceptable, and what is not [acceptable] becomes the rationale for the application of disciplinary control mechanisms given to individual women" (511).

Secondly, existing studies also draw attention to the point that police officers' perspectives of sex workers to a greater extent are shaped by "societal perceptions [that] stigmatize and dehumanize the 'prostitute' as a kind of trash, social blight and/or threat to public safety and order" (Saunders and Kirby 2010–2011, 110) (original emphasis). In this sense, Saunders and Kirby (2010–2011) argue that police misconduct toward sex workers is not random; instead, their actions are calculated and, clearly throughout, are measures to satisfy social elites' need to maintain their power and privilege by systemically oppressing the Other. In other words it is a relentless effort to keep the "social inequalities relating to class, race, migrant status, gender, sexual orientation, and age" (Saunders and Kirby 2010–2011, 110). In this regard, the social and moral panic about prostitution is used to justify the arrests, harassment, and exclusion of, for example, Latinos (who are perceived as security threats) and trans women of color (for gender nonconformity) from public spaces (Saunders and Kirby 2010–2011). Similarly, the white-savior panic about trafficking is used to justify policing and surveillance of massage parlors and other venues of immigrant congregation (Saunders and Kirby 2010–2011). Furthermore, Krüsi et al. explain that class, ethnicity, and gender influence how sex workers experience stigma and that "(s)ex workers of Indigenous ancestry face a multilayered reality of racism and discrimination that intersects and exacerbates sex work related stigmatization" (1139).

II. METHODS

Participants

This study draws on in-depth qualitative interviews with forty adults who fit the following two inclusion criteria: they self-identified as belonging to a racialized or Indigenous group and are currently or were formally engaged in the indoor sectors of the Canadian sex industry. Interviews were conducted between August 2014 and April 2015. Before the interviews, participants were informed of the objectives of the study and assured that participation was voluntary and their identities would be confidential. Participants received a cash honorarium of CAD 75.00 for their time and knowledge.

The purposive snowball sampling strategy was used to capture a wide range of racial groups. Research participants from nine different sites across Canada responded to a recruitment text circulated through email, Facebook, and Twitter. Ultimately, most research participants learned about this study through word-of-mouth. Data collection consisted of digitally recorded in-depth, face-to-face, and telephone interviews, which lasted between 40 minutes and 2.5 hours.

Thirty-eight individuals self-identified as women; two identified as gender non-binary and worked as women in the sex industry. Except for one participant who held a student visa, all participants identified as Canadian citizens or permanent residents. Participants self-identified as belonging to the following racial groups: Arab (2), East Asian (4), Indigenous (3), South Asian (6), Black (13), and mixed-race (12). At the time of the interview, two women had transitioned out of sex work, while the remaining thirty-eight were engaged in the indoor sectors of the sex industry, working for escort agencies, massage parlors, strip clubs, independent in-call and out-call services, and as webcam performers. Participants' tenure in the sex industry ranged from two months to over twenty-five years. Some participants also had transitioned from the street-based sectors, and some simultaneously worked in both the street-based and indoor sectors of the Canadian sex industry. Participants also identified as simultaneously being engaged in postsecondary education and/or in mainstream jobs. Some even identified as primary-care providers who had the responsibility of caring for their children and/or elderly parents.

Analysis

All interviews were transcribed verbatim and imported into NVivo 10 for coding. Three stages of inductive coding aimed to organize and separate the different themes that arose throughout the interviews. Descriptive coding was used to obtain a broad sense of primary issues. Following this analysis, two levels of subcodes were used to narrow the general descriptive codes. The final phase of coding involved reorganizing the codes into main themes for discussion.

III. DIRECT INFLICTION OF STATE VIOLENCE: ARBITRARY, HARSH, AND PUNITIVE LAW ENFORCEMENT

> I [hold a] university degree [and] I am a smart person [. . .] [But my interactions with police officers [are] always really, really, really, really, really, really demoralizing and dehumanizing for me. Being like a person of color without

> them [police officers] knowing I'm a sex worker is crazy awful. [. . .] I've been like arrested for nothing. I've like received tickets for being mouthy [. . .]. So then when it's like compiled with sex work which has happened, the police are just like [. . .] really shitty. [. . .] Like, I was completely sober, and I was just chilling with one of my friends in [name of the neighborhood], which is a pretty nice area. And I got arrested. [. . .] and they like called me awful names. One of them was just like, "You're a little shit." (Losliya)

Losliya is a Black massage parlor worker with experience working in the street-based sector of the sex industry. This participant's experience of interacting with police officers while working on the streets highlights two key issues. First, in addition to the historically tense relationship between police officers and sex workers, street-based sex workers are indeed subjected to unwarranted harsh policing practices (Krusi et al. 2016; Almodovar 2010; Socias et al. 2015). Second, the strict policing protocols, in addition to including punitive measures, are intended to push street-based sex workers out of public spaces (Hubbard 2004; also see Ritchie 2017). Losliya and other street-based sex workers' encounters with law enforcement in this study draw attention to the regulation of space and to the implications of particular types of people being in places where they "do not belong." In such police–sex worker interactions, it is evident that the responding police officers are concerned about the visual image of the city and the effect sex workers' presence has on the city streets. In other words, even when Losliya was not transgressing any laws, her appearance in the metropolis upset the supposed naturalness and image of a wealthy city (Cresswell 1996). Cresswell (1996) argues that expectations about who is an appropriate person and what is appropriate behavior in a particular place are essential components in the construction, maintenance, and evolution of the social elite's ideological values (also see Ritchie 2017).

The exclusion or eviction of particular types of people from public spaces for being *out of place* also takes a gender-specific form of police abuse. For instance, law enforcement personnel's power to punish gender and sexual nonconformity by engaging in sexual harassment, assault, and rape are well documented (Ritchie 2017; Stinson et al. 2014; Kraska and Kappeler 1995). Specifically, women in this study, who in the past worked as street-based sex workers, have experienced physical assault and rape by police officers.

Madhu, a Métis woman who currently works as an independent in-call and out-call service provider, used to work on the streets and consume drugs. Madhu recounts her experience interacting with police officers while she was on the streets.

> I only had experience with the police when I was living and working on the street. Oh, they didn't treat me well the last time they arrest me. When I arrive in the provincial woman jail close to [name of city], they asked me if I want to

> put a charge against my boyfriend and I was like actually, I don't have any boyfriend, but I just got arrested by your friend there, and they just did that to me. [. . .] They were very aggressive and violent [manhandled me], they broke my glasses, and I had like some blood and some sand in my mouth because they push me on the ground, and they had their feet on me. Actually, it's really, it was an aggression and assault. It was pretty brutal. [. . .] No, they didn't treat me well when I was on the street. As soon as they knew me and I was always visible in the street, they were harassing me. [. . .] They broke all my material for smoking crack. It was a just disaster and un-fun time of my life dealing with them. [. . .] I think it was because I was a sex worker and living on the street and using drugs and visible in public space. They hate me for that.

As a drug-using street-based sex worker, Madhu's eviction from public spaces by the responding police officers highlights the use of force that far exceeds their social and legal mandate. Furthermore, this participant's experience of police-inflicted violence is consistent with those of other Indigenous peoples in Canada (see Hunt 2015/2016, 2010; Kaye 2017). Thus, Madhu's violent encounter can also be attributed to the racial biases of the responding officers. Police officers, as moral guardians of civil society and as agents of public order and protection, are often able to justify their discretionary violence toward marginalized peoples (Sanders and Soothill 2011; Ritchie 2017; Williamson et al. 2007). Likewise, as Saunders and Kirby (2010–2011) argue, such police abuses of power and use of force toward sex workers are not random; instead, they are intentional and targeted and depend on the social tensions cohering to social groups. To this end, the historical dehumanization of Canadian Indigenous peoples and its linkage to their various social inequalities provides police officers with the necessary impunity for their violent actions and behaviors.

To further emphasize the intersectional nature (the raced, gendered, and sexual axes) of police abuses of power and uses of force, I provide the following example. This police–sex worker interaction along the axes of race, gender, and sexuality adds another dimension whereby the state inflicted violence upon my participant can also be understood as punishment for transgressing gender norms.

Vanitha is a mixed-race, White-passing trans woman who has been working in the sex industry for a long time. While she currently provides services to regulars (i.e., a set of clientele she has known for a long time and who seek her services frequently) in indoor settings, in the past, before the internet era, she used to stroll the streets of a large metropolitan area. Vanitha reflects on her experiences interacting with law enforcement:

> At one point, during the 70s, they were entrapping us. [. . .] They would entrap us and then charge us. So, there was an incident once when I was very young; I think I was 16 or 17. I was walking home one night—I had just been out with

> some friends, and a police car came along and started bothering me, asking me for ID, told me to get in the car—there was a police dog in the back. And the next thing I know, I'm down in [name of location] with this police officer, who I know carries a gun and a barking police dog, and I'm forced to perform oral sex [pause] yeah, at three in the morning, in [name of location], which is a very deserted place at that time.

Sanders's (2009) notion of public patriarchy can be applied here to Vanitha's sexual assault by a police officer. That is, the gendered and sexual dimension of control enforced by punitive policing practices is aimed at implementing "appropriate" conduct among those considered to be sexually "disordered" and "uncivil" (Sanders 2009). Vanitha's position as a trans sex worker subjects her to multiple oppressions and increased risk of police targeting. In this instance, structural stigma (Bruckert and Hannem 2013b) and institutional and social transphobia (Socias et al. 2015) shape disciplinary practices by police, which include disproportional targeting, arbitrary arrest, and subjection to physical and sexual violence.

As street-based sex workers, research participants' encounters with law enforcement featured thus far are consistent with existing literature on the police abuse of powers experienced by other street-based sex workers (Benoit et al. 2016, Miller 2002, Dewey and St. Germain 2014, Rhodes et al. 2008). However, it is necessary to note that, given police officers' discretionary powers toward enforcing sex-work-related laws (Williamson et al. 2007; Ritchie 2017), law enforcement personnel's tendency toward violence appears to be arbitrary. The following participant's encounter reveals the unpredictable nature of police officers' use of force and abuse of power.

Shereen is a mixed-race woman—half Black and half White—who successfully passes as White in her everyday life. She works simultaneously as an independent indoor escort and walks the downtown streets of a large metropolitan area. This participant also said that she used to have a drug habit and was known to police as a street-based sex worker and a drug user. Despite these intersecting marginalized identities, unlike most of the participants in this study, Shereen has never been arrested. According to Shereen, she has often been scolded for being in public and *out of place* as a drug user rather than as a sex worker. According to Shereen, the officers she has interacted with were all more concerned about her status as a drug user and how that affects the visual image of the city, rather than her presence as a sex worker.

> I have been stopped a lot by cops. Because of, my drug problem, the positions I get put into, usually if you get caught, or if I am out somewhere, "what you doing here" I am like "I'm a hooker" they're like "oh ok, don't worry about her," yeah, she got a reason, you know what I mean. *I solicited a cop accidentally, one night while I was walking* [participant's emphasis] this is a year ago,

> and he told me that [city name] police were not focusing on the workers, [. . .] they weren't really concerned with us as breaking laws as a whole, that it was the *pimps and the johns* [participant's emphasis]. [. . .] I don't really get hassled. I never ever had a cop like call me up off Backpage and come to my hotel room. I have never had the hotel call the cops on me [. . .]. I mean, I am not really worried about getting arrested.

Despite interacting with police officers as a street-based, drug-using sex worker, Shereen's different experiences interacting with law enforcement are, arguably, the result of the responding officer's assumption that she is a vulnerable White woman, whose involvement in the sex industry is involuntary and a consequence of her drug use. The binary categorization of the prostituted victim—the blameless *involuntary prostitute*, classified as a *vulnerable good victim* who deserves state protection and being rescued, and the classification of the *voluntary sinful deviant prostitute* as *undeserving victim* who is responsible for their own victimization and thus barred from seeking state protections—starkly shapes the responding officers' impressions. This binary categorization has its roots in the nineteenth-century white slave trade panic (Doezema 2000, 28; Faulkner 2018; Balgamwalla 2016; O'Connell Davidson 2010; Valverde 2008). In this case, Shereen's strategy to avoid arrest points to her ability to convert police officers' racial and occupational biases to her advantage.

IV. THE SUBTLETY OF STATE VIOLENCE: DENYING OF RIGHTS AND PROTECTIONS

Many participants in this study said that when they reported any type of victimization to police, they were not believed. According to participants, it is their position as a sex worker and a woman of color that shapes police officers' impressions that they are not credible witnesses. In the remainder of this chapter, I examine my participants' interactions with law enforcement to draw attention to the impact of social stratification and stereotypical assumptions that often position Indigenous women and women of color sex workers in the bottom ranks of the industry (see Razack 1998b). Moreover, it casts them all as less credible, hyper-disposable, and as second-class citizens who are less deserving of protection and/or wholly excluded from police protection (see Pratt 2005). Law enforcement officers' reliance on the racialized, gendered, and sexualized controlling images (see Collins 2000) impacts the lives of these research participants. To this end, despite their relative privilege as indoor sex workers,[1] many participants in this study were affected by such totalizing and stigmatizing rhetoric.

Divi's and Anu's accounts provide a glimpse into the negative implications of societal perceptions that stigmatize and dehumanize sex workers.

These participants' interactions also highlight how law enforcement practices lean on social tensions in their decision-making process that shapes their actions and behaviors. Divi, an Asian-Canadian massage parlor worker, reflects on an incident when she pursued the police to report a case of robbery by a client. According to Divi, even though she had enough information to identify the perpetrator, the responding officers disregarded her complaint, ignored the thief, and instead started questioning her about her involvement in the industry, making her feel like a criminal:

> One time, I had a problem. This person robbed me. And I called the police. Yeah, I called the police. When the person left, I called my manager's office. And I said, "take this person's picture." And they took the picture right away. From the lobby to the front door, they had pictures from different angles, enough to see what he looked like. And I called 9-1-1, the police came, and I told them "I have these pictures." They didn't go to take it. They were printed out. I asked my manager to print it out. They didn't take [. . .] Even if [sex work] is my business, you can't say someone won't come and rob me. If a person comes to rob me, he's the criminal, not me.

To similar effect, Anu, a South Asian-Canadian independent escort, reflects upon an incident in which she reluctantly reported a brutal sexual assault by a stranger to police:

> It was horrible. [. . .] I was on my way to meet a client, and I was walking, and I got attacked by a stranger. [. . .] I was viciously sexually assaulted by the stranger at gunpoint. [. . .] And then there was that moment of fuck should I, shouldn't I, am I calling the police [. . .] should I really [. . .] this is a stranger attack, he could be lurking anywhere, now other women are at risk. So that really put the, like oh, right. So I called the police. A guy came over, looked at how I was dressed—I was on my way to work, right—looked at how I was dressed. Questioned me like I was completely bullshitting or like "Are you sure that happened?" "Yes, I'm positive." I remember even saying, "I didn't even want to call you. And this is one of the reasons I didn't want to call you." "*What are you doing tonight, where are you going, why are you dressed like that?*" [participant emphasis] Oh, it was absolutely horrible. He must have asked me, I don't know how many times, "Are you sure that's what you want to say in your statement?" It was a horrible experience. I felt like I had done something wrong, that I had to prove myself to them. And then any follow-up I had about that file it was, you know "So you're sure you want to stick to what you said." I couldn't wrap my head around because I'm thinking, what are you trying to get at? Like if it was a client that did that to me that's still no different. So I wasn't even sure. It made no sense to me. I'm trying to think well why, okay, so he's figured it out, I work. But [. . .] how does that have any bearing on my statement of my horrible attack?

In this case, Anu felt that her sex worker identity and her race not only informed the impressions of the responding officer, but that they also affected her credibility as a *real* victim of sexual assault. In the quotation below, Anu reflects upon the moment when the officer nullified her experience with sexual assault and trivialized her pain:

> He [the police officer] kind of made me feel like there's something else going on. So I don't know if he thought I was a trafficked person, I can't say for sure. But the questions, the kind of things he was asking me and the way he was looking at me and kind of talking to me like I'm dumb, even though I speak pretty damn good English, right! I got the impression that he thought I was trying to protect somebody. Whether it be a pimp or [client].

Sexual assault victims in general struggle with establishing their credibility in society and within the criminal justice system (see McGregor et al. 2000; Masse 2004). Gotell (2008) and Randall (2010) argue that societal perceptions of risk management or risk avoidance and responsible and/or rational femininity are deployed within the Canadian judicial process to establish and maintain the boundaries of *good* and *bad* victimhood in sexual assault cases. Within this legal discourse, the *ideal victim* is the benchmark for the respectable sexual citizen (Smart 1985). The idealized sexual citizen "actively manages her behavior to minimize and/or avoid the ever-present risk of sexual violence through her responsible, security-conscious, crime-preventing" practices and actions (Gotell 2008, 879). The ideal and valorized/good victim, "characterized by her chastity and sexual morality, [. . .] is consistent, rational, self-disciplined and blameless" (Gotell 2002, 260).

Gotell (2008) argues that the idealized femininity/womanhood paradoxically establishes "new ways of victim-blaming and also functions as a standard for assessing the credibility of actual complainants. Complainants' behaviours are explicitly measured against the normalized risk-avoiding behaviours of the supposedly 'reasonable woman'" (808) (also see Randall 2010) [original emphasis]. The *ideal* victim undermines "the credibility of women who are seen to deviate too far from stereotypical notions of "authentic" victims and too far from what is assumed to be predictable and "reasonable" victim responses" (Randall 2010, 398) [original emphasis]. In this regard, the typical sex worker, who is often classified as sexually immoral and/or careless and irrational for not recognizing the risks inherent in the sex industry, is not only depicted as failing to behave responsibly and to manage risk effectively, but is also presented as lower class, loose, not credible, and ultimately as an unworthy victim (see Jiwani 2014; Sanders and Soothill 2011; Scoular and O'Neill 2007; Bruckert and Hannem 2013a).

Of course, the contexts in which Divi and Anu interacted with police officers are markedly different. Divi interacted with officers while working indoors in a third-party-managed massage parlor, and Anu was assaulted by a stranger on her way to work. However, the commonality in these stories is that their victimization was not believed, their status as sex workers became their master status (Hughes 1945) and was used to blame them for their own victimization; their experiences of violence, even when horrific, were trivialized or erased. To a great extent, the responding officers' actions and behaviors in these cases can be located with the historical dichotomous classification of victims of prostitution. This classification often identifies non-White sex workers as voluntary victims of prostitution who are not only responsible for their troubles but are also unworthy/undeserving of state protection (Faulkner 2018; Balgamwalla 2016; O'Connell Davidson 2010; Valverde 2008). The intersectionality of these women's identities creates particular impressions for police officers, and subsequent judgments about their experiences. Almodovar (2010) and Williamson et al. (2007) show that when responding to sex workers' complaints of sexual assault, police officers operate under the assumption that no one will believe a sex worker when she claims to be victimized. The normalization of violence inflicted upon sex workers (regardless of their race) distracts police from conducting objective, bias-free investigations to find the perpetrators, as is the case in the police–sex worker interactions outlined above.

The normalization of violence against sex workers serves multiple agendas. For abolitionist groups and law and policy makers, sex workers' experiences of violence let them emphasize the claim that sex work is inherently a risky business (see Farley 2004, 2003). Furthermore, in addition to the shame and stigma, the accusation of self-inflicted violence increases female sex workers' vulnerability, impairs their human rights, and impedes third parties from responding to such incidents (Scambler and Paoli 2008; O'Doherty 2011; Lewis et al. 2005). Socially constructed stereotypes and controlling images of Indigenous women and women-of-color sex workers not only as inherently and pathologically sexually deviant, and thus prone to promiscuity, but also as willing participants in prostitution, invariably help to imply relationships of superiority and inferiority and race-, gender-, and class-based hierarchy/oppressions (see Collins 2000; Ritchie 2017). To this end, law enforcement's reliance on such caricatures justifies their actions to deny sex workers state protection in cases of criminal victimization (Sherman et al. 2015; Krusi et al. 2016, 2014). As a result, many sex workers are reluctant to report crimes to law enforcement. This includes both sex-work-related offenses and other crimes that are not related to their job (Bruckert and Hannem 2013a; Saunders and Kirby 2010–2011; Krusi et al. 2016). These studies identify at least two main reasons: (1) sex workers do not trust law enforcement's willingness to respond to violence perpetrated against sex workers, and (2) sex workers fear that reaching out to police will make a bad situation worse by, for example, criminalizing their partners under sex-work-related laws, outing sex workers' locations of work, and discrediting, insulting, and/or humiliating sex workers.

The final participant account featured in this chapter emphasizes the differential treatment and abuse of power that participants in this study endured. This police–sex worker interaction informs another layer of state-inflicted violence that denies research participants their constitutional right to protection through the process of culturalization of violence they experience (see Razack 1998a). Gladys, a Black independent in-call service provider, reflects on an encounter she had with police officers at a time when she became ill while on vacation with her boyfriend. According to Gladys, the responding officers were not only unsympathetic but also insulted and humiliated her. The tone in which police officers spoke to her left her feeling inferior and disposable. Gladys feels that the responding officers, in this case, entered her hotel room with preconceived suspicions of criminal activity and/or sex-work-related activities:

> I have been in a situation recently where I was in a hotel room, and I became very ill. [. . .] Need to call the ambulance. We gave the hotel's name, and [. . .] cops came first. Before [my boyfriend] called, I said: "straighten up in here." Because something just [in my gut] told me, this might look this way to them, like a spot stray to them. And they came, and I was in extreme pain. The first thing the cops said, "*oh so what's going on here*" [pause] [participant emphasis] you know, [I'm] bent over in pain, and they were snickering to themselves. I was like, "what's the joke." That approach, that's not the approach of, "Are you in pain? Can you tell us what's wrong?" No. "*so what's going on in here*" [participant emphasis] hands in lock, you know. [. . .] I am reading the whole thing just as I feared. He's the John, I am the worker, and a whole lot is going on here.

The unsympathetic reaction to Gladys's pain from the responding officers gestures to the under-protection of minority communities and to the perception that Black communities are prone to criminality. This reaction aims to justify the differential approaches to policing stigmatized and marginalized communities (Razack 1998a; Monture-Angus and Conroy 1995; Jiwani 2002). The process of culturally normalizing violence among racialized and Indigenous populations then justifies police officers' practices of under-protection for women-of-color sex workers who report instances of exploitation and sex trafficking (as defined in Canadian Criminal Code ss. 279.04,[2] and ss. 279.01,[3] respectively) (Raguparan forthcoming).

It is important to note that female sex workers, in general, develop a distrust toward police at an early age. It is often further reinforced by interactions in their personal and professional lives (Sherman et al. 2015). Ultimately, negative encounters with law enforcement also contributed to research participants' mistrust in police officers and officers' ability to serve and protect marginalized populations. The negative experiences of these research participants are consistent with Indigenous sex workers' experiences reported by Krusi et al. (2016). Participants in the Krusi et al. (2016) study said that police officers' continued "denial of their citizenship rights for police protection and legal recourse by virtue of their 'risky' occupation" led to normalizing "their experiences of violence as an inherent part of selling sex," and that seeking police protection felt like experiencing a form of everyday/symbolic violence (1142).

V. CONCLUSION

This chapter explores Indigenous and women-of-color indoor sex workers' interactions with Canadian law enforcement personnel. The contributions of this chapter to the field of sex work studies, race, and intersectionality are twofold. First, this study supports existing literature on the tensions between sex workers, especially street-based sex workers, and police officers. Second, considering the fact that indoor sex workers' interactions with police officers is an understudied area (see Benoit et al. 2016), the lived realities of women-of-color sex workers who work in the indoor sectors fills the existing gap in literature and advances the conversation on women-of-color sex workers' experiences of state violence.

The individual stories of sex workers of color presented in this chapter highlight how at the intersection of race and sex work, women are not able to subvert power relations during their encounters with police officers. Here we see how socially constructed race-, class-, gender-based normative assumptions and discourses have a stronghold and shape policing practices concerning sex workers and the sex industry. Law enforcement's reliance on normative narratives at the intersection of race, gender, and sex work prevents some participants from escaping systemic stigmatization and criminalization through harsh and punitive policing protocols. Furthermore, the intersectional oppression of race, gender, and sexuality also result in raced and gendered forms of violence as punishment for transgressing social norms.

The raced and gendered forms of state violence experienced by participants in this study highlight yet another dimension of abuse of power: police officers' willful ignorance of sex workers of colors' complaints of criminal victimization. As a result, even when participants' victimhood is consistent with hegemonic policy discourse and public opinion, their intersections of race, gender, and sex work deny them the legal classification of victim and the emotional responses they deserve. Police offices' efforts to avoid serving and protecting sex workers and sex workers of color not only violate law enforcement's mandate to serve and protect the public, but they also violate sex workers' constitutional right to safety and protection and thus lead to civic exclusion. To this end, it is clear that the law and policy approach to sex work and race issues on the ground are incoherent and contradictory at best.

NOTES

1. Despite criminalization and the ongoing debate as to whether the industry fully, or in part, engages in the formal and informal economy, many of the indoor sites of the Canadian sex industry actively participate in the local economy in terms of financial investments and profits, human labor, and culture (for indoor sectors' economic participation in the global context, see Gall [2006]; Day [2007, 1996]; Pitcher [2015], Kempadoo [2003]; Kay Hoang [2011]). In this regard both prohibitionists and sex workers' rights advocates have classified the indoor sex industry as an "upscale" or "bourgeois" sector, such that relatively economically privileged women who may classify, or pass, as middle class more frequently operate through indoor sectors such as agencies, clubs, and private referrals (Day 2007; Mahdavi 2010, 2013; Razack 1998b; Bernstein 2007; Kay Hoang 2011).

2. Section 279.04 (Exploitation) states: "For the purposes of sections 279.01 to 279.03, a person exploits another person if they (a) cause them to provide, or offer to provide, labour or a service by engaging in conduct that, in all the circumstances, could reasonably be expected to cause the other person to believe that their safety or the safety of a person known to them would be threatened if they failed to provide, or offer to provide, the labour or service" (Canada 2012, 22).

3. Section 279.01 (Trafficking in persons) states: "Every person who recruits, transports, transfers, receives, holds, conceals or harbours a person, or exercises control, direction or influence over the movements of a person, for the purpose of exploiting them or facilitating their exploitation is guilty of an indictable offence" (Canada 2012, 22).

BIBLIOGRAPHY

Almodovar, Norma Jean. 2010. "The Consequences of Arbitrary and Selective Enforcement of Prostitution Laws." *Wagadu* 8.

Amnesty, International. 2016. *Sex Workers at Risk: A Research Summary on Human Rights Abuses against Sex Workers*. London: Amnesty International.

Anderson, Solanna, Jessica Xi Jia, Vivian Liu, Jill Chattier, Andrea Krüsi, Sarah Allan, Lisa Maher, and Kate Shannon. 2015. "Violence Prevention and Municipal Licensing of Indoor Sex Work Venues in the Greater Vancouver Area: Narratives of Migrant Sex Workers, Managers and Business Owners." *Cult Health Sex* 17 (7): 825–41. doi: 10.1080/13691058.2015.1008046.

Balgamwalla, Sabrina. 2016. "Trafficking in Narratives: Conceptualizing and Recasting Victims, Offenders, and Rescuers in the War on Human Trafficking." *Denver Law Review* 94 (1): 1–41.

Benoit, Cecilia, Michaela Smith, Mikael Jansson, Samantha Magnus, Nadia Ouellet, Chris Atchison, Lauren Casey, Rachel Phillips, Bill Reimer, Dan Reist, and Frances M. Shaver. 2016. "Lack of Confidence in Police Creates a 'Blue Ceiling' for Sex Workers' Safety." *Canadian Public Policy—Analyse De Politiques* 42 (4): 456–68. doi: 10.3138/cpp.2016–006.

Bernstein, E. 2007. "Sex Work for the Middle Classes." *Sexualities* 10 (4): 473–88. doi: 10.1177/1363460707080984.

Bruckert, Chris, and Frédérique Chabot. 2010. "Challenges: Ottawa Area Sex Workers Speak Out." Ottawa: POWER.

Bruckert, Chris, and Stacey Hannem. 2013a. "Rethinking the Prostitution Debates: Transcending Structural Stigma in Systemic Responses to Sex Work." *Canadian Journal of Law and Society/Revue Canadienne Droit et Société* 28 (01): 43–63. doi: 10.1017/cls.2012.2.

Bruckert, Chris, and Stacey Hannem. 2013b. "To Serve and Protect? Structural Stigma, Social Profiling, and the Abuse of Police Power in Ottawa." In *Selling Sex: Experience, Advocacy and Research on Sex Work in Canada*, edited by Emily van der Meulen, Elya M. Durisin and Victoria Love, 297–313. Vancouver: UBC Press.

Buffam, Bonar. 2017. "Racial Accountabilities: The Legal Legibility of Racial State Violence in the Special State's Attorney Report on Police Torture in Chicago." *Cultural Studies* 32 (2): 326–47. doi: 10.1080/09502386.2017.1354043.

Canada, Public Safety. 2012. National Action Plan To Combat Human Trafficking. Ottawa: Public Safety Canada.

Carter, Sarah. 2000. "Categories and Terrains of Exclusion: Constructing the "Indian Women" in the Early Settlement Era in Western Canada." In *Telling Tales: Essays in Western Women's History*, edited by Catherine A. Cavanaugh and Randi R. Warne, 60–81. Vancouver: UBC Press.

Collins, Patricia Hill. 2000. *Black Feminist Thought: Knowledge, Consciousness, and the Politics of Empowerment*. 2nd, rev. 10th anniversary ed. New York; London: Routledge.

Crenshaw, Kimberle. 1991. "Mapping the Margins: Intersectionality, Identity Politics, and Violence against Women of Color." *Stanford Law Review* 43 (6).

Cresswell, Tim. 1996. In Place/Out of Place: Geography, Ideology, and Transgression. Minneapolis: University of Minnesota Press.

Davis, Angela Y. 1998. "Race and Criminalization: Black Americans and Punishment Industry." In *The Angela Y. Davis Reader*, edited by Joy James, 61–73. Malden: Blackwell Publishers.

Day, Sophie. 1996. "The Law and the Market: Rhetorics of Exclusion and Inclusion among London Prostitutes." In *Inside and Outside the Law: Anthropological Studies of Authority and Ambiguity*, edited by Olivia Harris. London; New York: Routledge.

Day, Sophie. 2007. *On the Game: Women and Sex Work*. London: Pluto Press.

Dewey, Susan, and Patty Kelly. 2011. *Policing Pleasure: Sex Work, Policy, and the State in Global Perspective*. New York: New York University Press.

Dewey, Susan, and Tonia St. Germain. 2014. "'It Depends on the Cop'": Street-Based Sex Workers' Perspectives on Police Patrol Officers." *Sexuality Research and Social Policy* 11 (3): 256–70. doi: 10.1007/s13178-014-0163-8.

Doezema, Jo. 2000. "Loose Women or Lost Women? The Re-emergence of the Myth of White Slavery On Contemporary Discourses of Trafficking in Women." *Gender Issues*: 23–50.

Farley, Melissa. 2003. "Prostitution and the Invisibility of Harm." *Women & Therapy* 26 (3).

Farley, Melissa. 2004. "'Bad for the Body, Bad for the Heart'": Prostitution Harms Women Even if Legalized or Decriminalized." *Violence Against Women* 10 (10): 1087–1125. doi: 10.1177/1077801204268607.

Faulkner, Elizabeth A. 2018. "The Victim, the Villain and the Rescuer: The Trafficking of Women and Contemporary Abolition." *Journal of Law, Social Justice and Global Development* (21): 1–15.

Gall, Gregor. 2006. "The Political Economy of the Sex Industry." In *Sex Worker Union Organising: An International Study*, 36–45. New York: Palgrave MacMillan.

Goldberg, David Theo. 2002. *The Racial State*. Malden, MA: Blackwell Publishing.

Goldenberg, S. M., V. Liu, P. Nguyen, J. Chettiar, and K. Shannon. 2015. "International Migration from Non-Endemic Settings as a Protective Factor for Hiv/Sti Risk among Female Sex Workers in Vancouver, Canada." *J Immigr Minor Health* 17 (1): 21–8. doi: 10.1007/s10903-014-0011-1.

Gotell, Lise. 2002. "The Ideal Victim, the Hysterical Complainant, and the Disclosure of Confidential Records: The Implications of the Charter for Sexual Assault Law." *Osgood Hall Law Journal* 40.

Gotell, Lise. 2008. "Rethinking Affirmative Consent in Canadian Sexual Assault Law: Neoliberal Sexual Subjects and Risky Women." *Akron Law Review* 41.

Hubbard, Phil. 2004. "Cleansing the Metropolis: Sex Work and the Politics of Zero Tolerance." *Urban Studies* 41 (9): 1687–1702. doi: 10.1080/0042098042000243101.

Hubbard, Phil, and Teela Sanders. 2003. "Making Space for Sex Work: Female Street Prostitution and the Production of Urban Space." *International Journal of Urban and Regional Research* 27 (1) :75–89.

Hughes, Everett Cherrington. 1945. "Dilemmas and Contradictions of Status." *American Journal of Sociology* 40 (5): 353–59.

Hunt, Sarah. 2010. "Colonial Roots, Contemporary Risk Factors: A Cautionary Exploration of the Domestic Trafficking of Aboriginal Women and Girls in British Columbia, Canada." *Alliance News*, 27–31.

Hunt, Sarah. 2013. "Decolonizing Sex Work: Developing an Intersectional Indigenous Approach." In *Selling Sex: Experience, Advocacy, and Research on Sex Work in Canada*, edited by Emily van der Meulen, Elya M. Durisin, and Victoria Love. Vancouver: UBC Press.

Hunt, Sarah. 2015/2016. "Representing Colonial Violence: Trafficking, Sex Work, and the Violence of Law." *Atlantis* 37.2 (1).

James, Joy. 1996. *Resisting State Violence: Radicalism, Gender, and Race in U.S. Culture*. Minneapolis; London: University of Minnesota Press.

Jiwani, Yasmin. 2002. "The Criminalization of 'Race' and the Racialization of Crime." In *Crimes of Colour: Racialization and the Criminal Justice System in Canada*, edited by W. Chan and K. Mirchandani, 67–86. Peterborough, ON: Broadview Press.

Jiwani, Yasmin. 2006. *Discourse of Denial: Mediations of Race, Gender, and Violence*. Vancouver: UBC Press.

Jiwani, Yasmin. 2014. "Posthumous Rescue: The Shafia Young Women as Worthy Victims." *Girlhood Studies* 7 (1). doi: 10.3167/ghs.2014.070104.

Johnson, Karl. 2004. "Police-Black Community Relations in Postwar Philadelphia: Race and Criminalization in Urban Social Spaces, 1945–1960." *Journal of African American History* 89 (2): 118–34.

Kay Hoang, K. 2011. "'She's Not a Low-Class Dirty Girl!': Sex Work in Ho Chi Minh City, Vietnam." *Journal of Contemporary Ethnography* 40 (4): 367–96. doi: 10.1177/0891241611403481.

Kaye, Julie. 2017. "Settler Colonialism, Sex Work, Criminalization, and Human Trafficking." In *Responding to Human Trafficking: Dispossession, Colonial Violence, and Resistance among Indigenous and Racialized Women*. Toronto: University of Toronto Press.

Kempadoo, Kamala. 2003. "Globalizing Sex Workers' Rights." *Canadian Woman Studies* 22 (3–4).

Kempadoo, Kamala, Nicole McFadyen, Phillip Pilon, Andrea Sterling, and Alex Mackenzie. 2017. "Challenging Trafficking in Canada: Policy Brief." Centre for Feminist Research, York University.

Kraska, Peter B., and Victor E. Kappeler. 1995. "To Serve and Pursue: Exploring Police Sexual Violence against Women." *Justice Quarterly* 12 (1).

Krusi, A., T. Kerr, C. Taylor, T. Rhodes, and K. Shannon. 2016. "'They Won't Change It Back in Their Heads That We're Trash': The Intersection of Sex Work-Related Stigma and Evolving Policing Strategies." *Sociology of Health and Illness* 38 (7): 1137–50. doi: 10.1111/1467-9566.12436.

Krusi, A., K. Pacey, L. Bird, C. Taylor, J. Chettiar, S. Allan, D. Bennett, J. S. Montaner, T. Kerr, and K. Shannon. 2014. "Criminalisation of Clients: Reproducing Vulnerabilities for Violence and Poor Health among Street-Based Sex Workers in Canada—A Qualitative Study." *BMJ Open* 4 (6): e005191. doi: 10.1136/bmjopen-2014-005191.

Lam, Elene. 2016. "Inspection, Policing, and Racism: How Municipal By-Laws Endanger the Lives of Chinese Sex Workers in Toronto." *Canadian Review of Social Policy* 75: 87–112.

Lewis, Jacqueline, Eleanor Maticka-Tyndale, Frances Shaver, and Heather Schramm. 2005. "Managing Risk and Safety on the Job." *Journal of Psychology & Human Sexuality* 17 (1–2): 147–67. doi: 10.1300/J056v17n01_09.

Macdonald, John, Robert Stokes, Greg Ridgeway, and Jack Riley. 2007. "Race, Neighbourhood Context and Perceptions of Injustice by the Police in Cincinnati." *Urban Studies* 44 (13): 2567–85. doi: 10.1080/00420980701558400.

Mahdavi, Pardis. 2010. "Race, Space, Place: Notes on the Racialisation and Spatialisation of Commercial Sex Work in Dubai, UAE." *Cult Health Sex* 12 (8): 943–54. doi: 10.1080/13691058.2010.512393.
Mahdavi, Pardis. 2013. "Privileged Bodies in Pleasure and Leisure Spaces: Sex, Music, and Dance Clubs." In *Geographies of Privilege*, edited by France Winddance Twine and Bradley Gardener. London; New York: Routledge.
Masse, Mélanie. 2004. "Sexual Assault and Offender Conviction Rates." Sexual Assault Network and University of Ottawa—Faculty of Law Pro bono Students Canada.
Maynard, Robyn. 2015. "#Blacksexworkerslivesmatter: White-Washed 'Anti-Slavery' and the Appropriation of Black Suffering." *The Feminist Wire*. Accessed September 28, 2016.
Maynard, Robyn. 2017. *Policing Black Lives: State Violence in Canada from Slavery to the Present*. Winnipeg: Fernwood.
McGregor, Margaret J., Ellen Wiebe, Stephen A. Marion, Cathy Livingstone. 2000. "Why Don't More Women Report Sexual Assault to the Police?" *Canadian Medical Association Journal* 162 (5): 659–60.
Miller, Jody 2002. "Violence and Coercion in Sri Lanka's Commercial Sex Industry: Intersections of Gender, Sexuality, Culture, and the Law." *Violence Against Women* 8 (9): 1044–73.
Monture-Angus, Patricia, and Brenda Conroy. 1995. *Thunder in mySsoul: A Mohawk Woman Speaks*. Halifax, NS: Fernwood.
Moss, Wendy, and Elaine Gardner-O'Toole. 1991. *Aboriginal People: History of Discriminatory Laws*. Edited by Library of Parliament. Research Branch: Government of Canada.
O'Connell Davidson, Julia 2010. "New Slavery, Old Binaries: Human Trafficking and the Borders of 'Freedom.'" *Global Networks* 10 (2): 244–61.
O'Doherty, Tamara. 2011. "Criminalization and Off-Street Sex Work in Canada." *Canadian Journal of Criminology and Criminal Justice* 53 (2): 217–45. doi: 10.3138/cjccj.53.2.217.
Oliveira, A., and K. Murphy. 2014. "Race, Social Identity, and Perceptions of Police Bias." *Race and Justice* 5 (3): 259–77. doi: 10.1177/2153368714562801.
Pitcher, J. 2015. "Sex Work and Modes of Self-Employment in the Informal Economy: Diverse Business Practices and Constraints to Effective Working." *Soc Policy Soc* 14 (1): 113–23. doi: 10.1017/S1474746414000426.
Pound, Roscoe. 1910. "Law in Books and Law in Action." *American Law Review* 44 (12).
Pratt, Geraldine. 2005. "Abandoned Women and Spaces of the Exception." *Antipode* 37 (5).
Raguparan, Menaka. Forthcoming. "'Is It Because I'm Not Young and White with Blue Eyes?': Canadian Police Response to Sex Workers of Colour's Experiences of Exploitation and Trafficking." In *The Race and Coloniality of Anti-Trafficking*, edited by Kamala Kempadoo and Elena Shih. London; New York: Routledge.
Randall, Melanie. 2010. "Sexual Assault Law, Credibility, and "Ideal Victims": Consent, Resistance, and Victim Blaming." *Canadian Journal of Women and the Law* 22 (2): 397–433. doi: 10.3138/cjwl.22.2.397.
Razack, Sherene. 1998a. *Looking White Peopple in the Eye: Gender, Race, and Culture in Courtrooms and Classrooms*. Toronto: University of Toronto Press.
Razack, Sherene. 1998b. "Race, Space, and Prostitution: The Making of the Bourgeois Subject." *Canadian Journal of Women and the Law* 10.
Rhodes, T., M. Simic, S. Baros, L. Platt, and B. Zikic. 2008. "Police Violence and Sexual Risk among Female and Transvestite Sex Workers in Serbia: Qualitative Study." *BMJ* 337: a811. doi: 10.1136/bmj.a811.
Ritchie, Andrea J. 2006. "Law Enforcement Violence against Women of Color." In *Color of Violence: The Incite! Anthology*, edited by In Incite! Women of Color against Violence, 138–56. Boston: South End Press.
Ritchie, Andrea J. 2017. *Invisible No More: Police Violence aganist Black Women and Women of Colour*. Boston: Beacon Press.
Sanders, Teela. 2009. "Controlling the 'Anti Sexual' City: Sexual Citizenship and the Disciplining of Female Street Sex Workers." *Criminology and Criminal Justice* 9 (4): 507–25. doi: 10.1177/1748895809343403.
Sanders, Teela, and K. Soothill. 2011. "The Policing of Pleasure: 'What Kind of Police Service Do We Want?'" *The Police Journal* 84. doi: 10.1358/pojo.2011.84.2.557.

Saunders, Penelope, and Jennifer Kirby. 2010–2011. "Move Along: Community-Based Research into the Poiicing of Sex Work in Washington, D.C." *Social Justice* 37 (1).

Scambler, G. 2007. "Sex Work Stigma: Opportunist Migrants in London." *Sociology* 41 (6): 1079–96. doi: 10.1177/0038038507082316.

Scambler, G., and F. Paoli. 2008. "Health Work, Female Sex Workers and HIV/AIDS: Global and Local Dimensions of Stigma and Deviance as Barriers to Effective Interventions." *Soc Sci Med* 66 (8): 1848–62. doi: 10.1016/j.socscimed.2008.01.002.

Scoular, J., and M. O'Neill. 2007. "Regulating Prostitution: Social Inclusion, Responsibilization and the Politics of Prostitution Reform." *British Journal of Criminology* 47 (5): 764–78. doi: 10.1093/bjc/azm014.

Shannon, Kate, Thomas Kerr, Shari Allinott, Jill Chettiar, Jean Shoveller, and Mark W. Tyndall. 2008. "Social and Structural Violence and Power Relations in Mitigating HIV Rrsk of Drug-Using Women in Survival Sex Work." *Soc Sci Med* 66 (4): 911–21. doi: 10.1016/j.socscimed.2007.11.008.

Sherman, S. G., K. Footer, S. Illangasekare, E. Clark, E. Pearson, and M. R. Decker. 2015. "'What Makes You Think You Have Special Privileges Because You Are a Police Officer?" A Qualitative Exploration of Police's Role in the Risk Environment of Female Sex Workers." *AIDS Care* 27 (4): 473–80. doi: 10.1080/09540121.2014.970504.

Smart, Carol. 1985. "Legal Subjects and Sexual Objects: Ideology, Law and Female Sexuality." In *Women-in-Law: Explorations in Law, Family and Sexualities*, edited by Julia Brophy and Carol Smart, 50–70. London: Routledge & Kegan Paul.

Socias, M. E., K. Deering, M. Horton, P. Nguyen, J. S. Montaner, and K. Shannon. 2015. "Social and Structural Factors Shaping High Rates of Incarceration among Sex Workers in a Canadian Setting." *J Urban Health* 92 (5): 966–79. doi: 10.1007/s11524-015-9977-9.

Stinson, Philip Matthew, John Liederbach, Steven L. Brewer, and Brooke E. Mathna. 2014. "Police Sexual Misconduct." *Criminal Justice Policy Review* 26 (7): 665–90. doi: 10.1177/0887403414526231.

Valverde, Mariana. 2008. *The Age of Light, Soap, and Water: Moral Reform in English Canada, 1885–1925: With a New Introduction*. Toronto: University of Toronto Press.

Weitzer, Ronald, and Steven A. Tuch. 2004. "Race and Perceptions of Police Misconduct." *Social Problems* 51 (3): 305–25.

Williamson, Celia, Lynda Baker, Morris Jenkins, and Terry Cluse-Tolar. 2007. "Police-Prostitute Interactions." *Journal of Progressive Human Services* 18 (2): 15–37. doi: 10.1300/J059v18n02_03.

Williamson, Celia, and Gail Folaron. 2003. "Understanding the Experiences of Street Level Prostitutes." *Qualitative Social Work* 2 (3): 271–87.

Wortley, Scot, and Akwasi Owusu-Bempah. 2009. "Unequal Before the Law: Immigrant and Racial Minority Perceptions of the Canadian Criminal Justice System." *International Migration & Integration* (10). doi: 10.1007/s12134-009-0108-x.

III

Activist Politics of Resistance

Chapter Nine

Intersections of Gender and (In)Justice

Bibi Titi Mohamed and Women's Struggles during and after Independence in Tanzania

Catherine Cymone Fourshey and Marla L. Jaksch

In early June 1963, Bibi Titi Mohamed, president of the Women's Division of the Tanganyika African National Union (TANU), prepared to travel to Washington, DC, on official business. A formidable and undaunted force, she traveled to represent the interests of her fellow Tanganyikans on a leadership grant.[1] In preparation for Mohamed's arrival, Barrington King, a career Foreign Service officer appointed as ambassador to Tanganyika under President Kennedy, sent a memorandum on June 3, 1963 to his colleague, Mr. MacKnight. Though Mohamed remained an important activist and politician for a decade and arrived for purposes of further leadership development, King tried to diminish Mohamed's significance by commenting, "I don't think a sixth-floor meeting is necessary (her English is very poor). I will see her in any case, but I thought you might want to talk to her briefly."[2] As ambassador to Mohamed's country, King had to know the central roles she played politically and socially. King's memo foreshadowed the ways Mohamed would not only be marginalized internationally where she was perhaps little known, but also within her own nation, where she had skillfully mobilized the masses toward independence. Initiated in 1954, TANU, Tanganyika's founding political party, benefited greatly when Mohamed joined in 1955; members began to realize they were deficient with all-male leadership.[3] Despite her importance within and to TANU as an efficacious political activist who ignited the masses to action, Mohamed was ultimately sidelined and then ostracized by male leaders. At her 1969 trial, for example, Mohamed was impuned as disobedient not only politically but also in her married life. Attorney General Mark Bomani tried to discredit Mohamed by insinuating that she caused the dissolution of her marriage by failing to "bow down to your husband."[4] The implication was that she was a problem as a "very tough woman" who was undermining the state with her alternative perspectives. Mohamed's circumstances signaled—and are emblematic of—the in(justices) women in late colonial and independent Tanganyika (later, Tanzania) faced.

This chapter critically examines how gender in(justice) in post-colonial Tanganyika was amplified rather than reduced in a newly emerging nation that aimed to move radically away from a western colonial capitalist model rooted in nineteenth century social and historical constructions of gender. Notwithstanding rhetoric about wanting to build a nation founded in African socialism and equality that included leadership of women, the various men in positions of power failed to realize these goals.[5] This exploration of the case of Bibi Titi Mohamed (1926–2000) employs several theoretical approaches that bridge African feminist platforms and American intersectionality to highlight the complexities and missed opportunities of—and the imagined possibilities for—achieving gender justice.[6]

Bibi Titi Mohamed was one of many women who in a variety of ways contributed energies that brought about Tanzanian independence. She came to represent all women because postcolonial Tanzania replicated the gendered forms of power that dominated the colonial era (1885–1961) and the global political landscape in the Cold War era (1950s–1990s).[7] Women were and remain disproportionately excluded globally from power structures in nation-state politics and global economies of capital. Therefore, women must be more seriously included in discussions of history and politics as they continue to participate and critically animate political and economic discourses and action, even with the broader in(justices) they face. Bibi Titi Mohamed was, in the 1950s and 1960s, a relatively young urban, Muslim woman, who was once widowed, twice divorced, and thrice married. She had minimal formal schooling in a milieu where education was increasingly a critical form of capital for entering national politics. She was among a small cadre of political women in the leadership circle who were not the wife of a male official. At the same time, she owned land and conducted business while raising her child. She lived in a city with a large Asian population that dominated the business world while well-educated African and Anglo men dominated politics. In all of this context, Mohamed was undaunted by her role that included significant and regular travel to rural areas. She moved across the nation in order to use her voice for political action. Was Bibi Titi Mohamed an anomaly, or did she descend from a wide network of women who were both accustomed to carving out spaces of justice for themselves and clear about what their ability and authority was? It is worth considering precolonial examples of women shaping various definitions and strategies of injustice, as they might serve as models for directions that contemporary generations might move in.

Mohamed spent the late 1950s dedicated to the liberation of her nation. Men at the helm of independence found her useful toward that end, giving the impression that they saw her as a part of the inner circle. When she was selected in the early 1960s to travel to the United States on a leadership grant, it seems her role was becoming an obstacle for her challenges to the "justice" and "wisdom" of the male leadership.[8] When she did not fall in line or accept the perspective that men presented, she was ostracized. By the end of the 1960s, Mohamed, who clearly demonstrated herself to be a formidable organizer, was imprisoned. Her experience should not be taken as representative of all women, however. The aim here is hardly to reproduce a heroic narrative of one woman to rival heroic biographies of men. Rather, Mohamed's story reveals the ways in which a more layered approach to nationalist history that examines linkages and intersections provides a far more robust narrative of who was involved.

Considering Mohamed's unique position in the formal structures of Tanganyikan independence combined both with her role as a representation of an undifferentiated mass of ordinary rural and urban women (and men) and her skill as a networker across difference, it is important to critically analyze her work through an intersectional model rather than a heroic model. Applying an intersectional approach to this examination of Mohamed's lived experience not only provides insight into her leadership path but also serves as a gesture toward the many unacknowledged women who contributed to independence and nation building. This focus extends intersectional methodologies and epistemologies to an East African context for what they offer in terms of nuance in the narrative about gender and (in)justice.

With this aim, Kim Miller's work on women and commemorative practices in post-apartheid South Africa asks how historical truth is possible without an account of women's experiences.[9] Miller's simple but incisive question, applied to the exclusion of women from Tanzania's official narrative, reveals the problematic of the nationalist narrative genre. It provides us vignettes of "heroic" individual men and simply leaves us with a partial half story of how independence and nation building unfolded. By investigating the case of Mohamed, one of the many women politically and socially active, yet one of the few women ever mentioned in accounts of Tanzanian state building and politics, this chapter claims the necessity of intersectional approaches. Intersectionality is the key to a more comprehensive understanding of the complexity of in(justice) as it was experienced and instituted historically and what it says about the ability to achieve justice presently and into the future. This examination of Mohamed's work toward national independence and her own personal sovereignty is not meant to champion the heroic biography of leadership. Rather, the aim of this intersectional approach is to advocate an exploration of the diverse and intersectional ways that many contributed to liberation and nation building even when they did not hold a title or have support of official leadership.

We might draw parallels to the life of another coastal East African woman, Shamsha Muhamad Muhashamy, who was a contemporary of Mohamed. A Muslim Swahili woman who lived in Mombasa, Kenya, the British colony bordering British Tanganyika, Muhashamy was born in 1919, just six years before Mohamed came into the world in coastal Tanganyika. Muhashamy narrated her life as one full of lessons about East African women coming of age and involved in politics and activism.[10] She notes of her childhood that "back then children [girls] in our community were not to go out of doors after age five or six."[11] Muhashamy also narrates ample examples of women being trained for leadership in the home by their mothers and often encouraged to break social norms by their fathers. Her life was supposedly remarkable because her father deviated from the norm by enrolling her in school and teaching her to ride a bike.[12] What life histories reveal is that young women were often taught by their families to achieve and seek knowledge beyond the parameters defined as the norm. The idea that women operating in public and political spheres was against societal norms and constraints seems to be less of a reality and more of a perception or aspiration that could produce the kind of patriarchal nationalism some aimed to achieve.

It is not hard to imagine that Mohamed might have reminisced as Muhashamy did when she said, "I watched my mother creating all kinds of organizations. One time we did an organization for *leso*."[13] Between 1942 and 1943, Swahili Kenyans, led by women, boycotted and stopped purchasing when merchants monopolized cloth and caused price inflation of the important and versatile *leso* cloth, also known as *khanga*. The boycott is where Muhashamy notes, "At that time I realized that I had a voice, and I tried, even though I didn't succeed; I have become a leader."[14] She hardly stopped her involvement there; she continued through the nationalist and independence eras (1950s, 1960s, 1970s, and 1980s) to wield authority and influence in politics, from the local to the national level.[15] Muhashamy's life story, rooted in colonial and then independent Kenya, provides some important clues that her contemporary and fellow Muslim woman, Mohamed, was part of a larger eastern African tradition and praxis that actually allowed and encouraged women in a variety of ways to become "energetic organizers."[16] Both Muhashamy and Mohamed narrate how women engaged from an early age in embodied forms of knowledge such as *lelemama*, competitive dance associations that started in Zanzibar and spread to mainland Tanganyika and Kenya and had great social influence. *Lelemama* became a tool of political and social mobilization; the organizations provided women a voice to express their views and provided access to culturally important networks as they matured and came of age. Much like Mohamed, Muhashamy worked not just for her personal interests or women's issues. Both were highly interested in advocating for the needs and aspirations of people in their societies more generally.[17] Men who aspired to political influence in their communities sought the expertise of both Muhashamy and Mohamed to mobilize votes for the goals that men established.[18]

What is clear from Muhashamy's life history is that women could be and were highly influential even without an official political position or office in national or regional state institutions. Local community organizations and town affairs could have as much, if not more, impact than those at the nation-state level. Muhashamy grew up observing her mother leading and organizing family and community.[19] No doubt, Mohamed, though of a different social class, also grew up in eastern Africa watching elder women in her community do the same. It is worth pausing to think about the kinds of leadership women demonstrated and to frame it not as women's organizing, but as women who organized for larger social issues. In that pause, it becomes clear that cutting-edge methodologies are essential if we are to excavate women's societal influences. One such methodological approach is to combine national archival work with an examination of family archives, textile factory records, and personal *khanga* collections and archives. Researchers could examine the stories that *khangas* tell about individual women and their social networks.

The *leso* or *khanga* boycott that Muhashamy and so many others agitated for reveals that women recognized in(justice) and had great power to change the behaviors of traders and companies that went too far in their exploitation and manipulation.[20] The boycott sheds light on the tremendous importance that these cloths held in society.[21] It also provides insight into the importance of cloth prices and availability. This case reveals that examination of written sources alone may well deprive historians of realizing a full picture of who was involved and how these political and social movements evolved. This material item, cloth, that expresses sayings and incorporates culturally significant symbols was an important tool of commentary that women deployed to express their views and to network with each other. The cloth was not exclusively used by women, but East African women have had a particularly savvy ability to use the *leso/khanga* to claim authoritative voice in their communities.[22]

An African feminist intervention that illuminates new dimensions of women's political involvement aims to consider the social organizations, cultural associations, and material items that women produced and regularly used to convey their voice. *Lelemama*, *beni*, *ngoma*, and *khanga* are all critical examples of the important sources that reveal women's actions, raising awareness as political actors, even where written archives fail to record women's involvements. The *khanga* is a political archive, as well as legacy-building tool, and should be viewed as a form of African feminist praxis.

Worn by men in certain contexts, locations, and eras, the *khanga* is a material item predominantly controlled in its daily use by women. It is both communication and art. This relatively inexpensive cloth is ubiquitous and well understood in the popular imagination as a tool of discontent, agitation, and political statement. Though several scholars analyzed its meanings more broadly, it has not been regarded as a significant data source for understanding sites of women's knowledge production, resistance, and authority in the context of independent nation building. It also has hardly been examined as an archive of women's lives and their social-political networks.

Portuguese traders brought *leso* cloth into East Africa's coastal areas in the sixteenth century through a combination of local aesthetics and production in the context of transoceanic trade with Portuguese merchants. A *khanga* is a rectangle of cotton cloth with a standard measurement of five feet long by three feet high. It began as a hand-printed and hand-produced cloth. It became a factory-produced imprinted cloth with colorful designs that included a central motif called *mji* (central portion), a *pindo* (border that is folded for a hem) along all four sides, and a *msemo* (message along the bottom edge). Ordinary women across East Africa embraced the utility and beauty of *khangas* and hence continued to purchase, style, wear, and exchange them over the last two centuries. This type of cloth always comes in identical pairs imprinted with a wide variety of colorful motifs and designs. *Khangas* are typically wrapped as one piece around the waist with the msemo, the saying, positioned at the calves/ankles and squarely below the backside of the wearer, clearly visible to onlookers. The second, matching piece is worn typically over the hair and shoulders. It is worn over other clothing to protect it from grime and dust as women travel through town, on public transport, and while conducting work or household tasks. Often used in other utilitarian ways, *khangas* can be used to craft carrying slings for babies nestled on a back, to bundle a large load of goods, and to form a cushion to stabilize a large or small load of goods resting on the crown of the head. In more contemporary times, it has often been sewn and transformed into clothing and market bags.

Over the course of the twentieth century, as East African colonies pushed and negotiated for independence in the interwar and postwar eras, the *khanga* began to carry greater political weight even as it continued to be viewed as a commodity. Elisabeth Linnebuhr points out that British colonial representatives tried to control *khangas* because they contained messages that could, like a flag, be deployed to mobilize disloyal colonial subjects.[23] The messages of *khangas* were visual, verbal, and proverbial, so their meanings were always multiple.[24] Though they carry literal and transparent meanings that seem to express simple statements, *khanga* sayings typically hold provocative connotations embedded in more banal statements. Ambiguous meanings in the messages deftly employed can serve as a powerful social commentary.[25] The double entendre of the sayings also allows the *khanga* bearer plausible deniability, a chance for the wearer to proclaim innocence if accused of inciting discord. The motifs and words must reinforce each other with cultural codes that make sense and are imbued with layers of meaning. They must also be dynamic to accommodate shifting views, values, social concerns, and aesthetics. Almost exclusively an eastern African consumer goods and cultural item, more than half of mass production takes place abroad in Asia and Europe. These cloths embody cross-cultural interactions. Successful production and sale of *khanga* requires a dialogue among consumers and manufacturers.[26]

Women and girls craft powerful and subversive actions and messages through *khanga*. In addition to wearing a keen and effective message for a given moment, they have also built connections with other women and girls through *khanga* in a variety of ways, from gifting the cloth to collectively purchasing matching *khangas* for associations and events to signify their sodalities. While much of the scholarship on *khanga* has presented broad surveys of the cloth in the formation of identities along the Swahili coast and in its adjacent areas and periphery, several East African scholars have looked at the way women have seized upon it as an important political tool in personal and public domains. East African scholar Elinami Swai describes *khangas*' functioning as a form of "radical aesthetics of double-coding," which occurs when a saying has at least two meanings.[27] Since *khanga* sayings are almost always developed to capture multiple meanings, double coding is a strategy that *khanga* wearers employ to mobilize their message when direct speech is not possible or desirable.[28] Double coding is in this case being used as a way to subvert social norms and conventions through the use of visual speech, moving through social spaces on bodies. Further, Zanzibari feminist scholar Amina A. Issa situates women as central figures in the liberation struggle who used *khanga* as political interventions.[29] Zanzibari women crafted the idea of using the *khanga* as a "weapon of political struggles," and the *khanga* served as a foundational vehicle to raise women's consciousness about the struggle for independence.[30] In terms of serving as inventories and archives of social and political thought, the *khanga* has been used to communicate messages visually and linguistically to disrupt oppressive social orders.

Women's everyday cultural production and the values they aim to foster are embedded in what they say, wear, and do. This is reflected well in the stories that *khangas* reveal. The khanga in figure 9.1 expresses a value placed on unity among Tanzanian women. Through the imagery of motherhood, shared identity, interest, and connection are fostered. At the same time, the very words on the *khanga* claim women's unity as political, social, and economic aspirations.

Resistance is often encoded in personal choices, like clothing, that may be displayed in either the private or public sphere. While the private and public can have very different impacts and ramifications, as Stephanie Newell contends, popular culture, including clothing, can be used to shape and exhibit political and social resistance and self-defined authority. *Khanga* cloth has become a powerful tool for a woman to both create a positionality and to demonstrate her authority as an individual and within a community.

Relatedly, Saida Yahya-Othman argues that *khangas* are not only deeply symbolic of womanhood, they also represent a uniquely female form of communication and resistance.[31] It is important to note that Yahya-Othman does not make this argument from a biologically essentialized position. Rather, she points to modes of communication that women have defined for themselves, and the importance of the *khanga*. While connected to modes of production that women are not usually a part of, it is the meaning women give to the *khanga* that makes it unique and important. Women have made use of *khangas* to make strong statements about their concerns while at the same time avoiding direct conflict which might arise from their individual actions. As Nigerian feminist Obioma Nnameaka grapples with in her description of African "nego-feminism," the *khanga* functions as a clear example of a feminist approach in action.[32]

Figure 9.1. Umoja wa Wanawake wa Tanzania. *Photo Credit:* Marla L. Jaksch.

In the case of *khanga* messages, indirectness as a politeness strategy combined with resistance allows for additional avenues of expression and ways to make one's feelings known to both specific individuals and the community at large. In this way, one can work within and against the constraints placed upon one's life. The *khanga* was deployed in the early 2000s to call for justice by questioning the commitment and actualization of promises made to women during the liberation struggle. Women in the struggle expected leadership to address issues like gender inequalities and oppressions. Yet promises of gender equities remained unfulfilled two generations into the postcolony period. The promises made to women were more than political slogans; rather they were enshrined in the Republic of Tanzania constitution. These *khangas*, through their use of text, color, and imagery, combine the ways that women leveraged their interests during liberation struggles to more explicitly feminist concerns post-independence. In this way, *khangas* serve as another type of historical record. They can also serve as archives of political promises and thoughts that allow for national conversation and education. The messages captured in *khangas* collectively remind people of the past. Also used as a means of shared identity to build solidarity, *khangas* are frequently imprinted with political images and slogans. Like one of the many *khangas* to honor Mohamed, these popular cloths also hold to account those who had forgotten or refused to center women's rights in contemporary political, social, and advocacy work. *Khangas* very often are commissioned to honor nationally known figures whose contributions must be recognized. One *khanga* commemorating Mohamed reveals the endearment and honor expressed in the central motif and an undertone of disapproval for those who might fail to honor her (figure 9.2).

The work of transnational intersectional feminist justice must include consideration of the practices of representation—in terms of equal, fair, and truthful legal, political, and cultural representation. Tanzanian women embody this desire for justice through organizing and the creation and deployment of *khanga* messages in words and images draped across their corporeal form.[33] In this section, we linked the significance of the history and evolution of the *khanga* cloth as a necessary and potent symbolic and political form of representation that women have used throughout the colonial and postcolonial context. These forms counter the dominant archive of pre- and post-liberation leadership that exclusively reveal the experiences of men in museums, archives, and national monuments.

I. BUILDING A NATION OF PEACE AND JUSTICE

Based upon the written and photographic archive, the officially recognized African leadership in Tanganyika (1961–1963) and later, Tanzania (post-

Figure 9.2. Bibi Titi Mohamed khanga: Daima Tutakuenzi, 1926–2000. Title translation: Bibi Titi, we will glorify you forever and always. *Photo Credit:* Marla L. Jaksch.

Zanzibar Revolution in 1964). was exclusively male. This male cohort, led by Julius Kabaranga Nyerere, aimed to produce a new nation that would be the antithesis of the imperialistic colonial state. Although the rhetoric of the early nationalists implied full liberation for all Tanganyikans, which would also assume rights to positions of authority for both men and women. As late as 1967, documents like Nyerere's renowned Azimia la Arusha (Arusha Declaration) clearly called for a society built around the condemnation of all forms of exploitation. Its early declarations used the language of "all Tanganyikans/all citizens," having full access to dignity, respect, livelihoods, and resources. Like other socialist nations in Africa and the world, postcolonial Tanzania in its pan-African and socialist vision and approaches certainly aimed for a new kind of society after colonial rule. Despite proclamations of gender and class equality by nationalists, in a patriarchal context inherited from the colonial state, the socialist imaginings of equality were insufficiently realized. The new nation sought to produce an alternative to the colonial state that honored all individuals and brought greater in(justice); in fact, leaders failed to create justice for at least half of the population.

In many ways, political leadership replicated the injustices that it claimed it sought to eradicate. While race, ethnicity, and social class were addressed in various state policies to produce *umoja* (unity) in the aftermath of colonial rule, nationalist and postcolonial approaches mostly reinforced women's illegibility on the official landscapes of political and social movements and institutions. Policy and practice denied women the possibility of being treated justly, in spite of women's desires and concerted efforts to be recognized. Though they were present and active, women of Tanzania were not written into the political and economic nationalist narrative. The efforts and labors many women exerted were erased as all women were contracted and telescoped into one person's actions; Mohamed became the symbol of all women. To some extent, this is true for men as well; the difference is that men and all Tanzanians came to be embodied by a cohort of men. Though Nyerere stood at the apex, he was not alone on the stage. Once telescoped into the singular form of Mohamed, women could not be seen or read in the historical and political narrative for future generations to understand their centrality. Women were simply illegible as political or nationalist agents. The question becomes why political leadership failed to achieve gender justice even as it grappled more overtly to resolve issues of race, ethnicity, and class.[34]

Regardless of any precolonial equitable practices around gender, after nearly a century of colonial rule, a period when more than half the population—women and youth—were deprived of justice and equality, it proved difficult to eradicate gender injustice.[35] In a global context where binary imaginings of gender pervaded, Tanganyika's independence leaders had a great deal to overcome if they were to achieve freedom and self-determination for all. One conclusion to draw from the evidence is that gender, as a category that determined and conferred privilege, was deeply imbedded in mid-twentieth century Tanganyikan politics. As such, any imagining of gender justice would require tremendous effort to realize and maintain. In fact, gender injustice, rather than justice, was a predictable outcome of the pursuit of a nation-state agenda, itself a patriarchal model whereby imaginings of sovereignty hinged on notions of manhood.[36]

Applying an intersectional lens to the tensions regarding gender in(justice) reveals the ways that women were ultimately deemed insufficient for politics based upon gender as it overlapped with other identity categories. But for women, who experienced both sexism and other forms of oppression, it too often has been a liability and a precondition for their exclusion from politics and leadership. For instance, while the nationalist movement was decidedly masculinist, space was strategically made to include women once it became clear that women in the liberation struggle could result in the positive outcomes TANU leaders sought. However, in post-independence Tanzania, the full inclusion of women meant that not all men would have a seat at the table of power. Ironically, in the context of the socialist underpinnings of the Arusha Declaration and the ideology of *Ujamaa* that undergirded it, a form of elitism combined with sexism excluded women like Mohamed from politics, regardless of their qualifications and earlier work in the independence movement.[37] This did not work in the same ways for men. Though many of the men at the national level of politics came from a more educated elite, for men, being poor and/or undereducated did not result in political exclusion because their gender provided them with the necessary prerequisite for leadership.

II. BIBI TITI MOHAMED: ONE WOMAN REFLECTS MILLIONS

Ambassador King's dismissal of Bibi Titi Mohamed in Washington, DC, demonstrates the contradictions and tensions that existed as Tanganyika achieved independence. On the one hand, Mohamed was sent as a leader on a leadership grant to the United States in the midst of the Cold War. On the other hand, she was viewed as insignificant, diminished by a politics defined through patriarchal in(justice). Mohamed's case illustrates the glaring absence of Tanzanian (and African) women in the national arena as well as the global political landscape. It also reflects how access to authority and credibility was deeply inflected by race, class, and national origins. As a deeper consideration into this Tanzanian example reveals, founding nationalist documents that proclaimed equality and justice for all citizens did not sufficiently map a course for reaching the proclaimed goal. Additionally, such documents and proclamations did not account for the constraints that women faced on account of structural gender inequality. In contrast to issues of race, ethnicity, class, and gender, which were discussed in integrative ways, injustice within Tanzania deepened in the postcolonial era. Official rhetoric did not provide protection or promise justice in the ways outlined to the ideal, imagined subject of the nation. In retrospect, this projected ideal was clearly normatively male.

Mohamed's successful leadership in TANU emerged from her work as an *ngoma* singer.[38] *Ngoma* groups, largely comprising women, were already doing the work of nationalism—providing a sense of community that transcended ethnic, gender, religious, and other identities in Tanganyika. Women's successes as political activists in the context of struggle came with the necessity for women to fight against entrenched colonial, and in some cases, local gender norms. Examples include restrictions on women's movements in the public sphere. Being a part of *ngoma* groups was one socially accepted means around these restrictions. *Ngoma* required members to meet across cultural and social differences. Women often held prominent roles in *ngoma*. The notion of "segregated" living and working spaces was mediated by these critical social networks that fostered integrated social spaces. Regardless of often being identified and represented as universal, the women who made up much of TANU's membership represented both a breadth of divergences and remarkable similarities in marital status, parenthood, and age that shaped their collective agency.

Independence from colonial rule was by far the most pressing goal for Mohamed and the other women fighting to end colonial rule. Many of these women also imagined they would be part of the vision, planning, and building that would take place after independence. Considering that Mohamed, a woman put forward initially as a leader by male TANU members, struggled in the years after independence in her attempts to be part of the leadership, it is no surprise that women more broadly in independent Tanganyika and, later, Tanzania struggled to find a place in national and regional politics. In a less politicized environment in the context of TANU's discourse of equality, the forms of gender inequality, oppression, and in(justice) that emerged were no doubt greatly disappointing.

African feminists, such as Obioma Nnaemka and Oyèrónkẹ́ Oyěwùmí, rightly highlight and critically examine whether universalized notions of human rights are at all useful approaches to rectifying gender in(justices) and whether they actually support or hinder women's rights.[39] The deeper questions are whether and how women are subsumed under the rubric of human rights and how the representations of human rights are portrayed in ways that erase women's particular needs.

III. INDEPENDENCE ENVISIONED THROUGH SOCIAL EQUALITY: A VISION DEFERRED

Mohamed willingly joined the nationalist movement and TANU, whose early membership wisely made use of the energy and skills of this unknown twenty-something woman. Her effect as a political speaker and organizer was highly regarded by all who witnessed her action. Mohamed's poetic and deep knowledge of the Swahili language and metaphor, her ability to speak to everyday people, her use of culturally significant symbols through music, food, and clothes, and perhaps the fact that she was much more a reflection of everyday people than her male counterparts helped her succeed politically.

An analysis of Mohamed's experiences not only reveals how she was able to successfully mobilize, organize, and navigate a complex political landscape, but it also illustrates why her involvement in TANU was essential to the success of the liberation struggle. American scholars, such as Dorothy Hodgson and Susan Geiger, highlight that many of the women involved in the establishment of TANU were religiously Muslim and had minimal formal schooling.[40] As such, they were theoretically restricted by social norms. Yet, in reality, so many women adeptly navigated in and around these restrictions and maneuvered the landscape to participate in politics and nation making in substantial ways. Nevertheless, the social norms and expectations shaped how women were received as they moved through public, social, and political spaces.

It is indeed difficult to measure her contributions fully as no one to date has mapped Mohamed's social network and reach. Several male leaders, from Nyerere to Oscar Kambona noted Mohamed's central role in the level of success and direction of nationalism. Ironically, Kambona noted of Mohamed that "she has already made extensive tours of the Eastern Province and is likely to lead all the women of Tanganyika in a revolution that is without precedent. The present and future [mothers] of Tanganyika have refused to be left behind and are flowing with the current alongside of their men-folk. The problem of the emancipation of women at a later date has, in this way, been disposed of."[41] Women organizers, with Mohamed at their side, managed, in a very short period of time, to recruit thousands to join the cause of liberation. Through these women's efforts, TANU rose from 2,000 members in early 1955 to 40,000 by the end of the same year, and 1,000,000 by 1960, but women's emancipation became a problem in postindependence.[42]

It is critical to acknowledge that in the early postcolony, Mohamed's identity as a younger Muslim woman (aged thirty) was critical in shaping her relationship with President Nyrere, an educated Catholic man three years her senior. Mohamed's challenge to Nyerere's vision or Tanganyika and TANU had a disastrous aftermath in the context of these differences in identity and ideology. In fact, through an intersectional lens, we see how gender, culture, and power informed what she was expected to do and how she was ultimately punished for demanding full citizenship. In the Arusha Declaration, Nyerere guaranteed to "safeguard the inherent dignity of the individual in accordance with the Universal Declaration of Human Rights" and vowed to see "that the Government gives equal rights to all men and women irrespective of race, religion, or status."[43] Nyerere's vision rhetorically supported women's political and economic equality. However, this vision, as it connected to laws that were passed, retained the legacies of colonial power imbalances that had "enhanced the power of men as legal authorities, household 'heads,' political leaders, and property owners."[44] Perhaps Nyerere's earlier move to consolidate all the women's organizations, especially TANU's "women's section," into one national organization—Umoja wa Wanawake wa Tanzania (UWT)—is instructive. In order to promote and support women's interests so they aligned with TANU policies, Nyerere boldly moved to make other women's organizations illegal and therefore directly merged women's participation in women's groups into that of a single nationalist group. This move was a key moment in understanding both Mohamed's erasure and the turbulent gender relations that followed independence. After all, the women's section of TANU was started and run by Mohamed and was decidedly independent and more focused upon women's goals not just those of TANU male leadership. The process of transforming colonial subjects into national citizens was a deeply gendered process that largely denied women the benefits of the independence struggle.

In thinking about belonging to a nation, Patricia McFadden argues that for most newly independent African states, dominant notions of citizenship were largely derived from colonial practices that attached the status of citizenship to maleness and ownership of property. McFadden notes the possibility that anticolonial struggles allowed for a reimagining of the colonial-era paradigms. The contest for independence "provided a unique opportunity for black women to become political and to embark on the path toward citizenship."[45] Women's subjectivities, as self-determining actors who could aspire to become autonomous subjects, with a consciousness of rights and entitlements, might in McFadden's estimation enable women to demand protections and obligations from the state. The assumption of gender justice from the postcolonial state was quite reasonable, considering that nationalists often deployed a rhetoric that put them at the opposite end of the spectrum of the exploitative, patriarchal, and highly racially divided state.

African feminists and feminist scholars of Africa contend that to fully understand the totality of the liberation struggle, it is vital to know how women's knowledge shapes the movements in which they hold active leadership roles.[46] Further, Geiger argued that in fact "Tanganyikan nationalism centered on women activists and their narratives."[47] It is precisely this difference, that women made the core of the movement and Mohamed served as a partner to Nyerere, that makes this case so important and unique to the continent. Mohamed's knowledge was forged from her experience as an everyday citizen with no political voice in the colonial system. She did, however, establish a presence in her local community, where she developed her identity as a political voice for change. She understood the struggles of common people and their desire for meaningful justice in a postcolonial system. It seems that her knowledge of people's desire to gain access to land after being deprived and pushed from land through colonial-era plantation schemes shaped her political convictions. Mohamed's approach created tensions with Nyerere and those who supported him. Still, Mohamed remained committed to advocating for land and business ownership for the lower class. She recognized these components as essential to rural and urban, male and female, old and young Africans' security in a new nation, even if this meant she would be at odds with many in TANU.[48] Nigerian feminist Amina Mama argues that feminism originates in Africa providing clear examples of gender just epistemologies.[49] Yet in eastern Africa, where matrilineages had enough influence to reshape and impact the practice of Abrahamic religions (Christianity and Islam), we must ask how it is that in the transition from colonial rule to nationalist control, women fared so poorly?

Mohamed struggled in the changing landscape of post-independence Tanzania. First, she lost her parliamentary seat in the 1965 elections. This was due in part to changing ideas about who should hold political positions and could be the most effective leader. Significantly, an uneducated woman, even if a well-known former TANU leader, no longer fit this vision politically. Shortly thereafter she was rejected as the UWT's national candidate. She was forced to resign because of her conflicts over property ownership as outlined in the Arusha Declaration—the precursor to the Tanzanian constitution (explored further below) and its leadership code. Mohamed and Nyerere clashed over the principles articulated in the Arusha Declaration.[50] Arguably, what Mohamed expressed is an African feminist epistemology born out of her lived experiences. These standpoints informed the challenges she made to aspects of the founding document and leadership code that, on its surface, argued for equal rights. In its very articulation, however, this document made it *impossible* for women to be free because they could not simultaneously lead and own property based on official policy.

Mohamed's specific challenge to the founding document and to Nyerere's thinking emerged from the differential in effects of the policies on rural and urban populations as well as women and men who may have wished to enter the political arena. The Arusha Declaration (and early articulations of it) forbade members of parliament and cabinet ministers from profiting by renting property they owned. This move had its roots in anticorruption measures. However, due to the life Mohamed inhabited as a single woman, the rule against government officials owning land made it challenging for her to thrive. Moreover, it ensured that she would be removed from TANU party politics. As a Muslim woman involved in politics, she was already breaking with many conventions. Colonial systems in Tanganyika greatly eroded women's authority.[51] Often compounded by religious interpretations, colonial constructs of patriarchy minimized and constrained women's authority and abilities whether Muslim, Christian, or local religious practitioners. Further, while Mohamed was asked to travel across Tanganyika, often as the only woman, she was ridiculed and labeled as "promiscuous." The contradictory expectations and assumptions made successful political leadership a huge challenge.

Nyerere and his supporters deployed a language of justice against Mohamed to depict her as a threat to justice and the nation when she began to challenge some of the policies that the male leadership devised in the sphere of political decision making. She was cast as "treasonous" and worthy of "imprisonment." Yet the question must be asked: Were these accusations unjustly cast, and was their weight compounded by what Adrien Wing referred to as "multiplicative identities"?[52] Mohamed was in many ways an outsider: an "other," as a younger, informally educated woman who dared to challenge male leadership in what became a masculinist and patriarchal nationist circle. Though Nyerere sought to pursue a socialist agenda and espouse equality on all levels, the reality was far more complicated and challenging. Mohamed's case raises interesting issues for understanding how her identity—as a Muslim woman of limited economic means with minimal formal education, living in a socialist, developing postcolony—brought her into contest with the various states she lived through, first the patriarchal colonial state (birth–1961) post-colonial state (1961–1980), and neocolonial (1980–death). Tension arose in her home country when she challenged elements of the Arusha Declaration, which formed the core of the young nation's political identity and larger social and economic policies. Nyerere and his supporters devised what they perceived to be a revolutionary approach to the operation of a nation-state. Yet, with such narrow representation in the cohort, there were certain blind spots in the policies. The educated men inside Nyerere's circle were primarily of the same generation. Though there was some racial, ethnic, and religious diversity, the fact that women of a variety of backgrounds were not included raises questions about how in fact individuals, who were not educated, male, middle-aged, married, urban, Catholic, to name a few of the lenses Nyerere saw through, might perceive and experience the choices made in the Arusha Declaration.

The political elites of TANU certainly regarded their decisions as accounting for the interests of the masses in Tanganyika. In part I of the Arusha Declaration, known as the TANU Creed, the emphasis on the rights of all human beings and all citizens are clearly articulated. While the first section was barely contested, other sections were more controversial, and some contradicted aspects of part I. There was dissent from individuals, like Bibi Titi Mohamed and Oscar Kambona, on elements of part V in the declaration that prohibited TANU leaders, those in politics, from private business and ownership. Also, Mohamed opposed elements of the multiracial vision that Nyerere had for the nation. Mohamed was penalized for her opposition in ways that others, who were men, in the leadership circle were not. The treatment Bibi Titi Mohamed faced raises questions about justice and how justice is imagined and made possible to achieve. A closer look into the mechanisms at work in the conceptualization of justice and rights becomes paramount.

Applying an intersectional lens to the case of Mohamed allows us to see the various ways in which her overlapping identities become an important feature in understanding the rise and fall as a pre- and post-independence leader. Of course, intersectionality is a theoretical, methodological, and analytical framework that is critical for understanding inequality and injustice. First conceptualized by the Combahee River Collective (1979), it was expanded upon and named by Kimberlé Crenshaw, and further expounded upon by Patricia Hill Collins and Sirma Bilge.[53] This framework asserts that oppressions are in fact often based on interlocking and inseparable identities of race, gender, class, sex, and sexuality which are experienced simultaneously. In retrospect, it is important to consider whether Mohamed's multivalent identity as a woman—who was single, younger, Muslim, minimally schooled, and viewing the world through the lens of the disenfranchised—positioned her in a way that meant the educated and well-traveled men, who made up the vast majority of the nationalist leadership, were likely to dismiss her input. Mohamed was not merely discredited; she experienced a great injustice when she was accused of treason, imprisoned, and ostracized by the TANU leadership for over a decade.

Historian Susan Geiger's historical and ethnographic work provides a useful model to better understand nationalism, which also includes the struggles of women. Geiger's research provides a rich contextualization of Bibi Titi Mohamed's leadership in TANU. Her scholarship raised many questions regarding the rise of Mohamed through TANU's ranks. She identifies that while Mohamed is often mentioned as a phenomenon, the dominant official national narrative does not explain the multiple layers and complexities of Mohamed's leadership. For example, the remarkable fact in the 1950s of a twenty-something female singer in widely popular *ngoma* (music, drumming, and dance) groups, "Roho ni Mgeni" (the spirit/heart is a stranger) and "Bomba," (funnel, tap to beat, or excellence) becoming an effective political leader of TANU is hardly explored. Mohamed was, due to stereotypes about her age, profession, background, religion, and gender, an unlikely leader in the final years of colonial rule. Yet she managed to activate her skills and networks to recruit thousands of not only men, but also women, who had long been excluded from politics under colonial rule. Like the name of her music group "Bomba" proclaimed in Kiswahili slang, Mohamed was an individual who exuded "excellence" in all she undertook, including her political organizing and vision. Her acumen, enthusiasm, hard work, and networking drew other women in to become nationalist activists.[54] The in(justice) is that these thousands of individuals are forgotten in memories of Tanzanian history because they are telescoped into the single figure of Bibi Titi Mohamed. At the same time, Mohamed herself was in many ways treated unjustly while alive. Since her death, she has been given minimal credit in the larger narrative of Tanzanian independence and nationalist history. Hence, half the population is not reflected in the nation's imagining of its origins. Mohamed inhabited multiple identities, which allowed her to connect with many. Her different positionality from her male cohort and her own awareness of her intersectional existence allowed her to articulate perspectives different from what the male leadership collectively saw. It is precisely this set of ideas that we are most interested in, as they are questions at the heart of intersectional inquiry.

Mohamed is an important and complicated figure in Tanzanian liberation history. She was so central in Tanzanian independence work from 1955 to 1961 that she stood on the stage on December 9, 1961, with Julius Nyerere, the first president of Tanzania. Yet she lost her seat in parliament by 1965, resigned from TANU two years later in 1967, was on trial for treason by 1969, and was in prison until 1972. She lived a meager existence economically until she regained possession of her home in 1976 which she used as a source of rental income. Then, in the 1980s, the ruling party in Tanzania began to resurrect and redefine her image partially. A decade later, in 1991, the ruling party claimed her and proclaimed her a national heroine. Her history reflects not a linear rise to power, but rather it models a much more circuitous route toward goals that mirror Tanzania's own paths to independence and nation building.

Relatedly, in 1997, Susan Geiger published a seminal body of work on TANU women, with a particular focus on Bibi Titi Mohamed. Since that time little academic attention has been focused on Mohamed or the thousands of women who worked with her or contemporaneously.

The dearth of critical examinations of particular women in the larger processes of independence is emblematic of the in(justice) of gender in the postcolonial Tanzanian context. When the fifty-year commemorations were held between 2011 and 2012 for Tanzanian liberation, very little time and space was dedicated to celebrating the women of the independence era. If recognized at all, they were an addendum to the main workings of, and set apart from, the central core of the liberation struggle. Further, efforts to show the full spectrum of society involved in independence and nation building have been minimal. Whether in efforts of memorialization or historical accounts, officials and scholars have not sustained diverse representations of women in museum displays or scholarly analysis. Oversight of Mohamed rested in the ruling party's view that her story complicated the dominant, official nationalist history of Nyerere's heroic rise to power and success in Tanzania.

Although typically presented as linear and heroic, neither independence movements nor nationalist projects are achieved in such a tidy fashion. This is something that cutting-edge Africanist scholars of the 1990s revealed with their careful ethnographic and historical excavation of women's life histories.[55] What life history reveals is that such endeavors are always the result of overlapping, converging, conflicting, and contested endeavors. Indeed, the narratives of women activists in TANU disrupt the view that liberation happened in uncontested and progressive stages that produced a shared nationalist consciousness borrowed heavily from Western forms and ideals.[56] There were a number of challenges to women receiving just representation for their roles in independence and nation building in Tanzania.

IV. CONCLUSION: TOWARD A TRANSNATIONAL FEMINIST INTERSECTIONAL JUSTICE

In 1963, written records reveal that both Bibi Titi Mohamed and Julius Nyerere visited Washington, DC. As president, Nyerere's visit garnered far more attention than Mohamed's did. Nyerere was illustriously photographed at the White House with President Kennedy and many other dignitaries. Mohamed, given her tremendous efforts to free Tanganyika by mobilizing the people to join TANU's undertaking, evidently did not warrant a sixth-floor visit with officials in Washington.[57] But this discrepancy was about more than just political status; it was also a function of global and national gender in(justices).

In Tanzania, one of the many acts undertaken by the independent government, thus it strove to create unity and to celebrate liberation after independence, was to rename many of the major roads in the city of Dar es Salaam in honor of significant heroes of African liberation history. Bibi Titi Mohamed was identified as sufficiently significant to be recognized. Indeed, she was an important TANU leader, one of the few women among many African men. A road was named in her honor. This recognition of Mohamed is significant for many reasons, including the overall reluctance to acknowledge any individual women as leader or pivotal player in the Tanzanian liberation struggle. This is supported by the fact that so few memorials exist in Tanzania commemorating women in liberation history. However, after Mohamed was imprisoned, the road was renamed with a generic title representing women as a collective, Umoja wa Wanawake wa Tanzania (Union of Women of Tanzania). Not only were her significant contributions folded into a collective, but one street named for a particular woman, who could represent a mass, or one that was literally named after an undifferentiated mass to encompass all women's contributions, was perceived as sufficient. The number of streets and buildings named after Tanzanian and foreign men were in the meantime numerous. On the one hand, this designation is reflective of the larger experience of women in Tanzanian politics. In an unexpected twist, the road was eventually renamed again, as Bibi Titi Mohamed Road, which it remains to the present (see figure 9.3). This occurred in the mid-1980s, during the nation's thirty-year independence celebrations.

Mapping the city and nation reveals that there are interesting ways in which the geography of location names has mirrored the heroic male-centric biography of the nation. Yet, like the cultural spheres that women often

Figure 9.3. Bibi Titi Mohamed Road, Dar es Salaam, Tanzania. *Photo Credit:* Marla L. Jaksch.

deployed to express their messages in music, cloth, dance, and other important political and social formats, the landscape may be another opportunity for rethinking the ways in which the nation has unfolded. Symbolically, Bibi Titi Mohamed Road serves as a critical junction between the city center and the arteries to various neighborhoods; thus, it serves as a well-known landmark and reference point for directions between corridors of Dar es Salaam. Bibi Titi Mohamed was just such a critical figure that networked the leadership and the population intersectionally. She continues to be a symbol of the centrality of women broadly in nation building and the simultaneous in(justices) women face as both central and marginal figures in Tanzanian politics. Intersectional investigations of justice allow us to see the ways in which Mohamed and other women activists saw themselves as political actors. Women had a deep sense of collective agency that shaped Tanzanian history. These women engaged in this work to liberate not only themselves but their daughters, sons, elders, and the many generations to follow.

NOTES

1. Tanganyika formed part of German East Africa from 1885 until 1919. When the Germans lost their colonies at the end of World War I, the colonized territory was placed under British control, though it was officially a mandate under the United Nations until its independence in 1961. Tanganyikans were the people who inhabited the territory. Tanganyika became Tanzania in 1964 when Zanzibar's population led a revolution that called for the joining of the island off the coast of Tanganyika with the mainland. Thus, mainland Tanganyika combined with the islands of Zanzibar and became Tanzania.

2. National Archives RG 59 Box 4, General Records of the Department of State, Bureau of African Affairs, Office of Eastern and Southern African Affairs, College Park, Maryland. Several weeks later President Julius Nyerere visited Washington, DC, an event that was well documented in photos and memos. These can be found in the US National Archives, College Park Maryland.

3. TANU lasted from 1954 to1974, until the Chama cha Mapinduzi (CCM), the Revolutionary Party, emerged.

4. Geiger, *TANU Women*, 183.

5. Julius Nyerere, *Arusha Declaration* written for Tanganyika National Union 1967. See Particularly part 1, the TANU Creed, "Whereas TANU believes: (a) That all human beings are equal and (c) That every citizen is an integral part of the nation and has the right to take an equal part in Government at the local, regional, and national level."

6. Oyèrónkẹ́ Oyěwùmí, *African Women and Feminism: Reflecting on the Politics of Sisterhood* (Trenton, NJ: Africa World Press, 2003).

7. Susan Geiger, Nakanyike Musisi, and Jean Marie Allman, *Women in African Colonial Histories* (Bloomington: Indiana University Press, 2002).

8. National Archives RG 59 Box 4, General Records of the Department of State, Bureau of African Affairs, Office of Eastern and Southern African Affairs, College Park, Maryland. Several weeks later President Julius Nyerere visited Washington, DC, an event that was well documented in photos and memos. These can be found in the US National Archives, College Park Maryland.

9. Kim Miller, "Selective Silence and the Shaping of Public Memory in Post-Apartheid Visual Cutlure: The Case of the Monument to the Women of South Africa." *South African Historical Journal* 63, no. 2 (2011): 295–317.

10. Sarah Mirza and Margaret Strobel (eds.), *Three Swahili Women: Life Histories from Mombasa Kenya* (Bloomington: Indiana University Press, 1989, 110–14; Susan Geiger, "Women in Nationalist Struggle: Tanu Activists in Dar Es Salaam," *International Journal of African Historical Studies* 20, no. 1 (1987): 1–26.

11. Mirza and Strobel, *Three Swahili Women*, 95.

12. Mirza and Strobel, *Three Swahili Women*, 95.

13. Mirza and Strobel, *Three Swahili Women*, 102.

14. Mirza and Strobel, *Three Swahili Women*, 102.

15. Mirza and Strobel, *Three Swahili Women*, 89–115, 139–44.

16. Mirza and Strobel, *Three Swahili Women*, 90.

17. Mirza and Strobel, *Three Swahili Women*, 92.

18. Mirza and Strobel, *Three Swahili Women*, fn. 11, 143; Geiger points to external pressures that may have prompted male leaders of TANU to pull in charismatic women like Bibi Titi Mohamed, in Geiger, "Women in Nationalist Struggle," 1–26.

19. Mtoro bin Mwinyi Bakari, *The Customs of the Swahili People: The Desturi za Waswahili of Mtoro bin Mwinyi Bakari and Other Swahili Persons,* ed. and trans. J. W. T. Allen (Berkeley: University of California Press); Mirza and Strobel, *Three Swahili Women*, 89–115, 139–44.

20. *Leso* were handkerchief-sized cloths in eastern Africa, which date to the sixteenth century. Often sewn together, *leso* could be combined to form the *khanga*, which emerged in the nineteenth century as the larger version of *leso*.

21. Mirza and Strobel, *Three Swahili Women*, 89–115, 139–44.

22. Elinami Veraeli Swai, "Beyond Women's Empowerment in Africa: Exploring Dislocation and Agency," in *Speaking through Fashion: Khanga as Mediator of Women's Knowledge System* (New York: Palgrave Macmillan, 2010), 81–99.

23. Elisabeth Linnebuhr, "Kanga: Popular Cloths with Messages," in *Readings in African Popular Culture*, ed. Werner Graebner (Amsterdam: Rodopi, 1992), 138–41.

24. Fair, Laura. *Pastimes and Politics: Culture, Community, and Identity in Post-Abolition Urban Zanzibar, 1890–1945* (Athens: Ohio University Press, 2001); *Tanzania National Symbols* (Dar Es Salaam: Information Service Division, Office of the Prime Minister and First Vice President), 198u.

25. Rose Marie Beck, "Gender, Innovation and Ambiguity: Speech Prohibitions As a Resource for 'Space to Move,'" *Discourse & Society* 20, no. 5 (2009): 531–53; Mackenzie Moon Ryan, *The Global Reach of a Fashionable Commodity: A Manufacturing and Design History of Kanga Textiles*. PhD diss., University of Florida, 2013; Elinami Veraeli Swai, "Beyond Women's Empowerment in Africa: Exploring Dislocation and Agency," in *Speaking through Fashion: Khanga as Mediator of Women's Knowledge System* (New York: Palgrave Macmillan, 2010), 81–99; T. Troughear, "Khangas Bangles and Baskets," *Kenya Past and Present* 16, no. 1 (1984): 11–19.

26. Chris Spring, "Not Really African? Kanga and Swahili Culture," in *East African Contours: Reviewing Creativity and Visual Culture*, ed. Hassan Arero and Zachary Kingdon (London: Horniman Museum, 2005), 80.

27. Elinami Veraeli Swai. *Beyond Women's Empowerment in Africa: Exploring Dislocation and Agency*. New York: Palgrave Macmillan, 2010), 74.

28. Rose Marie Beck, "Gender, Innovation and Ambiguity, 531–53; Rose Marie Beck, "Texts on Textiles: Proverbiality As Characteristic of Equivocal Communication at the East African Coast (Swahili)," *Journal of African Cultural Studies* 17, no. 2 (2005): 131–60.

29. Amina Issa,"Women, Kanga and Political Movements in Zanzibar, 1958–1964," *JENdA:A Journal of Culture and African Women Studies*, no. 28 (2016).

30. Issa, "Women, Kanga and Political Movements."

31. Yahya-Othman, Saida. "Covering One's Social Back: Politeness among the Swahili," TEXT 14, no. 1 (1994): 141–61.

32. Obioma Nnameka, "Nego Feminism: Theorizing, Practicing, and Pruning Africa's Way," *Signs* 29, no. 2 (2004): 375–85.

33. Nasra M. Hillal, "Khanga: A Medium of Communication among Women," *Sauti ya Siti*, 6 (June 1989): 16–19.

34. Seth Markle, *A Motorcycle on Hell Run: Tanzania, Black Power, and the Uncertain Future of Pan-Africanism, 1964–1974* (East Lansing: Michigan State University Press, 2017).

35. While much of the scholarship to date on authority women held and the strategic power of youth in precolonial Africa is focused on western Africa, there are also numerous allusions to this authority women held in eastern (and other regions) Africa as well. For western Africa, see Onaiwu Ogbomo, *When Men and Women Mattered: A History of Gender Relations among the Owan of Nigeria* (Rochester, NY: University of Rochester Press, 1997); Oyèrónkẹ́ Oyěwùmí, *The Invention of Women: Making an African Sense of Western Gender Discourses* (Minneapolis: University of Minnesota Press, 1997); Flora Edouwaye S. Kaplan (ed.), *Queens, Queen Mothers, Priestesses, and Power: Case Studies in African Gender* (New York: New York Academy of Sciences), 1977. For southern Africa, see Pfarelo Eva Matshidze, "The Role of Makhadzi in Traditional Leadership among the Venda," PhD diss., University of Zululand, 2013; P. E Matshidze and T. P. Mulaudzi "Investigating the Role of Modern Practices on Women's Rites of Passage among the Vhavenda in Vhembe District, Limpopo," *The Oriental Anthropologist: A Bi-Annual International Journal of the Science of Man* 16, no. 2 (2016): 291–302. For eastern Africa, see Paul Bjerk, *Building a Peaceful Nation: Julius Nyerere and the Establishment of Sovereignty in Tanzania, 1960–1964* (New York: Boydell and Brewer, 2015), 101; Rhonda M. Gonzales, *Societies, Religion, and History: Central-East Tanzanians and the World They Created, c. 200 BCE to 1800 CE*. (New York: Columbia University Press, 2009). On youth, see Thomas Burgess, "Imagined Generations: Constructing Youth in Revolutionary Zanzibar," in *Vanguard or Vandals: Youth, Politics, and Conflict in Africa*, ed. J. Abbink and Ineke Van Kessel (Leiden: Brill, 2005).

36. Bjerk, *Building a Peaceful Nation*, 148–49.

37. Marjorie J. Mbilinyi, "Education, Stratification and Sexism in Tanzania: Policy Implications," *African Review* 3, no. 2 (1973: 327–40; Marla L. Jaksch, "Feminist Ujamaa: Transnational Feminist Pedagogies, Community, and Family in East Africa," in *Family, Community, and Higher Education*, ed. T. Jenkins (New York: Routledge, 2013); Van den Berg, "On a Communitarian Ethos, Equality and Human Rights in Africa" *Alternation* 6 no. 1 (1999): 193–212.

38. Geiger, *TANU Women*, 11.

39. Regina M. Rweyemanu, "In Search of Women's Human Rights: How to Capture 'Living' Customary Law in Tanzania" in *Against Neoliberalism: Gender, Democracy and Development*, ed. S. L. Chachage and Marjorie Mblinyi (Dar es Salaam: E & D Ltd., 2004); Obiomo Nnameka, "Nego Feminism: Theorizing, Practicing, and Pruning Africa's Way," *Signs* 29, no. 2 (2004): 375–85; Oyěwùmí, *African Women and Feminism*; O. Oyěwùmí, "Conceptualizing Gender: The Eurocentric Foundations of Feminist Concepts and the Challenge of African Epistemologies." *JeNdA* 2, no. 1 (2002): 1–6.

40. Geiger, *TANU Women*, 42; Dorothy Hodgson, *Gender, Justice, and the Problem of Culture: From Customary Law to Human Rights in Tanzania* (Bloomington: Indiana University Press, 2017).

41. Oscar Kambona, Organizing Secretary-General of TANU, to Fabian Society, October 18, 1955, FCB papers 121; Rhodes House cited in Susan Geiger, "Women in Nationalist Struggle, 1–26.

42. Bjerk, *Building a Peaceful Nation*, 39.

43. Julius Nyerere, "The Arusha Declaration" in *Ujamaa: Essays on Socialism* (London: Cambridge University Press, 1968).

44. Dorothy Hodgson, *Gender, Justice, and the Problem of Culture*.

45. Patricia McFadden, *Becoming Postcolonial: African Women Changing the Meaning of Citizenship* (Meridians: Feminism, Race, Transnationalism, 2005), 5.

46. Amina Mama, "What Does It Mean to Do Feminist Research in African Contexts?" *Feminist Review* 98, supplement 1 (2011): e4–e20.

47. Susan Geiger, "Tanganyikan Nationalism as 'Women's Work': Life Histories, Collective Biography and Changing Historiography," *Journal of African History*, 37, no. 3 (1996): 465–78.

48. J. Dibua and B. Ibhawoh, "Deconstructing Ujamaa: The Legacy of Julius Nyerere in the Quest for Social and Economic Development in Africa," *African Journal of Political Science* 8, no. 3 (2003): 59–83.

49. Mama, "What Does It Mean to Do Feminist Research in African Contexts?"

50. Julius Nyerere, Arusha Declaration, written for Tanganyika National Union 1967; Julius Nyerere, "Good Governance for Africa," October 13, 1998.

51. Rhonda M. Gonzales, Christine Saidi, and Catherine Cymone Fourshey, "The Bantu Matrilineal Belt: Reframing African Women's History," in *Gendering Knowledge in Africa and the African Diaspora*, ed. Toyin Falola Falola and Olajumoke Yacob-Haliso (New York: Routledge, 2017), 19–42; Catherine Cymone Fourshey et al., "Lifting the Loincloth: Reframing the Discourse on Gender, Identity, and Traditions—Strategies to Combat the Lingering Legacies of Spectacles in the Scholarship on East and East Central Africa," *Critique of Anthropology* 36, no. 3 (2016): 302–38.

52. Adrien Wing, "Brief Reflections toward a Multiplicative Theory and Praxis of Being," in *Back to the Drawing Board: African-Canadian Feminism(s)*, ed. Njoki Nathani Wane, Katrina Deliovsky, and Erica Lawson (Toronto: Sumach Press, 2002), 262–72.

53. Combahee River Collective, *The Combahee River Collective Statement: Black Feminist Organizing in the Seventies and Eighties*, 1st ed. (Kitchen Table/Women of Color Press, 1986); Kimberlé Crenshaw "Mapping the Margins: Intersectionality, Identity Politics, and Violence against Women of Color." *Stanford Law Review* 43 no. 6 (1991): 1241–99; Patricia Hill Collins and Sirma Bilge, *Intersectionality* (Cambridge: Polity Press, 2016).

54. Geiger, *TANU Women*, 11.

55. Examples of life histories that reveal the ways all kinds of proceses from abolition of slavery to nationalism are in fact both macro and micro events include: Gracia Clark, *African*

Market Women: Seven Life Stories from Ghana (Bloomington: Indiana University Press, 2010); Marcia Wright, *Strategies of Slaves & Women: Life-Stories from East/central Africa* (New York: Lilian Barber Press, 1993); Belinda Bozzoli and Mmantho Nkotsoe, *Women of Phokeng: Consciousness, Life Strategy, and Migrancy in South Africa, 1900–1983* (Portsmouth, NH: Heinemann, 1991); Landeg White, *Magomero: Portrait of an African Village* (Cambridge: Cambridge University Press, 1987); Marcia Wright, *Strategies of Slaves and Women*, Belinda Bezzoli, Claire C. Robertson, *Sharing the Same Bowl? A Socioeconomic History of Women and Class in Accra, Ghana* (Bloomington: Indiana University Press, 1984).

56. Geiger, *TANU Women*, 15.

57. Nyerere visit July 1963 Folder 2, Box 4 and 5, Department of State. Bureau of African Affairs. Office of Eastern and Southern Africa Record Group 59, A13110G, Tanganyika and Zanzibar 1958–1963, National Archives, College Park, Maryland.

BIBLIOGRAPHY

Bakhari, Ali, Mhd. (2003). "Leadership Succession and Democratization in Tanzania." *Indian Journal of Political Science* 64(1/2): 79–95.

Bjerk, P. (2015). *Building a Peaceful Nation: Julius Nyerere and the Establishment of Sovereignty in Tanzania, 1960–1964*. Woodbridge: Boydell and Brewer.

Clark, G. (2010). *African Market Women: Seven Life Stories from Ghana*. Bloomington: Indiana University Press.

Collins, P. H. (1990). *Black Feminist Thought: Knowledge, Consciousness, and the Politics of Empowerment*. New York: Routledge.

Collins, P. H., and Sirma Bilge (2018). *Intersectionality*. Cambridge, UK: Polity Press.

Combahee River Collective (1986). *The Combahee River Collective Statement: Black Feminist Organizing in the Seventies and Eighties*. First edition. Albany, NY: Kitchen Table/Women of Color Press.

Crenshaw, K. (1989). "Mapping the Margins: Intersectionality, Identity Politics, and Violence against Women of Color." *Stanford Law Review* 43(6): 1241–99.

Decker, A., and G. Baderoon (2018). "African Feminisms: Cartographies for the Twenty-First Century." *Meridians: Feminism, Race, Transnationalism* 17(2): 219–31. https://doi.org/10.1215/15366936-7176384.

Fourshey, C. C., et al. (2016). "Lifting the Loincloth: Reframing the Discourse on Gender, Identity, and Traditions—Strategies to Combat the Lingering Legacies of Spectacles in the Scholarship on East and East Central Africa," *Critique of Anthropology* 36(3): 302–38.

Geiger, S. (1996) "Tanganyikan Nationalism as 'Women's Work': Life Histories, Collective Bibliography and Changing Historiography." *Journal of African History* 37(3): 465–78.

Gieger, S. (1997). *TANU Women: Gender and Culture in the Making of Tanganyikan Nationalism, 1955–1965*. Portsmouth, NH: Heinemann Press.

Geiger, S., and Nakanyike Musisi (2002). *Women in African Colonial Histories*. Bloomington: Indiana University Press.

Gonzales, R., C. Saidi, and C. C. Fourshey. (2017). "The Bantu Matrilineal Belt: Reframing African Women's History." In *Gendering Knowledge in Africa and the African Diaspora*, edited by Toyin Falola Falola and Olajumoke Yacob-Haliso, 19–42. New York: Routledge.

Herr, R. S. (2014). "Reclaiming Third World Feminism: Or Why Transnational Feminism Needs Third World Feminism." *Meridians: Feminism, Race, Transnationalism* 12(1): 1–30. doi:10.2979/meridians.12.1.1.

Hilal, N. M. (1989). "Khanga: A Medium of Communication among Women " *Sauti ya Siti,* 6 (June): 16–19.

Hodgson, D. (2017). *Gender, Justice and the Problem of Culture: From Customary Law to Human Rights in Tanzania*. Bloomington: Indiana University Press.

Issa, Amina A. (2012). "Wedding Ceremonies and Cultural Exchange in an Indian Ocean Port City: The Case of Zanzibar Town." *Social Dynamics* 38(3): 467–78.

Issa, A. A. (2016). "Women, Kanga and Political Movements in Zanzibar, 1958–1964." *JENdA: A Journal of Culture and African Women Studies*, no. 28.

Jaksch, M. L. (2014). "Mapping Differential Geographies: Women's Contributions to the Liberation Struggle in Tanzania." In *Global Perspectives on Gender and Space: Engaging Feminism and Development*, edited by A. M. Oberhauser and I. Johnston-Anumonwo, 138–60. New York: Routledge.

Jaksch, M. L. (2013). "Feminist Ujamaa: Transnational Feminist Pedagogies, Community, and Family in East Africa." In *Family, Community, and Higher Education*, edited by T. Jenkins, 116–31. New York: Routledge.

Lal, Priya (2012). "Self-Reliance and the State: The Multiple Meanings of Development in Early Post-Colonial Tanzania." *Africa: Journal of the International African Institute* 82(2): 212–34.

Lewis, D. (2001). "Introduction: African Feminisms." *Agenda: Empowering Women for Gender Equity* 50, 4–10.

Linnebuhr, E. (1992) "Kanga: Popular Cloths with Messages." In *Readings in African Popular Culture*, edited by Werner Graebner. Amsterdam: Rodopi.

Machava, Benedito (November 2019). "Reeducation Camps, Austerity, and the Carceral Regime in Socialist Mozambique (1974–79)." *Journal of African History* 60(3): 429–55.

Mama, A. (2011). "What Does It Mean to Do Feminist Research in African Contexts?" *Feminist Review* 98(supplement 1): e4–e20.

Markle, S. (2017). *A Motorcycle on Hell Run: Tanzania, Black Power, and the Uncertain Future of Pan-Africanism, 1964–1974*. East Lansing: Michigan State University Press.

Mbilinyi, M. J. (1973) "Education, Stratification and Sexism in Tanzania: Policy Implications." *African Review* 3(2): 327–40.

Mbilinyi, M. (2015). "Transformative Feminism in Tanzania: Animation and Grassroots Women's Struggles for Land and Livelihoods." In *The Oxford Handbook of Transnational Feminist Movements*, edited by R. Baksh and W. Harcourt, 507–30. New York: Oxford University Press.

McFadden, P. (2005). "Becoming Postcolonial: African Women Changing the Meaning of Citizenship." *Meridians: Feminism, Race, Transnationalism* 6(1): 1–22.

Miller, K. (2011). "Selective Silence and the Shaping of Public Memory in Post-Apartheid Visual Culture: The Case of the Monument to the Women of South Africa." *South African Historical Journal* 63(2): 295–317.

Moulidi, Salma. (2011). "Between Law and Culture: Contemplating Rights for Women in Zanzibar." In *Gender and Culture and the Limit of Rights*, edited by D. Hodgson, 32–54. Philadelphia: University of Pennsylvania Press.

Nadar, Sarojini, and Sarasvathie Reddy (2016). "From Instrumentalization to Intellectualization." *Journal of Feminist Studies in Religion* 32(1): 136–42.

Nnameka, O. (2004). "Nego Feminism: Theorizing, Practicing, and Pruning Africa's Way." *Signs* 29(2): 375–85.

Oyěwùmí, O. (2003). *African Women and Feminism: Reflecting on the Politics of Sisterhood*. Trenton, NJ: Africa World Press.

Oyěwùmí. O. (2002). "Conceptualizing Gender: The Eurocentric Foundations of Feminist Concepts and the Challenge of African Epistemologies." *JendA* 2 no. 1.

Saidi C., C. C. Fourshey, R. M. Gonzales (2019). Gender, Authority, and Identity in African History. In *The Palgrave Handbook of African Women's Studies*, edited by O. Yacob-Haliso and T. Falola, 1–17. Cham, UK: Palgrave Macmillan.

Spring, Chris (2005). "Not Really African? Kanga and Swahili Culture." In *East African Contours: Reviewing Creativity and Visual Culture*, edited by Hassan Arero and Zachary Kingdon. London: Horniman Museum.

Swai, Elinami Veraeli (2010). *Beyond Women's Empowerment in Africa: Exploring Dislocation and Agency*. New York: Palgrave Macmillan.

Wing, Adrien, K. (2008). "Women's Rights and Africa's Evolving Landscape: The Women's Protocol of the Banjul Charter." In *Africa: Mapping New Boundaries in International Law*, edited by Jeremy I. Levitt. Oxford: Hart.

Wing, Adrien, K. (2002). "Brief Reflections oward a Multiplicative Theory and Praxis of Being." In *Back to the Drawing Board: African-Canadian Feminism(s)*, edited by Njoki Nathani Wane, Katrina Deliovsky, and Erica Lawson, 262–272. Toronto: Sumach Press.

Wright, M. (1993). *Strategies of Slaves & Women: Life-Stories from East/Central Africa.* New York: Lilian Barber Press.
Yahya-Othman, S. (1994) "Covering One's Social Back: Politeness among the Swahili." *TEXT* 14(1): 141–61.
Yahya-Othman, S. (1997) "If the Cap Fits: Kanga Names and Women's Voice in Swahili Society." *AAP* 51, 135–49.

Chapter Ten

Policing and Place-Making

Trans Persecution and Resilience*

Ava Ladner

On October 8, 2019, the U.S. Supreme Court heard three cases that pertain to workplace discrimination. The three cases, *Bostock v. Clayton*, *Altitude Express v. Zarda*, and *Harris Funeral Homes v. EEOC* all pertain to LGBTQ persons fired from jobs and with their sexuality or identity involved as a focal part of the action. After the court issued its ruling, the matter remained unfinished. In fact, if anything, the appearance of these cases before a Supreme Court that is considered conservative in 2019 brings into focus the ideological divides that exist in this country and the obstacles that many people face with regard to "normative rights." Not to mitigate the importance of the first two cases, the *Harris Funeral Homes* (*HFH*) case is of most concern here. The first two cases deal with cisgender White men who may occupy a certain less-than status because of their homosexual orientation, but they still enjoy more privilege than many others. The *HFH* case, however, problematizes the existence of transgendered persons in the workplace.

Before going any further, it is important to address vocabulary. There are several different distinctions under the T part of LGBTQ. The word "transgender" is the preferred placeholder, but under it are a variety of different classifications of identities that consist of any of the following: transgender, transsexual, transvestite, gender nonconforming, and non-binary. Some even prefer the use of gender queer. It is thus important to recognize that for this discussion, *trans** will be the all-inclusive term. The use of this term works to erase some of the differences that permeate the subject of gender identity in the modern context but allows for a melding of historical views surrounding the topic. That is, to assert that, because the term *transgender* did not come into use until the latter half of the twentieth century, other words have filled its void throughout history, and it is difficult to determine the relation to contemporary definitions.

Another element that is consequential to this topic is that *transgender* did not become a prevalent word in the American lexicon until the late 1990s. Even though Christine Jorgenson entered public stardom in the 1950s as a notable Ex-GI who traveled to Europe for gender reassignment surgery and returned a celebrity, her presence did not shift public dialogue into using the term *transgender*. Indeed, often trans* persons who sought public spaces were considered transvestites and cross-dressers rather than people who may have deeper or constructed identities. The vocabulary, then, is an important aspect of control and one that had been until the 2000s in the hands of the other; rather than gender non-conforming persons being able to determine what they should be called, the powerful structures and people above them established the terms. The word *trans** has then liberated many people, giving them the opportunity to marry their identity with a word that helps to define them more accurately.

To return to the intent of this chapter is to wonder where trans* persons fit in the world and what challenges they face. The overwhelming truth is that trans* people face challenges that present themselves almost constantly and in different environments and forms. As they make up roughly 1 percent of the population (as far as we know), the low number indicates that they are not a collective voice with the power of multitudes.[1] That means many battles are personal and experienced in public. Often, they involve law enforcement, the workplace, family, insurance companies, the state, education, and online forums.

That the challenges that trans* persons face can be all encompassing makes safeguarding their rights a vigilant fight and offers insight to American culture. Angela Davis, the well-known civil rights advocate, speaking at an engagement on the University of Hawai'i campus, stated that taking care of transgender people was of enormous importance, going beyond just the trans* community. The position she espoused was that if we could not take care of such a small percent of the population, how could this country ever hope to take care of anyone else?[2] Her statement gives a bleak look at the prevailing attitude of the country, where trans* persons must fight to prove that they are even worthy of care. Trans* persons are at once ostracized from society and then further subdivided by race and class to challenge further their existence.

The division of race and class, even among trans* persons, is important because Black trans* women are often the ones paying the highest cost of being out, doing so with their lives, but on the whole, trans* persons as a group are attacked, ignored, and ostracized in similar ways. We need not subdivide trans* persons from the start but better establish how their identities are built as a group. To start as trans* is to already be placed into a position outside of normative identity. The concept of intersectionality can be reimagined using what Columbia law professor Kimberlé Crenshaw refers to as "multiple discrimination," a way of seeing that trans* people face discrimination as a given and that there may be additional biases at work.[3] Though differences exist within the trans* community, they do not preclude recognizing that trans* people are all part of one small subgroup, between 0.7 to 3 percent of the United States population, that continually faces discrimination.[4]

Of course, discrimination presents in many forms, be it the workplace, family, society, online, health care, dating, the military, or even internally. What created this atagonistic policing of trans* persons seems to have been established by religious attitudes and practices that have ignored, invalidated, criminalized, and dismissed views of gender and sexuality that challenge heteronormative ideals. Therefore, analyzing an early documented case of trans* elimination helps to better understand the current attitudes. One place that provides historical context to this examination of gender, justice, and intersectionality is to consider a cultural alternative to the hegemonic structures that permeate the United States. Rather than focus on policing and the criminal justice system, this chapter details how trans* persons are denied their places in society, be it historically, socially, or critically and that they face constant pressure to be excludeed. While focusing on Hawai'i and the issues of identity may seem like a peculiar place to argue for the broader issues of trans* identities and justice, what should be made clear is that it is exactly the perfect place to examine the various troubles that challenge trans* persons. In Hawai'i, the māhū were non-binary people of color who could be easily ostracized for their nonconformity. This was true even if their role and talents within society warranted celebration. Christian missionaries were able to inculcate attitudes of negativity toward this small percentage of the people. It served well to move beyond that segment of the population to form exclusive attitudes. It forced māhū into the shadows and the world of sex work. This confused construction extends beyond the islands and is found in other elements of society.

I. HISTORICAL ERASURE

The omission and erasure of trans* lives are not new concepts and in fact are practices extant for centuries. One of the more recognized omissions from history is found in Hawai'i in the form of four large stones situated in Waikiki, a major tourist destination. These boulders are commonly referred to as the "Wizard Stones" but are formally known as the Stones of Life, or Na Pohaku Ola Kapaemāhū a Kapuni. The story that coexists with these stones establishes the rhetoric that is part of the practice of denying the existence of trans* persons, or māhū, in the islands. Thus, trans* persons are removed from the narrative of people who used to be considered, like priests/priestesses and the keepers of culture.

In James Boyd's depiction of the Wizard Stones, the first known written account, the author describes the story behind the stones. In Boyd's narrative, four healers, or wizards, from Tahiti visited the island of O'ahu around 400 AD. The four were Kapaemāhū (the leader), Kinohi, Kahaloa, and Kapuni and were described as "unsexed by nature, and their habits coincided with their feminine appearance although manly in stature and bearing."[5] Such a description aligns with the realization of māhū existence and further establishes their position as people of importance in society. That they were accepted as they were also indicates that the peoples of the island, in general, did not see their identity as problematic. If they had, it stands to reason that they would have been asked to leave the island long before the four Tahitians actually chose to leave.

When the four healers decided that they would leave Hawai'i, they had four large boulders quarried from a nearby area and brought to Waikiki in remembrance of their visit. These stones were blessed and consecrated with the sacrifice of a young priestess—whose bones would later be found under one of the stones—in a ritual that lasted one full-moon phase. Once the healers felt their powers were transferred to the stones, they left and were never seen by the people of Hawai'i again.

This story in many ways seems to be simply a friendly telling of benevolent people who visited the island of O'ahu and were able to bring wellness. The retelling of the tale is more startling, however, because over time the fact that the four Tahitians were māhū has been forgotten or ignored. Though the stones were moved twice before finding their current home near the Pacific Ocean, the story is one that endured revision through the lens of the colonial settlers that brought transphobic and homophobic ideals. The Presbyterian missionaries that began occupying Hawai'i in 1820 did not adopt the Hawaiian's perspective on gender identity or sexuality, instead imposing their beliefs of two genders. Further, coupledom was between those two groups.

The erasure did not happen immediately but over time. As the stones were moved from their original position to another spot in the area and then moved again, the accompanying story became more normative. The stones had originally been all but forgotten, lost among the development, as Hawai'i's native population decreased while the overall population increased. However, in 1905, a newspaper article mentions the stones. Yet the then-owners of the property, Princess Likelike and her husband Samuel Cleghorn, knew only that the peculiar boulders had some sort of religious significance.[6] The missionaries had done well to remove any sense of importance of the stones by lessening the importance of the story, especially one that they might be in conflict with their own religious teachings. In the 1940s, the stones were moved for the construction of a bowling alley. After the condemnation of the bowling alley and the takeover of the area by the City and County of Honolulu, the municipality relocated the boulders and held a dedication ceremony in 1963. The ceremony did not mention the healers' gender identity. The stones found a new home again in 1980, about 50 feet from their previous position on the beach and by a sewer pipe, drawing the ire of local Hawaiians. By the time the stones reached their present home in 1997, the story evolved into one that ignored all notes pertaining to māhū (see figures 10.1 and 10.2).

The story of the stones highlights the work of the missionaries' attempts to dismiss Hawaiian culture and to enforce their views on the people of the islands. The plaque by the stones (figure 10.3) omits the interesting element of gender identity and shows how the 170 years of Christian influence allowed those practices and attitudes to flourish. The narrative surrounding the stones is one that should be celebrated by a culture that had previously honored māhūs but became one that highlighted a newly ingrained disdain. Recognizably, the narrative reflected internalized transphobia and racism. The key is the internalized racism, which is to say that the missionaries cultivated a mindset that acted contrary to the notions of community by

Figure 10.1. The Stones of Life/Na Pohaku Ola Kapaemāhū a Kapuni positioned on Waikiki Beach, Hawai'i. *Photo Credit:* Ava Ladner.

Figure 10.2. The Stones of Life/Na Pohaku Ola Kapaemāhū a Kapuni sit just off busy Kapahulu Ave in Hawai'i. *Photo Credit:* Ava Ladner.

encouraging self-centeredness. This position valued the ideology and behaviors of whiteness, antagonizing cultural traditions.[7] Hence, the aloha spirit of welcoming and befriending that Hawaiians generated toward missionaries is the same attitude that allowed and encouraged new ideas to flourish. Moreover, it inspired Hawaiians to adopt negative views about their culture. The internalized transphobia stands as a byproduct of this racism, as the White colonizers brought with them a binary structure of gender.

This situation is further represented by a Hawai'i law passed in the 1960s, specifically targeting māhū persons. It was during this decade that Honolulu enacted measures that required māhū wahine to wear badges when they were in public. These badges marked the women as men.[8] These efforts were meant to single out the māhūs with violent repercussions, as the police often handled matters violently. Aleandro Zhangellini notes that there were two distinct elements involved with the passage of the badge law. The first was that it "socially stigmatized *māhū* as dangerous bearers of an inauthentic gender identity."[9] Hostility to the māhū wahine involved embarrassing them with the badges they wore. It othered them and defined them as lesser people. "There were also racist undercurrents to the requirement, pitting as it did the

Figure 10.3. The plaque commemorating the "Wizard Stones" or the Stones of Life/Na Pohaku Ola Kapaemāhū a Kapuni. *Photo Credit:* Ava Ladner.

supposedly devious and predatory *māhū* sex-workers (in all likelihood the principle target of the provision, even if this was on its face race- and profession-neutral) to their 'innocent' and 'unsuspecting' customers—the non-Polynesian soldiers or tourists unfamiliar with Hawaiian gender-variance, whom the *māhū* were supposedly intent on deceiving and taking advantage of."[10] This two-pronged assault on the māhū population treated them as criminals and deviants, positioning them outside the normative constraints of society. Forced to work in the world of prostitution, māhū people further developed a negative portrayal. In many ways, this practice adhered to the desires of early missionaries.

When examining how missionaries changed the perception of nonconforming gender persons, Kalaniopua Young, a Hawaiian scholar, asserts that the intolerance placed on māhūs was part of maintaining the settler-colonizing project. Young notes that "Honaleimoana Wong-Kalu, a very well-known and respected māhū wahine, has described the term *māhū* as a place in the middle, a transitory and fluid gender construct that emerges, moves and falls beyond the confines of "male" and female."[11] This position challenges the norms of male and female, the constructed binary scripted on most of society. In the traditional Hawaiian sense, this bifurcation is too simplistic, and māhū allows for different interpretations. It presents the possibility for an individual to make the self as one wants to see oneself. This management of the self brings friction to settler ideals for the islands and is the reason why Young presents the concept of māhū as more comfortable with modern life than the constructed binary.

Moreover, Young sees Janet Mock and Mock's depiction of self as an argument that reasons for the use of māhū. It is instrumental to indicate how indigenous identities are ignored and how they present life beyond their ostensible eradication. The issue that Young sees with Mock pertains to how Mock refers to herself. Mock's journalism career helped to spread awareness of trans* struggles through her own coming-out story in the magazine *Marie Claire* in 2001. This exposure led Mock to become a celebrity over time. Her two memoirs, *Redefining Realness* (2014), a *New York Times* bestseller, and *Surpassing Certainty* (2017), brought her into the social consciousness. She has since appeared on *The Colbert Report*, *Real Time with Bill Maher*, and a number of other shows. She has also produced the HBO documentary *The Trans List* (2016) and then became a writer and producer on the FX show *Pose.* To say that she is one of the more high-profile trans* persons in the United States in the late 2010s would be an understatement. Indeed, she has become one of *the* most prominent voices. Her career is commendable as is her story as an ethnically diverse transgender woman who grew up in Hawai'i. For the most part, she established herself as a notable presence. In many ways, she is a role model of trans* people, succeeding in the world and coming out of the shadows; her genealogical background makes her story more compelling as she is of African American, Portuguese, and Hawaiian descent. It is in a different area of self-identifying that Young sees a problem.Mock states that she is a transgender woman of color. On the surface, such a description is nothing to find offense about. Recognize that she is, in modern lexicon, all of those things. Her varied background allows for such an assertion, but Young sees Mock's depiction of self as entirely troubling. "It is as if going mainstream means that she must negate the Native and participate in the settler-colonial erasure of indigenous terminology." Young's critique aligns with internalized colonialism and indicates how people, who may be proud to call themselves māhū, find trouble in doing so. Further, Young argues, "I think that distancing oneself from the language of these struggles can delegitimize our power not only as Native Hawaiian transwomen, but as transwomen of color. . . . Hawaiian transwomen who are of aboriginal ancestry, are of critical import to the work of prison abolition and a broadly envisioned collective movement for land, life, and self-determination."[12] Young contends that Mock is eschewing the identity of her people and that by adopting a mainstream categorization, Mock is no longer able to speak for the group nor able to help them break free from the constraints that society has placed upon them.

The overall elements of identity, and the problematic components that situate themselves within any construct, remain evident in how Young sees Mock and how Mock sees herself. As both are māhū wahine/trans women, they both argue for their positions and are informed about the difficulties of being trans*. Mock acknowledged her labor as a sex worker during her teenage years in Honolulu's Chinatown. Young stated that she has lived in a tent city in Waianae on the western coast of O'ahu. Both have endured, and both bring the ability to express confidence in how they see themselves. Further, consider how the colonization of Hawai'i led to the term "māhū" becoming pejorative to many and that how dividing people from their culture makes it easier to break their relationship with their land, or in this case 'āina. It is the compounding of the elements of identity, class, and gender that challenges normative ideals that allow this practice to become easier.

II. HISTORICAL NORMATIVITY

While *trans** is a term used here, for many cultures, the term *third gender* applies to those persons outside the common established definitions. Western notions of gender inform the current attitudes toward gender as it stands, with many indigenous or native persons once having attitudes that mirrored those of Hawaiians and māhū.[13] And while it is easy to continue to vilify missionaries or Western paradigms as the reason for the hostility directed toward trans* people, the continued disparaging of trans* or māhū persons has moved into being a cultural practice that is widely accepted.

The ideologies that took shape during the twentieth century have much to do with how we perceive gender and thus determine what is questionable outside of the general constructs. The development of societal statistics works as a method of discovery but also as one of control. As Leibler and Leibler state, most research located statistics as a tool of the state and revealed how the tool is used to invent society, meaning that the constructs of any accumulated statistics are meant to reify established perceptions.[14] For example, by offering only two gender options on a questionnaire, the state is structuring gender to be either one of two things; the same goes for race, occupation, or any other measures where the nation-state is inclined to collect data. This interpretation indicates that it is how things are coded, be it occupation, ethnicity, family, or any of a number of elements that reveal as much about a society as anything else. For a concept like gender, statistics present limited options. If not female, then male is the only other possibility.

This limited world is one that was crafted either with a lack of foresight or an intended simplicity, and possibly both. One way of contemplating society is to consider that gender identity of sexuality were not topics that were categorized prior to the twentieth century, and by recognizing this aspect, a whole world of ideas opens. Academics, like Michel Foucault or George Chauncey have argued that while homosexual relationships have existed forever that they did not find a label until after the industrial revolution.[15] That is not to say that they had no name but, rather, that no standard name existed and that once one was adopted, it became the accepted nomenclature for not only depicting but also ostracizing and hating persons of that ilk. By being named, homosexuality became something identifiable and something that went against what was thought to be normal. Halberstam goes further in this examination by using Foucault and states: "Normativity, we know from Foucault, is a central part of modern power systems, and it works by disciplining complex societies through self-policing mechanisms. In his *History of Sexuality*, Foucault, using the example of the "masturbating child," sees the child body as a place where social expectations are enforced over and against, through and within, whatever expressions of identity and desire may emerge in the oversurveyed and multiply interpreted terrain of childhood.[16] There are a number of aspects of Halberstam's statement that are worth mentioning beginning with the concept that norms are power systems at their base. That discipline comes in the form of self-policing that means that society works in tandem with the state apparatuses to ensure that the norms are kept in line, and often other institutions can help to maintain such a relationship.

In looking at trans* lives, their existence is policed not only through the laws that have denied them access and incarcerated them, but it can also be seen in the efforts of religion. Much as the depiction of māhū and Hawai'i was one based primarily on religious intervention that became the basis for sociocultural practices and attitudes, modern society employs many different institutions to enforce its belief structure. Consider that the term *transgender* did not even exist until 1965, and there is reason to find issue with its deployment and its significance. Dr. John F. Oliven first brought the term to the fore with its use in a medical text to describer persons who go beyond cross-dressing and have longings for surgery. This myopic view is one that conflates the differences between transgender and transsexual, but it also places the term in the gated medical community, its usage meant for clinical use and by highly educated persons. Four years after Oliven coined the term, activist Virginia Prince used *transgenderal* as her descriptor, proclaiming that she was not a transsexual but rather someone that had decided to transition the way she saw fit.[17]

While Prince's efforts sought to claim the word for the queer community, the medical establishment was still the one regulating its existence even if while trying to understand what it meant to be transgender, transvestite, or transsexual, in an attempt to make sense of the various identities and practices that a small subset of society comprised. But the word *transgender* largely fell away, being ignored or forgotten. The Stonewall Riots in 1969 in New York spawned a wave of queer activism, but by the 1980s, transgender persons were overlooked as the AIDS/HIV epidemic decimated the queer community, and the public and overall health focus shifted toward homosexuality. The transgender community, small as it was, fell into the shadow of gay and lesbian rhetoric, meaning that even in their own segment of queerness, they failed to carry the same weight as the other voices in their community. In this ideology, transgender persons rested in a particular nexus, a liminal position to the rest of their queer compatriots while also being constrained and abutting gender and the roles that accompany those performances. Any further identities that rest on top of this difficult position just made life more challenging for those individuals.

III. METHODS OF DISCRIMINATION

On June 25, 2017, Ava Le'Ray Barrin was killed in Athens, Georgia. The terrible news was fraught with a myriad of distressing details, but the obvious one was that Barrin was a trans* woman of color. The story, originally reported by the *Athens Banner-Herald* omitted the fact that Barrin was trans* and "deadnamed" her, choosing to go with her legal name and male pronoun rather than the name she had chosen and how she identified herself.[18] The story, as ugly as it is, highlights the various ways that trans* woman of color endure hostility and violence in both life and after life. The goal here is to analyze why the death of even one trans* woman of color is representative of what many other women face. At the time, Barrin was the fourteenth trans* woman of color to be killed that year, and this segment of society continues to face brutal violence.

The first element that should be addressed is that Barrin was called by her deadname; deadnaming occurs when someone, intentionally or not, refers to a transgender person by the name they used before they transitioned.[19] This practice is hurtful for a number of reasons, but the biggest one deals with not respecting the person being named, an act that invalidates their existence by allowing parameters placed upon them to flourish in the face of someone who is actively trying to construct themselves. Many people who question and confront systems of thought or practice refer to their efforts as "queering the system," that is, disrupting it and allowing for more than just normative binary constructions. Deadnaming is an attempt to make people feel comfortable at the expense of the victim, but there are other elements at play and not the least of them pertains to the costs associated with legal names.

Many trans* persons, regardless of race, lose support when they come out, transition, or emerge. (It is important to include all terms in this description because the nomenclature is shifty and depends on the person and the community.) Families frequently turn away their trans* sons and daughters, leaving them homeless. The National Center for Transgender Equality (NCTE) has stated that trans* persons face difficulties in many aspects of housing, including one in ten having been evicted, one in five has been discriminated against in attempting to find housing, and one in five has been homeless at some point in their lives. In addition, shelters often turn trans* persons away because of their gender nonconformity, finding trouble in properly placing them.[20] Without a home, trans* people frequently lack the support and resources that it takes to handle aspects of their lives, including obtaining proper documentation. But even with support, navigating the legal system to acquire name and gender documents can take time and money. The NCTE U.S. Trans Survey (2015) offers data that illustrate the troubling aspect of documentation, noting that only 11 percent have all identifying documents with their correct name and gender, meaning that their passport, driver's license, birth certificate, and Social Security card were all amended. Furthermore, 30 percent of respondents completed a legal name change, with cost being a notable barrier to adjusting as thirty-four percent of people who were granted a legal name change reported that they had spent over $250, and 11 percent spent over $500. Thirty-five percent (35 percent) of those who did not try to change their legal name did not try because they could not afford it.[21] These documents are ones that cisgender persons take for granted, ones that begin to be handed out at birth and continue to accumulate as part of growing up. For a trans* person, these documents all represent hurdles to being able to identify as desired.

Between the costs associated with altering documents, to the barrier placed by the state, as only nine percent of trans* people in the survey were able to change their birth certificates, becoming one's true self is difficult if not impossible. Again, many people may take for granted the privilege they enjoy without considering how the systems that exist have been built to maintain a status quo. The survey mentioned above notes that "as a result of showing an ID with a name or gender that did not match their gender presentation, 25 percent of people were verbally harassed, 16 percent were denied services or benefits, 9 percent were asked to leave a location or establishment, and 2 percent were assaulted or attacked."[22] In the US, the treatment of minorities has become a notable issue during President Trump's time in office as stories of White Americans telling people of color to go back to where they came from, or to speak English or American when POC use a language other than what is commonly accepted in the US.[23] This hostility has extended to trans* persons that also move about in the country and when those people make headlines the reaction is vicious.

When Tiffany Moore visited a GameStop store in January 2019, she encountered a situation where the store's employee misgendered her several times. The verb "mis-gender" refers to the act of referring to someone using terminology which does not reflect their gender identity.[24] In this respect, misgendering is much like deadnaming in that it references a person's past rather than acknowledging their present. This kind of slight is problematic and destructive, one that invalidates a trans* person's identity, thus putting them in a place of having to reconcile with a past that they may or may not want to address while allowing the power dynamic to be dictated by the individual expressing a lack of care. In this case, Moore responded by becoming infuriated, and her reaction was captured on a cell phone camera that was then posted and joined the viral circus that permeates the news cycles. In the video, Moore can be seen and heard vigorously reacting to the employee, kicking over a display and then storming from the store.

Her actions brought about an unfair public discourse, one that sought to disrespect, condemn, celebrate, challenge, support, and ridicule. An article like the one posted on Yahoo! allows for reactions from all kinds and amassed over 14,000 comments.[25] While the queer community constructed an online form of solidarity with Moore, the online vitriol focused on Moore's incensed reaction, finding permission in being able to mock everything about her but especially her claims of being a woman. Without even bothering to check the coverage on any of the right-wing sites, one can already imagine that narrative that basically calls Moore a man and then decides to use the tired argument that if a person was born with male genitalia that the person is a male. While some people may see pronouns and names as something that is of little consequence, that they are free to dismiss how a person wants to be called, this denigration serves as an example of the microaggressions that evince themselves against trans* persons that then fester and grow into the larger issues of violence. These interactions all showcase how the balance of power rests with the comfort of being traditionally male or female rather than recognizing modern possibilities. If a simple transaction like visiting a store is problematic, consider then the difficulty in dating, employment, or going to the bathroom, or dealing with criminal justice system.

Anything involving the criminal justice system is a moment of concern for a trans* person and it begins the moment that any contact is made with the police. The system has not kept up with the changing of the times and continues to adhere to attitudes and practices that were ostensibly established during the Eisenhower administration. Humor aside, the police have yet to adjust their ways of dealing with trans* persons. As seen with Barrin's murder, being misgendered and deadnamed is one of the most obvious problems, one that serves to denigrate the victim while allowing the perpetrator to enjoy a peculiar amount of leeway, and that is because the police are complicit in treating trans* people horribly. The police bring with them both expectations and prejudices about the trans* community, and one that relates to how Hawai'i saw intolerance spread which is by either locating or assuming that trans* people are involved in the sex trade.[26] Thus, law enforcement frequently approaches them with suspicion or hostility. Many trans* women have been forced to work in the sex trade as an only form of available employment, but this fact should not encourage the police to treat all trans* persons as being in that line of work. In addition, the power bias that exists when addressing sex work is problematic—mainly because the majority of the blame is placed on the individual seeking to make money from sex rather than the desires and fetishization fueling the need to keep trans* persons in a specific locale, and notably away from affluent areas.

Incarceration, of course, is a part of this narrative and has two elements that traumatize a trans* person at the onset. The first has to do with how law enforcement sees transgressions (pardon the word choice), that anything outside of acceptable or approved behavior is worthy of punishment. This concept can best be seen in how law enforcement may ignore a person's choice of identity—even with the proper documentation. For instance, in January 2019, Linda Dominguez of false personation or knowingly misrepresenting her identity; even though Dominguez had legally changed her name, the police felt that her representation of self was a falsehood.[27] This belief then shifts to law enforcement believing such an idea which encourages deadnaming and misgendering; making the whole experience a very real hell. The efforts of the police position themselves as the model of behavior for incarceration.

Trans* persons face a difficult time in jail or prison, which is an understatement, as they are plagued by abuse from both other inmates and the staff of the prison. The United States Transgender Survey 2015 (USTS) found, transgender people are ten times as likely to be sexually assaulted by their fellow inmates and five times as likely to be sexually assaulted by staff.[28] Eric A. Stanley and Nat Smith compiled a book that addresses the relationship between trans* lives and the law and how people resist the structures that bind them.[29] While the scholarly attention is necessary, the NCTE took a practical approach and crafted the report "Failing to Protect and Serve: Police Department Policies Towards Transgender People," which examined the relationship between the police and trans* persons, noting that 58 percent are unwilling to call police because of their identity.[30] The contentious relationship between law enforcement and trans* people does not end with the brutality by the police, or the violence that they face in prison but also manifests itself in the courtroom.

One of the troubling concepts that has infiltrated crimes against trans* people is that a trans* person deserved violence. A prominent example of this strategy accompanied the murder of Jennifer Laude, a Filipina trans* woman who died at the hands of Scott Pemberton, a nineteen-year-old U.S. marine who was on leave in the Philippines. This story offers a layered perspective on the denigration and negativity surrounding trans* lives. Laude, was a twenty-six-year-old, who was engaged to a German person out of the country at the time. Laude met Pemberton in a disco and chose to leave with him, going to a nearby hotel for sex in what is believed to be a transaction for sex. About thirty minutes later, Pemberton had gone, and Laude's body was found in the bathroom, asphyxiated. The ensuing trial brought forth simmering U.S.-Filipino relations, but the focus was on Laude and what she represented.[31] Laude, as the U.S. government argued was, a troubled person because of her trans* identity, and more problematically, a prostitute.

One of the first tactics employed to disparage Laude was to position her as a sex worker. This position would not be uncommon in the Philippines, especially in Olongapo Bay, where the options for work are minimal for a trans* woman. In fact, Laude's status as a sex worker was an open secret. It was one that most people in the area knew about, and one that she shared with many other trans* women.[32] The tactic of focusing on Laude's exploits in sex work can be regarded as a way of trying to indicate that Laude's life was of lesser value, that sex workers do not occupy the same place as people with so-called normative careers. That Laude was a woman of color and Pemberton a White U.S. marine inevitably placed the U.S. soldier in a position of power and even more so when the U.S. government gave him full support at his trial. What makes Laude's murder even more frustrating is the defense strategy employed.

Pemberton's lawyer used a tactic that has become more prevalent in the past decade, one that essentially blames the victim for the crime. What Pemberton said on the stand was that he had been with Laude but that he did not kill her outright, that he did so in self-defense when he found out that Laude was transgender.[33] The idea is that Pemberton grew so alarmed when he discovered that Laude was trans*, after believing her to be cisgender, that the "false" representation of herself caused him to respond violently, thereby killing her. This tactic is an evolution of the homophobic panic response, that when confronted with a homosexual, an unsuspecting heterosexual can justify their actions through panic. In this case, Laude's death is the result of trans* panic.[34] While Laude enjoyed the privilege of being able to pass—move through spaces without being noticed for being trans*—the acknowledged assumption is that in that area, one can assume that there is a strong chance that a sex worker might be trans*. Of course, making such a statement is full of folly because when the situation was separated into its core elements, whether Laude is trans* or not should not matter; her life matters regardless. The attempt to give Pemberton permission to murder Laude through a panic defense is downright disgusting, but it is a tactic that has become increasingly common in assaults against queer people.[35] Pemberton was found guilty of homicide but not murder and sentenced to six to ten years in jail, a conclusion that feels rather disappointing. The Laude case accentuates another element of the intersections of being trans* and notions of justice, and that is how trans* bodies are employed as a fetish.

IV. FETISH

The construct of seeing trans* persons as a fetish is one that rests with the categorization of bodies existing outside the White heteronormative gaze. Thus, it is not just trans* bodies that are fetishized but especially bodies of color. The terminology is often meant offensively, much like calling a trans* person a "tranny" places them in the state of being the other and having their identity crafted by a group other than themselves that focuses on one particular identifier.[36] Trans* scholar C. Riley Snorton posited that Black bodies were established as a fetish early in the Republic's formation. This occurred especially through the lens of medical practitioners, who considered Black bodies, especially those of Black women, to be different and also a curiosity.[37] This attitude extended to Asian bodies as they became a part of U.S. culture, especially in the mid-nineteenth century. The response to the accompanying "Yellow Peril" was regarded by two methods of subjugation: violence toward and creation of the highly sexualized female Asian body.[38] The latter provides a template for viewing trans* women as a fetish, by hypersexualizing Asian women and limiting further elements of identity. The extreme limit of this is that it was possible to order one through the mail. Haualani asserts that this unequal power structure maintains hegemonic themes: romance, commodification, oppositional images and inoculation, and euphemizing, and racist ideology. These various groups endured the traumatic experiences of being other, and these same processes were projected onto trans* bodies.

The combination of trans* bodies and fetishization often existed in reference to the self. Magnus Hirschfeld, a German medical doctor and queer activist, was one of the first to offer a thorough examination of the division between bodies and fetish. He detailed how male-bodied persons that sought to wear women's clothes were described by the medical community as engaging in a fetishistic practice, and one that was framed as inherently bad or troubling. As the *Diagnostic and Statistical Manual of Mental Disorders* (*DSM*) evolved, so have attitudes toward transvestites and other trans* persons, as these behaviors are regarded as conditions rather than as syndromes to be corrected. Thus, being trans* often accompanied negative inward beliefs that created negative self-images and senses of self-worth. This reality facilitated manipulation by the hegemony. With such a frustrated existence, it is no wonder that trans* people were often pushed to the periphery of society or forced into sex work or to hide their identities. To create a shift in the status quo requires the possibility of fulfilling existence, that moving from the periphery requires seeing and believing in what seems impossible, that trans* lives can exist outside of these limiting constructs.

One of the earliest and best examples of seeing the potential of living fulfilling lives came with the documentary *Paris Is Burning* (1991), which provided a new way for trans* persons to see and construct their world, especially those outside of city centers. The film provides a glimpse into the world of drag, trans* lives and ball culture and predominantly features trans* women of color. This film was the first to treat trans* persons as strong, vibrant people, an incarnation of resilience that has come to life in the margin of society.[39] Rather than being limited by their position in the world, the community in *Paris* thrives in the face of oppression. Ramón Rivera-Servera argues that this space is where queer persons establish a place of safety and community and provides the benefit of shielding participants from violence: law enforcement, or otherwise.[40] But, as a film, it opens audiences eyes to a new space where queerness and trans* persons exist, even if some have argued that the film is a fetishistic venture into the world of trans* people.[41] As trans* people began to assert more of a presence in society, pop culture followed. A song like "Lola" (1971) by the Kinks presages Lou Reed's "Walk on the Wild Side," with both depicting moments of trans* queerness. The problem with the two songs is that they are narrations about trans* people rather than songs from that perspective. This difficulty manifested itself in film. A film like *Boys Don't Cry* (1999), a biographical drama about the murder of trans* man Brandon Teena, brought attention to the serious issue of violence perpetrated against trans* persons. However, in the film, the character Teena is played by Hilary Swank, a cisgender straight woman. Swank's performance earned her an Oscar, but it also brought awareness to the aspect of cisgender people playing trans* persons, an issue that is made more problematic when trans* actors do, in fact, exist. Having trans* persons appear in films and on television increases their visibility and, with it, a broader acceptance in society, even if that change is slow.

Films bring with them many elements, but one of the key elements is that they are a money-making endeavor, and filmmakers argue that casting cisgender persons will bring a better return on investment. For example, in the film *Anything* (2018), cisgender male actor Matt Bomer was cast as the trans* character because the filmmakers felt they had a better chance of getting financing with Bomer in the lead rather than a trans* actress.[42] The prevailing thought is that films or shows need identifiable actors to make money, and trans* persons do not make the cut. There has, however, been a shift in the late 2010s, one filled with trans* persons being focal points of production. The prominent example is the reality show *I Am Jazz* (2015–present). It follows the life of trans* woman Jazz Jennings from her early teenage years through her gender confirmation surgery. Netflix produced the show *Sense 8* (2015–2018), which had the Wachowski sisters, both trans* women and of *The Matrix* (1999) fame, and features a trans* woman in a starring role; the Chilean film, *A Fantastic Woman* (2017), starring trans* woman Daniela Vega (which won the Oscar for Best Foreign Picture at the ninetieth Academy Awards), which followed a grieving trans* woman who is confronted by her lover's family when he dies; perhaps the best media representation can be found with the show *Pose* (2018–present).

Pose, created by Ryan Murphy, centers on the ballroom culture that was presented in *Paris Is Burning* and features trans* women of color, notably MJ Rodriguez and Indya Moore, in starring roles. The show freely acknowledges the place of trans* persons on the periphery, depicting scenes about sex work or the difficulty of employment or featuring transphobia enacted on the characters. While these stories are told with deft seriousness *Pose* also highlights the resilience of their community and how queer persons thrive. What has added legitimacy to the production is that Janet Mock, previously mentioned, is both a writer and director of the show, meaning that the stories are shaped by lived experiences in the trans* community. The efforts of this show represent what queer scholar Mia Mingu avowed, specifically, that we must shift from a politic of desirability and beauty to a politic of ugly and magnificence. This shift would move us closer to bodies that disrupt.[43] It is possible to see trans* bodies as both beautiful and repulsive, that they need not conform. And the disruption is what brings about the necessary change to see trans* persons as people worthy of the same rights and privileges as anyone else.

V. AUTHOR'S NOTE

As a White trans* woman, I enjoy elements of privilege in comparison to my trans* sisters of color. I attended universities and worked to make a career as an academic. Nevertheless, I too face challenges. I may or may not "pass," depending on who is deciding the criteria which singles me out in a crowd. The fear of losing my insurance has wrapped itself around me like a boa constrictor at times. The job market is unforgiving for everyone but provides a real challenge for me. Eating at restaurants is always difficult because of the looks/sneers that often surround any outing. I was born in Pennsylvania, but I call Hawai'i my home. I know that I am an outsider, but I also feel comfortable because of the island's more welcoming attitude toward trans* people. I mention all of this to note that I face many of the issues mentioned, as does anyone else who is trans*—that the current structures, even when trying to include, can still leave us feeling ostracized.

Things may be getting better, but there is still a long way to go. I feel wonder and love for the next generations who are dismissive of the cultural norms that shaped society for the past few centuries. I give thanks to those who fought for a better world before me. I end with one anecdote: while sitting in the clinic in Honolulu, waiting for my estradiol (synthetic estrogen) shot, a māhū wahine and I started talking. We asked each other what we did for a living, and I told her that I was currently working toward my PhD. I said this with a sense of shame, feeling bad about my privileged position when she was working as a flight attendant. She responded by saying, "Yasss! We need trans people to be professors and at the college." She knew that rather than leaving anyone behind, every time a trans* person moves into new areas, they carry others with them.

NOTES

1. Andrew R, Flores, Jody L. Herman, Gary J. Gates, and Taylor N. T. Brown. "How Many Adults Identify as Transgender in the United States?" *Williams Institute UCLA School of Law*, June 2016, 13.
2. Author notes. Angela Davis spoke at the UH Campus in the spring of 2018 as part of the Daniel K. Inouye series.
3. Crenshaw, Kimberle. "Demarginalizing the Intersection of Race and Sex: A Black Feminist Critique of Antidiscrimination Doctrine, Feminist Theory and Antiracist Politics." *University of Chicago Legal Forum* 1989, no. 1 (December 7, 2015). https://chicagounbound.uchicago.edu/uclf/vol1989/iss1/8.
4. Human Rights Campaign, "Understanding the Transgender Community." Human Rights Campaign. Accessed October 24, 2019. https://www.hrc.org/resources/understanding-the-transgender-community/.
5. "Boyd, James H. 1907. 'Tradition of the Wizard Stones Ka-Pae-Mahu.' *Hawaiian Almanac and Annual,* Ed. Thomas Thrum."
6. "Sacrificial Stones Idols and Skeleton—Relics of a Barbarian Past Uncovered." *Pacific Commercial Advertiser*, February 23, 1905, 1.
7. Rice, Julian. "'It Was Their Own Fault for Being Intractable': Internalized Racism and Wounded Knee." *American Indian Quarterly* 22, no. 1/2 (1998): 63–82.
8. Matzner, Andrew. *O Au No Keia: Voices from Hawai'i's Mahu and Transgender Communities*. Xlibris Corporation, 2001.
9. Zanghellini, Aleardo. "Sodomy Laws and Gender Variance in Tahiti and Hawai'i." *Laws* 2, no. 2 (June 2013): 51–68. https://doi.org/10.3390/laws2020051.
10. Zanghellini, Aleardo. "Sodomy Laws and Gender Variance in Tahiti and Hawai'i." *Laws* 2, no. 2 (June 2013): 51–68. https://doi.org/10.3390/laws2020051.
11. Kalaniopua Young, in Tourmaline, Eric A. Stanley, and Johanna Burton, eds. *Trap Door: Trans Cultural Production and the Politics of Visibilty*. Critical Anthologies in Art and Culture. Cambridge, Massachusetts: MIT Press, 2017, is referring to Wilson, Joe, and Dean Hamer. *Kumu Hina*. Passion River, 2015.
12. Ibid.
13. Hollimon, Sandra E. "Third Gender." In *The International Encyclopedia of Human Sexuality*, 1355–1404. American Cancer Society, 2015. https://doi.org/10.1002/9781118896877.wbiehs509. Simple overview with links to sources that delve further into how third-gender people populated native cultures.
14. Leibler, Anat E., and Anat Leibler. "Statisticians' Ambition: Governmentality, Modernity and National Legibility." *Israel Studies* 9, no. 2 (2004): 121–49.
15. Chauncey, George. *Gay New York Gender, Urban Culture, and the Makings of the Gay Male World, 1890-1940*. New York: Basic Books, 1994. Foucault, Michel. *The History of Sexuality: An Introduction.* New York: Vintage Books, 1990. http://hdl.handle.net/2027/heb.00516.

16. Halberstam, Judith. *Trans*: A Quick and Quirky Account of Gender Variability*. Oakland: University of California Press, 2018.

17. "What Does the Word 'Transgender' Mean?" them. Accessed October 28, 2019. https://www.them.us/story/inqueery-transgender.

18. Human Rights Campaign. "HRC Mourns Ava Le'Ray Barrin, Trans Woman Killed in Georgia." Human Rights Campaign. Accessed November 5, 2019. https://www.hrc.org/blog/hrc-mourns-ava-leray-barrin-trans-woman-killed-in-georgia/.

19. Clements, K. C. "Deadnaming: What Is It and Why Is It Harmful?" Healthline. Accessed November 5, 2019. https://www.healthline.com/health/transgender/deadnaming.

20. NCTE. "Housing & Homelessness." National Center for Transgender Equality. Accessed November 5, 2019. https://transequality.org/issues/housing-homelessness.

21. NCTE. "2015 U.S. Trans Survey." 2015 U.S. Trans Survey. Accessed November 6, 2019. http://www.ustranssurvey.org/reports.

22. Ibid.

23. Mezzofiore, Gianluca. "People's Experiences of Being Told to 'Go Back to Where You Came From.'" CNN. Accessed November 20, 2019. https://www.cnn.com/2019/07/15/us/go-back-where-you-came-from-trnd/index.html.

24. Gratton, Chantal. "Resisting the Gender Binary: The Use of (ING) in the Construction of Non-Binary Transgender Identities." *University of Pennsylvania Working Papers in Linguistics* 22, no. 2 (December 1, 2016). https://repository.upenn.edu/pwpl/vo22/iss2/7.

25. Parker, Maggie. "Trans Woman Explains Why She Cursed at Gamestop Cashier in Viral Video: 'It Was Blatant and Malicious Hate.'" Accessed November 6, 2019. https://www.yahoo.com/lifestyle/trans-woman-explains-cursed-gamestop-cashier-viral-video-blatant-malicious-hate-162919129.html.

26. Whitford, Emma. "When Walking While Trans Is a Crime." *The Cut*, January 31, 2018. https://www.thecut.com/2018/01/when-walking-while-trans-is-a-crime.html.

27. NBC News. "Transgender Woman Sues NYPD Officers Over 'False Personation' Arrest." Accessed November 6, 2019. https://www.nbcnews.com/feature/nbc-out/transgender-woman-sues-nypd-officers-over-false-personation-arrest-n962236.

28. NCTE. "Police, Jails & Prisons." National Center for Transgender Equality. Accessed November 6, 2019. https://transequality.org/issues/police-jails-prisons.

29. Stanley, Eric A., and Nat Smith, eds. *Captive Genders: Trans Embodiment and the Prison Industrial Complex*. Oakland, CA: AK Press, 2011.

30. National Center for Transgender Equality. "Failing to Protect & Serve: Police Department Policies Towards Trans People," May 6, 2019. https://transequality.org/issues/resources/failing-to-protect-and-serve-police-department-policies-towards-transgender-people.

31. Talusan, Meredith. "The Aftermath of a Marine's Conviction in the Death of A Philippine Trans Woman." Accessed October 24, 2019. https://www.buzzfeednews.com/article/meredithtalusan/the-aftermath-of-jennifer-laude-and-joseph-scott-pemberton.

32. Raval, P. J. "Call Her Ganda (2018)." Accessed July 28, 2019. https://www.imdb.com/title/tt7288562/.

33. Diebel, Matthew. "U.S. Marine Found Guilty of Killing Transgender Filipino." Accessed October 7, 2019. https://www.usatoday.com/story/news/world/2015/12/01/marine-guilty-transgender-filipino-killing/76597936/.

34. The National LGBT Bar Association. "LGBTQ+ Panic Defense." *The National LGBT Bar Association* (blog). Accessed November 5, 2019. https://lgbtbar.org/programs/advocacy/gay-trans-panic-defense/.

35. The National LGBT Bar Association. "LGBTQ+ Panic Defense." *The National LGBT Bar Association* (blog). Accessed November 5, 2019. https://lgbtbar.org/programs/advocacy/gay-trans-panic-defense/.

36. "Identity Formation and the Processes of 'Othering': Unraveling Sexual Threads—ProQuest." Accessed October 24, 2019. https://search.proquest.com/openview/773cd83ad36af0bbf974963be489de7c/1?pq-origsite=gscholar&cbl=2031152.

37. Snorton, C. Riley. *Black on Both Sides: A Racial History of Trans Identity*. Minneapolis: University of Minnesota Press, 2017.

38. Halualani, Rona Tamiko. "The Intersecting Hegemonic Discourses of an Asian Mail-Order Bride Catalog: Pilipina 'Oriental Butterfly' Dolls for Sale." *Women's Studies in Communication* 18, no. 1 (April 1, 1995): 45–64. https://doi.org/10.1080/07491409.1995.11089787.

39. Singh, Anneliese A., Danica G. Hays, and Laurel S. Watson. "Strength in the Face of Adversity: Resilience Strategies of Transgender Individuals." *Journal of Counseling & Development* 89, no. 1 (2011): 20–27. https://doi.org/10.1002/j.1556-6678.2011.tb00057.x.

40. Rivera-Servera, Ramón H. *Performing Queer Latinidad: Dance, Sexuality, Politics*. Triangulations: Lesbian/Gay/Queer Theater/Drama/Performance. Ann Arbor: University of Michigan Press, 2012.

41. Lodge, Guy. "Boys Don't Cry at 20: In Praise of the Divisive Transgender Drama | Film | the Guardian." Accessed November 24, 2019. https://www.theguardian.com/film/2019/oct/22/boys-dont-cry-at-20-in-praise-of-the-divisive-transgender-drama.

42. Romano, Nick. "How Matt Bomer's Role in 'Anything' Sparked a Controversy and a Conversation." EW.com. Accessed November 24, 2019. https://ew.com/movies/2018/05/11/anything-matt-bomer-controversy/.

43. Mingus, Mia. "Moving Toward the Ugly: A Politic Beyond Desirability." *Leaving Evidence* (blog), August 22, 2011. https://leavingevidence.wordpress.com/2011/08/22/moving-toward-the-ugly-a-politic-beyond-desirability/.

BIBLIOGRAPHY

"ACLU Says It Will Sue NC If Transgender Inmate Isn't Moved." *Raleigh News & Observer*. Accessed November 6, 2019. https://www.newsobserver.com/news/state/north-carolina/article227119669.html.

Adair, Cassius. "Bathrooms and Beyond: Expanding a Pedagogy of Access in Trans/Disability Studies." *TSQ: Transgender Studies Quarterly* 2, no. 3 (August 2015): 464–68. https://doi.org/10.1215/23289252-2926428.

"A Startling Look at How Cops Mistreat Trans People." VICE. Accessed November 6, 2019. https://www.vice.com/en_us/article/wjvnw9/police-department-policies-toward-transgender-people.

Bakshi, Sandeep, Suhraiya Jivraj, and Silvia Posocco, eds. *Decolonizing Sexualities*. Oxford: Counterpress, 2016.

Boyd, James H. 1907. "Tradition of the Wizard Stones Ka-Pae-Mahu." *Hawaiian Almanac and Annual*, edited by Thomas Thrum. Accessed October 22, 2019. https://www.google.com/search?q=Boyd%2C+James+H.+1907.+%E2%80%9CTradition+of+the+Wizard+Stones+Ka-Pae-Mahu.%E2%80%9D+Hawaiian+Almanac+and+Annual%2C+ed.+Thomas+Thrum.&oq=Boyd%2C+James+H.+1907.+%E2%80%9CTradition+of+the+Wizard+Stones+Ka-Pae-Mahu.%E2%80%9D+Hawaiian+Almanac+and+Annual%2C+ed.+Thomas+Thrum.&aqs=chrome..69i57.777j0j1&sourceid=chrome&ie=UTF-8.

Clements, K. C. "Deadnaming: What Is It and Why Is It Harmful?" Healthline. Accessed November 5, 2019. https://www.healthline.com/health/transgender/deadnaming.

Clements-Nolle, Kristen, Rani Marx, and Mitchell Katz. "Attempted Suicide among Transgender Persons: The Influence of Gender-Based Discrimination and Victimization." *Journal of Homosexuality* 51, no. 3 (October 11, 2006): 53–69. https://doi.org/10.1300/J082v51n03_04.

Crenshaw, Kimberle. "Demarginalizing the Intersection of Race and Sex: A Black Feminist Critique of Antidiscrimination Doctrine, Feminist Theory and Antiracist Politics." *University of Chicago Legal Forum* 1989, no. 1 (December 7, 2015). https://chicagounbound.uchicago.edu/uclf/vol1989/iss1/8.

Diebel, Matthew. "U.S. Marine Found Guilty of Killing Transgender Filipino." Accessed October 7, 2019. https://www.usatoday.com/story/news/world/2015/12/01/marine-guilty-transgender-filipino-killing/76597936/.

Duran, Antonio, and Z. Nicolazzo. "Exploring the Ways Trans* Collegians Navigate Academic, Romantic, and Social Relationships." *Journal of College Student Development* 58, no. 4 (2017): 526–44. https://doi.org/10.1353/csd.2017.0041.

Edison, Avery. "I'm Trans and on Tinder, but I Am Not a Fetish for Your Sexual Bucket List." *Guardian*." Accessed November 7, 2019. https://www.theguardian.com/commentisfree/2014/dec/12/trans-tinder-sexual-bucket-list.

Ellison, Treva, Kai M. Green, Matt Richardson, and C. Riley Snorton. "We Got Issues: Toward a Black Trans*/Studies." *TSQ: Transgender Studies Quarterly* 4, no. 2 (May 2017): 162–69. https://doi.org/10.1215/23289252-3814949.

Flores, Andrew R, Jody L. Herman, Gary J. Gates, and Taylor N. T. Brown. "How Many Adults Identify As Transgender in the United States?" *Williams Institute UCLA School of Law*. June 2016, 13.

Gratton, Chantal. "Resisting the Gender Binary: The Use of (ING) in the Construction of Non-Binary Transgender Identities." *University of Pennsylvania Working Papers in Linguistics* 22, no. 2 (December 1, 2016). https://repository.upenn.edu/pwpl/vol22/iss2/7.

Haas, Ann, Phillip Rodgers, and Jody Herman. "Suicide Attempts among Transgender and Gender Non-Conforming Adults: Finding of the National Transgender Discrimination Survey." American Foundation for Suicide Foundation, 2014. https://doi.org/10.13140/RG.2.1.4639.4641.

Halberstam, Judith. *Trans*: A Quick and Quirky Account of Gender Variability*. Oakland: University of California Press, 2018.

Halualani, Rona Tamiko. "The Intersecting Hegemonic Discourses of an Asian Mail-Order Bride Catalog: Pilipina 'Oriental Butterfly' Dolls for Sale." *Women's Studies in Communication* 18, no. 1 (April 1, 1995): 45–64. https://doi.org/10.1080/07491409.1995.11089787.

Hollimon, Sandra E. "Third Gender." In *The International Encyclopedia of Human Sexuality*, 1355–1404. American Cancer Society, 2015. https://doi.org/10.1002/9781118896877.wbiehs509.

Human Rights Campaign. "HRC Mourns Ava Le'Ray Barrin, Trans Woman Killed in Georgia." Human Rights Campaign. Accessed November 5, 2019. https://www.hrc.org/blog/hrc-mourns-ava-leray-barrin-trans-woman-killed-in-georgia/.

———. "Understanding the Transgender Community." Human Rights Campaign. Accessed October 24, 2019. https://www.hrc.org/resources/understanding-the-transgender-community/.

"Identity Formation and the Processes of 'Othering': Unraveling Sexual Threads." ProQuest. Accessed November 24, 2019. https://search.proquest.com/openview/773cd83ad36af0bbf974963be489de7c/1?pq-origsite=gscholar&cbl=2031152.

"Kapaemāhū." Wikipedia, August 19, 2019. https://en.wikipedia.org/w/index.php?title=Kapaem%C4%81h%C5%AB&oldid=911527078.

Leibler, Anat E., and Anat Leibler. "Statisticians' Ambition: Governmentality, Modernity and National Legibility." *Israel Studies* 9, no. 2 (2004): 121–49.

"LGBT Demographics of the United States." Wikipedia, October 24, 2019. https://en.wikipedia.org/w/index.php?title=LGBT_demographics_of_the_United_States&oldid=922877769.

Leyva, Marizol, with Michelle Ruiz. "Marizol Leyva: 'I Refuse to Be Someone I'm Not.'" *Cosmopolitan*, December 2, 2015. https://www.cosmopolitan.com/sex-love/a49285/mariol-leyva-interview/.

Lodge, Guy. "Boys Don't Cry at 20: In Praise of the Divisive Transgender Drama." *Guardian*. Accessed November 24, 2019. https://www.theguardian.com/film/2019/oct/22/boys-dont-cry-at-20-in-praise-of-the-divisive-transgender-drama.

Matzner, Andrew. *O Au No Keia: Voices from Hawai'i's Mahu and Transgender Communities*. Xlibris Corporation, 2001.

Messman, Jenna B., and Leigh A. Leslie. "Transgender College Students: Academic Resilience and Striving to Cope in the Face of Marginalized Health." *Journal of American College Health*, April 19, 2018, 1–13. https://doi.org/10.1080/07448481.2018.1465060.

Meyerowitz, Joanne J, (Joanne Jay), and American Council of Learned Societies. *How Sex Changed a History of Transsexuality in the United States*. Cambridge, MA: Harvard University Press, 2004.

Mezzofiore, Gianluca. “People’s Experiences of Being Told to ‘Go Back to Where You Came From.’” CNN. Accessed November 20, 2019. https://www.cnn.com/2019/07/15/us/go-back-where-you-came-from-trnd/index.html.

Mingus, MIa. “Moving toward the Ugly: A Politic Beyond Desirability.” *Leaving Evidence* (blog), August 22, 2011. https://leavingevidence.wordpress.com/2011/08/22/moving-toward-the-ugly-a-politic-beyond-desirability/.

Minkowitz, Donna. “How I Broke, and Botched, the Brandon Teena Story.” *Village Voice* (blog), June 20, 2018. https://www.villagevoice.com/2018/06/20/how-i-broke-and-botched-the-brandon-teena-story/.

Mogul, Joey L, Andrea J. Ritchie, and Kay Whitlock. *Queer (in)Justice: The Criminalization of LGBT People in the United States*. Boston; Enfield, CT: Beacon Publishers Group, 2012.

National Center for Transgender Equality. “Failing to Protect & Serve: Police Department Policies Towards Trans People,” May 6, 2019. https://transequality.org/issues/resources/failing-to-protect-and-serve-police-department-policies-towards-transgender-people.

National LGBT Bar Association. “LGBTQ+ Panic Defense.” *National LGBT Bar Association* (blog). Accessed November 5, 2019. https://lgbtbar.org/programs/advocacy/gay-trans-panic-defense/.

NBC News. “Transgender Woman Sues NYPD Officers over ‘False Personation’ Arrest.” Accessed November 6, 2019. https://www.nbcnews.com/feature/nbc-out/transgender-woman-sues-nypd-officers-over-false-personation-arrest-n962236.

NCTE. “2015 U.S. Trans Survey.” NCTE. Accessed November 6, 2019. http://www.ustranssurvey.org/reports.

———. “Housing & Homelessness.” National Center for Transgender Equality. Accessed November 5, 2019. https://transequality.org/issues/housing-homelessness.

———. “Police, Jails & Prisons.” National Center for Transgender Equality. Accessed November 6, 2019. https://transequality.org/issues/police-jails-prisons.

Nuttbrock, Larry, Sel Hwahng, Walter Bockting, Andrew Rosenblum, Mona Mason, Monica Macri, and Jeffrey Becker. “Psychiatric Impact of Gender-Related Abuse across the Life Course of Male-to-Female Transgender Persons.” *Journal of Sex Research* 47, no. 1 (January 22, 2010): 12–23. https://doi.org/10.1080/00224490903062258.

Parker, Maggie. “Trans Woman Explains Why She Cursed at Gamestop Cashier in Viral Video: ‘It Was Blatant and Malicious Hate.’” Accessed November 6, 2019. https://www.yahoo.com/lifestyle/trans-woman-explains-cursed-gamestop-cashier-viral-video-blatant-malicious-hate-162919129.html.

Pflum, Samantha R., Rylan J. Testa, Kimberly F. Balsam, Peter B. Goldblum, and Bruce Bongar. “Social Support, Trans Community Connectedness, and Mental Health Symptoms among Transgender and Gender Nonconforming Adults.” *Psychology of Sexual Orientation and Gender Diversity* 2, no. 3 (2015): 281–86. https://doi.org/10.1037/sgd0000122.

Pluralist. “WATCH: Trans Beefcake Who Rampaged Through GameStop Drops Must-Hear Rap Single.” Pluralist. February 19, 2019. https://pluralist.com/transgender-gamestop-saratonin-tiffany-moore/.

Pryor, Jonathan T. “Out in the Classroom: Transgender Student Experiences at a Large Public University.” *Journal of College Student Development* 56, no. 5 (2015): 440–55. https://doi.org/10.1353/csd.2015.0044.

Raun, Tobias. “Interview with Blogger/Vlogger FinnTheInficible.” *TSQ: Transgender Studies Quarterly* 5, no. 2 (May 1, 2018): 281–89. https://doi.org/10.1215/23289252-4348722.

Raval, P. J. “Call Her Ganda (2018).” IMBD. Accessed November 7, 2019. https://www.imdb.com/title/tt7288562/.

“Review: ‘Call Her Ganda’ Explores the Murder of a Transgender Woman.” *New York Times*. Accessed November 5, 2019. https://www.nytimes.com/2018/09/20/movies/call-her-ganda-review.html.

Rice, Julian. “‘It Was Their Own Fault for Being Intractable’: Internalized Racism and Wounded Knee.” *American Indian Quarterly* 22, no. 1/2 (1998): 63–82.

Rivera-Servera, Ramón H. *Performing Queer Latinidad: Dance, Sexuality, Politics*. Triangulations: Lesbian/Gay/Queer Theater/Drama/Performance. Ann Arbor: University of Michigan Press, 2012.

Romano, Nick. "How Matt Bomer's Role in 'Anything' Sparked a Controversy and a Conversation." EW.com. Accessed November 24, 2019. https://ew.com/movies/2018/05/11/anything-matt-bomer-controversy/.

Singh, Anneliese A., Danica G. Hays, and Laurel S. Watson. "Strength in the Face of Adversity: Resilience Strategies of Transgender Individuals." *Journal of Counseling & Development* 89, no. 1 (2011): 20–27. https://doi.org/10.1002/j.1556-6678.2011.tb00057.x.

Singh, Anneliese A., and Vel S. McKleroy. "'Just Getting out of Bed Is a Revolutionary Act': The Resilience of Transgender People of Color Who Have Survived Traumatic Life Events." *Traumatology* 17, no. 2 (2011): 34–44. https://doi.org/10.1177/1534765610369261.

Snorton, C. Riley. *Black on Both Sides: A Racial History of Trans Identity*. Minneapolis: University of Minnesota Press, 2017.

Spencer, Leland G. *Transgender Communication Studies—Histories, Trends, and Trajectories*. Lanham, MD: Lexington, 2016.

Stanley, Eric A., and Nat Smith, eds. *Captive Genders: Trans Embodiment and the Prison Industrial Complex*. Oakland, CA: AK Press, 2011.

Stryker, Susan, and Stephen Whittle, eds. *The Transgender Studies Reader*. New York: Routledge, 2006.

Talusan, Meredith. "The Aftermath of a Marine's Conviction in the Death of a Philippine Trans Woman." Buzzfeed. Accessed October 24, 2019. https://www.buzzfeednews.com/article/meredithtalusan/the-aftermath-of-jennifer-laude-and-joseph-scott-pemberton.

Tourmaline, Eric A. Stanley, and Johanna Burton, eds. *Trap Door: Trans Cultural Production and the Politics of Visibilty*. Critical Anthologies in Art and Culture. Cambridge, MA: MIT Press, 2017.

"Trans Women and Femmes Speak Out about Being Fetishized." them. Accessed November 7, 2019. https://www.them.us/story/trans-women-femmes-fetishization.

"USTS Full Report—FINAL 1.6.17.Pdf." Accessed November 6, 2019. http://www.transequality.org/sites/default/files/docs/usts/USTS%20Full%20Report%20-%20FINAL%201.6.17.pdf.

Waiton, Stuart. "Transgender Fetish Is a Truly Shameful Modern Invention," November 27, 2017, sec. Scotland. https://www.thetimes.co.uk/article/transgender-fetish-is-a-truly-shameful-modern-invention-g7036fr0g.

"What Does the Word 'Transgender' Mean?" them. Accessed October 28, 2019. https://www.them.us/story/inqueery-transgender.

Whitford, Emma. "When Walking While Trans Is a Crime." The Cut, January 31, 2018. https://www.thecut.com/2018/01/when-walking-while-trans-is-a-crime.html.

"Why Trans Woman Cursed at Cashier in Video." Accessed November 6, 2019. https://www.yahoo.com/lifestyle/trans-woman-explains-cursed-gamestop-cashier-viral-video-blatant-malicious-hate-162919129.html.

Wilson, Joe, and Dean Hamer. *Kumu Hina*. [DVD]. Passion River, 2015.

Zanghellini, Aleardo. "Sodomy Laws and Gender Variance in Tahiti and Hawai'i." *Laws* 2, no. 2 (June 2013): 51–68. https://doi.org/10.3390/laws2020051.

Chapter Eleven

Becoming Theodore

Spatial Legal Consciousness and Transgender Name Changes

Theodore Davenport

On February 17, 2016, transgender man Rowan Elijah Feldhaus attended a hearing in the Superior Court of Columbia County, Georgia, after filing a petition to change his legal name as part of his gender transition.[1] Feldhaus testified that he "had a 732 credit score, was not delinquent on any bills, had no criminal history and had no allegations of fraud in his past," in addition to providing medical testimony from his therapist, who confirmed his gender dysphoria diagnosis. Yet, Superior Court judge David Roper denied his petition based on his personal disapproval of Feldhaus's transition, and in the final petition denial, Judge Roper even argued that name changes for transgender people are "a type of fraud upon the general public."

For many transgender and gender nonconforming (GNC) people, changing one's given name is a major milestone in social transition. Julia Sinclair-Palm offers the following insight on the significance of trans renaming:

> Even before a child can talk, they are called into language through their identification with and internalization of [a] name. . . . Paradoxically, names have the power to represent and make us intelligible, and to render us strange and alienated both from our families and from social conventions. This meditation on names takes on significant urgency for trans people. Often, choosing a name is one of the first ways trans people begin to assume a different gender from the one they were assigned at birth. . . . The act of selecting a name separate from the one their parents assigned them, then, is central to identity formation, enacting simultaneously the pull back into the home and the push out into the world.[2]

Transgender people experience a myriad of challenges within legal systems. Critical trans legal scholarship has well explored how binary sex categories within legal administrations uniquely affect transgender people and shape legal consciousness around gender markers on identity documents.[3] Further, work on LGBT legal consciousness has almost exclusively focused on lesbian and gay legal challenges with partnership and parenting.[4] However, less work has explored how transgender people experience legal consciousness around names. In most places in the United States, the process for making a social name change legible to the state requires a court order, regardless of gender modality, or "how a person's gender identity stands in relation to their gender assigned at birth."[5] Obtaining a court-ordered name change is a more common and accessible legal signifier of gender transition than legally changing gender markers nearly everywhere in the United States. Yet, obtaining a court-ordered name change and subsequently changing names on identity documentation is still a confusing, expensive, time-consuming, and highly fragmented process. Particularly for a marginalized group affected by high rates of poverty and violence, I argue that trans spatial experiences of legal consciousness around names present unique challenges. Related issues include economic barriers, increased securitization, and gender transition performance limited to linear and binary ascriptions.

In this chapter, I ask how transgender people experience legal consciousness around names and name changes. I begin with a brief history of identification documents as a tool for racial surveillance in the United States. Then, I detail current legislation and scholarly work around gender markers as regards identification documents. After explaining the legal process for obtaining a court-ordered name change (and the unique barriers that exist for transgender people to obtain it), I explore my personal experiences as a trans person navigating the uniquely complex experience of legally changing names within the United States. This work draws from a rich history of trans scholars using autoethnographic methods to reclaim narratives. I am particularly inspired by Petra Doan, Dean Spade, and Susan Stryker, whose autoethnographic works seamlessly weave their life stories with deeper analyses of gender and space.[6]

I. SITUATEDNESS

My experiences as a white, transmasculine, and binary-presenting U.S. citizen are central to the experiences I describe in this chapter. If need be, I have the privilege and luxury of modifying my body and habitus to fit within the bounds of what scholars like Evan Vipond have named "transnormativity," or "narratives of transition [that] reinforce medical discourses of what it means to be trans and how to be trans."[7] Salvador Vidal-Ortiz articulates how, in rhetorically invoking trans women of color without including them in academic spaces, white academics reinscribe whiteness within trans studies.[8] Instead, I adopt the approach of critically evaluating my own whiteness and hope to make space for name experiences beyond whiteness. My work is also geographically situated within the legal context of the United States and thus may contribute to the geographic limitations of current scholarly work within trans studies.[9] Further, the legal landscape of gender identity legislation is changing rapidly in the United States. While detailed information around state laws is true as of the time of this writing, it may quickly become outdated as laws are updated to reflect increasing transgender legal consciousness. I anticipate that general arguments around the gendered nature of identification documents will remain relevant for some time after publication.

II. IDENTIFICATION DOCUMENTS AND SECURITIZATION

Particularly in the United States, identification documents have a history as technology for racial surveillance. Cass Adair traces the Progressive era origin story behind driver's licensing requirements in the United States.[10] Adair analyzes how pro-licensing organizing was steeped in anti-Black and pro-eugenic cultural narratives, and the inclusion of racial categories on driver's licenses served as a mode for data collection and surveillance. While careful not to conflate the unique experiences of racialized and trans peoples, Adair observes that (particularly white) transgender activists rarely acknowledge how they draw upon racial legal consciousness when discussing the role that identification documents serve in transgender discrimination.

Increasing securitization, particularly in the post-9/11 era, has led to social and often legal expectations that one must be ready to present legal identification at nearly all times. Populations perceived as security threats are subject to intense state surveillance, particularly people of color, immigrants, and trans/gender-nonconforming people.[11] Toby Beauchamp details how U.S. state security measures assume that nonnormative gender presentations constitute a form of deception.[12] Trans organizational responses to a Department of Homeland Security advisory, which explicitly named gender nonconformity as a basis for increased scrutiny, recommended "strategic visibility." This advisory included preemptive measures, such as bringing court-ordered name changes and any paperwork related to a gender change to the airport. Thus, trans/GNC people who do not wish to be visible, who lack suitable documentation of their transition, or who for other reasons cannot meet transnormative standards that would render their trans status understandable to security forces are understood as potential security threats when identification documents do not match their visual appearance, chosen name, or preferred gender marker.

Beyond the threat of state violence, the expectation that one's identity must be verified by legal documentation extends to nearly all aspects of daily life. Access to employment, housing, social services, and education requires legal identification to prove one's safety vis-à-vis identification verification. Owning legal identification that reflects one's chosen name thereby increases access to formal institutions, improves personal safety, and allows one to participate in daily life.[13] This practice is supported by historical moments in trans rights. For example, Susan Stryker detailed how providing identity documentation with one's preferred name and gender allowed transgender people medically transitioning through Stanford University during the late 1960s to access essential opportunities, such as opening up bank accounts and accessing employment.[14]

Gender Markers

An overwhelming amount of popular and academic discourse around transgender legal rights centers the role of gender markers within administrative systems. In *Invisible Lives* (2000), Vivian Namaste details how Québec, like many places in the United States, legally required proof of lower surgery in order to change gender markers on identity documents. In practice, this rule was applied unpredictably, based on the whims of an individual case worker, meaning that some transgender people undoubtedly "illegally" obtained access to their correct gender marker. However, for the majority assigned rule-abiding caseworkers, Namaste rightfully argues that this rule both misunderstood goals for gender transition and grossly overestimated the accessibility of lower surgery for a group who is systematically excluded from employment and denied transition health care.

While the process for changing gender markers on documents has since been simplified in Québec, this legal landscape remains highly fragmented, complex, and often antiquated in the United States.[15] Each individual identification document corresponds to a different set of requirements for updating a gender marker, and document requirements are inconsistent across geography. For example, changing gender markers on a driver's license from Massachusetts only requires the completion of a short form requesting a new gender designation, whereas a Louisiana license requires proof of surgery.[16] Transgender people born in Tennessee are outright forbidden from changing gender designations on birth certificates, whereas Idaho, Ohio, and Puerto Rico have instituted policies or practices that *de facto* forbid a change.[17] Other states like Texas technically allow (or do not explicitly forbid) a gender-designation change but make it prohibitively difficult so that it is practically impossible to obtain.[18] While many federal- and state-level documents require proof of surgery to change a legal gender marker, the 2015 US Transgender Survey (USTS) found that only a quarter of all trans and non-binary people underwent transition-related surgery, whether due to financial inaccessibility or a lack of interest for surgery.

Finally, states with allegedly progressive gender marker policies generally limit available gender markers to two or three options. An increasing number of states (such as Oregon, Arkansas, and Indiana) offer X as a gender marker option on select identity documentation.[19] X can be affirming for transgender, non-binary, intersex, or otherwise gender-nonconforming people who find that M or F markers do not adequately capture their gender or sex. Yet, the X gender marker is an imperfect solution to the complicated problem of existing outside a legally recognized gender binary. First, the X gender marker flattens all identities that fall outside the gender and/or sex binaries into a single category, serving as a proxy for "other." Further, X immediately outs members of these vulnerable groups as falling outside the gender and/or sex binary, potentially rendering them more vulnerable to both state and personal violence. Finally, the X marker is currently offered only on a limited basis. Some states do not offer X as an option on all identity documentation, such as Washington, which allows for an X on birth certificates but not driver's licenses. Such mismatches in documentation are tied to increased rates of administrative violence, as the gender-variant body is once again perceived as deceptive.[20]

Administrative systems will never fully capture every possible gender identity, and they serve as a form of surveillance for trans and GNC populations. Many trans socio-legal scholars argued for eliminating gender markers on identity documents altogether. The reason given relates to how infrequently gender is (or rather, *should be*) relevant for daily life. Further, the mere inclusion of gender categories outside of *male* and *female* on legal documents does not indicate the absence of transphobia within legal systems. Particularly in spaces with a veneer of high security (such as airports), gender classification is arbitrarily enforced. Rarely does it in fact prevent fraud or security issues. Moreover, it mainly serves to discriminate individuals who do not fit into racialized gender norms.[21]

Both easing requirements to change gender markers and eliminating gender markers on identity documentation are essential strategies toward improving daily life for transgender people. Because names are often implicitly gendered as male or female, the mere inclusion of legal names on identification documents presents additional challenges that cannot be easily alleviated via elimination.

Legal Name Changes

In the United States, the process for legally changing one's name is highly fragmented. It depends on the individual's state (and sometimes county) of residence and the reason for the name change.[22] Name changes due to personal factors (which gender transition usually defers) generally require that one submit a petition to the Superior Court for the county of residence, pay court dues, and attend a name-change hearing. Some states require a wait time; others require that one publish one's name change petition in the local newspaper to allow for objections. Certain populations, including formerly or currently incarcerated people or those who have previously undergone a name change, are often subject to additional scrutiny and requirements during the legal name-change process.[23]

The 2015 USTS revealed that just over half of its 27,715 respondents owned any form of identification with their preferred name.[24] The report found that this figure varies wildly by document; for example, while 44 percent of those who wanted to change the name on a state ID/driver's license had done so, only 18 percent had changed their name on a birth certificate. Unsurprisingly, transgender people remain confronted by a number of barriers for obtaining court-ordered name changes and corresponding identification documents. Significantly, respondents were over twice as likely than the cisgender population to live in poverty. Half of USTS's respondents reported that their court-ordered name change cost between $100 and $499, and a frightening 10 percent reported that their name change cost more than $500. Further, trans people, particularly women of color, are more likely to be currently or formerly incarcerated, and nineteen states place restrictions or additional requirements on name change petitions filed by someone with a criminal record, adding confusion to the petition process.[25] Finally, trans people often lack access to legal aid sensitive to their identities and needs—which was the very inspiration for Dean Spade's creation of the Sylvia Rivera Law Project.[26] Given how few trans people are able to consistently access legal documentation with their chosen name, there exists a theoretical need to understand how transgender people experience legal consciousness around their own names.

III. AUTOETHNOGRAPHY

I draw from a rich history of queer and trans scholarship that uses autoethnography to situate personal experiences within broader cultural, geographic, and legal contexts. Petra Doan conceptualizes her spatial experiences as a trans woman as a "tyranny of gendered spaces" that require careful navigation.[27] Connecting Foucault's theorizing of governance to the gatekeeping of medical transition, Dean Spade draws from his personal experiences unsuccessfully attempting to obtain letters from counselors for top surgery.[28] Perhaps most famously, Susan Stryker reclaims "transgender rage" and the transgender body as monstrous in a textual adaptation of a 1993 conference performance piece that reflects and theorizes around her complex emotions following the birth of her lover's child.[29] I am indebted to these scholars' willingness to be vulnerable, among countless others not named here.

Moreover, Stacy Holman Jones and Tony Adams beautifully articulate that autoethnography, like queer theory, "open[s] up definitional boundaries" by embracing fluidity, instability, and a politic of change.[30] Jones and Adams note that the permanency of autobiographical texts creates the illusion of a fixed and singular self. Likewise, this chapter represents an incomplete snapshot of how I relate to my*self* vis-à-vis legal consciousness around my name.

For some personal historical context: I first began socially transitioning and using my new name, Theodore, in the summer of 2017, when I was living in a small city in my home state of Georgia. Later that year, I began medically transitioning while not fully *out* as trans in my daily life. I was accepted into graduate school and moved to the state of Washington the following summer. Throughout this time period, I wrote about my experiences via detailed journal entries, which now constitute my field notes.

Why Not Georgia?

Choosing not to change my name legally after beginning my social transition was a painful decision centered around several financial, legal, and social barriers. First, like one-third of trans people who report not attempting to change their legal name. I had a low annual income and simply did not have the capacity to pay the legal name-change fee of several hundred dollars.[31] Later, I learned that courts sometimes grant fee waivers regarding name changes to low-income petitioners, although the application process is quite opaque and not mentioned on my state or county websites. Moreover, Rowan Feldhaus's name-change case was also fresh in my mind during this time. While only about 1 percent of all attempted court-ordered name changes for trans people are denied, the notoriety around this case contributed to my anxiety toward attempting my name change in Georgia.[32]

Second, I believed that legally changing my name at that time could have severely compromised my livelihood. Georgia does not have antidiscrimination laws that recognize gender identity or sexual orientation as protected categories.[33] Thus, coming out as transgender publicly could have resulted in myriad negative consequences for which I would have no legal recourse. I personally knew of transgender people forced out of their housing after coming out or being outed. While I had a good rapport with my property manager, I had no way of knowing whether she would understand, let alone accept, my transition. Allegedly LGBT-friendly property managers in my city often used this notoriety as a marketing tactic, reminiscent of strategies financiers employ to drive rent costs in urban gayborhoods.[34] Since Georgia is a right-to-work state without employment protections for transgender people, I also could have lost my job without legal recourse, as I was living outside of the only city in Georgia with broad antidiscrimination protections for transgender people.[35]

Finally, legal name changes in Georgia require advertising the name change petition in the local county newspaper once weekly for a month with "a statement admitting the right of anyone interested to object to your name change."[36] As if gender transition was not already an exercise in vulnerability, the prospect of announcing my name change intent via the county newspaper in anticipation of objection struck me as a horrifyingly draconian requirement. Like most trans people, I certainly had people in my life who would disapprove of my name change. Why should they have any avenue to object to my name change?

All Rise: Courtroom Jitters

Three months after moving to Washington, I walked into a small courthouse wearing a gingham button-down shirt, comically small oxford shoes from the boy's section, and a nearly fresh haircut. I am worried that the judge will not take my name change seriously if I do not present myself and act as masculine as possible. So just for that day, I ditch my smudged eyeliner and practice speaking through my diaphragm to deepen my tinny voice. My partner, who accidentally tries to bring a pocketknife through the security metal detector, returns to the car to put his would-be weapon away while I shyly walk up to the court's main desk. I am relieved when the person running the desk does not respond visibly to the paperwork I submit, and I am told that I can be seen in the next civil court hearing, which would be in about half an hour. Great!

The judge quietly peers down at his paperwork for a minute, looks up, and announces, "It looks like we have a name change today! If that's you, could you come up to speak with me privately, please?" I was deeply relieved that he did not announce my birth name but irrationally worried I am somehow in trouble. My heart pounding loudly, I trip over my shoes in my haste to get to the podium. Clearly sensing my anxiety, the judge tells me to take a deep breath once I finally arrive. He smiles and slowly asks me several questions. He calls me "sir" and "young man." It becomes clear to me that I am not the first trans person he granted a name change to. I find this realization calms me. Our interaction takes fifteen minutes, and I leave the courthouse later that day with a certified copy of my name change. Success!

The Perils of Public Existence

In late October 2018, two of my close friends married and honeymooned in Washington. They stopped to visit me and my partner in Seattle, and we suggested a restaurant for dinner. The place was busier than usual, and the host asked if we wanted to sit at the bar instead of waiting for a table. We readily agreed.

We put in drink orders, and I asked for just a water. (It was a weekday, after all!) The bartender immediately asked for ID. Although Washington State Department of Licensing assured me that the temporary driver's license with my new name would permit me to order alcohol, prior personal experience proved otherwise, and bartenders had most often asked me to present both my hole-punched license with my old name and my temporary paper license with the new name. I showed both to the bartender, still a little confused about why I was asked for ID to order water.

The smile slid off her face, and her confusion was quickly replaced by a scowl. "The name isn't even the same on these," she snapped. I tried to explain how *that was the whole point*, and I had a new license on the way because of a name change. Previously, people checked my license and made snarky comments, but this was the first time my identity was questioned so intensely. The bartender refused to accept either ID, instructing me to leave the bar. I insisted that I had no intention to drink alcohol and remarked that I did not carry additional identification. The bartender begrudgingly let me stay seated at the bar on the condition that I not tell other wait staff she had let me do so. I felt exceptionally embarrassed by the encounter; after all, this was supposed to be a celebratory event for our newly married friends. We took our food to go and quickly left.

Later, I learned about Washington's complicated legislation about the age allowing someone to sit at a bar. Rules depend on whether an establishment is classified as a food counter, liquor bar, or a service bar.[37] After this encounter, I began to carry most of my legal documentation. In fact, I used my passport with my previous name to order drinks and for other identity-verification purposes as I waited for my new license to arrive. This strategy generated some strange looks from bartenders, who were likely unaccustomed to patrons using passports as ID. I simply hoped that I looked enough like the unsmiling woman with a bob haircut and unfashionably orange button-down in my passport photo to avoid further questioning.

What I remember most after this incident is that, after all the uproar at the restaurant's bar, *I was allowed to stay*. In an attempt to make myself more palatable to bewildered ID checkers, I ironically took on strategic visibility to position myself as a trans person "deserving" of existing in spaces: *Here is my ID—do you need to see my name change paperwork? I don't want one of your establishment's fun cocktails, only a water, thanks. I don't want to cause trouble.* As Sarat famously argues, the law is "all over" and permeates everyday spaces, even environments that are not directly under the surveillance of the state.[38] While my identification was scrutinized in this space, some combination of my whiteness and masculinity-as-assertiveness perhaps unwittingly convinced the bartender to overlook what she understood to be suspect identification credentials, a "kindness" she may not have afforded me had I not fit the transnormative ideal.

IV. CONCLUSION

Although it has been more than a year since I received my court-ordered name change, I still have not successfully updated my name on all identity documentation. I recognize that without matching documentation, I am at increased risk for discrimination and violence. Regardless, the fatigue and financial exhaustion of changing my name became overwhelming quickly. Each institution required a different set of documentation, forms, fees, and uncomfortable phone calls that required me to out myself. Occasionally, "helpful" employees aimed to "correct" my mistake when they could not conceive of *Theodore* as a legitimate progression from my feminine birth name. After experiencing the process firsthand, I understood why only 11 percent of USTS respondents had their preferred name and gender on all their records.[39]

I assumed erroneously that Washington's trans-friendly laws meant that changing my legal name would be safer in Washington than in Georgia. In retrospect, I did not adequately question what "safety" meant in this context. When I decided to wait to change my name legally until I moved from Georgia to Washington, I failed to realize several ironies. First, proving discrimination under antidiscrimination measures is extremely difficult to do. Drawing from Critical Race Theory, Dean Spade argues that these laws grossly misunderstand discrimination through a victim-perpetrator model or those who perpetrate acts of violence based on hatred and fear, rather than stemming from systemic oppression.[40] Minor microaggressions, such as those I experienced in the restaurant, while mortifying and humiliating, do not meet legal criteria for discrimination. Such incidents are not likely to be addressed by legal frameworks that punish perpetrators. Second, even if I experienced an act of discrimination that met the required criteria, I did not have the means to hire a lawyer and, as Spade notes, I would not likely win in court anyway.[41] Yet, other safety concerns, such as potential violence through the publication of my name in the newspaper, still haunt my imagination. In both states, obtaining my court-ordered name change still required hundreds of dollars and a public performance of my gender expression in front of a judge with the power to deny my petition.

Relatedly, Kylar Broadus notes how emphasizing legal rights discourse as a main avenue for change often limits other political imaginaries.[42] Also, Broadus invokes Patricia Williams in arguing that legal rights serve an important symbolic role in reconceptualizing marginalized peoples as fully human. The complexity around the role of legal rights for trans people was highlighted by scholars, such as Spade, who argues for strategic legal rights interventions that help improve living conditions for the entire trans population, rather than those who already fit the transnormative mold.[43] Further, Isaac West well conceptualizes this complexity via an "impure transgender politics" which moves beyond an unwavering (and often paralyzing) commitment to Left political ideals. Rather, it recognizes multiple modes of transgender politics that may find opportunities in existing systems and legislation.[44]

In a modern world where identification documents are a prerequisite to exist in public spaces, trans people must be able to access documentation that reflects their chosen name. I therefore suggest the following strategic interventions to complement a politic that recognizes the problematic, racialized history of identification requirements.

First, lowering the high costs of legally changing one's name via the U.S. court system would greatly help to increase access to proper identification for trans people. As noted earlier, over a third of trans people in the United States have not attempted to change their name due to financial constraints.[45] This figure is hardly surprising when two-thirds of USTS respondents report their legal name change cost between $100 and over $2,000. Reducing or eliminating this cost would particularly benefit trans people, who have an increased likelihood of being impoverished.

Second, states should consider eliminating unnecessary name-change requirements that disproportionately affect or harm transgender people. Placing additional restrictions or requirements on people with a criminal history bolsters the prison-industrial complex. Barring this population from accessing documentation that reflects their chosen name severely restricts their ability to participate in daily life. Removing such name-change restrictions can legitimize transgender inmates' requests for prison staff to use their chosen name and can increase access to daily life for those formerly incarcerated.

Finally, while petition-publication requirements like those in Georgia are somewhat uncommon, the Movement Advancement Project reports that around 16 percent of LGBT people live in states with this requirement.[46] Requiring public announcement of one's intent to legally change names in anticipation of potential objection portends disaster for trans people, who are more likely in fraught personal relationships. Significantly, name-change publications place transgender people who wish to remain stealth (i.e., not out as trans) at particular risk. Legal name changes should not be subject to public scrutiny and approval to be legitimized.

A long-term solution for addressing inequities in the legal name-change process in the United States may involve decoupling name changes from civil courts altogether. Several countries, such as the United Kingdom, use deed polls to render name changes visible to legal systems.[47] In the UK, a name-change deed poll costs a maximum of £36, a significantly lower amount than most court-ordered name changes in the United States.

While gender markers are a core component of transgender administrative violence, scholars and activists risk neglecting other issues trans people face vis-à-vis bureaucratic systems. As demonstrated through this work, transgender people like me, Rowan Feldhaus, and countless others tend to experience significant frustration and harm around attempting to change legal names. Addressing the unnecessarily complex and expensive legal name-change systems within the United States (and countries with similar processes) would allow transgender people greater access to documentation that reflects their chosen name. This would result in increased access to daily life while still allowing for robust critiques of a state which increasingly relies on identification technologies as a form of gendered and racialized social control.

NOTES

1. Littrell and Levasseur, "In Re Feldhaus."
2. Sinclair-Palm, "What's in a Name?," 5–6.
3. Sally Engle Merry defines *legal consciousness* as "the ways people understand and use law . . . [how] people conceive of the 'natural' and normal way of doing things, their habitual patterns of talk and action, and their commonsense understanding of the world" (Merry, *Getting Justice and Getting Even*, 5). See also: Spade, *Normal Life*.
4. Hull, "Legal Consciousness in Marginalized Groups."
5. Ashley, "'Trans' Is My Gender Modality: A Modest Terminological Proposal," 1.
6. Doan, "The Tyranny of Gendered Spaces."
7. Vipond, "Resisting Transnormativity."
8. Vidal-Ortiz, "Whiteness."
9. Aizura et al., "Introduction: Decolonizing the Transgender Imaginary."
10. Adair, "Licensing Citizenship."
11. Ferguson, *The Rise of Big Data Policing*; Stuesse and Coleman, "Automobility, Immobility, Altermobility"; and Beauchamp, "Artful Concealment and Strategic Visibility."
12. Beauchamp, "Artful Concealment and Strategic Visibility."
13. Spade, *Normal Life*.
14. Stryker, *Transgender History*, 99.
15. Gouvernement du Québec, "Change of Sex Designation."
16. Movement Advancement Project, "Equality Maps: Identity Document Laws and Policies."
17. Lambda Legal, "FAQ about Identity Documents."
18. Transgender Law Center, "State-by-State Overview: Rules for Changing Gender Markers on Birth Certificates."
19. Movement Advancement Project, "Equality Maps: Identity Document Laws and Policies."
20. Spade, *Normal Life*, 77–80.

21. Currah and Mulqueen, "Securitizing Gender."
22. Streissguth, "Steps to Legally Change Your Name."
23. Movement Advancement Project, "Equality Maps: Identity Document Laws and Policies."
24. James et al., "The Report of the 2015 U.S. Transgender Survey."
25. Movement Advancement Project, "Equality Maps: Identity Document Laws and Policies."
26. Spade, *Normal Life*.
27. Doan, "The Tyranny of Gendered Spaces."
28. Spade, "Mutilating Gender."
29. Stryker, "My Words to Victor Frankenstein."
30. Jones and Adams, "Autoethnography Is a Queer Method," 199.
31. James et al., "The Report of the 2015 U.S. Transgender Survey."
32. Ibid.
33. Human Rights Campaign, "HRC Georgia."
34. Bell and Binnie, "Authenticating Queer Space."
35. City of Atlanta, "Atlanta, GA: LGBTQ."
36. State of Georgia, "Name Changes."
37. Washington State Legislature, "WAC 314-02-014: What Is a Food Counter?"
38. Sarat, "The Law Is All Over."
39. James et al., "The Report of the 2015 U.S. Transgender Survey."
40. Spade, *Normal Life*.
41. Ibid., 41.
42. Broadus, "The Evolution of Employment Discrimination Protections for Transgender People."
43. Spade, *Normal Life*, 91.
44. West, *Transforming Citizenships*, 163–94.
45. James et al., "The Report of the 2015 U.S. Transgender Survey."
46. Movement Advancement Project, "Equality Maps: Identity Document Laws and Policies."
47. Government of the United Kingdom, "Change Your Name by Deed Poll."

BIBLIOGRAPHY

Adair, Cassius. "Licensing Citizenship: Anti-Blackness, Identification Documents, and Transgender Studies." *American Quarterly* 71, no. 2 (July 6, 2019): 569–94. https://doi.org/10.1353/aq.2019.0043.

Aizura, Aren Z., Trystan Cotten, Carsten/Carla Balzer/LaGata, Marcia Ochoa, and Salvador Vidal-Ortiz. "Introduction: Decolonizing the Transgender Imaginary." *TSQ: Transgender Studies Quarterly* 1, no. 3 (August 1, 2014): 308–19. https://doi.org/10.1215/23289252-2685606.

Ashley, Florence. "'Trans' Is My Gender Modality: A Modest Terminological Proposal." In *Trans Bodies, Trans Selves*, edited by Laura Erickson-Schroth, 2nd ed. Oxford: Oxford University Press, forthcoming.

Beauchamp, Toby. "Artful Concealment and Strategic Visibility: Transgender Bodies and U.S. State Surveillance after 9/11." *Surveillance & Society* 6, no. 4 (June 26, 2009): 356–66. https://doi.org/10.24908/ss.v6i4.3267.

Bell, David, and Jon Binnie. "Authenticating Queer Space: Citizenship, Urbanism and Governance." *Urban Studies* 41, no. 9 (August 1, 2004): 1807–20. https://doi.org/10.1080/0042098042000243165.

Broadus, Kylar. "The Evolution of Employment Discrimination Protections for Transgender People." In *Transgender Rights*, edited by Paisley Currah, Richard Juang, and Shannon Price Minter, 93–101. Minneapolis: University of Minnesota Press, 2006.

City of Atlanta. "Atlanta, GA: LGBTQ." City of Atlanta, GA, 2019. https://www.atlantaga.gov/government/mayor-s-office/executive-offices/office-of-equity-diversity-and-inclusion/lgbtq.

Currah, Paisley, and Tara Mulqueen. "Securitizing Gender: Identity, Biometrics, and Transgender Bodies at the Airport." *Social Research: An International Quarterly* 78, no. 2 (2011): 557–82.

Doan, Petra. "The Tyranny of Gendered Spaces—Reflections from Beyond the Gender Dichotomy." *Gender, Place & Culture* 17, no. 5 (August 25, 2010): 635. https://doi.org/10.1080/0966369X.2010.503121.

Ferguson, Andrew G. *The Rise of Big Data Policing: Surveillance, Race, and the Future of Law Enforcement*. New York: NYU Press, 2017.

Gouvernement du Québec. "Change of Sex Designation." Directeur de l'état civil, June 13, 2016. http://www.etatcivil.gouv.qc.ca/en/change-sexe.html#rrq-b.

Government of the United Kingdom. "Change Your Name by Deed Poll." Gov.UK. Accessed September 20, 2019. https://www.gov.uk/change-name-deed-poll.

Hull, Kathleen E. "Legal Consciousness in Marginalized Groups: The Case of LGBT People." *Law & Social Inquiry* 41, no. 3 (2016): 551–72. https://doi.org/10.1111/lsi.12190.

Human Rights Campaign. "HRC Georgia." Human Rights Campaign, 2019. https://www.hrc.org/local-issues/georgia/.

James, Sandy E., Jody Herman, Susan Rankin, Mara Keisling, Lisa Mottet, and Anafi Ma'ayan. "The Report of the 2015 U.S. Transgender Survey." Washington, DC: National Center for Transgender Equality, 2016. https://transequality.org/sites/default/files/docs/usts/USTS-Full-Report-Dec17.pdf.

Jones, Stacy Holman, and Tony E. Adams. "Autoethnography Is a Queer Method." In *Queer Methods and Methodologies*, edited by Kath Browne and Catherine Nash, 2nd ed., 195–214. New York: Routledge, 2016. https://doi.org/10.4324/9781315603223-13.

Lambda Legal. "FAQ about Identity Documents." Lambda Legal, 2019. https://www.lambdalegal.org/know-your-rights/article/trans-identity-document-faq.

Littrell, Beth, and M. Dru Levasseur. "In Re Feldhaus." Initial Brief of Appellant. State of Georgia: Court of Appeals, June 9, 2016. https://www.lambdalegal.org/sites/default/files/feldhaus_ga_20160609_initial-brief-of-appellant.pdf.

Merry, Sally Engle. *Getting Justice and Getting Even: Legal Consciousness among Working-Class Americans*. Chicago: University of Chicago Press, 1990.

Movement Advancement Project. "Equality Maps: Identity Document Laws and Policies." 2019. http://www.lgbtmap.org//equality-maps/identity_document_laws.

Namaste, Viviane. *Invisible Lives: The Erasure of Transsexual and Transgendered People*. Chicago: University of Chicago Press, 2000.

Sarat, Austin. "The Law Is All Over: Power, Resistance and the Legal Consciousness of the Welfare Poor." *Yale Journal of Law & the Humanities* 2 (1990): 343–80.

Sinclair-Palm, Julia Helen. "What's in a Name? Trans Youths' Experiences of Re-Naming," October 28, 2016. https://yorkspace.library.yorku.ca/xmlui/handle/10315/33434.

Spade, Dean. "Mutilating Gender." In *The Transgender Studies Reader*, 331–48. New York: Routledge, 2013.

———. *Normal Life: Administrative Violence, Critical Trans Politics, and the Limits of Law*. Vol. 2. Durham, NC: Duke University Press, 2015.

State of Georgia. "Name Changes." Georgia.gov, March 16, 2012. https://georgia.gov/popular-topic/name-changes.

Streissguth, Tom. "Steps to Legally Change Your Name." Legal Zoom. Accessed September 19, 2019. https://info.legalzoom.com/steps-legally-change-name-20369.html.

Stryker, Susan. "My Words to Victor Frankenstein above the Village of Chamounix: Performing Transgender Rage." In *The Transgender Studies Reader*, edited by Susan Stryker and Stephen Whittle, 1:244–56. New York: Routledge, 2013.

———. *Transgender History*. 2nd ed. New York: Seal Press, 2017.

Stuesse, Angela, and Mathew Coleman. "Automobility, Immobility, Altermobility: Surviving and Resisting the Intensification of Immigrant Policing." *City & Society* 26, no. 1 (April 1, 2014): 51–72. https://doi.org/10.1111/ciso.12034.

Transgender Law Center. "State-by-State Overview: Rules for Changing Gender Markers on Birth Certificates." Oakland, CA: Transgender Law Center, April 2017.

Vidal-Ortiz, Salvador. "Whiteness." *TSQ: Transgender Studies Quarterly* 1, no. 1–2 (May 1, 2014): 264–66. https://doi.org/10.1215/23289252-2400217.

Vipond, Evan. "Resisting Transnormativity: Challenging the Medicalization and Regulation of Trans Bodies." *Theory in Action; Fair Lawn* 8, no. 2 (April 2015): 21–44.

Washington State Legislature. "WAC 314-02-014: What Is a Food Counter, a Liquor Bar, and a Service Bar and Are Minors Allowed in These Areas?" Washington State Legislature, November 24, 2005. https://apps.leg.wa.gov/wac/default.aspx?cite=314-02-014.

West, Isaac. *Transforming Citizenships: Transgender Articulations of the Law*. New York: NYU Press, 2013.

Chapter Twelve

The Model Speaks?

Obscenity Laws in the United States

John Felipe Acevedo

The First Amendment to the Constitution purports to protect the free-speech rights of persons within the United States (U.S. Const. amend. I). However, in the area of sexualized speech—and obscenity jurisprudence, in particular—the person speaking the most, the model, is ignored, indeed silenced. This creates a paradox as the model is one of two persons, along with the artist, doing the most speaking, yet they are seldom heard in legal doctrine and make virtually no appearance in case law. Instead it is the gallery director, store proprietor, theater owner, seller, or shipper who are the most often heard in the law. This first paradox is a paradox of irony—to be heard in court, the artwork that a model appears in must be censored or silenced, but if the artwork a model appears in is not censored, then he or she is ignored or silenced. This is linked to the more general problem of censorship—to censor something, the censor must describe that which they do not want described (Butler 1997, 130).

The origin of the paradox can be explained by quirks in the development of legal doctrine, which focused on the distribution and sale of obscene materials more than on its production. In addition, structural anomalies within the American legal system, which restrict potential plaintiffs to only those who meet narrow standing requirements, limit who can bring a case involving obscenity. This is combined with the adversarial nature of American law to create a discursive binary around each case: state versus criminal, victim versus tortfeasor. This structure limits the voices heard in each instance. But, these do not explain stasis in the law. Stasis is the preference of the hegemonic culture of America: Christian, middle-class, heteronormative. Indeed, stasis is the nature of obscenity itself. The legal definition of obscenity has not changed since 1973, and individual definitions are tied to the gaze of the individual view not society (*Miller v. California* 1973). These limitations are enhanced with regard to child models, who are bounded by their parent's consent and decisions made for them while they were minors. This disregard of models' speech reveals the intersection of gender, age, class, and sexual orientation in both the relationships of models to artists and the law. Finally, the nature of sex speech itself works to silence the model because it inverts the subject and object gaze of the viewer, indeed of the law. Even when the models themselves are deemed First Amendment speakers, such as in erotic dancing, the court has discounted their voices by providing them less protection than similarly situated performative speakers (*City of Erie v. Padp's A.M.* 2000).

The focus of this chapter is on the obscenity laws of the United States, which currently focus on visual depictions of models through digital, photographic, and video mediums. The law developed such that it is rare that written words or painted art will qualify as pornographic (*Miller v. California* 1973, 24–25). In the realm of child pornography, the court also held that children, persons under the age of eighteen, must be depicted in an image in order for it to be prosecuted. Computer-generated images or depictions of adults posing as children do not qualify because the goal of the law is the protection of actual children (*Aschroft v. Free Speech Coalition* 2000).

Feminist scholars have debated the plight of models in sexual speech, some of whom see it as degrading and brutalizing to women (MacKinnon 1989, 200–201); meanwhile, others characterize it as a way for marginalized communities to express themselves (Rubin 2011, 124–125). And although there has been some attempt to give voice to models in both academic (Phillips 2006) and public settings (MacKinnon and Dworkin 1997), most models remain largely silent. Artists, models, and others wrote memoirs and collected the artifacts of speech, predominantly photos, but these are rarely used for the creation of laws that govern the lives of models (Dean et al. 2014, 44–55).

In contrast, live performers, primarily erotic dancers, have been separated from obscenity discussion and held to be expressive conduct protected under the First Amendment (*Schad v. Borough of Mount Ephraim* 1981, 65). Instead, local governments use zoning ordinances to limit and often prohibit nude dancing, which are routinely upheld by the court as valid time, place, and manner restrictions (*Barnes v. Glen Theatre, Inc.* 1991, 566–67). As in the case of models, dancers are rarely heard (*City of Erie v. Pap's A.M.* 2000). The cases focus instead on the dispute between the government entity and the owner or operators of the venue (*Schad v. Borough of Mount Ephraim* 1981; *Barnes v. Glen Theatre, Inc.* 1991; City of Erie v. Pap's A.M, 2000).

Although there are similarities in the silencing of models and live performers, they are of a different quality because the dancer has more protection in their performative work. The law has applied the same standard as required for political expressive speech, which requires that there be a "sufficiently important governmental interest," to justify impinging free speech rights (*United States v. O'Brien* 1968). In contrast, work that is found to be obscene is wholly without First Amendment protection (*Roth v. United States* 1957). But, a non-obscene work is then protected by the most searching scrutiny against governmental regulation (*American Booksellers Assn. v. Hudnut* 1985, 324). Interestingly, this means that once a work is deemed to be non-obscene, it gains full First Amendment Protection; but, the dancer will always be subjected to some form of governmental regulation at a lower level of protection.

Relatedly, Amy Adler made a compelling theory based on Freud's "Medusa's Head," that the court's different treatment of exotic dancers is attributable to "anxieties about castration (Adler 2009, 228). For Freud, the terror of Medusa's head is the terror of castration, which he links to a male child seeing adult female genital for the first time, thus contemplating his own castration (Freud 1953, 273). Adler asserts that live performers are Medusa-like because they cannot be elided through the shield of cinematic or photographic depiction, which tames the image of women, just as Perseus's shield protected him from Medusa's gaze (Adler 2009, 242–44). While a compelling theory, its basis on simple castration obscures the deeper cultural problem with nudity, which is based in the dominant hegemonic culture. Although this cultural hegemony can be used to explain the court's discomfort with both live performers and those captured on film, this chapter focuses on models in pornographic and obscene works.

Moreover, drawing on subaltern studies, queer theory, and postmodern theories, this chapter examines why courts have been unwilling, indeed unable, to hear the model speak. It is asserted that the intersection of categories prevents the court from hearing the model as it would then have to grapple with the law's implicit preference for Christian, middle-class, heteronormative hegemony. The problem of silencing could be approached through numerous methodologies, but subaltern studies was selected for two reasons. First, is its focus on the relationship between power and knowledge (Chakrabarty 2000, 15) in a legal context is especially important since who speaks shapes the case law, or knowledge, of the law. Second, as one of the major reasons for the silencing of models is the historical development of the law, subaltern studies' historiographic emphasis is important to disentangle the development from cultural hegemony (Chakrabarty 2000, 15–16).

I. ART, EROTICA, PORNOGRAPHY, OR OBSCENITY

Adler's theory that the gaze of the female performer is tamed through the medium of film or print does not fully address the question of "whose gaze?" For Adler, it is an unabashedly male gaze, which reflects the power division in society—the tale of Medusa and Perseus becomes an allegory for the struggle over possession of the gaze (Adler 2009, 243–45). This points to the second paradox within sexualized speech as the silenced model serves as both object and subject of the gaze. The problem of the gaze in turn illuminates the difficulty in distinguishing between obscenity, pornography, erotica, and art nudity present in both legal and nonlegal discussions of sexual imagery.

Arguably, models are the object of the speech as they, or their image, are being observed. But, they are also the subject of the artwork because they are speaking through their actions. Lucan focuses on the artist as the speaker. In paintings, this is absolutely true since the model is only represented and not literally seen (Lucan 1981, 110–12). For Lucan, what the audience sees, is "the gaze of those persons who, when the audience are not there deliberate in this hall. Behind the picture it is their gaze that is there" (Lucan 1981, 113). This refers to the gaze of the audience that the artist was initially creating for (Lucan 1981, 111–13).

But in photography and film, a direct representation of the model is captured. And, while it is true that the artist still directs the action of art, the model's speech comes through much more clearly. Building from Lucan, Žižek asserts that the gaze of the viewer of sexual imagery, specifically pornographic speech, transforms the viewer into both the subject and object of the work. They are the object because when we gaze at pornographic imagery our gaze "falls into ourselves, the spectators." (Žižek 1989, 37). This inversion occurs because the goal of pornographic imagery is the arousal of the viewer rather than the model or the artist. Therefore, any degradation or stigmatization fall on the person viewing the image and not the person depicted. The real subjects become the actors or models and "we, the spectators, are reduced to a paralyzed object-gaze," (Žižek 1989, 37).

If Žižek's theory is expanded, the paradox of definition among art nude, erotic, pornographic, and obscene becomes clear. If the viewer becomes the object of the image, then the model becomes the subject. Thus, they invert roles. More accurately, both the model and the viewer are simultaneously both the subject and the object. In other words, what is seen and what is intended to be seen can never be separated. This leads to the fact that the agency of the model is ignored in favor of the viewer, but the model's agency still exists independent of the law or culture more generally (Butler 1990, 195).

In law, art, eroticism, pornography, and obscenity are held to be within the viewer, and the model is silenced. The law defines what is licit or illicit sexualized speech from the impossibly knowable viewpoint of the viewer. "Pornography is a term of judgement but not of law" (Rubin 2011, 261). As discussed later, the current legal test for determining whether an image is obscene includes asking "whether 'the average person, applying contemporary community standards, would find that the work, taken as a whole, appeals to the prurient interest?" (*Miller v. California* 1973, 24–25) This question can only be answered at the level of the viewer.

"Obscenity, at bottom, is not crime. Obscenity is sin" (Henkin, 1963, 395). Beliefs that once dominated American society become apparent. Although not an explicit element of obscenity, works that are deemed to be obscene almost always require nudity by the model (*Miller v. California* 1973, 29; but see *FCC v. Pacifica Foundation* 1978). In Abrahamic religions, nudity, sexuality, and sin are inextricably linked through theological discussion of man's fall (Gen. 3:7), as depicted in Genesis (Agamben 2011, 57). Part of the knowledge gained by humans in the Edenic fall was awareness of their nakedness—implying that their previous state of nudity had been, "clothed in a garment of grace" (Augustine 1998, 615). This was a nakedness without obscenity, lust, or the taint of original sin (Augustine 1998, 615–16). From the association of nudity with sin comes the extrapolation that sexual intercourse should be hidden from the gaze of others, regardless of who is engaging in the act (Augustine 1998, 617–20). Until the late twentieth century, obscenity laws were used to challenge written works as well as visual depictions (*Memoirs v. Massachusetts* 1966). But virtually all obscenity cases since the 1960s have dealt with visual works, which is the focus of this chapter (Strub 2013, 201–7).

This association of nudity, sexual intercourse, and sin is not unique to Augustine but common in Western cultures since early Christianity (Agamben 2011, 71–73). Of course, neither nudity nor sex alone is obscene. Obscenity is often associated with uncontrollable sexuality. Augustine defined obscenity as the lack of control of genitalia, which he attributed to the presence of lust (Augustine 1998, 618–19, 625–26, and 628–29). Similarly, Sartre viewed obscenity as the "certain involuntary waddlings" of the body (Sartre 1956, 519). Linking obscenity to involuntary bodily motion persists to this day; it is considered unprofessional conduct for a male model to have an erection, and almost all models have poses they will not take out of belief they are pornographic in nature (Phillips 2006, 60–63). In contrast, the law looks not to the model but to the viewer to determine if the image appeals to prurient interests (*Miller v. California* 1973).

Art and art modeling maintain the fiction that the work strives to portray "the chaste clothing of nakedness" (Gualdoni 2012, 12). Pornography's goal is certainly not chaste, but so long as it does not run afoul of the law's definition of obscenity, it enjoys the same First Amendment protection as art. That is, the law is concerned only with the end result, not the goal of the artist or model. Because the intent of the artist and model is not a legal consideration, all models have the potential to appear as obscene, regardless of intention (Stone 2017, 278–79). The law does not distinguish among pornography, erotica, or art. Instead, it registers a binary: obscene or non-obscene, illicit or licit (*Roth v. United States* 1957). The feminist debate of what is pornographic versus erotica is absent from the law (Rubin 2011, 263–65).

The law's elimination of the distinctions between these forms elides the motives behind the creation of art works and places all models of artworks, obscene or not obscene, outside the discourse of law. That is, the law does not ask why an artwork was made, but rather if it meets the legal definition for obscenity. This distinction necessitates focusing on the viewer's gaze (*Miller v. California 1973*, 29). This means that the model who poses has virtually no role in any subsequent legal action about a photo that they have posed in. The law's binary places all models together for the purpose of its analysis. It is at the discretion of the object-gaze of the viewer to determine if the image is obscene, pornographic, merely erotic, or perhaps just the chastity of nudity.

Perhaps unsurprisingly, the law has not specifically distinguished what is licit or illicit sexualized speech (Stone 2018, 278). The only thing the law has agreed upon is that some speech is obscene and thus not worthy of First Amendment protection (*Roth v. United States* 1957). Indeed, a decade after the Supreme Court began to grapple with the segregation of obscenity from other erotic speech, Justice Stewart conceded the problem of defining obscenity: "I shall not today attempt further to define the kinds of material I understand to be embraced within that shorthand description; and perhaps I could never succeed in intelligibly doing so. But I know it when I see it" (*Jacobellis v. State of Ohio*, Stewart concurring 1964, 197).

In the intervening years, the court settled on a definition of obscenity that combines community standards, artistic merit, and a clear definition of what type of sexual activity is defined as obscene (*Miller v. California* 1973, 24–25). But contemporary legal analysis ignores the primary speakers, the models. and, to a lesser extent, artists, relying instead on the object-gaze of the viewer, juror or judge. Indeed, even in the area of child pornography, which explicitly focuses on the characteristics of the models, the opinion and motives of the models are ignored. The law focuses which side of the arbitrary age limit of eighteen the model falls on. In the area of sex crimes, the use of arbitrary ages, such as the defense that a male under the age of fourteen cannot commit rape, or a minor under twelve cannot give testimony, have existed for centuries (Blackstone 2016, 141–42), and if the depiction is sufficiently "lascivious" to run afoul of the statute (18 U.S.C. 2256). Still, the object-gaze of the viewer dictates the outcome.

The following sections discuss the reasons that models have been silenced, focusing on the structure of the legal system; development of obscenity law; and the hegemony of masculine heteronormative Christian beliefs. Child pornography is then discussed as an example of the law seeming to let the model speak, but actually silencing him or her further. Finally, the chapter discusses whether the model can speak in either legal discourse or academic discourse.

II. STRUCTURAL LIMITATIONS OF THE LAW

In December 2017, an online petition began, seeking the Metropolitan Museum of Art to remove the painting "Thérèsa Dreaming," by Balthus. Allegedly, its depiction of the young model in a sexually suggestive pose was offensive. The painting depicts the model reclining with eyes closed, and her left leg is raised, revealing her white underwear (Bellafante 2017). The Met declined to remove the picture, but the petition sparked discussion about the exploitation of models in the production of artwork (Papenfuss 2017). Lawyers and legal scholars were absent from this discussion. Under the law, there was no issue to discuss; the painting was clearly not obscene since the model was clothed and not engaged in sexual activity (Chemerinsky 2019, 1112–14).

Significantly, the model would not have been party to any obscenity action. Instead, it would be the Met or the curator of the exhibit. In other words, the law punishes the person who disseminates the obscenity and not the person who appears in it (Chemerinksy 2019, 1112–14). Thus, the model does not enter the legal arena. But if the model could be given a voice in legal discourse, their conduct of posing, like that of the erotic dancer, would likely be held to be communicative conduct, which has been recognized as a form of protected speech under the Constitution (*Cohen v. California* 1971, 19). Since the performance of sex and erotica creates the normative gender roles of society, the silencing of models is particularly problematic because it removes them from the discussion (Butler 1990, xi).

On a societal level, the dominant masculine heteronormative Christian viewer speaks; meanwhile, the model performing gender roles is silenced (Ruben 2011, 145–49). Legally, this means that "licit" and "illicit" are defined neither by the models who participate in the creative act nor the artists who direct it, but by the viewers who often have radically different views about gender and sexuality from those involved in the creative process (Ruben 2011, 160–62). There are three structural elements of American law that silence the model. First is the adversarial system, which limits each case to only two viewpoints. Second, the requirement that all federal laws be based on some federal power has dictated the form of obscenity law. Finally, the standing requirements limit who can be a party to a lawsuit.

The adversarial legal system arose with the introduction of defense counsel and transformed the judge from an active participant into an arbitrator between warring counsel (Langbein 1978). The adversarial process requires that each case be reduced to two sides, thus creating a binary system and limiting the points of view that are represented in any single lawsuit. Even when numerous parties are allowed into an aggregate case, their interests and causes of action must be aligned for the parties to be joined (*Principles* 2018, §1.02). The problem is that models are not a unified class nor do they view their work as the same. Models' interests are sometimes aligned with the state, sometimes with the defendant, and sometimes with neither.

The binary nature of the legal system is compounded by the necessity that all federal laws be based on an enumerated grant of power within the Constitution (*McCulloch v. Maryland* 1819). In addition, the federal government lacks a generalized police power for the entire nation and therefore cannot criminalize any activity, including obscenity, without justifying the law under a power granted to it under the Constitution (*United States v. Lopez* 1995, 564–65). As a result, the original obscenity laws, the Comstock laws, were justified under Congress's power to regulate the postal system (*Ex parte Jackson 1877 and United States v. Bott* 1873).

When the Comstock laws were expanded to capture a greater degree of obscene materials, Congress relied on its power to regulate foreign and interstate commerce (Schauer 1976, 21). Congress's reliance on its Commerce Powers resulted in the focus of obscenity law on the senders and sellers of obscenity, not on the models in it nor producers of it. This is because the act needed to touch interstate commerce, and initially the court held that production was part of intrastate not interstate commerce (*Carter v. Carter Coal Co.* 1936). Even when the court overturned its holding to declare that Congress can reach production via interstate commerce, obscenity laws did not change (*NLRB v. Jones & Laughlin Steel Co.* 1937). Instead, the court emphasized the right to privacy by holding that private possession and viewing of obscene materials is protected under the First Amendment (*Stanley v. Georgia* 1969). Once an obscene object has come into personal possession, it is beyond the reach of the law unless it re-enters commerce. Although, the court carved out an exception, allowing for the criminalization of child pornography possession (*Osborn v. Ohio* 1990).

Finally, the United States Constitution requires that any lawsuit be brought by a person who has standing. Standing requires that the plaintiff must allege they have suffered an injury or imminently will suffer one, that the injury is traceable to the defendant's conduct, and that a favorable court decision will redress the harm (Chemerinsky 2019, 63–64). In obscenity law, this severely limits the ability of models to enter into court since they have signed contracts that bind their rights (*Shields v. Gross* 1983). MacKinnon and Dworkin sought to introduce a new form of action to prohibit pornography based on the civil rights of women (Mackinnon and Dworkin 1997). But, the federal court struck the law down for unconstitutionally burdening protected, non-obscene, speech (*American Booksellers Assn. v. Hudnut* 1985). This decision is also why involuntary models, such as victims of revenge porn, have been able to gain some protection and why they do not fit neatly within the scope of this chapter (Stokes 2014).

Some countries, such as India, sought to eliminate this problem by creating public interest litigation (PIL), which removes traditional standing requirements for issues that are of general public concern (Das Acevedo 2017, 5–6). If this approach was adopted in the arena of obscenity law, it could provide a way for models to bring suits to redress harms that they have suffered within the coverage of their contracts that are currently non-justiciable. But as the Indian practice has demonstrated PILs most likely will result in meddlesome interlopers using the suits to advocate their own views of society (Das Acevedo 2017). This is exactly what happened in the Indian sodomy cases where religious advocates and social reformers were parties to the suit rather than the LGTBQ community (Das Acevedo 2017). PILs are no panacea, and the silencing of models will continue within the law. This silencing constitutes more than legal blindness; it strips the models of their voice, supposedly guaranteed under the First Amendment, since they cannot enter court.

III. AMERICAN OBSCENITY LAW

The law's focus on publishers and sellers of disfavored works can be traced to the licensing laws of early modern England (Johns 1998, 230–35). Although in England, works were only sporadically targeted for obscenity until the nineteenth century (Schauer 1976, 3–7). The sustained criminalization of obscenity in America was part of the growth of Federal criminal law following the Civil War and the establishment of postal and treasury criminal departments (Dale 2008, 137–38). Indeed, the criminalization of obscenity was part of a broader criminalization of immoral behavior in the second half of the nineteenth century (Dale 2008, 138).

The campaign to criminalize victimless crimes of vice and sexual propriety was driven by Protestant reformers and funded by elite society (Friedman 1993, 134–35). In the area of obscenity, the primary instigator was a dry goods salesman, Anthony Comstock, who became obsessed with preventing sexual immorality in the country (Friedman 1993, 135). Comstock was actively involved in the Young Men's Christian Association (YMCA) and served as a lay minister before he began to be involved in enforcing Sunday-closing laws against saloons and morality against published items (Horowitz 2003, 366–68). The link between Protestant evangelism and obscenity laws is not limited to Comstock. Indeed, the Comstock Act was part of a wider effort to codify Christian morality into the laws of the United States (Werbel 2018, 66–67).

But advocates for greater regulation of morality at the national level were themselves restricted by the limited powers of government. Advocates were able to circumvent this limitation by basing the Comstock laws on the power of Congress to regulate the post office. In addition, when federal law could not directly be applied, political pressure was used to persuade industries to self-regulate, as seen by the Motion Picture Association of America's adoption of the Hays Code, which effectively removed sex from the cinema (Stone 2017, 172–74). By the middle of the twentieth century, criminalized obscenity was broadly defined to include not only pornographic movies but also literary works, such as *Fanny May* and *Ulysses* (Woodward and Armstrong 1979, 234–35). In order to counteract the over inclusiveness of obscenity, the court began to move toward a definition that exempted works that had serious artistic merit (Stone 2017, 176–77). But the court failed at its goal as evidenced by the 1990 prosecution of the curator of the Cincinnati Contemporary Arts Center for exhibiting Robert Mapplethorpe's photography ("Justice in Cincinnati" 1990).

Modern jurisprudence on obscenity began in 1957 with *Roth v. United States*, in which the court sought to maintain obscenity outside of First Amendment protection, while limiting the definition of obscenity to works that lacked redeeming social merit (Strub 2013, 161–65). The Model Penal Code, which was seen as progressive for advocating the abolition of sodomy laws, advocated keeping obscenity laws (American Law Institute 1985, 199–200). However, the proposed code limited obscenity to only those images that have a "predominant appeal to the prurient interest, that is, a shameful or morbid interest, in nudity, sex or excretion" and only to those images intended for sale (American Law Institute1985, 297 and 199–200).

By 1966, a plurality of the court seemed on the verge of abolition of obscenity. It held that material could only be found as obscene if it was "utterly without redeeming social value," but criminal obscenity would persist (*Memoirs v. Massachusetts* 1966, 418; *Final Report* 1986, 13). For a few decades, it appeared that the court would end the criminalization of obscenity, and it overturned obscenity convictions in over thirty cases. The court decided on an ad hoc basis (Chemerinsky 2019, 1112). The court "knew it when it saw it," but could never articulate it (*Jacobellis v. Ohio* 1964; *Redrup v. New York* 1967). The court's inability to formulate a coherent doctrine led to the continued criminalization of obscenity (Friedman 2002, 234).

Chief Justice Burger and the other Nixon appointees took advantage of the Warren Court's inability to reach a consensus on an approach to obscenity. They forged their own approach to obscene material (Strub 2013, 213). Burger believed that by expanding the definition of obscenity, and including local standards in the new test, obscene and pornographic material would wane (Stone 2018, 291–93 and 296). In *Miller v. California*, the court set forth the current legal standard for obscenity. To determine if a work is obscene the court asks,

> (a) whether the average person, applying contemporary community standards, would find that the work, take as a whole, appeals to the prurient interest; (b) whether the work depicts or describes, in a patently offensive way, sexual conduct specifically defined by the applicable state law; and (c) whether the work, take as a whole, lacks serious literary, artistic, political or scientific value. (Chemerinsky 2019, 1112–13)

The first part of the test is local in nature since it measures the prurient interests on a local level, thus allowing for variation across the nation (Strub 2013, 213–17). In contrast, the third element continues to evaluate the artistic merit of works on a national level (*Pope v. Illinois* 1987, 500–501). The goal was to eliminate local prejudices or the local object-gaze, but the court failed to do so. Even if it had succeeded, the model would still have been silenced because the other elements focus on the work and not the model.

The new *Miller* test failed to stop the growth of either obscenity or pornography because changes in technology simultaneously overwhelmed society with the volume of materials and altered national views about the division between pornographic and obscene material. (Stone 2018, 301–3). But, the *Miller* test did provide a basis for the continuation of obscenity prosecutions. Obscenity prosecutions fluctuate as each new presidential administration refocuses its law-enforcement priorities (Stone 2018, 308–10). Starting with the Clinton administration, resources were redirected from obscenity toward prosecuting child pornography. Nevertheless, obscenity laws still exist at the federal and state levels (Strub 2013, 303). As a result, the threat of obscenity prosecutions remain; meanwhile, the volume of sexual speech is largely unregulated.

IV. HEGEMONY

Common law courts are inherently conservative and rarely, if ever, bring about radical social change, instead ratifying extralegal societal changes (Rosenberg 2008, 420–22). Social changes must therefore derive from outside courts. Indeed, the inability of the court to adequately define obscenity contributed to the proliferation of obscenity cases. But it is the hegemonic conservative masculine Christian heteronormative ethics, enforced by politicians and the courts, that has retarded progress in providing protection to sexual speech. This is a cultural hegemony of American society—an elite group dominating the subaltern.

In its original sense, *hegemony* refers to the "predominance of one nation over another" (Simon 2015, 17). Gramsci expanded on the concept to describe that cultural hegemony within a society creates the "ideological terrain, determines a reform of consciousness and of methods of knowledge: it is a fact of knowledge, a philosophical fact" (Gramsci 2000, 192). For Gramsci, hegemony was a tool to be used by a class, preferably the proletariat, to lead and dominate their state working people (Gramsci 2015, 19). But cultural hegemony is the power of persuasion, not force. It is coercion and not forceful domination (Anderson 1976, 22). In an attempt to gain knowledge about "the art of government," subalterns educate themselves in the dominant ideology. In doing so, subalterns place themselves under the dominant hegemony (Gramsci 2000, 197). Within a state, there is both civil hegemony, which influences the culture of the state, and political hegemony, which asserts political power (Anderson 1976, 22–23). Cultural hegemony, therefore, can only change when a class or portion of a class builds alliances to displace the current hegemony (Simon 2015, 20–21). But any class can use hegemony to dominate other classes within a society and make its own beliefs dominant (Anderson 1976, 18).

In America, and most of Western Europe, the middle class (bourgeoisie) has been the hegemonic class, dominating workers (Simon 2015, 30–31; Anderson 1976, 44). Once gained, the hegemony of a class must be maintained (Simon 2015, 35). Since the French Revolution, and arguable before, force and consent have been merged and thus reinforce each other to create greater hegemonic stability of the bourgeoisie (Anderson 2017, 20). In America, middle class hegemony is primarily Christian, white, masculine, and heterosexual (Kivel 2013, 11–36). It is unsurprising that in the realm of obscenity, indeed all sexual speech or interests, these hegemonic principles distort our laws, ideas, and practices. Indeed, as discussed, the entire conflation of sin, nudity, and sexuality can be traced to Christian thinkers (Agamben 2011, 80–82).

Moreover, American obscenity law and sex-speech repression is inextricably tied to notions of a "good Christian nation." The first advocate for obscenity law, Anthony Comstock, was an active member of the YMCA, and his early supporters were Christian activists (Werbel 2018, 46–47; Horowitz 2003, 371–76). These early Christian moralists also conflated issues of obscenity, contraceptives, and sex because they viewed them all as corrupting married and unmarried women alike. All three encouraged women to sinful deeds and sex and helped them cover it up via abortion and contraception (Werbel 2018, 68–69). The conflation of sexual imagery with sex as sin, abortion, and contraception has not been fully excised to this day (Martin 1996, 101).

Some historians have tied the rise of the religious right in the 1960s to an alignment of church and business leaders seeking to rehabilitate free enterprise in the wake of the Great Depression and New Deal (Kruse 2015). Others have attributed its rise and the wedding of evangelical Christianity to conservative politics as a response to John Kennedy's election as president, which presented a threat to Protestant Americans (Martin 1996, 54–58). Whatever its cause, by the end of the Nixon administration, the religious right was able to exert pressure on politicians of both parties to promote its view of sexuality, obscenity, and contraception (Perlstein 2008, 288–89, 406–11).

In the area of obscenity, indeed in most sex-related regulation, the zenith of the religious right was the Reagan administration (Strub 2013, 224–25). Calls against obscenity and pornography began in earnest in 1983 with separate campaigns by the Morality in Media, an anti-pornography organization, to appoint a "smut czar," and Roman Catholic and Eastern Orthodox bishops calling for action against pornography (Alilunas 2016, 167–68). The push against sexual speech was not limited to pornography or obscenity; it also manifested in the area of educational sexual speech. Here, the Reagan administration limited sexual discussion by mandating abstinence education in all programs receiving federal funding (Moran 2000, 204–5). The religious right's direct assault on obscenity and pornography came in 1985 with the creation of the Meese Commission (Alilunas 2016, 167–77).

The Meese Commission was created with the explicit ideology that pornography must be suppressed. Its goal was to stop pornography's circulation by focusing on the social harms of pornography in emotionally charged hearings (Stone 2017, 297). Importantly, the Meese Commission aligned anti-porn feminists and the religious right in their common cause against pornography and obscenity by praising the anti-pornography statutes drafted by MacKinnon and Dworkin (Alilunas 2016, 179–80). Although many social scientists complained that the commission distorted their work by finding links between "adult pornography and child pornography, abuse against women, and other social ills," in contrast, anti-porn feminists largely embraced the report and its gesture toward their belief that pornography subjugated women (Alilunas 2016, 180; Strub 2013, 224). The report was too little, too late; changing technology and general views about nudity, pornography, and obscenity blunted the report's impact (Stone 2017, 301–5).

The Meese Commission emboldened conservative Christian groups to pressure retailers into removing undesirable magazines from the shelves, including *Playboy*, *Penthouse*, *Forum*, and *Playgirl* (Alilunas 2016, 180–81). There was also an increased number of obscenity cases in the latter half of the 1980s, but this was not to last (Stone 2017, 302–3; Alilunas 2016, 180–89). One of the last major targets of the obscenity crusade was Ferris Alexander, who sold pornography and obscenity in Minnesota (Stone 2017,

300). Alexander was convicted of selling four magazines and three videotapes that were found to be obscene by a jury under the *Miller* test (*Alexander v. U.S.* 1993, 544). Alexander's conviction was upheld as was the controversial forfeiture of his warehouse, inventory, and stores (*Alexander v. U.S.* 1993). Despite the continued vitality of the religious right, its ability to expand obscenity prosecutions waned. Instead, the Justice Department continues its focus on child pornography and only the most extreme obscenity (Strub 2013, 228).

What has not fully waned is the continued hegemony of masculine heteronormative views of sexuality, which at times lauds pornography as masculine behavior (Fausto-Sterling 2000, 199). This hegemony is intertwined with Christian hegemony as exemplified by Jesse Helms's reference to Robert Mapplethorpe's homoerotic art as "sick and polluting" American culture, in the 1990s (Meyer 2018, 218–19). The hegemony of male heterosexuality in pornography produced two opposite effects. The first is the tenuous, and often fraught, alliance between some anti-porn feminists and the religious right; both regard obscenity and pornography as subjugating women (*Final Report* 1986, 39–47). This alliance sought to remove First Amendment protection from pornography, as well as expand the definition of obscene materials (Alilunas 2016, 177–80). The second is a resistance among feminists to the religious right's attempt to define any non-heterosexual or non-mainstream sexuality as obscene (Martin 1996, 346–49 and Rubin 2011, 111–16). Gale Rubin explained the heightened danger that obscenity prosecutions pose to smaller erotic communities, such as sadomasochists, because they are not only targeted by conservatives but also unprotected by other groups (Rubin 2011, 110–14, 136, 273–75).

Just as the Protestant Reformation ended some forms of oppression, the Christian oppression can only be ended when a new hegemony is created, and the standards of moral conduct are reformed (Simon 2015, 22). The sexual revolution of the mid-twentieth century died in the court's inability to narrowly define obscenity. Although the paternalistic edifice of obscenity law was partially breached in the sexual revolution of the 1970s, it enabled a wide range of formally obscene material to be widely circulated (Stone 2018, 301–3). However, the revolution fell short, leaving the hegemony of the old order in place (Friedman 2002, 234). The silencing of models was perpetuated, and the gaze of the viewer was given primacy over the intent, beliefs, and speech of the model.

V. CHILD PORNOGRAPHY

The one area of law where the model appears to speak is in child pornography. After all, the entire genre of speech is defined by the model's age, but as will be shown, the model is still silenced. Federal statute prohibits shipment in interstate or foreign commerce of child pornography (18 U.S.C. 2256). Child pornography, or the depicting of children in sexually explicit conduct, is defined as "sexual intercourse . . . whether between persons of the same or opposite sex; bestiality; masturbation; sadistic or masochistic abuse; or lascivious exhibition of the anus, genitals, or pubic area of any person" (18 U.S.C. 2252). Unsurprising, the key to defining child pornography is nudity. The statute's narrow focus on sexual activity almost avoided the issue of the viewer's object-gaze, but the final clause, "lascivious exhibition," once again introduces the object-gaze of the viewer as in obscenity (Žižek 1989). But even if this last clause had been eliminated, the model would be silenced. All that the model contributes in a child pornography case is their age; once established, they are no longer needed for the case.

Since the early 1980s, the court recognized protecting children as a valid governmental interest (*New York v. Ferber* 1982). However, the court has required that an image "depicts *real* children engaged in *actual* sexual conduct" (Stone 2017, 302). The Clinton administration promised to aggressively enforce federal obscenity statutes to gain votes in the 1992 election, but instead, it shifted its focus to child pornography (Stone 2017, 302–3). This enabled the continued prosecution of sexualized pictures, despite the waning of obscenity laws, and because intergenerational sexual contact is widely stigmatized, thus making them easier targets (Rubin 2011, 111–12; Stone 2017, 302–3).

Although the goal of child pornography statutes is to protect children, it is a poor tool because it does not reach the issue of American society's sexualization of children, especially female children, and the subsequent exploitation of that sexualization (Kincaid 1998, 13–14). In addition, advertisements and fashion industries trade on the erotization of child models, and the infantilization of adult models, in order to sell a range of products (Kincaid 1998, 104–6). Finally, the bodies of female athletes of all ages are being sexualized and exploited for attendance through the use of revealing uniforms (Krane et al. 2007, 87–89). Given this rampant, and legal, sexualization of minors, it is unsurprising that the law does not care to hear child models speak.

Importantly, the statute seems targeted at criminalizing adults more than protecting children. For example, in 1976, a series of pictures was produced of a naked pre-pubescent girl. Her face was incongruous with her body, with makeup applied as if she were an adult, and her hair was styled as though she were older (Robert 1976, 40–41). The setting further increases the erotic feel of the images; she is posed in a marble bathtub complete with telephone, a pink rose, and nude female statues for decor. The untitled work by Garry Gross is unabashedly erotic. Indeed, the editor of *Sugar and Spice*, in which the photos were included, wrote, "Garry's premise in creating them was simply to demonstrate his feeling that a little girl often projects an identifiable sensuality, into which she grows as she becomes a woman. Obviously, a child's and a woman's expressions of that sensuality will differ, but Garry is intrigued by the fact that it so clearly exists in both: inside that little girl there's a sexy woman hiding" (Robert 1976, 36). Despite the overtly sexualized blurb, the photo, along with another image of the same model, have not been held to be either child pornography or obscene, although published by Playboy Press. In contrast, the images were withdrawn from the Tate Modern Gallery in London after police suggested it violated the country's obscenity law (Turner 2009).

Several years after the pictures were first published, the model, Brooke Shields, sued to have the continued distribution of the photos enjoined (*Shields v. Gross* 1983). She asserted that the photos were harming her career because they were now being distributed by the photographer beyond their original intended use in the Playboy book *Sugar and Spice*. A New York court held that Shields did not have a cause of action to enjoin the distribution of the images because her mother had signed a binding contract granting use rights to the photographer (*Shields v. Gross 1983*, 345–46). The repurposing of photographs by unknown models, who later become famous, is not limited to child models. It represents a source of unexpected, and often high, revenue to the photographer since unknown models are underpaid (MacKinnon and Dworkin 1997, 224–25). Thus, the law does not protect the interest of the model unless the image is obscene. Then, it is concerned with the prosecution of the seller but not in hearing the model.

Society claims to protect the child, but the child model can no more speak than an adult model. They are relevant to the statute only in so far as their age is below the legal limit of consent. The anomalous case of Brooke Shields shows the limitations of the law. Once a picture is deemed to be neither child pornography nor obscene, contract law governs, and the voice of the parent supplants that of the child model. This is particularly troubling given how many models are underage. But it also reveals a way to give models voice. Although she lost the case, Shields's disapproval of the photos and the way they were being used was recorded in the legal record (*Shields v. Gross* 1983). She lost the case, but the law heard her speak and recorded it.

VI. CAN THE MODEL SPEAK?

Although models speak through their poses and actions in sexual materials, they are still silenced. Like the subaltern before (Spivak 1984, 104), the model cannot speak. Or rather, the model cannot communicate beyond the body. In legal discourse, this is due to historical, structural, hegemonic, and genre limitations. Under the current criminal obscenity regime, there is no place for the model to speak. Even in criminal investigations of child pornography, the model is only relevant insofar as their age establishes an element of the crime. Otherwise, like other models, they are excluded from legal discourse.

The absence of models from obscenity law is not completely negative given the propensity of prosecutors and police to target racial, ethnic, gender, and sexual-orientation minority groups generally (Acevedo 2016), specifically using obscenity laws (Meyer 2018). There is thus a positive side to the law's silencing of models. It has placed them beyond the reach of police and prosecutors under current obscenity laws and other sex-suppressive laws (Almodovar 2006, 149–53).

Ending the criminal legal regime of obscenity would contribute to end of the targeting of intersectional communities, especially those including the LGTBQ community, by law enforcement (Meyer 2018). Rubin argued for the complete abolition of all sex–speech crimes, including child pornography, because of their past use to target marginal communities (Rubin 2011, 112–13). This is of course not a cure-all for police mistreatment of intersectional communities, but it is the removal of one tool of oppression. The remedies for police misconduct are more varied and must include remedies for both individuals harmed and the communities targeted by the state (Acevedo 2016).

Significantly, decriminalizing obscenity would not fully enable the model to speak because of the inherent genre limitations of sexualized speech. Even legal pornography inverts the subject and object so that the viewer's "gaze falls into ourselves, the spectators. . . . It is only we who gaze stupidly at the image that 'reveals all'" (Žižek 1992, 110). Indeed, the lines between pornography, obscenity, and erotica are drawn by the individual viewer through claims about the level of sexual explicitness (Rubin 2011, 261–62). The viewer, therefore, imposes their own fantasies, beliefs, and speech onto the body of the model. This practice renders the model silent.

The only way to hear models' voices in the law is to provide them a place. Their names must appear on one side of the *versus* in case titling. This will of course not ensure a positive outcome, but as Brooke Shields's case demonstrated, the model can then be heard. Shields's views that the photos taken of her by Gross were harming her and that she did not want them to continue to be displayed was made clear (*Shields v. Gross* 1983, 342–434). Although she lost the case, her voice is recorded in case law; she spoke and was heard (*Shields v. Gross* 1983).

Scholars sought to provide voices to models, as well as other marginalized groups. Social historians sought to expand the discourse of history beyond politics and "great men" by examining a more diverse group of people and aspects of society (Kessler-Harris 1997, 231–33). Similarly, Marxist historians looked for nascent class struggles by examining the ideology and actions of common people (Rigby 1997, 900–902). From Marxist historiography emerged subaltern studies, which initially sought to study the non-elite Indian population rather than Indian or foreign elites (Chakrabarty 2000, 15). All of these theoretical moves sought to give voice to non-elites, but none of them can because, in the end, they are bounded by the view of elites (Spivak 1984, 90–93).

In addition to historians, feminist scholars attempted to give voice to marginalized groups. But, in the area of sexual modeling, they have been deeply divided, perhaps unsurprisingly, along their views of sexual imagery. Feminists such as Butler and Rubin view sexual imagery in a generally positive light—or at least fear censorship more than masculine hegemony (Rubin 2011, 260–62; Butler 1997, xiii). In contrast, others viewed most sexual speech, pornography as well as obscenity, as suppressing women (MacKinnon 1993, 22–25). This division reveals the inability of feminist scholars to speak for models; rather, the model's body is the site for their contested views of feminism. Although anti-porn feminists are motivated to un-subjugate women, the use of the model's body to assert their views echoes the English imperialist project to "make a better" India (Spivak 1984, 98). Thereby, "there is no space from which the sexed subaltern subject can speak" (Spivak 1984, 103).

Relatedly, critical race theory scholars sought to give voice to marginalized racial communities in legal scholarship by engaging in legal storytelling and narrative analysis (Delgado and Stefancic 2001, 37–39). These methods have been successful in making law students, legal scholars, and judges think about alternative voices in both well-known cases and those ignored by the legal canon (Delgado and Stefancic 2001, 39–43). In the area of speech, critical race theory focused on expanding the Fighting Words Doctrine to include hate speech (Butler 1997, 64, 99). Critical race theory has started to provide a remedy for the silencing of entire communities (Delgado and Stefancic 2001, 43–44), but it cannot encompass all sex-speech models. The reason is that, as an advocacy model, critical theory is compelled to defend the marginalized and view sex speech as a form of assaultive speech (Matsuda et al. 1993, 7). Thus, critical theory has difficulty comprehending the model who is not oppressed by their work.

All of these theoretical traditions sought to break the dominant narrative, focus on elites, and end the silencing of marginalized groups. These theories succeeded to varying degrees, but in the area of models, they have proven inadequate. The inability of scholars to adequately capture subalterns is further complicated on the issue of models because they are not heterogeneous; some look back on their work with pride and others with embarrassment; some viewed their work as a voluntary profession and others were coerced through circumstance or directly; some consider themselves empowered and others victims (Phillips 2006, 97–101; MacKinnon and Dworkin 1997, 60–66, 108–12, 224–25).

Spivak noted that the immolated widow, or sati, served as a cite for the discussion of what made India a good or bad society, but the widow herself was never allowed to speak. So too the body of the model serves as a cite for determining what makes an image obscene or acceptable even as they are silenced (Spivak 1984, 93). No matter how much law reforms try, "one cannot put together a 'voice'" of the model (Spivak 1984, 93). Just as with the act of sati, all that recounters can hope to achieve is a description. The image persists but without the substantive voice of the model. Indeed, we have a fragment of the model's speech in pictures, film, oil, and numerous other mediums, but we still do not, cannot, hear their voices. The speech of these images is the speech of the censor, prosecutor, defendant, judge, legislator, or other viewer, but they are not the voice of the muted model. "The subaltern cannot speak" (Spivak 1984, 104). Herein lies the irony of obscenity, indeed of all sex speech. The person baring all, sometimes literally, cannot speak. Until the law changes, they will be forever silenced.

BIBLIOGRAPHY

Acevedo, John Felipe. "Restoring Community Dignity Following Police Misconduct," *Howard Law Journal* 59 (2016): 621–49. HeinOnline.

Adler, Amy. "Performance Anxiety: Medusa, Sex and the First Amendment," *Yale Journal of Law and the Humanities* 21 (2009): 227–50. HeinOnline

Agamben, Giorgio. *Nudities*, translated by David Kishik and Stefan Pedatella. Stanford: Stanford University Press, 2011.

Alilunas, Peter. *Smutty Little Movies: The Creation and Regulation of Adult Video*. Oakland: University of California Press, 2016.

Almodovar, Norma Jean. "The Battle between Feminist Theory and Reality, Free Speech, and Free Spirits." In *Prostitution and Pornography: Philosophical Debate about the Sex Industry*, edited by Jessica Spector. Stanford: Stanford University Press, 2006.

American Law Institute. *Model Penal Code: Official Draft and Explanatory Notes*. Philadelphia: American Law Institute, 1985.

Anderson, Perry. "The Antinomies of Antonio Gramsci," *New Left Review* 100 (1976): 5–78.

———. *The H-Word: The Peripeteia of Hegemony*. London and New York: Verso, 2017.

Augustine. *The City of God against the Pagans*, edited by R. W. Dyson. Cambridge: Cambridge University Press, 1998.

Bellafante, Gina. "We Need to Talk about Balthus." *New York Times*, Dec. 8, 2017, MB 1. NYTimes.com.

Blackstone, William. *Commentaries on the Laws of England, Book IV of Public Wrongs*, edited by Ruth Paley. Oxford: Oxford University Press, 2016.

Butler, Judith. *Excitable Speech: A Politics of the Performative*. New York: Routledge, 1997.

———. *Gender Trouble*, second edition. New York: Routledge, 1990.

Chakrabarty, Dipesh. "Subaltern Studies and Postcolonial Historiography." *Nepantla: Views from South* 1, no. 1 (2000): 9–32. ProjectMUSE.

Chemerinsky, Erwin. *Constitutional Law: Principles and Policies*, sixth edition. New York: Wolters Kluwer Law and Business, 2019.

Dale, Elizabeth. "Criminal Justice in the United States, 1790–1920: A Government of Laws or Men?" In *The Cambridge History of Law in America: Volume II The Long Nineteenth Century (1789–1920)*, edited by Michael Grossberg and Christopher Tomlins. Cambridge and New York: Cambridge University Press, 2008.

Das Acevedo, Deepa. "Sovereignty and Social Change in the Wake of India's Recent Sodomy Cases," *Boston College International and Comparative Law Review* 40 (2017): 1–26. HeinOnline.

Delgado, Richard, and Jean Stefancic. *Critical Race Theory: An Introduction*. New York: New York University Press, 2001.

Fausto-Sterling, Anne. *Sexing the Body: Gender Politics and the Construction of Sexuality*. New York: Basic Books, 2000.

Final Report of the Attorney General's Commission on Pornography Michael J. McManus Introduction. Nashville: Rutledge Hill Press, 1986.

Freud, Sigmund. "Medusa's Head." In *The Standard Edition of the Complete Psychological Works of Sigmund Freud*, vol. 18, 273–74, edited by James Strachey. London: Hogarth Press, 1953.

Friedman, Lawrence M. *Crime and Punishment in American History*. New York: Basic Books, 1993.

———. *American Law in the 20th Century*. New Haven and London: Yale University Press, 2002.

Gramsci, Antonio. *The Antonio Gramsci Reader: Selected Writings 1916–1935*, edited by David Forgacs. New York: New York University Press, 2000.

———. *The Southern Question*, translated by Pasqual Verdicchio. New York: Bordighera Press, 2015.

Gualdoni, Flamnio. *The History of the Nude*, edited by Eileen Romano; translated by Sylvia Notini. Milan: Skira, 2012.

Henkin, Louis. "Morals and the Constitution: The Sin of Obscenity," *Columbia Law Review* 63 (1963): 391–414. HeinOnline.

Horowitz, Helen Lefkowitz. *Rereading Sex: Battles over Sexual Knowledge and Suppression in Nineteenth-Century America*. New York: Vintage Books, 2003.

Johns, Adrian. *The Nature of the Book: Print and Knowledge in the Making*. Chicago: University of Chicago Press, 1998.

"Justice in Cincinnati," *New York Times*, October 6, 1990, 22. NYTimes.com

Kessler-Harris, Alice. "Social History." In *The New American History: Revised and Expanded Edition*, edited by Eric Foner. Philadelphia: Temple University Press, 1997.

Kincaid, James R. *Erotic Innocence: The Culture of Child Molesting*. Durham, NC, and London: Duke University Press, 1998.

Kivel Paul. *Living in the Shadow of the Cross: Understanding and Resisting the Power and Privilege of Christian Hegemony*. Gabriola Island, British Columbia: New Society Publishers, 2013.

Krane, Vikki, Precilla Y. Choi, Shannon M. Baird, Christine M. Aimar, and Kerrie J. Kauer. "Living the Paradox: Female Athletes Negotiate Femininity and Masculinity." In *Women and Sports in the United States: A Documentary Reader*, edited by Jean O'Reilly and Susah K. Chan, 81–100. Boston: Northeastern University Press, 2007.

Kruse, Kevin M. *One Nation under God: How Corporate America Invented Christian America*. New York: Basic Books, 2015.

Langbein, John. "The Criminal Trial before the Lawyers," *University of Chicago Law Review* 45 (1978): 263–316. Westlaw.

Lucan, Jacques. *The Four Fundamental Concepts of Psychoanalysis: The Seminar of Jacques Lacan Book XI*, edited by Jacques-Alain Miller, translated by Alan Sheridan. New York: W.W. Norton, 1981.

MacKinnon, Catharine A. *Only Words*. Cambridge, MA: Harvard University Press, 1993.

———. *Toward a Feminist Theory of the State*. Cambridge, MA: Harvard University Press, 1989.

MacKinnon, Catharine A., and Andrea Dworkin. *In Harm's Way: The Pornography Civil Rights Hearings*. Cambridge, MA: Harvard University Press, 1997.

Martin, William. *With God on Our Side: The Rise of the Religious Right in America*. New York: Broadway Books, 1996.

Matsuda, Mari J., Charles R. Lawrence III, Richard Delgado, and Kimberle Williams Crenshaw. *Words That Wound: Critical Race Theory, Assaultive Speech, and the First Amendment*. Boulder, CO: Westview Press, 1993.
Meyer, Richard. *Outlaw Representation: Censorship and Homosexuality in Twentieth-Century American Art*. Brattleboro, VT: Echo Point Books, 2018.
Moran, Jeffrey P. *Teaching Sex: The Shaping of Adolescence in the 20th Century*. Cambridge, MA: Harvard University Press, 2000.
Papenfuss, Mary. "NYC Met Museum Refuses to Remove Painting That Petition Says 'Sexualizes' Girl." Huffington Post, Dec. 5, 2017. https://www.huffpost.com/entry/therese-dreaming-petition-metropolitan-museum_n_5a260869e4b0f9f0203ec645.
Perlstein, Rick. *Nixonland: The Rise of a President and the Fracturing of America*. New York: Scribner, 2008.
Phillips, Sarah R. *Modeling Life: Art Models Speak about Nudity, Sexuality and the Creative Process*. Albany: State University of New York Press, 2006.
Principles of the Law of Aggregate Litigation Scope Information. New York: Thomas Reuters, 2018.
Rigby, S. H. "Marxist Historiography." In *Companion to Historiography*, edited by Michael Bentley. London and New York: Routledge, 1997.
Robert, Francois (ed.). *Sugar and Spice*. Chicago: Playboy Press, 1976.
Rosenberg, Gerald N. *The Hollow Hope: Can Courts Bring About Social Change?*, second ed. Chicago and London: University of Chicago Press, 2008.
Rubin, Gayle. *Deviations: A Gayle Rubin Reader*. Durham, NC, and London: Duke University Press, 2011.
Sartre, Jean-Paul. *Being and Nothingness: A Phenomenological Essay on Ontology*, translated by Hazel E. Barnes. New York: Washington Square Press, 1956.
Schauer, Frederick F. *The Law of Obscenity*. Washington, DC: Bureau of National Affairs, 1976.
Simon, Roger. *Gramsci's Political Thought: An Introduction*, third ed. London: Lawrence & Wishart, 2015.
Spivak, Gayatri Chakravorty. "Can the Subaltern Speak?" In *Colonial Discourse and Post-Colonial Theory, A Reader*, edited by Patrick Williams and Laura Chrisman, 66–111. New York: Columbia University Press, 1984.
Stokes, Jenna K. "The Indecent Internet: Resisting Unwarranted Internet Exceptionalism in Combating Revenge Porn," *Berkeley Technology Law Journal* 29 (2014) 929–52. Westlaw.
Stone, Geoffrey. *Sex and the Constitution: Sex, Religion, and Law from America's Origins to the Twenty-First Century*. New York: Liveright, 2018.
Strub, Whitney. *Obscenity Rules: Roth v. United States and the Long Struggle over Sexual Expression*. Lawrence: University of Kansas Press, 2013.
Turner, Christopher. "Sugar and Spice and All Things Not So Nice," *Guardian*, October 3, 2009, Global. www.theguardian.com.
Werbel, Amy: *Lust on Trial: Censorship and the Rise of American Obscenity in the Age of Anthony Comstock*. New York: Colombia University Press, 2018.
Woodward, Bob, and Armstrong, Scott. *The Brethren: Inside the Supreme Court*. New York: Simon & Schuster, 1979.
Žižek, Slavo. "Looking Awry." *October* 50 (1989): 30–55. JSTOR.
———. *Looking Awry: An Introduction to Jacques Lacan through Popular Culture*. Cambridge, MA and London: MIT Press, 1992.

Cases

Alexander v. U.S., 509 U.S. 544 (1993).
American Booksellers Assn. v. Hudnut, 771 F. 2d 323 (1985).
Aschroft v. Free Speech Coalition, 535 U.S. 234 (2000).
A Book Named 'John Cleland's Memoirs of a Woman of Pleasure' v. Massachusetts, 383 U.S. 413 (1966).
Carter v. Carter Coal Co., 298 U.S. 238 (1936).

City of Erie v. Pap's A.M, 529 U.S. 277 (2000).
Cohen v. California, 403 U.S. 15 (1971).
Ex Parte Jackson, 96 U.S. 727 (1877).
FCC v. Pacifica Foundation 483 U.S. 726 (1978).
Jacobellis v. State of Ohio, 378 U.S. 184 (1964).
McCulloch v. Maryland 17 U.S. 316 (1819).
Miller v. California, 413 U.S. 15 (1973).
New York v. Ferber, 458 U.S. 747 (1982).
NLRB v. Jones & Laughlin Steel Co., 301 U.S. 1 (1937).
Osborne v. Ohio, 495 U.S. 103 (1990).
Pope v. Illinois, 481 U.S. 497 (1987).
Redrup v. New York, 386 U.S. 767 (1967).
Roth v. United States, 354 U.S. 476 (1957).
Schad v. Borough of Mount Ephraim, 452 U.S. 61 (1981).
Shields v. Gross, 58 N.Y.2d 338 (1983).
Stanley v. Georgia, 394 U.S. 557 (1969).
United States v. Bott, 24 F. Cas. 1204 (S.D.N.Y., 1873).
United States v. Lopez, 514 U.S. 549 (1995).
United States v. O'Brien, 391 U.S. 367 (1968)

Statutes

Constitution of the United States of America.
18 U.S.C. 2256 (2018).
18 U.S.C. 2252A (2018).

Index

About the Editor

Elaine Wood is lecturer of women's and gender studies, affiliated with the Center for the Study of Race, Ethnicity & Gender at Bucknell University. She serves as the code of conduct ombudsperson for the International Flann O'Brien Society. Holding a PhD in English and gender and women's Studies from the University of Illinois at Urbana-Champaign and a JD emphasis in immigration law from the University of Miami, her research and teaching interests focus on theoretical practices and linguistic representations of intersectionality. Prior to her academic appointment at Bucknell, she served as a law clerk for the United States Department of Justice.

About the Contributors

John Felipe Acevedo is assistant professor in residence at the University of Alabama School of Law. He earned his PhD in history from the University of Chicago with an emphasis on early modern legal history; his JD from the University of Southern California Gould School of Law, where he was a fellow in the Center for Law, History, and Culture. He received his BA in history from California State University, San Bernardino. His research focuses on the interplay between law and society in both contemporary and historical examples with an emphasis on property, criminal law, and procedure.

Lisa Beckmann studied English and German literature as well as Anglophone literary, cultural, and media studies at Justus-Liebig-University Giessen, Germany, and the University of Sheffield, United Kingdom. She is currently a PhD student and a research assistant at Justus-Liebig-University Giessen. Her PhD project explores the cultural and legal politics of disability in the United States eugenics movement at the beginning of the twentieth century with an emphasis on constructions of disability, gender, and sexuality through the law.

Arunita Das is a master's degree student in the Socio-Legal Studies Program at York University. She holds an Honors BA in sociology from York University. Broadly, her research interests lie within historical injustice, colonialism; race and racialization, crime and regulation, and feminist/postcolonial/critical race theories. Das's current research examines the overrepresentation of Indigenous peoples in federal and provincial prisons. She applies critical feminist discourse methodology to broadly examine the criminalization of Indigenous women in Canada to better understand the role of Canadian courts in providing a culturally appropriate space for Indigenous women to access meaningful justice.

Theodore Davenport (he/they) is a master's degree student in geography at the University of Washington. Theodore obtained a bachelor's degree in geography at the University of Georgia, where he worked as a research assistant for a political ecology lab and a community mapping lab. Theodore's research interests include trans geographies, care geographies, and digital scholarship. His thesis project draws from community oral history archives to explore how transgender people in the United States engage with feminist care ethics within and beyond traditional institutions of care (particularly the home, medical institutions, and "caring" bureaucracies) from the mid-twentieth century to 2019.

Catherine Cymone Fourshey is associate professor of history and international studies and acting director of the Griot Institute for Black Lives and Culture at Bucknell University.

Marla L. Jaksch is associate professor of women's, gender, and sexuality studies, with affiliations in the departments of African American Studies and International Studies, in the Africa concentration at the College of New Jersey.

Ava Ladner is a PhD candidate in the American Studies department. Prior to beginning her studies at the University of Hawai'i at Mānoa, she earned a masters in writing from the University of Southern California and a masters in sports studies and physical education from the University of Georgia, where she looked at antitrust collusion in the National Football League. Ava has worked in libraries at the University of Georgia, University of Mississippi, and Hawai'i Pacific University. She has also taught at Hawai'i Tokai International College. Her dissertation is focused on the influence of southern (American) culture and its influence throughout the United States, using the sport of NASCAR as a conduit and lens for the delivery of the messages. Ava has also concentrated on transgender studies, developing, implementing, and teaching the first course at UH that is solely dedicated to the topic. She has taught Contemporary American Issues, Early U.S. History in the History and Film Studies Departments. When she finds free time, Ava enjoys running, pilates, and spending time with her two dogs.

Laura Lane-Steele graduated cum laude from Harvard Law School in 2016. She clerked for the Honorable Judge Jane R. Roth for the United States Court of Appeals for the Third Circuit. Her scholarship focuses on the intersections of race, gender, and sexuality in American equality law, family law, and education law. She currently practices law in Washington, DC.

Shirley Lin is acting assistant professor at New York University School of Law, and adjunct professor of employment law at City University of New York (CUNY) School of Law. Professor Lin's scholarship focuses on the intersection of workers' rights, constitutional and administrative law, critical race feminism, and class critical theories. Prior to joining the faculty, she was a senior associate at Outten & Golden, LLP, a national labor and employment law firm where she advised and litigated on behalf of civil rights plaintiffs. She previously served as a law clerk for the Honorable Denny Chin of the U.S. Circuit Court of Appeals for the Second Circuit, and as a Skadden Fellow at the Asian American Legal Defense & Education Fund. Professor Lin publishes and speaks frequently on topics including sex and disability discrimination, the rights of LGBTQIA workers, litigation, and professional ethics.

Lissa Lincoln is a scholar of critical theory, gender studies, and French literature, whose interdisciplinary research explores normativity, exclusion and violence within marginalized communities, with particular emphasis on gender and caste. She is interested in questions linked to stigma, systemic violence, discrimination, and historical silencing and in the ways that literature and testimony emerge as forms of resistance against oppression. Co-founder and head of the Gender, Sexuality and Society Program at the American University of Paris, her work in feminist and postcolonial theory, Dalit literature and testimonio, twentieth-century continental philosophy, and law and literature are all informed by a commitment to interrogating the intersecting politics of race, class, caste, gender, and sexuality.

Christin M. Mulligan is a feminist scholar of Irish and global Anglophone literatures at Caldwell University. In 2019, she published her first monograph, *Geofeminism in Irish and Diasporic Culture: Intimate Cartographies*. She has been a Fulbright-Hays FLAS Scholar in the Gaeltacht and a Werner Friedrich Fellow at the Zurich James Joyce Foundation. Her work has also appeared in *Hypermedia Joyce Studies*, *Literature Interpretation Theory*, and *Humanities*. Christin earned her doctorate from the University of North Carolina at Chapel Hill and her AB from Bryn Mawr College, where she was an Andrew W. Mellon Foundation Hanna Holborn Gray Fellow.

Menaka Raguparan is assistant professor in the Department of Sociology and Criminology at the University of North Carolina, Wilmington. Her research includes policy-based analysis for the Canadian government and non-profit agencies in the areas of marginalization, systemic exclusion, identity, race, and gender. Menaka is the founder and co-chair of "Sex, Work, Law and Society," a collaborative research network (CRN 6) at the Law and Society Association (LSA). Her current research examines the racial impacts of state-led human trafficking initiatives in the United States.

Rebecca Smyth is a PhD candidate at the University of Edinburgh Law School. She holds an LLM (Distinction) in human rights law from the same university, an MPhil (Distinction) in gender and women's studies from Trinity College Dublin, and a first-class honors degree in European studies, also from Trinity. Committed to intersectional feminist research, teaching, and activism, her doctoral thesis concerns feminist critiques of international human rights law, and the ways in which the language and mechanisms of international human rights law can be used to advance women's human rights, specifically in relation to abortion access.

www.ingramcontent.com/pod-product-compliance
Ingram Content Group UK Ltd.
Pitfield, Milton Keynes, MK11 3LW, UK
UKHW041841031026
15587UKWH00002B/928